U2 FAQ

U2 FAQ

Anything You'd Ever Want to Know About the Biggest Band in the World . . .

and More!

John D. Luerssen

Backbeat
Books

An Imprint of Hal Leonard Corporation

Published in 2010 by Backbeat Books
An Imprint of Hal Leonard Corporation
7777 West Bluemound Road
Milwaukee, WI 53213

Trade Book Division Editorial Offices
33 Plymouth St., Montclair, NJ 07042

Printed in the United States of America

Book design by Snow Creative Services

Library of Congress Cataloging-in-Publication Data

Luerssen, John D.
    U2 FAQ : anything you'd ever want to know about the biggest band in the world—and more! / John D. Luerssen.
        p. cm. — (FAQ)
    Includes bibliographical references and index.
    ISBN 978-0-87930-997-8
    1. U2 (Musical group)—Miscellanea. I. Title. II. Title: U2 frequently asked questions.
    ML421.U2L84 2010
    782.42166092'2—dc22
                                                                    2010037243

www.backbeatbooks.com

For Heidi—my everlasting love

and

Meredith, Hayley, and Jack

Contents

32 Space Junk Coming in for the Splash: Ten Totally Random U2 Facts 282
33 Jesus Never Let Me Down: U2 and Religion   284
34 I See an Expression: U2's Essential Music Videos   288
35 I Never Bought a Lotto Ticket: *Pop*   292
36 Cigars and Big Hair: U2 Enjoys Its Fame and Wealth   303
37 They Said Be Careful Where You Aim: U2's Controversies   312
38 I Got No Home in This World: *The Million Dollar Hotel*   331
39 See the World in Green and Blue: U2 on Home Video   334
40 The Heart Is Abloom: *All That You Can't Leave Behind*   337
41 It's You When I Look in the Mirror: Bono on Bob Hewson   343
42 I Won't Heed the Battle Call: Can Bono (and the Rest of U2)
    Save the World?   345
43 I'm Hanging Out to Dry with My Old Clothes: Side Projects,
    Collaborations, Compilation Tracks, Soundtracks, Benefits,
    Books, Movie Roles, and More   361
44 It Could Be Yours Tonight: Gettin' Paid   381
45 I Have No Compass, and I Have No Map: U2's Side Businesses   386
46 The Songs Are in Your Eyes: *How to Dismantle an Atomic Bomb*   389
47 I Believe You Can Dance with Me: Rare, Unreleased, and
    Collectible Releases   396
48 Papa Sing My Sing My Song: Tunes U2 Has Written for Others   405
49 Joyful Noise: U2's Hits Compilations   407
50 Three Chords and the Truth: U2 and the Rock and Roll
    Hall of Fame   411
51 Shine Like a Burning Star: ZooTV to 360°: U2's Tours (1992–2010)   415
52 I Know You're Looking Out for Us: Post-Millennium Honors
    and Awards   426
53 We Need New Dreams Tonight: U2's Grammy Awards   432
54 The Future Needs a Big Kiss: *No Line on the Horizon*   434
55 Is That All You Want from Me?: Quotes About U2   444

    Selected Bibliography   447
    Index   451

Foreword

In spring 1985, my band, Red Rockers, had the unique privilege of opening some dates for U2 on their *Unforgettable Fire* Tour. To us, it seemed a natural pairing and could not have come at a better time. We had been doing tours of this size for the previous couple of years, though at the time, it seemed like we were being slighted publicity-wise by our label (they were placing all their efforts into an album from some New Jersey guy; *Born in the U.S.A.*, I think it was called). In that respect it was bittersweet, but still, we recognized that we were a part of the biggest tour of the decade.

That it came about at all was something of a fluke. We were at an MTV shindig in NYC at the Radio City Music Hall. Band members from both acts were in attendance and we knew they were about to release *The Unforgettable Fire* and tour. When we were all in the lobby, chatting amongst ourselves, our drummer, Jim Reilly, sprang the question right then and there. (It must've helped that he was Irish.) They accepted without reservation right there on the spot. A tour was born. The guys in U2 were generous and were well aware of what we were going through at that stage of our career; let's say they were very astute and perceptive of their surroundings and what was about to happen to them and what it took to get there.

U2 fans, I believe, were a reflection of the band's demeanor. Gracious, kind, forgiving, and accepting. I can't remember ever having a bad night on that tour. Again, I have to say the match could not have been more appropriate, from sound to substance, from theory to message. Both bands carried flags and had their own political messages. The messages in general were closely tied together in a world view, yet slightly different due to geographic backgrounds, obviously. In all, the message from both bands was the same: Take your world that YOU live in and make it a better place, and have fun while you do it. The fans came to hear that message and they got it.

Red Rockers had joined the band at the opening of *The Unforgettable Fire* Tour in Houston, Texas. The original scheduling was for us to perform roughly two dozen dates which would cover the entire west coast, including Hawaii, and back through the Midwest, ending in Chicago. When we played in Denver, we got in an argument with our business manager, and for some reason, unannounced, he flew to Colorado, hijacked our tour bus and drove it back to Missouri. All our clothes and other belongings went with it. To make this short, the guys in U2 found out and that night after the show, they presented us with $4,000—a nice chunk of money in 1985—to buy new clothes and get transportation. It was given to us no questions asked and they requested we not pay it back. We were stunned. That's the kind of people they were.

For whatever reason, Lone Justice was to play the second of two nights in Chicago and stay the opening act for the remaining dates of the tour. Two or three weeks passed, we'd moved on to our own tour schedule, and our tour manager got a call from our agent asking how soon and probable would it be that we could get to the next closest U2 date, which was the Atlanta Omni Dome. We never got the full details of why Lone Justice was not working out on the tour and didn't have time to really think about it, so we scrambled like jet fighters and got to Atlanta as fast as we could. We finished the last four dates. Atlanta, Tampa, and two gigs in Hollywood. We were certainly thrilled to be asked back. It was a glorious feeling. It did a lot for our psyche.

On the tour our interactions with U2 were limited—just your average, everyday casual hellos and goodnights. They had a lot going on with interviews, radio, the usual career building work. We did also. We would all share a glass of wine backstage once in awhile and talk shop. Edge was really getting into the new electronics that were coming out, and he I would discuss some of the cool new features of certain products.

As an aside, I escorted Jim to Belfast in the summer of 1983, to somehow assure his safe return to the States after his brother Thomas Reilly was murdered. He was shot in the back by a British Army paratrooper. The U.S. State Department was calling my parents, asking them to plead with me to come back home. The embassy in Northern Ireland was calling Jim's parent's house asking me to please leave. I understood they were worried something tragic would happen to me and it would just blow up into some diplomatic clusterfuck, but I never felt safer and less apprehensive in my life there. As Jim dealt with his family I hooked up with Ali McMordie, bassist from Jim's first band, Stiff Little Fingers. He and I drove down together from Belfast to Dublin's Phoenix Park for U2's big homecoming festival. It was great because a lot of the bands on that bill had not been to America yet. Big Country, Simple Minds, the Eurythmics. It was an incredible bill. Bono dedicated "I Fall Down" to Jim's brother, who they called "Kidso."

The one memory I've often spoken of to folks is my favorite to tell. It was the last night of our original run with U2 in Chicago. While in San Francisco a week or so earlier I had bought some microdot acid. I was waiting to take it on a special occasion such as this. My girlfriend at the time had flown up from New Orleans—where I am from—to celebrate. We dropped the acid no sooner than our set had ended. I will say that during this period U2 were simply on fire (no pun intended). No props, no special staging. Pound for pound, they were the best concert experience ever! On acid . . . there are no words in *Webster's* to describe it. Needless to say, somewhere during the second half of the show I peaked and thought I was in heaven. Suddenly at the end of the show, I see the crew scrambling around, and my tour manager walks up to me and says, "The band wants you to join them onstage for the last song, to sing '40' with them." And we did. As we approached the second verse, Bono just handed me the mic and left the stage, leaving me to finish the song tripping my brains out. Little did he know. There's a cassette tape floating around of the event, and it sounds remarkably good, I will say.

JTG
Los Angeles, CA
April 2010

John Thomas Griffith *co-founded the New Orleans punk outfit Red Rockers in 1979. Their 1983 hit "China" was an MTV favorite. After three albums and numerous national tours opening for acts like the Cars, Men at Work, Joan Jett, the Go-Gos, and U2, the group folded in 1987. Currently, Griffith fronts Cowboy Mouth. He lives in Los Angeles.*

Introduction

We Get to Carry Each Other: U2—A Band of Brothers

U nlike most bands, which are formed with the idea of playing together for a while for fun, U2's existence was, as Bono would say, "very much a complete thing." U2 were always four rock and roll horsemen with a singular cause.

Brian Eno told *Pitchfork* in 2009 that U2 should be studied in the Smithsonian, explaining that "the politics of it work, the accommodation of each other by each other, it's quite something." Few bands through history have had the same allegiance to one another.

U2 has endured divorce, drug busts, critical mauling, a cult-like religious group and commercial flops among its many artistic, financial, and personal achievements. Remarkably, the band has remained unaltered since 1978 when The Edge's older brother Dick Evans was asked to leave.

And despite those Who, Stones, and Bowie records that they were all weaned on, their biggest influences have always been each other.

When Larry Mullen, Jr. lost his mother unexpectedly in a 1978 car crash, Bono—who lost his mother some four years earlier—was there to console the drummer. With the experience of bereavement they became the closest of friends.

After multiple years where bassist Adam Clayton was the lone dissenter in a group of otherwise devout Christians, Bono worked to bridge the members together by having the hell raising bassist assume the role of best man when he married in 1982.

At industry parties, they would mingle around for a while but ultimately end up back talking to one another, even when they had been on a tour bus together all day long. U2 was, and still is, one.

Bono tried to express this closeness to *Rolling Stone* publisher Jann Wenner in 2005. "The truth is I need them more than they need me," the singer said. "They raise my game. I'm terrified of being in a room on my own . . . I'm a better person for being around these men."

Exultation

I discovered the music of U2 the way many kids learned about up and coming bands in the days before the internet—through a classmate. In the early months of 1982, when I was in the eighth grade at Roosevelt Junior High School, we had a substitute teacher for our eighth-period Boys Choir class. The sub, who had no musical abilities to speak of, said we could listen to the radio at a reasonable volume while we worked on our homework for the forty-minute session.

It was tuned to WPLJ, the big and enormously popular New York album-oriented rock station. At the time the station's idea of new music was J. Geils, Journey, Billy Squier, the Rolling Stones, and Styx. After about thirty-five minutes of what the station called "kick-ass rock and roll," a guy named Sean Minogue approached the tape deck with some kick-ass rock of his own. It was "Gloria" from U2's *October* cassette.

As the song played—if memory serves me right—he told me how he was turned onto this great new Irish band during a visit by some of his Dublin cousins. I couldn't believe what I was hearing. It was amazing, innovative . . . like nothing I had ever heard. At this point I was mostly into Springsteen, the Who, the Doors, the Kinks, and had only recently discovered *London Calling* by the Clash. My horizons were broadening. I wrote the name of the band inside my notebook for fear I'd forget and went on my merry way. Regrettably, I did forget for a while.

When my older sister, Liz, came home with *War* in March of the following year, it became an instant favorite of mine. I listened to it religiously and was consumed by its melodic power and opinion. By this point I was mesmerized by the likes of the Clash, Elvis Costello, Joe Jackson, the Sex Pistols, the Lords of the New Church, and, of course, U2's first albums.

When friends told me about the epic U2 show they had seen that June at Pier 84 in Manhattan, I couldn't help but feel jealous. Of course I righted those wrongs on subsequent treks, and although I went on to dig really deep into music of the rock, punk, and alternative varieties in subsequent years, playing in bands as a teenager and writing about music as an adult, the music of U2—which has had its amazing highs and iffy lows—has always been with me. For that I thank Sean Minogue. Cheers, wherever you are.

Putting this book together, I was reminded just how omnipresent U2 has become. They really are the biggest band in the world. It's virtually impossible to turn on a rock station for an hour and not hear a song from the band's catalog. The milestones in my own life—be it "With or Without You" at my wedding or the band's rendition of "Everlasting Love" coming through the radio as my oldest daughter was born—have been accompanied by Bono, Edge, Adam, and Larry.

Thanks to my beautiful, wonderful wife Heidi for putting up with the long hours I have put into this book, and my amazing, sweet, and tolerant children Meredith, Hayley, and Jack. I also have to thank Dave and Pinky Luerssen; Liz Luerssen; Marie Garner; Ann and John Crowther; Karen Fountain and Tom Jardim; Dennis McLaughlin and Yvette Scola; Michael Connelly; Marc McCabe; Sheldon Ferriss and Michelle Weintraub; Beth and Kenneth Hoerle; Scott Simon plus Bill Crandall, Jessica Robertson, Dan Reilly, and everyone from *Spinner*.

The following folks also deserve acknowledgment for their assistance with the collectible art found in the pages of *U2 FAQ*. Major thanks to Mike Kurman, Angelo Deodato, Cathryn Draper at 991.com, Sophie Ashley, EIL.com, Chris Raisin, Cathleen Penyak, Mike Stein, Ninnee from Norwich, U2 Feedback, Guax Guax, Remy at U2Start.com, Aaron J. Sams and U2Wanderer.org, Tracy Sigler, YAT Records, Aaron Sapoznik, the Hugh Lynn Collection, Riza Abdullah, and Alex Da Real Beat Digger.

Finally, thanks to Robert Rodriguez and Bernadette Malavarca for support, direction, and encouragement; Diane Levinson for her enthusiasm; John Griffith for a great foreword; and John Cerullo for everything else.

I think we're being shut down.

John D. Luerssen
Summer 2010

Into the Heart of a Child

The Members of U2 as Children

Bono

Bono, a.k.a. Paul David Hewson, was born on May 10, 1960, at the Rotunda Hospital in Glasnevin, Dublin. Along with his brother Norman, who was nearly eight years his senior, the future U2 singer was raised in the Dublin suburb of Ballymun, in a semi-detached three bedroom home at 10 Cedarwood Road.

Bono's home for the first twenty years of his life was discovered nearly built in the early summer of 1960, when Paul's mother Iris and his Aunt Ruth were out walking him in a stroller in the neighborhood where the latter lived with her husband Ted. Iris pitched the idea of buying a new home to Bono's dad, Bob, who agreed, and they—along with Paul's older brother Norman—moved in upon its completion.

Bobby Hewson and Iris Rankin

Bono's parents were proud Dubliners who both came from the modest and respectable Oxmantown Road area of the city, just to the north of the River Liffey. His father, Brendan Robert "Bobby" Hewson went to Brunswick Street Secondary School in Eamon De Valera's Ireland of the early 1940s. The school was run by the Christian Brothers, who were powerful men in the Republican movement and helped shape Bobby's principles as an Irishman.

Although Bobby considered himself Republican at heart, he was nonviolent in his convictions, and once revealed that he could never see himself shooting anybody. The son of a technician in the General Post Office, Bobby left Brunswick Street Secondary School at fourteen with his Intermediate Certificate and followed his dad into the same line of safe and pensionable work the following year.

Although the Christian Brothers begged Bobby's mother to keep him in school because he was one of their better students, Bono's father moved forward with his decision to work as a Post Office clerk. Bobby became a member of the Catholic Young Men's Society and thrived socially, as an outgoing and personable young man with a love of music that included everything from Al Jolson and Bing Crosby to arias.

By the time he was nineteen, Bobby first got up the nerve to talk and dance with Iris Rankin at a CYMS event. A dark, pretty, and petite girl of the same age, Iris was raised on Cowper Street, just around the corner from Bobby's parents' home. Both were reared in the working class area of Dublin in the Cowtown District, near the cattle market, the two had spotted each other in the neighborhood through the years.

As for his mother's looks, Bono once suggested that his mother's side of the family looked like taxi drivers from Tel Aviv. Rankin can be a Jewish name, the singer pointed out, hinting that someone in Iris's ancestry may have been Jewish.

Just the same, Iris, the second of eight siblings, was raised Anglican Protestant in the Church of Ireland. As a young adult, after leaving school, she found work as a bookkeeper.

Religious Controversy

As Iris and Bobby fell in love and decided to marry, their proposed matrimony was met with controversy. The mere thought of a Roman Catholic man and a Protestant woman defied Éamon de Valera's edict of the 1940s. Proper living among Ireland residents in 1949 was Catholic living, and marriage to a Protestant was unforgivable. Five and a half decades after this union, Bono would tell those during his speech and sermon at the 2006 National Prayer Breakfast that, "One of the things that I picked up from my father and my mother was the sense that religion often gets in the way of God."

Despite the hullabaloo, Bobby and Iris went forward with their marriage on August 6, 1950, marrying in St. John the Baptist Church of Ireland on Church Avenue in Drumcondra. Although Bobby's actions were considered quite defiant at the time, his marriage to Iris was ultimately blessed by a Catholic priest, which enabled him to make peace with his own Church.

Stillorgan

Bobby and Iris briefly rented for a few months before buying a house in Stillorgan, which was six miles out of Dublin on the Southside of the Liffey. In 1952, their first son Norman was born, and although the couple had agreed to raise any boys they had in the Roman Catholic Church and any girls they had as Protestants, Bobby had a change of heart and opted to have all of his children raised in the faith of their mother. Norman would go to church with Iris on Sunday and Bobby would go to mass on his own.

The Hewsons were a happy young couple. Iris was a natural homemaker who took to cooking, sewing, and knitting and was close with her younger sisters Ruth and Stella. Meanwhile, Bobby was promoted to Survey Overseer in the Post Office and his hobbies included golfing and painting.

The Town Crier

Paul was an irritable baby who supposedly cried most of the day for the first two years of his life. When he wouldn't stop, his mother eventually took him to a specialist at Crumlin Children's Hospital, where he was kept for observation. After a week's stay during which he was deemed healthy and normal, Iris came to the conclusion that her youngest son was attention starved. As a result, Bob would stay outside in his car, an NSU Prinz, after his return from work. There he would read the evening newspaper in the quiet, away from his crabby young lad.

Just after Paul's third birthday, his father took him and Norman to see U.S. President John F. Kennedy's motorcade pass by on Drumcondra Road, during the Irish American hero's June 1963 visit to Dublin. By now, the future singer had stopped crying his days away and instead started talking incessantly. Although Paul would rarely shut up, he revealed himself to be affectionate, curious, and fully spirited.

Bono once told a story of having his photography taken with Norman around the age of three, which he objected to. As a result, young Paul destroyed one of two leopard ornaments his parents kept on the mantel in the family's home. For the misdeed, he was sent to his room as punishment.

Bono loved music as a toddler, and at a young age seemed interested in making his own on his grandmother's piano. He would climb under the instrument and listen to the music reverberate, touch the keys, and listen to the notes.

A "Proddy" Outsider

Raised Protestant in a predominantly Roman Catholic neighborhood, Bono was different from the other kids on Cedarwood Road. He attended a different primary school—the Protestant-run Glasnevin National—and a different church—St. Canice's Church of Ireland—than his neighbors, which made him something of a "Proddy" outsider.

According to Bono, on his first day at Glasnevin National, a boy came up to his best friend at the time, James Mahon, and bit his ear. Reacting, he took the biter's head and smacked it against some iron railings. Remembering the incident forty-plus years on, U2's singer—who liked to take bullies to task—revealed he tended to retain the violent and aggressive incidents from his youth.

Enter Guggi

In 1967, Bono befriended Derek Rowen, another Protestant boy from the neighborhood, and they became fast friends. Guggi—as he would become known—wanted to try the swing in the Hewsons' backyard, and Bono let him. The Rowens lived around the corner from the Hewsons and were part of a Protestant sect called the Plymouth Brethren.

The blond-haired and artistic Derek—who came from a boisterous family of eleven children—and the dark haired Paul were best mates. Shunning football for painting in the Hewsons' garage, Paul found comfort in the manic, cramped environment at the Rowens.

A Confident Boy

As a boy, Paul spent a lot of time outdoors and had a lust for life. An adventurer, he would explore the neighborhood, including the fields and trees behind the family home. On summer weekends, he would accompany his family to the Rankin's beach chalet in Rush, on the Co. Dublin coast, and also canvas that area—to see what he might discover.

Outside of his friendship with Derek, who was a year ahead of him, Bono was an independent spirit at the time. Intellectually able, confident, and somewhat haughty, he wasn't much interested in other kids.

Operatic Bob

Bob Hewson was an opera fanatic. Playing his music really loud, Bono's father would stand in front of the stereo speakers with Iris's knitting needles, pretending to conduct.

Although he resisted it for years, begging his father to "turn that down," Bono eventually came to appreciate the style. Of course, Norman's collection—which counted the Who and Hendrix—was much more to his liking. Bono was also exposed early on to the likes of Engelbert Humperdinck and Tom Jones, two of his mother's favorites, and eventually co-wrote a song, "Sugar Daddy" for the latter.

The Chess Champion

By 1971, Bono had proven himself as a talented chess player, but when he became famous, music journalists made more of his talent than was actually true. Bob Hewson—who taught his boy to play the game—told *Unforgettable Fire* author Eamon Dunphy in 1987, "I think that's been blown up. The press got it and blew it up. He did join a chess club and he won a couple of medals. He beat the chairman of the club and in order to maintain the chairman's reputation he more or less exaggerated Paul's prowess."

On the ZooTV trek, Bono indicated that he was hesitant to admit his love of chess early on because it was an uncool pursuit. A chess geek would be the polar opposite of a rock and roll singer. So he kept the fact that he played in adult tournaments and internationally when he was ten or eleven quiet until he was an established music personality.

St. Patrick's

In the summer of 1971, Paul Hewson had finished primary school in Glasnevin, graduating second in his class. Despite the marks, he hadn't earned a scholarship to high school like his older brother Norman had done, and the tuition was too expensive for Bobby. Therefore Paul was sent to attend Dublin's less prestigious and more working class St. Patrick's Secondary School, reluctantly.

After school, he would hang out in Griffith Park, and talk with a clique of music aficionados about Jimi Hendrix, the Beatles, and the Who, artists his older brother had turned him onto. Still, Bono was unchallenged and unhappy and began to ditch classes to wander around Grafton Street.

Frustrated by a bitchy Spanish teacher called Biddy, the twelve-year-old and some friends had followed her into St. Pat's Cathedral Park, where she would often eat her lunch. Hiding behind a bush, Paul took revenge as he flung dry dog shit at her. He was caught and while he wasn't expelled on the spot, he was quite ecstatic when he learned that he wouldn't be allowed to return for the 1972–73 academic year.

Mount Temple

Faced with a dilemma about where their son might go to school, Bob and Iris had learned about Mount Temple, the first comprehensive, co-ed, non-denominational school in Dublin. With the religious and social barriers removed, twelve-year-old Bono felt free. There were no uniforms, encouraging individuality. The teachers not only taught; they listened.

In between classes and at lunchtime, the students were free to roam the Mall, a corridor that ran the length of Mount Temple. It was here that Bono thrived socially and had his first real interaction with girls. Paul's empathy with women was an extension of his close relationship with his mother, as he formed relationships with classmates like Zandra Laing, the daughter of St. Candice's Vicar, and, later, Maeve O'Regan.

At this age, Bono had become well versed in the CIE bus schedule, which took him the five miles to Dublin City Centre. From here, he would connect on another bus to the school. He became quickly familiar with the city's best record shops like Golden Discs and Pat Egan's, where he would browse for hours.

On May 17, 1974, that same bus route nearly became Bono's end. He just escaped being a casualty in one of the worst bombings ever in Southern Ireland, when Loyalist paramilitaries planted three car bombs in the City Centre. Passing through on his way home, he often stopped at a coffeeshop known as Graham Southern's, which was near his bus stop. On this day, some fifteen minutes after his bus departed from Marlborough Street, a bomb blew up just outside the business.

Despite that near miss, Bono spent part of the summer of his fourteenth year in Criccieth, North Wales. He attended a YMCA summer camp there while his parents vacationed to Rome. Camping on the beach, attendees studied the Bible in the morning and were free to roam and relax in the afternoon. Here, he met a girl named Mandy, with whom he had a brief romance. Although he was sad to part her company, he left Criccieth feeling elated and secure as he returned home to Dublin.

Iris Hewson Passes Unexpectedly

Despite that confidence, the tragic, sudden loss of his mother rattled Bono to the core. In September 1974, Iris and her family came together to celebrate her parents' fiftieth wedding anniversary. The day after the party, her father died abruptly. As the second of eight siblings, she stepped up to help handle his funeral. But during his burial, at the Military Cemetery on Blackhorse Avenue, Iris collapsed with a brain hemorrhage. Norman picked her up and carried her to the car, driving her to the Mater Hospital, where she died four days later.

On September 10, Iris's sudden passing forever changed Bono's world. The death of his mom greatly altered his self-assurance. Bono would return to the house after school, but it didn't feel much like a home. He felt forsaken and often times afraid.

After the sudden death of Larry Mullen's mother Maureen in a traffic accident in November 1978, the drummer and Bono forged a brotherly bond. It was U2's singer—who had lost his mother when he was just fourteen—who urged Larry to start living life again. This early picture from 1980 reflects that closeness.

© B. C. Kagan/Retna Ltd.

Bono Mourns

After four days, Paul, Norman, and Bob were brought in to say goodbye to her and she was taken off life support. According to a neighbor, Mrs. Onagh Byrne, who lived at 14 Cedarwood and was one of her best friends, Paul came home from the funeral and retreated to his room. She could hear the sound of a guitar strumming upstairs.

It was that emptiness Bono suddenly felt that shaped who he became as an artist. When his world collapsed at age fourteen, his creative life took form. The first thing he started writing about was death.

For a time after his mom's death, Bono still held onto his fascination with chess. It comforted him during this very troubling time, until the pursuit took a backseat to music. The game allowed him to temporarily clear the troubles from his mind so that he could focus on the task at hand.

After her passing, Bob Hewson rarely ever spoke of Iris. As a result, Bono had few memories of his mother, who collapsed at the funeral of her own father, only to be picked up and carried away by her husband.

Bono and Norman were never quite clear if Iris ever regained consciousness in the short time she lived after that incident. But whenever Bob was at his breaking point with his younger son during their challenges in subsequent years, he would suggest to Bono he promised his mom on her deathbed that he would look after her boys.

Two and a Half Men

With his wife now gone, Bobby—running an all male-household—designed a system to keep the house in order. Bobby would split the chores with Norman and Paul, making the beds, cleaning the house, doing the wash—once they figured out how to turn the washing machine on—and trying to keep a general sense of order.

Meanwhile, Iris's sisters Ruth and Barbara tried to look after their nephew although he was barely receptive to it. He was in an "obnoxious teenager" phase, as he would call it. While his aunts came to his defense when they thought Bob was too rough on him, three decades later Bono couldn't help wondering if his father was hard enough.

Looking to religion at the time, Bono joined the Saturday prayer group at school. Mount Temple's Christian Union offered him a spiritual connection while providing him with some much-needed solace.

Handbag Hanvey

Overcome with grief in the absence of his mother, and with Bob and Norman at work, Bono was often left in an empty house. Feeling lonely and looking to fill that void, Bono was drawn closer to Derek, who by now was nicknamed Guggi, and another mate, Fionan Hanvey, who was nicknamed Gavin Friday.

Describing the impact of his mother's death to author Michka Assayas, the singer explained how his best friends growing up took a lot more abuse from their fathers than Bono. "Guggi's now a painter, Gavin's a great performer, writing songs for a kind of 'nouveau cabaret' and score for movies. But what separated them, I guess, is that they ran from the scold of their respective fathers to the bosom of their mothers. And I probably would have too, but she wasn't around. So that created its own heat, and looking back on it now, some rage."

Together Bono, Guggi, and Gavin formed a surreal gang, a means to escape from the conventions of the real world. Called Lypton Village, the group resisted the alcohol abuse that plagued many of their peers in Ballymun and Finglas. Considerably wiser and aspiring to be hipper than the other teen boys in the area, the crew that formed Lypton Village invented their own language, came up with nicknames for one another and dressed differently.

By this time, the forest that backed up onto Cedarwood Road had been torn down and replaced with the Ballymun Flats, the first high-rise housing projects in the country. With the Seven Towers Bono would sing about in 1987's "One Tree Hill," urban blight—including gangs—began creeping into the area. With two rough neighborhoods—Ballymun and West Finglas—surrounding them, Bono, Gavin, and Guggi had learned to defend themselves from the skinheads and bootboys.

Adept at violence, Bono and his friends spent a lot of time in the streets. Studying people on street corners, they laughed at how others talked and the expressions they would make. Mocking the adult world, the trio made a pact, according to the future singer. They agreed they would never grow up.

Bono's friends were peculiar, and Bob Hewson's reaction to his unusual group was an understandably worried one. If the Doc Martens and Mohawks weren't enough, Gavin might show up in a dress. Then there was the time Guggi came to the door on a horse. Surrealists from their early teen years onward, hilarity among the future singer's early friends didn't often translate to Bono's perplexed postal-worker dad.

Blood Brothers

Bono's relationship with his brother, Norman—who, in spite of their age difference, first taught Bono to play guitar—had become strained, and continued to be as the time since Iris's death elapsed. They would physically fight. Bono, who once described himself as a "sixteen-year-old little

Antichrist who resents the house he's living in," recounted how Norman, then twenty-four, would come home from work and take exception to his little brother and his friends lounging around in front of the TV.

During an argument, Bono went so far as to throw a knife at Norman, just to scare him. It stuck into the door, which made him realize he could have killed his older brother. Together they wept, spoke of their shared anger and the fact that no one ever gave them the opportunity to grieve what they had lost.

Sweet Revenge

Although he always knew he was a bright kid, Bono became a classic under-achiever in his teenage years, doubting his abilities and briefly thinking he was stupid. He didn't give a fuck about school work, so his concentration wasn't there. He found solace in music, but it was also a conduit for his rebellion. It was his sweet and colorful revenge on the black-and-white world.

The Edge

David Howell Evans was born at Essex, England's Barking Maternity Hospital on August 8, 1961, to Garvin and Gwenda Evans. His parents, who were both raised among Llanelli, Wales' middle class, came from Protestant families. Garvin Evans was reared a Presbyterian, while Gwenda Richards was brought up Baptist.

Garvin and Gwenda

Garvin's father was a pharmacist in London—where he lived until he was evacuated during World War II. Sent to live with his grandparents in Llanelli, he met Gwenda—the daughter of a grocer—at secondary school. Both attended University College London in the 1950s, where he studied to be an engineer and she pursued a teaching career.

Soon after their graduation, Garvin and Gwenda married. With Garvin committed to serve two years in the Fleet Air Arm of the National Service, he asked to be kept close to home, but he was instead sent to Eglington, Northern Ireland. When his time was up, in 1962 he was offered a job in Dublin with Plessey Engineering, and the Evans settled in Malahide, in a nice, comfortable section of the suburb called St. Margaret's Park.

Before Garvin had left the service, he and Gwenda had already started a family. In 1959, their first son, Richard—who was informally called Dick—arrived. David—or Dave as he was called—followed in 1961, with a younger sister, Gill, rounding out the Evans clan.

The family was a musical one: Edge's father co-founded the Dublin Male Welsh Voice Choir. Meanwhile, his mom served as an active member of the Malahide Musical Society. Garvin also played piano, and although Gwenda was a mere beginner on the keys, she played for her children's entertainment.

St. Andrews

Dave's mom also tried to instill the Welsh traditions in her children—rugby, singing, church on Sunday. Dave attended St Andrew's Church of Ireland School in Malahide, where he briefly befriended his future bandmate, Adam Clayton. He was a strong student, who may have been quiet much of the time, but he had a crafty, sarcastic side, and thrived in the small classroom environment.

Dave and Dick

Dave and Dick were very close and had a secret fascination with fire and explosives at a young age. Loose parenting, inquisitiveness, lack of inhibition, and access to a fully stocked school chemistry lab all contributed to the Evans boys' pursuit of danger and destruction.

Edge has said his first exposure to rock and roll was a Christmas airing of the Beatles' movie *A Hard Day's Night* on television. The first two records he and his older brother bought were *Sgt. Pepper's Lonely Hearts Club Band* and *A Hard Day's Night*. Their next purchase, Ringo Starr's *Sentimental Journey*, was their first Fab Four–related disappointment.

By 1968, Dave obtained his first toy guitar, a Spanish-styled six-string that was a gift from Gwenda. Another guitar, bought for a pound in 1971, was meant for Dick, but the Evans brothers shared it and before long Edge could play complete songs.

Music continued to be an essential part of Dave's life as he discovered records by Led Zeppelin, Creedence Clearwater Revival, the Rolling Stones, Jimi Hendrix, Bowie, and more. By 1972, he had started two years of piano lessons, but really didn't care for it. Sight-reading music was far less exciting than playing songs by Slade and T. Rex on his axe by ear.

Mount Temple

By the time Edge stepped up to Mount Temple in 1973, he began to take guitar lessons. A relatively shy boy who was small for his age, Dave found the bigger environs of his next school, Mount Temple, and the action on the Mall somewhat intimidating. Throughout 1974 and 1975, he mostly kept to himself and focused on his studies, while honing his musical skills.

Edge did make a couple of friends, including future Leeds United soccer player Stephen Balcombe. Another friend, named David "Barney" Barnett, was a drummer in a garage band. After witnessing their practice, Dave Evans was sure he had found his calling.

Meanwhile, Dick had grown tired of playing the Beatles' catalog on an acoustic guitar and was determined to do something about it. Dick wanted to go electric, and much like Garvin he had a talent for building things. Inspired by a magazine at the time called *Everyday Electronics*, which boasted a cover story on how to build an electric guitar, the Evans' oldest son did in fact craft the instrument—a yellow guitar in the shape of a flying swan—in the family shed with the help of a friend, Barry O'Connell, while Dave watched in awe.

When he was fourteen, Dave first met Bono on the grounds of Mount Temple when the latter—by now a notorious personality on the Mall—witnessed him playing songs from the Fab Four's songbook on an acoustic guitar during a lunch break. A brief conversation about guitar ensued, but the discussion was short lived.

In September 1976, Edge, now fifteen, learned from his mother that a boy from his past, Adam Clayton, was going to Mount Temple. Looking, as Edge would later describe him, as "an albino Bootsy Collins," the weird new hippie kid he saw with the rest of the sixth-form smoking fraternity was indeed the guy he had known when he was seven.

Days later, Dave's music teacher, Albert Bradshaw told him that a younger classmate, Larry Mullen, had posted a flyer around the school announcing that he was starting a band. After tracking down the aspiring drummer, he explained he wanted to attend the audition at Larry's house. He would bring his older brother Dick, and his homemade electric guitar.

Adam Clayton

Adam Clayton was born on March 13, 1960, to Brian and Jo Clayton in Chinnor, Oxfordshire, England. The first of three children, he was initially raised in his grandparents' house by his mother—who in the absence of her pilot husband—had the help of her parents and his two aunts. Adam's father was a Royal Air Force pilot who became a flying instructor upon his release and then a civil aviation pilot for what ultimately became British Airways.

Adam's family also included a sister Sindy, who was four years younger, and would later count a younger brother, Sebastian, born in 1970. In 1964, Brian and Jo moved their young family to Nairobi, Kenya when he found work as a pilot for East African Airways. The following year, with job offers in Hong Kong and Ireland, the Claytons picked the latter, as it was closer to England. They settled in Malahide, an affluent town just outside of Dublin.

In his fifth year of life, Adam briefly attended St. Andrews Church of Ireland, where he met Dave Evans for the first time. The Clayton and the Evans families became social in the community largely comprised of Protestants and British ex-pats, with the future U2 members playing together occasionally. But because of their age difference (Adam is a year and a half older than Dave) they didn't become close friends.

Castle Park

By the time he was eight years old, Adam was sent to Castle Park, a British-styled boarding school in nearby Dalkey, which was about fifty-five minutes away by car from his home. Although it was a tough decision, his parents were supposedly thinking of their son's future and had concerns about Brian's employment—by then with Aer Lingus—which at the time seemed uncertain for some reason.

Adam had minimal interest in sports at a school where athletics were held in high regard. As a result, he loathed Castle Park from the outset. He was forbidden from listening to pop music, which was considered decadent in 1968. Watching television during the school week was equally taboo. Not surprisingly, he loved the weekends, when he could return to the comforts of home. Of course, Sunday evenings were hell on Adam as his father drove him back to the cold dorms.

Unhappy with the school's formalities—which included rituals like wearing brown shoes indoors, black shoes outdoors—he grew to despise the establishment at Castle Park. At first he played along, politely deceiving his instructors, but by 1969 his true colors were reflected in poor marks. If he committed what the school called a "misdemeanor," he would be beaten with a sneaker, but the physical punishments stopped as he grew older, as they just didn't have any affect.

For Adam, the school's one saving grace was the Gramophone Society, which met twice a week to listen to classical music. He took comfort in and grew to appreciate classical music in these forty-five-minute sessions. This steered him toward piano lessons until that pursuit was derailed by his lack of motivation and dexterity, coupled with a yearning to learn the guitar.

By 1970, Adam had made friends with a group of students who would tape the Top Twenty on Radio Caroline each Sunday. During the week they would secretly gather to listen to the playback. The students at Castle Park were also allowed to listen to rock operas, like *Hair* and *Jesus Christ Superstar*, which bridged classical with pop. It may not have been Led Zeppelin or Cream, but it was better than nothing.

St. Columba's

Entering his teens, Adam spent the summer of 1973 in Malahide, where his parents had purchased a seafront home. With his maternal grandparents close by, the thirteen-year-old rode his bicycle, explored the beach and hung out with his grandfather. That fall, he moved to St. Columba's College, an Irish public boarding school in Whitechurch. Despite being an avid reader, his grades continued to be mediocre.

Adam was slow to make companions, but he found one in a classmate named John Leslie. Leslie played guitar and had smuggled in a vast collection of musical cassettes, including the likes of the Who, Cream, Crosby, Stills, Nash & Young, and the Grateful Dead. In the fall of 1974—after realizing that Eric Clapton didn't begin playing guitar until he was fifteen—Adam plunked down £12 on his first guitar, a used acoustic. He learned to play a few songs and even took a few lessons.

At St. Columba's, a fellow student named Stuart Dolan had convinced the powers at be at the College to let him convert one of the horse stables into a music room in his third year. Here, he formed a band of his own and upon witnessing this group play songs by John Lennon and Santana, Adam and his friend John became inspired to follow suit.

With Dolan set to graduate, Clayton and Leslie set their eyes on his music room. Hatching a plan for their own band, John—a much more accomplished guitarist—suggested to Adam that they could do so if he switched to bass. With Leslie committed to teach him the instrument, Clayton—about to turn fifteen—petitioned his parents to get him one. They agreed.

"I Always Wanted to Be a Rock Star"

Upon receiving the bass—a dark brown Ibanez copy that Jo bought him for £52—her son fell in love with the instrument and—according to U2's 1987 *Time* Cover Story—pledged, "I'll play till I'm bigger than the Beatles." Adam, who was without an amp at this stage—also vowed to try harder with his school work and his enthusiasm showed, with improvements in English, Math, and Biology.

Although his demeanor in a St. Columba's evaluation was described as "excellent" and "pleasantly eccentric" by his House Warden, the latter remained a doubter, and insisted that "not nearly enough work is being done." Clayton was clearly distracted. He had made his career choice, all he had to do was figure out how to make it. With his bass in hand, Adam imagined himself onstage in front of thousands. From this point onward it was his goal in life to be a rock star.

Rebel, Rebel

In the summer of 1975, Adam traveled to visit his parents, who were living temporarily in Singapore. Upon his return, he had a pair of cool prescription sunglasses which he often wore in place of his regulation glasses. He was soon enough called to the Headmaster's office and told that he could not wear his "shades" around the school.

Another time, the housemaster spotted Clayton, whose parents had by now returned home to Ireland, in full hippie gear and his sunglasses, ready to go home for the weekend. Confronting him for violating the dress code as he was getting into their car, the House Master ordered him to change. Adam complied but when he returned on Sunday, he was informed he was "gated," or restricted to certain parts of the school.

As its resident rebel and a hippie at St. Columba's boarding school, Adam's days were numbered in the spring of 1976 because of poor grades and an increasingly defiant attitude. Much of his focus in what became his final year was spent with Leslie, plotting their band and beginning work on an Irish rock opera. It was based on the Celtic myth of the Children of Lir—where children are turned into swans by their wicked stepmother.

In his final days at the school, after breaching his "gated" order by revealing he had ventured up into the mountains to smoke with a couple of girls, Clayton supposedly relayed to the House Master disrespectfully that the rules were stupid, and he refused to do something stupid just for the sake of appearances.

Although he was never officially expelled—his parents just decided to stop spending money on his expensive tuition because they weren't getting a return on the investment—Adam would ultimately return to the college a hero.

As arguably its most famous former student in May 2009, Clayton presented it with the bass guitar he previously played in a concert in New Orleans to aid those displaced after Hurricane Katrina. Adam spoke of his time at St. Columba's and acknowledged some of his shortcomings while he attended.

He also praised the inspiration of some of his teachers, especially his art teacher of the time, Chris Vis, before closing out his visit by spending time talking with the pupils and giving autographs.

Mount Temple

Although he was bound for a new school in the fall, the summer of 1976 offered sixteen-year-old Adam a rare opportunity to see another part of the world. He was invited by Gordon Petherbridge, a friend of his from St Columba's whose father was the Australian Ambassador to Pakistan and Afghanistan, to join him on a holiday in Rawalpindi, Pakistan.

Here he smoked hash for the first time and discovered the sounds of Bob Marley. In a side trip up to Kabul for a week, he picked up his soon to be notorious Afghan coat. Having the time of his life, the trip had clearly expanded his horizons. When he reluctantly returned to Ireland, his parents—as planned—sent him to the nearest free school, Mount Temple, that September.

On the Mall at Mount Temple, Adam—clearly an independent spirit—quickly latched onto a group of cigarette and dope smokers. A proud burn-out with a unique presence, the kid with the posh accent, the corkscrew blond hair and the AFGHANISTAN '76 T-shirt sported his prized long Afghan coat and mirrored sunglasses. Adding to his mystique, he would routinely bring his own coffee thermos into classes.

By the time he landed at Mount Temple, his rebellious streak was in full effect. With an attitude and general haughtiness on display, he was able to keep any real vulnerabilities from surfacing.

Larry Mullen, Jr.

Larry Mullen, Jr. was born on October 30, 1961, to Larry and Maureen Mullen. Their second child and only son, young Larry was a well-mannered, albeit hard-headed boy—a notion affirmed when he supposedly smashed it into a plate-glass window in Killester Shopping Center when he was just four years old. Born four years after Cecilia and three years before Mary—who died in 1973—Larry and his family lived at 60 Rosemount Avenue in Artane, a northern suburb of Dublin.

Larry's Parents

Larry's father was born and raised on the city's Northside. One of seven siblings in a Roman Catholic family, his father became a carter, driving the horse-drawn vehicle for a famous bakery known as Johnson, Mooney, and O'Brien, delivering bread and cake orders throughout Dublin.

In his teens, Larry, Sr. mulled the priesthood at the encouragement of the Christian Brothers who ran St. Joseph's School in Marion. When he was sixteen, he entered a seminary in Ballinafad County, Mayo.

Although the decision to pursue the priesthood made his family proud, he found seminary life—including hard beds, meager meals, and cold water—very difficult. He stuck with it, studying in Cork and later at university in Galway, until he came to realize that he wasn't sure he could endure the loneliness. He approached the Order for guidance, and was sent home for a year to ponder the irrevocable step of ordination. Finally, in 1948, when he was twenty-five, he decided against the priesthood.

That decision itself brought Larry, Sr. loneliness. Most of his friends had become priests, while people from his childhood had already moved on to careers and families of their own. He wound up taking a civil-servants exam and went to work for the Department of Health and Environment.

Several years later, in the summer of 1954, Larry Mullen, Sr. went on a holiday to Ballymoney on the Wexford coast of Ireland with a friend from his seminary days. Here he met Maureen Gaffney, who was staying with friends who ran a boarding house. On their first date they saw *High Noon*, the Gary Cooper movie.

Maureen Gaffney was born in 1922 in Anna, part of Leitrim in the West of Ireland. Her mother died giving birth to her, leaving her to be raised by her maternal grandmother. When she was ten, she was sent to Dublin's Southside to live with her mother's sisters, where she could receive a better education than the economically depressed area from which she came could provide.

Maureen attended the Sacred Heart Convent School and moved on to Alexandra College while staying under the roof of her maiden aunts. Aside from her studies, she fought off loneliness by learning piano and eventually earned medals for her talent at area festivals. After college, Maureen found work as a typist clerk for the credit and finance firm Bowmakers, and spent her weekends ballroom dancing.

In 1956, after two years of dating, Larry and Maureen married, moving to Harmonstown Avenue, which would later be rechristened Rosemount Avenue, in Artane. Both in their thirties, they were anxious to have a family; and within a year, they became parents.

Scoil Colmcille

Larry Mullen, Jr. went to a local national school for his first year before his parents moved him to Scoil Colmcille, an all-Irish school on Marlborough Street. With all of his lessons taught in Gaelige, the first Irish language, Larry's father felt his only son would have an easier time with his studies later, when he might want to go to university. The Mullen men would travel the four miles to town together by train in the morning and Maureen would retrieve her son by car in the afternoon.

Larry was close with his mother, who served as his Cub Scout leader. Maureen would play piano for him, and after his sister Cecelia took lessons, Larry also expressed an interest. But after a year of struggling, his piano teacher told his mother to stop wasting her money. He turned his interest to drums, but because his parents had paid for his piano lessons, Maureen told him he would have to finance drum lessons himself.

Still nine years old when he began taking Joe Bonnie's drum class in the fall of 1971, Larry would do household chores and later mowed lawns and washed cars, to earn the nine quid for the first term. When he showed he was sticking with it, his parents paid for additional terms.

Larry soon grew bored with the military-style drumming taught by Bonnie—a veteran session drummer who had played in show bands—and he started to develop his own unique playing style. Although he was developing his own unique approach to the kit, Bonnie—who would die in 1974— appreciated Larry's passion for his instrument.

Using the kind of rubber pad that many young drummers get their start with for practice, Larry would drum along to the radio and *Top of the Pops* with the acts of the day, like Sweet, T. Rex, and Slade. "I wasn't very good at learning or technique," Larry told *Modern Drummer* in 1985. "I didn't practice much, because I was far more interested in doing my own thing. I wanted to play along with records like Bowie and the Stones."

By 1973, Larry was petitioning his parents for his own drum kit. His sixteen-year-old sister Cecilia had a friend with a brother who was selling his old Hohner toy set for £12. Larry had some money saved up and his father gave him the rest. Larry put his set in the box room, which also served as his bedroom, and added to it—additional drums, cymbals, sticks—whenever he could. He was only allowed to practice at certain times, in an effort to keep the neighbors from complaining. Larry could be found every day after school, in that small room, experimenting on his kit, teaching himself and working through his mistakes.

Rock On

With Cecilia's record collection to guide him, the first record Larry ever bought was Bowie's *Space Oddity*. He also became a fan of David Essex's "Rock On," Bruce Springsteen, the Eagles, and Roxy Music. He actively studied the drum work on most of the rock music and pop music of the day. Larry also listened to legendary drummers like Buddy Rich, Gene Krupa, and Sandy Nelson when he wasn't grooving to Sweet, T. Rex, and the Glitter Band.

Although his father wanted Larry to go to Chanel College or possibly St. Paul's, and he was pressured to take the entrance exams, his dad eased off when the Mullens lost their youngest child, Mary, in 1973. She was just nine years old, however little else has ever been discussed about her passing.

By the time Larry moved up to Mount Temple in 1974, his parents, recognizing their son was just a satisfactory student, felt it offered him a wide range of subjects. With the possibility that Larry might become a

professional musician someday, his dad even suggested he consider joining the army, so that he could play in the band and get a proper musical
education. But with a seven-year commitment, and the thought that he'd be
away from his mother and her cooking, not to mention the friends he had
established, Larry dismissed the idea.

Despite his good looks and long blond hair, Larry kept to himself around
Mount Temple from the outset. He was nicely mannered, but guarded
around other kids. Clad in a leather jacket—the beginnings of a look he
cultivated during U2's 1980s ascension—Mullen stood out and had a confidence undoubtedly bolstered by his musical ability. Furthermore, he was a
walking bullshit detector who had no time for phonies.

Speaking of Larry's hair, it was what kept him from joining the Artane
Boys Band for very long. Members of the ABB were given the distinction
of playing on All-Ireland Day in Dublin's Croke Park, but in order to join a
young man's hair needed to be a suitable length. At the first rehearsal, the
bandmaster informed he would need a trim. Larry agreed. But when the
next rehearsal came the following week, he was told his hair was still too
long. That was enough for the drummer, who politely agreed to cut it again,
but knew when he walked out, he was never going back.

Larry Sr. instead managed to get his son a position in the Post Office
Workers' Union Band. Playing a variety of styles, from traditional Irish music
to popular hits at festivals and fairs throughout Ireland, Larry proudly
debuted with the band in the 1975 St. Patrick's Day Parade through Dublin.
He was having the time of his life during his two-year tenure with the
POWUB. Traveling with the other members of the band, and socializing
with some of the attractive females, he suspected that this kind of fun could
be multiplied if he started his own rock band.

So, in September 1976, Larry Mullen, Jr.—at the encouragement of his
father—posted a notice up at Mount Temple about forming a band.

And I Can Grow

The Early Years

U2 Is Formed

Well before U2's first-ever practice/meeting, Bono had observed Edge—who was a year behind him at Mount Temple—in the corridors of the school with some albums by Taste, Rory Gallagher's first band, under his arm. Later, Bono spotted him sitting in a hallway of the school playing Neil Young's "The Needle and the Damage Done."

Larry Mullen, Jr.'s Flyer

The seeds of U2 were sown after Larry Mullen, Jr. posted a note on the Mount Temple bulletin board in September 1976 seeking other musicians to start a band. The flyer—according to *Star Hits* writer Chris Heath—revealed that he had "money wasted on a drum kit" and wondered if there were "others out there who had done the same on guitars?"

Although Paul Hewson didn't see the note, he had gotten word about it and approached Larry to inform him that he could play guitar. Of course the reality was that he only knew a few chords.

Elsewhere, Dave Evans—who had pondered starting his own band—learned from one of Mount Temple's music teachers that a younger student was looking to form a band.

Less than a month after coming to Mount Temple, Adam Clayton was approached rather timidly by Larry, two years his junior, to inform him that he was a drummer looking to form a band. Adam had actually seen Larry's flyer on the walls of Mount Temple but dismissed it when he thought it was a school-related activity. When he found out it wasn't, he was receptive to the idea and told Larry to give him a call.

First Practice

On September 25, 1976, the six interested respondents congregated at the Mullen's house. Dave and Dick Evans brought a homemade yellow "Flying V" electric guitar, Adam Clayton had his Ibanez-styled bass in tow, Ivan McCormick brought a Stratocaster knock off, Paul Hewson brought himself, and a curiosity seeker named Peter Martin showed up to suggest he would manage the group.

With Mullen's drum kit occupying the area between his parent's kitchen and back entranceway, those with instruments joined in on spotty renditions of the Rolling Stones' "Brown Sugar" and "Satisfaction" when they weren't tuning up. One of the first things that the others uniformly noticed was that Larry could really play the drums.

"The Edge could play," Larry remembered in *Time* back in 1987. "Adam just looked great—big bushy hair, long Afghan coat, bass guitar, and amp. He talked like he could play, used all the right words, like 'gig.' I thought, this guy must know how to play. Then Bono arrived, and he meant to play the guitar, but he couldn't play very well, so he started to sing. He couldn't do that either. But he was such a charismatic character, that he was in the band anyway, as soon as he arrived."

Arriving on the back of his friend Reggie "Bad Dog" Manuel's motorbike, Bono made quite a grand entrance at the Mullens' home in Artane. But it was still clearly Larry's show on that first day. And with his parents and sister Cecilia present, Adam couldn't help wondering if he was auditioning for Larry or his parents.

The Larry Mullen Band

"It was the Larry Mullen Band for about ten minutes, so as not to hurt my feelings," the drummer laughed to the *Toronto Sun* in 2009. "Then Bono came in and that was the end of that."

At first Larry was the star. When he hit the skins, everyone was astounded. Larry had a real ability that came from his years of practice. He played the drums with agility and determination, as if his life depended on it.

Although Dick Evans had already left school, he and The Edge had always played music together, so it only made sense that they came together, replete with the homemade electric guitar Dick had built in the Evans' garden shed. Thinking back on the day, Bono would tell *Hot Press*, jokingly, in 1983, "There was Edge and his brother Dick—two people who were anti-guitar heroes, anti-heroes full stop. Edge would only take his guitar out on formal occasions—not a man to sleep with it. Or even put new strings on it!"

Touchstones for everyone at the audition were T. Rex and Bowie, and although it was hardly spectacular, the first-ever practice of the band that would become U2 was encouragement enough to work forward.

Before parting company, the aspiring musicians planned for a second practice. Coming away from that first meeting, they all seemed to get along, which was an important first step. They were happy to find kindred spirits.

Practice, Practice, and More Practice

On the heels of its first gathering, the newly formed group approached two teachers at Mount Temple to see if they would let them rehearse on Wednesday afternoons, when the school typically had half days. With the help of a history teacher named Donald Moxham, and the willingness of music teacher Mister McKenzie, who let them use his classroom, their rehearsal schedule was cemented.

Despite his guitar and amp, Peter Martin was the band's first sacrificial member because of his inability to play and age difference. Within the first few rehearsals, Ivan McCormick was also out of the mix. And even though Adam couldn't really play, the fact that he owned a bass made him a keeper.

By this point, Bono's lack of a guitar, and playing skills that were deemed inferior to Dave's and Dick's, he was left with little else to do but sing, even if his voice wasn't all that great. The guitars, bass, and microphone went through one little amp and a large part of their rehearsal time was spent on tuning and arguing.

Feedback

In search of a name, someone—either Clayton or Hewson—suggested "Feedback" and the others agreed it was apt. After all there was plenty of it to be heard during its early rehearsals. When they realized one practice for one hour a week wasn't enough of a commitment, the group began to rehearse on the weekends, coming into the school each Saturday.

In November 1976, the band performed its first gig in the cafeteria at Mount Temple School, but without Dick, because he wasn't a student. In front of their academic peers and as part of a school talent show, with Bono's microphone running through the guitar amp, they played covers of Peter Frampton's "Show Me the Way," a couple of Beach Boys tunes, and the Bay City Rollers' "Bye Bye Baby." When pressed for an encore, Feedback—with no other tunes it its repertoire—performed "Bye Bye Baby" again. High on the audience reaction, it changed the way they thought about their future.

"When I first heard that D chord, I got some kick," Bono remembered of that liberating moment, speaking to Neil McCormick. "It was like starting up a motorbike." They must have seemed like a group of unrefined and inexperienced players to most onlookers, but the young men in Feedback were in all of their discordant joy. They were—like any young band that ever performed their first triumphant gig—high on their own sonic supply.

There was a definite chemistry that sustained the band and gave them the courage to move forward. It was a magical touchstone—a significant event that sustained the group in the coming months and years. When the band struggled to keep it together, they could look back on the elation they felt that first time they performed in front of a supportive audience.

Bono Meets Alison Stewart

Bono began dating Alison Stewart in November 1976. A fellow Mount Temple student, she was a year behind him (born March 23, 1961) in Edge's class.

When Bono first saw Alison—who was in the fifth year with Adam and Dave—he was smitten. A beauty with dark hair, tan skin, a wonderful smile, and a gorgeous body, he courageously approached her on her first day of school, but she shunned his early advances.

Smart and sensible, Alison still found something alluring about Paul Hewson, and after a few years, she softened to him, and they began a relationship that would survive and thrive, despite Bono's choice for a career in rock and roll.

Of course, Paul wasn't your usual rocker. And although the band was getting off the ground, the two began to attend meetings of the religious group known as the Christian Movement by the spring of 1977. Together with the group, they would study the Bible and pray in unison.

Their relationship wouldn't be without its challenges in the years to come, but despite a brief split in the late 1970s, Bono pledged to be true to Ali. Somehow managing to stay monogamous to the woman who would become his wife and the mother of his children, Bono was quoted by TheInsider.com in 2008 as saying: "I met the most extraordinary woman and I couldn't let her go."

First Gig in Front of a Paying Audience

With Adam beginning to act as the band's manager, Feedback secured a gig at St. Fintan's High School in Dublin on April 11, 1977. In preparation for the event and with Adam's parents away, the band rehearsed at his home in

This shot of U2 circa late 1979 is downright amusing. Be it Edge's funny expression, Bono's pose, Adam's fashion sense, or Larry's bowl haircut and disinterested look, the band had yet to acquire its photoshoot savvy.   © Scott Weiner/Retna Ltd.

Malahide over the Easter weekend. The show was held on Easter Monday at the school's assembly hall.

For the gig, opening for Rat Salad and the Arthur Phybbes Band, Bono suggested they recruit two female backing singers. Stella McCormick—sister of Ivan—and Orla Dunne joined on to fill out the sound and give the group some sex appeal. But the ladies didn't exactly care for their frontman and they approached Edge just before the gig to ask him if he would sing instead. In their opinion, Bono wasn't very good and he tended to shout too much.

Edge brushed off Stella and Orla's suggestion and the forty-minute set got underway. Although there were microphone problems during the gig, they fire off uneasy takes on the Moody Blues' "Nights in White Satin," the Eagles' "Peaceful Easy Feeling," and Chuck Berry's "Johnny B. Goode."

After the gig, having endured boos from attendees and ridicule by the members of Rat Salad, they realized their experiment with backing singers was a mistake. Feedback reverted to a five-piece and elected to change their name. Adam suggested "the Hype" and it stuck, for a while.

Adam's management vision early on helped carry the band. The bassist instilled a belief in the others that the group could go beyond Mount Temple and one day make records and conquer the world. Clayton's perseverant outlook and motivational words made him an essential component, even if his musicianship was pretty poor.

Adam Clayton's Substandard Bass Playing

Because of his rock and roll guise, it wasn't immediately evident just how bad Adam was on bass. He carried himself like a musician, plus he was the only one with an amplifier. Only later, did they realize he wasn't playing the right notes.

Although Bono's close friend Maeve O'Regan told him quite matter-of-factly after watching a rehearsal that the bassist had no idea what he was doing, was often out of tune and completely out of time. But what Adam lacked in natural talent, he made up for with heart, dedication, and image. So even though his contribution was undisciplined and formless, his commitment meant that there was never a chance that they would actually fire him.

Larry Pushes for a Foursome

In Larry Mullen's estimation, Dick Evans's role in Feedback seemed increasingly dispensable in the group's first year. Although Dick was as capable as his younger brother, he was a bit unconventional and at times out of step with the others in the band. In Dick's absence, Mullen was pushing Edge and the others to do something about Dick's status with the group.

Dick's eccentricities didn't sit well with the drummer. He didn't quite match the band in terms of image and drive, and Larry ultimately felt the band made more sense as a four piece. Although Larry didn't get his wish right away, he definitely had insight about the matter and would eventually win out.

Bono Writes His First Song

Over the Easter Weekend rehearsals at Adam's parent's house for the St. Fintan's performance, Bono managed to write his first-ever song, making up his own chords. Titled "What's Going On?"—long before the future members of U2 would discover Marvin Gaye—the tune supposedly had a strong mood and tone.

When asked for his memories of the tune, Larry remembered it differently. He was of the belief it was called "Wednesday Afternoon" in honor of their weekly after-school rehearsals.

Regardless of that song's true name, Bono had come to the conclusion that writing his own songs was as easy, if not easier, than trying to learn songs by the Rolling Stones and others. He convinced the group to work to incorporate more original material and eventually to reduce the cover songs in its repertoire.

Punk Influences Surface

By 1977, punk had made a significant chart impact in the U.K. Although it was a little slower to travel to Ireland, Adam Clayton was fortunate enough to have had a neighbor who was one of the first punks in Malahide. Through this rebellious associate, Adam and ultimately the rest of the Hype found themselves exposed to the Sex Pistols' first few singles, plus early seven-inch discs by the Stranglers, the Clash, the Buzzcocks, and the Damned.

Summer 1977 Hiatus

The Hype went on hiatus in the summer of 1977 when Adam was sent to London to work in the Billingsgate fish market. The Claytons, having grown concerned that their son—who was unproductive academically and an inferior musician—might end up a loser and wanted him to experience what it would feel like to actually have to support himself.

Although the assignment may have felt like tough love at first, it became quickly tolerable. The fish trading began at 6 AM and was over by midday, which allowed Adam to establish a work ethic while carousing in pubs and hitting the record shops in his spare time. When he returned to Malahide in the fall, he not only asserted that he could maintain a job, but that he had a new and improved musical taste. He couldn't wait to show his bandmates treasures like Television's *Marquee Moon*, Patti Smith's *Horses*, and *The Clash*.

Back in Dublin, Adam made a gesture to show his increasing dedication to the band. Using some of the money he'd saved working in Billingsgate, he bought a fifteen inch speaker that he could connect to his existing Marshall amp. He also paid for a cabinet that Edge could play through.

Bono Attends University College Dublin for Two Weeks

After doing quite well on his Leaving Cert. Exam, earning enough points to apply to attend university, Bono had made an arrangement with his dad that Bob would pay for his first year. But when he entered University College Dublin in September 1977 to study for an arts degree in English and History, the Bursar demanded a meeting with Bono's dad. The UCD admissions office hadn't realized that he had failed Irish.

Concerned about how this might affect his son, Bob Hewson pleaded with the school to see if something else could be done. The folks at UCD refused to budge. Although he had been accepted on his other results, he couldn't speak the national language as required. Paul David Hewson had "falsely matriculated."

UCD advised Bob Hewson that if his son was to pass his Irish the second time around, he would be guaranteed entrance in the fall of 1978. With this in mind, Bob sent Bono back to Mount Temple. That decision more than any other would ultimately shape the singer's future. Besides studying Irish, he had little else to do but work on his budding career as a rock star.

Although he never did end up going to UCD, Bono did eventually end up becoming a fan of Gaelic. By the time he was twenty-three and supporting the *War* album, Bono spoke of his love of the language, and the fact that he regretted recoiling against it as a teen. He also suggested that he resisted at the time because his teachers were forcing it upon him.

The Shoe Salesman Goes Punk

In his seventeenth year, Bono exited Mount Temple still of the belief that he was headed to Dublin's University College. Alongside Guggi, Bono landed a summer job working in the Dublin shoe shop known as Justin Lord's. Inspired by punk rock and with some money in their pockets, the lifelong mates boldly opted to change their images.

After learning he would not be attending UCD and would be heading back to Mount Temple for the 1977–78 academic year, Bono shocked the entire student body by showing up dressed as a punk, replete with spiky hair, winklepicker shoes, and safety pins through his ear and mouth.

The safety pins were later revealed as clip-ons and the look was just temporary, but the power of punk was in the air and on the minds of the Hype's members. Edge also went for a cool look, and began wearing his dad's National Service military naval jacket.

The Hype

To reflect the group's shift toward the exploding punk scene, the Hype—which the band later discovered was the name of David Bowie's first band—stuck as the new moniker for the quintet in the fall of 1977. By October, the

Hype began learning to play "Glad to See You Go" by the Ramones, plus songs by the Sex Pistols, Wire, and the Stranglers for shows at the Marine Hotel in Sutton and the Suttonians Rugby Club.

Yet for all of his bandmates' enthusiasm toward punk music, Larry heavily resisted the rebellious imagery. Having just turned sixteen and still in jeans and long hair—which was almost conservative at the time—he was hesitant to be labeled part of "a punk band." Perhaps this was due to pressures from his conservative father, and in the wake of the publicity and controversy of the Sex Pistols, who spat on their fans and used foul language on television.

NME Classified Ad

Adam Clayton placed a classified ad under the guise of "Brian," a manager, in the January 14, 1978, set off issue of *New Musical Express*. Purportedly seeking "the whereabouts of the Hype after an amazing Howth gig," the ad was a stunt designed to raise interest in the band. Based on the band's rising star in 1978, it was at least a hint of things to come.

Adam Clayton Becomes Serious as the Hype's Manager

In March 1978, Adam Clayton was kicked out of Mount Temple after being caught running naked through the campus. Leading up to this reprehensible act, Adam bet a bunch of classmates fifty pence that he'd wear a skirt in school.

Those controversies aside, School Principal J. T. Medlycott released Clayton with a letter of reference in which he praised the bassist. "He has shown considerable initiative and organizing ability, especially in relation to his music 'group,' which has had considerable success," Medlycott wrote in a letter that Eamon Dunphy had acquired in his 1987 book *Unforgettable Fire*.

"With Adam out of school," the principal contended, "he's able to spend much more time managing the band's affairs, and he continues to make valuable contacts with other musicians, industry insiders and media."

Dick's Exit

By early 1978, it had become apparent that Dick Evans was no longer the best fit for the band. The four-piece was spending a lot of time together, perfecting their originals, while Dick—an honors student at Trinity College pursuing a career in science—was missing rehearsals.

Because Edge had such a close bond with his older brother, the line-up change weighed heavily on his mind, and he elected not to take a position. But Dick's beard didn't bode well for the group's image, and his absences were problematic, so the rest of the band finally had to confront him.

Things got sticky. There was an altercation that resulted in the oldest Evans brother hitting a stunned Mullen in the stomach. Still it was Edge who called Dick to formally deliver the bad news. The Hype were being phased out, he told Dick. He was beginning a new band with only four members, to be known as U2. Around this time, Gavin and Guggi were plotting their own band with others from the Lypton Village and Edge encouraged his brother to give the Virgin Prunes a try.

Heckled in Howth

During a gig in Howth sometime in early 1978, Bono was frustrated that he didn't have the attention of everyone in his audience. Two girls at the front of the stage were dancing together and ignoring the singer, who tried to engage them.

Asking their names and putting his microphone in their faces, one girl blushed. The other apparently took the bait and according to witnesses, they told him, "Fuck off, dickhead! Get on with the bleeding music. Who do you think you are anyway, David Bowie?"

Humiliated, Bono was unsure how to respond to the sneers of those around him. But those wounds healed quick enough, and the show moved forward.

Life on a Distant Planet

U2 Insiders

Derek Rowen

In addition to the band, Bono's friends in Lypton Village continued to play an essential role in his life in his teen years. Of course, there was Derek Rowen—one of Bono's oldest friends. Alongside U2, Rowen, a.k.a. Guggi, created the avant-garde punk band the Virgin Prunes in 1978 with Bono's other close friend, Gavin Friday, and The Edge's older brother Dick Evans.

Upon meeting him, Edge thought Derek was a frail little blond-haired Iggy Pop lookalike. But Rowen was funny, tough, and incredibly smart and because of his intelligence and drawing ability, he was sent to a technical school early on.

By early 1977, when Guggi was seventeen, he left school to work for the family business. As a tradeoff, he was able to afford a car—a used NSU Prinz like the one Bob Hewson once had. The small car gave the young men of Lypton Village a newfound freedom, and the ability to go beyond the confines of the local bus routes.

Fionan Hanvey

Although Fionan Hanvey also grew up on Cedarwood Road, Bono and Guggi didn't meet him until they were about thirteen. Hanvey, never a stranger to controversy, crashed a party they were attending with a friend. Despite the fact that Fionan tried to steal something from the house where the bash was being held, they all wound up getting to know each other and discovered they shared an affinity for David Bowie.

Fionan—who would later earn the nickname Gavin Friday—was a huge T. Rex fan who often mimicked how Marc Bolan looked. Of course the skin-heads and bootboys in the area had a field day with him over his long hair, dubbing him "Handbag" Hanvey. Because of this, Fionan, would frequently carry an enormous handbag to taunt his detractors. Not surprisingly, he eventually threw himself into the punk movement.

Friday was an antagonist in the way he acted and the way he dressed. He was the first to walk around Dublin with an *Eraserhead* haircut and military storm-trooping boots. Because he dared to be different, thugs in the street found his appearance offensive and felt compelled to let him know with their words, spit, and fists. Fionan seemed to like the attention, and would happily push the boundaries of style just to get a reaction from the punters.

Arguably more aesthetic than Guggi, with whom he went on to form the Virgin Prunes, Gavin would judge people by their record collections. He was into Brian Eno and Roxy Music.

Reggie Manuel

Reggie Manuel was a motorcycle enthusiast and a natty dresser, who gave Bono a lift on his moped to the first-ever U2 practice at Larry Mullen's house. One of his first friends at Mount Temple, Reggie was a Protestant boy from Ballymun, who was cool and confident.

In earlier years, Bono looked up to Reggie and was inspired by his confidence. Despite this allegiance, Bono was quite attracted to his friend's girlfriend, Zandra Laing, and he eventually lured her away from Manuel. Still, Bono and Reggie's friendship remained intact and Manuel was there for the singer when he lost his mom.

Zandra Laing

Bono's first serious girlfriend, Zandra was the daughter of Rev. Laing, Vicar of St. Canice's—the church he and Norman attended with their mother. Extremely attractive, she had long legs and regularly wore miniskirts, which made her the object of his affection.

In an effort to bring Zandra closer, Bono approached her father and asked if he could use an old schoolhouse at St. Canice's to launch his own weekend disco. Calling the club "the Web," he called himself the spider. She was known as the fly.

Maeve O'Regan

While Bono always had girls who were friends, Maeve O'Regan stood out. Her beauty, intelligence, confidence, and willingness to listen as Bono sorted his way past his mother's death was essential to the strengthening of his fragile character.

Under Maeve's influence, Bono discovered books and became an avid reader. While it has been suggested that they may have been friends with benefits, and Bono may have wanted their friendship to be more than it was, there is no real evidence their relationship was serious or romantic.

The friends—who talked music, art, literature, and religion—remained close, even when he started going out with Ali. Maeve, with her American basketball playing boyfriend, was a free-thinking hippie chick who was always a full step ahead of Bono and, as such, kept him on his toes.

The Lypton Village Expands

As Paul Hewson, Derek Rowen, and Fionan Hanvey grew older, their circle of friends got larger. A unique group of characters, the Village members would put on arts installations when they were sixteen and seventeen.

Climbing onto a bus with an electric drill and a stepladder, Bono and his friends would take their inspiration from *Monty Python*. At times they'd put on impromptu performances in the heart of Dublin. To the lads in the Village it was a way of expressing their humor. To onlookers trying to go about their business, they must have seemed like a bunch of oddball fuck-up kids.

Nicknames

An extension of their desire to create an alternate existence, the group invented names, mythical places, and even its own language. The Village members' logic was, if you don't want the life you've been given, you probably don't like the name you were given, either.

But even if that was the case, you weren't, as a general rule, allowed to choose your own name. Bono's nickname, for instance stemmed from a joke. His friends in the Lypton Village named him after a hearing-aid shop in Dublin. The nicknames were instantly contagious among his friends. People would just start repeating them, and they would stick.

Bonovox

Before he was Bono, he was "Steinvic von Huyseman," then just "Huyseman" and then "Houseman" before becoming "Bon Murray" then "Bon Smelly Arse" and ultimately, "Bono Vox of O'Connell Street."

Walking down O'Connell Street with Paul Hewson and the other Villagers, Derek Rowen became intrigued by the name of a shop near the Gresham Hotel called "Bonavox." Discovering it was a hearing-aid shop, Guggi felt it was the perfect name for his mate, although he altered the "a" for an "o."

Bono—who served as the Judge of Lypton Village, ruling on decisions regarding the collective of friends—was elusive, sometimes mysterious, and evoked any number of personalities depending on the hour of the day. Only later, with his new position in U2, did it take on another meaning.

Gavin Friday

Fionan Hanvey liked confrontation, and as a result, he struggled at the local Christian Brothers school. But resisting the ways and means of the world didn't stop his friends from giving him the nickname "Gavin." He was handsome, smooth with the ladies, and daring . . . Man Friday. He was in charge of being in charge.

Guggi

The usually leather-clad Derek Rowen was into bikes and had silver studs covering his jacket. Known to wear thigh high boots with stiletto-heels, this was not your average kid from the neighborhood. Derek, who was the group's official giver of names, had also evolved into a talented oil painter, but the basis for his nickname had something to do with something indefinable about his lower lip.

Strongman

Derek Rowen's brother Trevor was an asthmatic. All the more reason for the Lypton Village to dub him "Strongman." He was in charge of handling ignorance within the group.

Day-Vid

David Watson was a very bright kid who looked a little peculiar because he had contracted spinal meningitis as a child. The illness caused him to become physically incapacitated, but his sense of humor made his membership in the Village essential. Originally a friend of Gavin's, he also had a wicked record collection and a brother who was affiliated with the group, who went by the name of "Niggles."

Because he talked slowly, people tended to think he was an idiot, but the opposite was the case. So he began to call himself "Day-Vid" in order to startle people he would meet, telling them "I'm mad. Quite mad."

Bad Dog

This handle was modified from a name given to Reggie Manuel by Bono in their early days at Mount Temple. Originally known as "Cocker Spaniel," Manuel was a bona fide ladykiller, with a nickname to match.

Pod

Born Anthony Murphy, his friends gave him this name because he reminded Gavin of a fictional character, Sir Poddington, the Bravest Knight of All. In charge of maintaining the group's morale, Pod—who would later become the drummer in the Virgin Prunes and ultimately U2's first official roadie—was impulsive and had no time for fakers.

The Edge

Although he was never an official member of the Lypton Village, Dave Evans had become a significant part of Bono's life by 1977. At first he was named "Inchicore," for a small town on the outskirts of Dublin. But soon enough he was nicknamed "The Edge."

Not only did it have something to do with the shape of his head and his jaw, but the guitarist also had a thrill-seeking penchant for walking on the edges of very high walls, bridges, and buildings.

The Best of the Rest

The other members of Bono's band would earn unofficial names. Larry was known as the "Jam Jar" for some inexplicable reason, and Adam was known as "Mrs. Burns" because he sometimes came across as an old woman.

The Virgin Prunes

Mirroring the Hype, Gavin and Guggi launched the Virgin Prunes out of the Lypton Village in 1978. Inspired by punk and the notion that music should shock, confront, and offend—which was altogether different from Bono's belief that music should strive for truth and honesty—Gavin, Guggi, and Pod approached Dick Evans—who was no longer part of the Hype—about joining their new group.

Designed to fuse performance art with music, the outspoken and instigative Gavin would sing while Guggi would join him out in front. Pod would learn the drums, Strongman would play bass, Dick (who would soon spell his name Dik) would play guitar and write the music, and Day-Vid (who also went by Dave-iD Busaras) would also appear, while Reggie Manuel acted as manager for the Prunes.

Before they had their line-up in place, the Prunes made their first appearance at a garden party held in Glasnevin with Edge, Adam, and Larry backing Gavin and Guggi. They performed originals like "Art Fuck," a punk anthem of Gavin's that attacked pub life, the Beatles, Holidays in Spain, and the middle class in general.

Playing small shows in and around Dublin, they built a cult audience that enjoyed the band's creative fusion of art, social conflict, and sonic power. When Pod elected to leave left the group after a year, the band replaced him with Daniel Figgis, who took on the name Haa-Lacka Binttii. In 1980, Figgis was replaced by Mary D'Nellon.

The band released singles like "Twenty Tens (I've Been Smoking All Night)" and "In the Greylight" in 1980 and 1981 respectively, which it followed up with an EP, *A New Form of Beauty*. In 1982, the band aligned with Wire's Colin Newman, who produced their debut album . . . *If I Die, I Die*, which surfaced that November.

By 1984, Dik and Guggi both quit the band, prompting Mary to assume guitar chores while Pod returned to the band on drums. The Virgin Prunes' lost album, *Sons Find Devils*, was the result of this line-up. After releasing the studio disc *The Moon Looked Down and Laughed* in July 1986, Gavin left the group, effectively ending the band.

The Shalom

In the spring of 1978, Bono and some friends met a man named Dennis Sheedy in a Dublin McDonald's. Observing Sheedy reading his Bible, Bono and his Lypton Village mates began a conversation with the stranger about God. Sheedy told them all about Shalom, a Christian group he was involved in.

Led by a preacher named Christopher Rowe, at its hub the members of Shalom believed in surrendering one's ego to God. Bono, Edge, and some members of the Village investigated Shalom, while still staying active in the Monday night prayer group they had been involved with alongside their fellow students from Mount Temple.

Bono was drawn to the group's passion about Christ and their appreciation of humor. He was intrigued by their lack of material desire. In hindsight he looked back on his experience with Shalom as insatiable intellectual curiosity. He responded to the way they approached the Scriptures—it was very similar to what he had been taught as a Protestant boy on Cedarwood Road.

The Shalom remained a fixture in the lives of certain U2 members for several years.

4

New Direction

U2's Early Original Songs

"The Fool"

ne of the first songs U2 ever built in an improvised way. Lyrically, Bono was looking to create a personality that was uncool and childlike, the opposite of David Bowie's Ziggy Stardust.

When it came time to record a demo of the song with Barry Devlin of Horslips, Bono was in a quandary. He never wrote the lyrics down because he changed them every time he sang it. Upon doing so, he realized they were "kind of shite," as he explained in *U2 by U2*. If it's true that his lines (*"Alive in the ocean, a world of glad eyes, insane! They call me the Fool, I'm gonna break all the rules"*) weren't poetic, they were still better than the lyrics of most young, hopeful rock bands.

During the demo recording of the song, Larry—who ran over his foot with a motorbike in the days before the session—had to try and record his drum part the song with an injured leg. If that wasn't enough, the fifteen-year-old's father had shown up to yank his boy out of the studio—it was a school night after all.

"Life on a Distant Planet"

The first song written by Edge for the band, "Life on a Distant Planet," was performed on Irish TV in late March 1978. Inspired by Bono's ambition to write and record originals, the guitarist took a crack at it and found the process of fusing his own riffs and melodies together exhilarating.

"Street Missions"

"Street Missions" was first hatched by Edge and Adam at their rehearsal space in the Evans family's shed. Bono helped them build on the basic verse and establish the chorus. His lyrics, *"Oh no man, I just got here/You got me thinking I'm about to leave someday, maybe tomorrow, new direction"* may have been stream of conscience, but the song's energetic launch and Edge's guitar solo made it an immediate favorite within the band.

For a time U2 would actually begin and end its live sets with the song. With its dramatic changes of mood and direction, which were a testament to Edge's increasing guitar prowess, the group couldn't help but be proud of their accomplishment. "It was our 'Free Bird,'" Adam would later remember of the song, which was also performed on their first-ever TV appearance.

"The TV Song"

Performed at the Harp Lager contest that U2 won in March 1978, the song was named for the fact that it resembled the sounds of the New York band Television. Mid-tempo and melodic, the tune's main appeal to the band was that they were able to end it.

"Shadows and Tall Trees"

Debuted live at the group's gig on March 20, 1978, at the Presbyterian Church in Howth, "Shadows and Tall Trees" would remain in the band's live set for several years and finally surface on U2's 1980 debut *Boy*. Like many of the group's early numbers, the music for the song developed out of a jam session, with Bono seeking out a melody to fit the chords that Edge was working out with Adam and Larry.

"Out of Control"

After spending his eighteenth birthday celebrating at McGonagle's in Dublin with Guggi and Gavin, Bono woke up the next morning, May 11, 1978, and began writing what would become one of the most memorable songs in U2's catalog.

With its lyrics, *"It was one dull morning, woke the world with bawling. They were so glad. I was so sad,"* a teenage Bono wrote of his objection to being born.

Aside from its topical stance, the song's power and enthusiasm—so pure and so potent—is the main reason it has endured.

"Cartoon World"

Written by Edge, Bono had to be persuaded to sing the lyrics to this song. But not before the singer could tweak the lyrics.

With lines like, *"Jack and Jill went up the hill/They dropped some acid and they popped some pills,"* the song affirmed that the band was still very much in its development stage.

The band was trying to figure out its language, its message, if you will. "Cartoon World" was never properly released, but has been available through internet file sharing sites on the internet.

"Concentration Cramp"

A short-lived song that Bono built around a children's word game. *"Let's go, concentration, let's go,"* he sang, using nursery rhymes and other childish references in his quest to find U2's sound.

5

Play for Real

U2 Gets Serious

U2 Wins a Demo Session with CBS Ireland

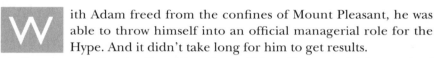

With Adam freed from the confines of Mount Pleasant, he was able to throw himself into an official managerial role for the Hype. And it didn't take long for him to get results.

Spotting the *Evening Press*–Harp Lager Talent Contest, which promised a £500 prize and the opportunity to audition for CBS Ireland, the bassist enrolled the group in the event, and promptly arranged the trip down to Limerick by train.

Just days after Clayton's eighteenth birthday, the band competed against seven other acts in the finals of the Civic Week Pop '78 Talent Contest on March 18. Performing early staples "Street Missions," "Life on a Distant Planet," and a song called "The TV Song," which was supposedly inspired by the Tom Verlaine–fronted New York favorites Television, the band—billed erroneously as U2 Malahide—won the contest, which resulted in a trophy, £500, and a demo session with CBS Ireland.

"I knew we had something," Bono said of the 1978 competition victory in the 1981 *NME* article "Kings of the Celtic Fringe." "I knew the effect we had over the audience compared to the other bands with their tight music and their pompous playing."

"We made use of the fact that we were slightly fragile and when we recorded our early demos in a four-track studio, we couldn't get a big sound out of it so we had to work on the fragile sound," he continued. "Whatever we were good at we worked around, not trying to be like anyone else just looking for what was best in ourselves."

Stoked on their prize money, Bono told an *Evening Press* journalist in 1978, "This means we can solve our money problems in a big way, particularly with regard to equipment." He also suggested the band might buy a van, but it ultimately paid for new clothes and a formal photo shoot.

Nearly thirty years after first posting a flyer at Dublin's Mount Temple School, U2's founder, Larry Mullen, Jr. rocks his drum kit during the group's 2005 world trek.
Photo by Mike Kurman

According to Matt McGee's 2008 chronicle *U2: A Diary*, CBS marketing manager, Jackie Hayden was quoted at the time saying, "Maybe someday U2 might achieve the level of success enjoyed by the great Limerick band Reform."

Keystone Studios

In April 1978, the band recorded its first demo at Keystone Studios as part of the Limerick competition prize. Overseen by CBS Ireland's Hayden, who had little production experience, the band had studio time but little guidance.

They were inexperienced and overwhelmed. It was hard enough playing together onstage. The results were pretty shitty. Adding to their troubles, Larry's dad—as previously mentioned—showed up to retrieve his fifteen-year-old son before the school night session was complete because he had exams the next day. As a result, the band only finished one song, "Inside Out."

Just the same, Graham, wrote an approving feature on the band called "Yep! It's U2," based on his time observing U2 at Keystone for

The sleeve for U2's official debut single, released in 1979 on CBS Eire. On the strength of airplay of the A-side, "Out of Control"—one of U2's very early compositions—the band cracked the Irish Top Twenty, reaching #19.   *Author's collection*

the April 28, 1978, issue of *Hot Press*. The exposure helped raise the band's profile in and around Dublin and attendance at their gigs began improving. Describing the studio experience, Graham reported in his article, "It wasn't the happiest of sessions, the band's inexperience showing up on what was a rush job."

Jackie Hayden Offers U2 a Deal

Jackie Hayden—the CBS Eire A&R man who oversaw U2's March 18 contest win and subsequent demo audition—offered U2 a record deal around this time. But the terms weren't the best—a skimpy deal for two or three singles in exchange for world rights to the label for possibly five years.

The band considered the offer and talked to some insiders before declining Hayden's deal. Surprisingly, Hayden was less disappointed than impressed with the group's business acumen and began talking up the band to the CBS bosses in London.

Farewell to Mount Temple

In June 1978, U2 headlined its final Mount Temple performance in the school parking lot. With Adam out of the school since March, and Bono, Edge, and Larry all planning to exit within a few days, the band performed in the parking lot after an opening set by Frankie Corpse and the Undertakers.

What Now?

The summer of 1978 was one spent in the rehearsal shed the band had set up behind the Evans' house. With Edge's mom, Gwenda, there to provide moral support and lunch, U2's members were clearly dedicated to their art. With Adam having already made the band his full time pursuit, Bono's father and Edge's parents had given their boys a year to have a go at the band.

There was one snag, however. Larry could only be present in the evenings. After leaving school before his sixteenth birthday, the drummer was forced to take a job when his family fell on tough economic times. Working for the American company Seiscom—which was involved in oil exploration off the coast of Ireland—Larry became committed to his job in the purchasing department as a courier. He even considered working his way up to a computer programmer in the geology department.

Larry Nearly Sacked

Because Larry was at times late to evening rehearsals and gig soundchecks, his availability to the band had become a concern to the others. Then, he suffered an injury on the job—running over his toe on his courier's motorbike—which continued to keep him sidelined from U2.

Out of concern, Larry found a drummer named Eugene from a Dublin metal band called Stryder to cover for him in his absence, and Guggi—with his blond hair—filled in for Mullen at a photo shoot. Meanwhile the others located a substitute drummer named Eric Briggs who played at rehearsals and even a few gigs. Around this time, the others in U2 pondered the ramifications of getting a new drummer.

Briggs was handsome, easygoing, capable, and donned a leather jacket. The rest of the group—sensing Larry might indeed step out of U2 for good—approached him about the possibility of officially joining the band. He agreed to join if Larry left. The band went back to Larry and forced his hand. Deep down, Bono, Adam, and Edge might have been bluffing, but they didn't show their cards.

Larry was trying to stay committed to the band, but he had pressures his bandmates didn't. Bono's father and brother could support him, while Edge and Adam's families had far more financial stability. Larry's parents wanted their son to work for a year, and take advantage of the experience that Seiscom could offer him. This way he would have something to fall back on in case things in his musical life failed.

Religious Dissension in the Band

With Bono and Edge religious allies pretty much since the dawn of the band, Adam took a stance against spirituality in these early years. For a rock and roll band, he thought of it as a threat to future pursuits.

By the summer of 1978, Adam had made his pessimism about organized religion and spiritual interests known. Clayton confronted Edge, and accused him of following Bono's lead, suggesting it wasn't something the guitarist truly believed in. Adam was upset, suspicious, and confused. He was frightened that Bono was turning their rock band into a Christian group.

Members of the Shalom also started coming to U2 gigs, which Adam thought was strange. He was turned off by the cult-like vibe the religious group was projecting. They were cliquey and although they were attending the shows, they weren't into the music. He felt the spiritual group had ulterior motives.

Revolver and Advertising

In August 1978, U2 opened for Revolver and Advertising at McGonagle's in Dublin. The band's *Hot Press* ally Bill Graham reviewed the gig and wrote, "Revolver had better not stand still, U2 are ready to pass everyone out. Oh, and both bands slew last week's British import, Advertising. Guaranteed Irish, guaranteed quality."

The Stranglers

At the Top Hat Ballroom in Dun Laoghaire on September 9, 1978, U2 performed in front of 2,500 contemptuous Stranglers fans. The band discovered that the punk ethos that the hit group known for singles like "Peaches" and "No More Heroes" supposedly upheld didn't bode well for its support acts.

With manager Paul McGuinness attending a wedding, the unrepresented members of U2 were screwed out of a dressing room, didn't get a sound-check, and were flat out infuriated. After U2's opening, Bono confronted the band's bassist J J Burnel in their dressing room and told him how heroes ought to treat opening bands.

In Bono's words, Burnel was an "arsehole." He posed as a punk, but he was really just an affected douchebag rock star. For retribution, the band broke into the Stranglers' dressing room and stole a bottle of wine.

The Greedy Bastards

Playing at Dublin's Stardust Ballroom on December 11, 1978, U2 opened for the Greedy Bastards—a group featuring Thin Lizzy's Phil Lynott and former Sex Pistols' guitarist Steve Jones. At an impromptu jam at U2's show at either the Baggot or McGonagle's the night before, Jones borrowed Edge's beloved Explorer. During the performance, Edge was a nervous wreck.

The members of U2 were grateful for the fact that they were treated much more graciously by Philo's side outfit than they had been by the Stranglers a few months earlier. Still unable to soundcheck, the band took the stage one at a time, turning "Out of Control" into a lengthy number so that Edge and Adam could set their sound levels.

Afterward, the exposure to such rock and roll excess—with the drugs and sex backstage—alarmed the group from Malahide. Bono, for one, had observed a member of the Bastards come offstage during the show, vomit into the room, and then go back onstage.

Back to Keystone

On November 1, 1978, U2 went back to Keystone for its second attempt at a proper demo. This time, Barry Devlin of Horslips fame produced the session. Paul McGuinness—who was friendly with Devlin through his connection to Michael Deeny—coaxed him into doing it. They managed to record four songs: "Street Missions," "Shadows and Tall Trees," "The Fool," and one called "The Dream Is Over."

Larry's Mother Is Killed

In mid-November 1978, Larry's mother, Maureen, was killed tragically in a traffic accident. Her death affected the drummer—who was extremely close with his mom in the first sixteen years of his life—very deeply.

After moving away from the band in the previous six months, Larry decided that he wanted to leave his job altogether to put his full focus into U2. With his sister Cecilia's encouragement, his father—impressed by the friendship his bandmates had shown his son—gave his blessing.

After the sudden passing of his mom, Larry found it difficult to focus on certain tasks. He recoiled and stayed inside. It was Bono who came to his house and urged him to get out and embrace life again. Sitting on Mullen's front stoop, Bono opened up about losing his own mother when he was merely fourteen. In that moment, a brotherly bond was forged as they shared similar tragedies. That friendship and understanding brought Larry back into the band with a renewed commitment, a feeling of belonging, and a sense of purpose.

"I was younger than him. I didn't have any brothers," Larry added in Bill Flanagan's 1995 book, *U2 at the End of the World*. "My father was out of whack anyway, so Bono was the link. He said, 'Look, I understand a bit what you're going through. Maybe I can help you.' And he did. Through thick and thin, he's always been there for me. Always."

Looking for comfort in his time of sorrow, the band rallied behind him. Bono and Edge drew Larry in, and he started to attend prayer meetings with his U2 mates.

No Deals

By late 1978, McGuinness began sending U2 demo tapes to A&R representatives at record labels in London and in America. There was a general lack of interest, but on the rare occasion when someone would come to Ireland to check out the band, things would fall apart.

Released as a proper single in North America in March 1981, U2 performed their debut hit on *The Tomorrow Show with Tom Snyder* two months later. Some copies included a fold out, six-panel poster sleeve. The front featured a poster of the band, while the back featured praise from press, radio, and retail people with the proclamation: U2 IS MAKING PEOPLE VERY TALKATIVE. *U2Wanderer.org*

Maybe it was just that U2's demo wasn't that good. At least that was some of the feedback the band was getting. Due to his schmoozing, however, Adam was invited to Charles O'Connor of Horslips' Christmas party. Here he handed off U2's new demo to Dublin scenester and musician B. P. Fallon, leaving him to criticize it later. Said Fallon in his book *U2—Faraway So Close,* "The singer was crap, the rhythm section was lumpy, but the guitarist had the magic with traces of Tom Verlaine's shimmer and—although he'd never heard of him—the fluid tones of Barry Melton from Country Joe and the Fish." Yikes.

6

There's a TV Show

U2 on the Idiot Box

The Hype on TV: RTE's *Our Times* and *Youngline*

When Bono learned that an RTE producer was coming to inter-view Mount Temple music teacher Albert Bradshaw about his children's choir in early 1978, he approached the instructor about bringing the television man around to meet this young band. The pitch was that the Hype was a group of kids who wrote and played their own tunes.

In anticipation of the producer's arrival, the band was in a predicament. They had spent too much time disagreeing and hadn't perfected their own compositions. So when the RTE employee came to meet the group and asked to hear one of their own numbers, they faked it, instead playing a lesser-known Ramones song, "Glad to See You Go."

The producer was impressed and offered to put them on the network's *Youngline* program. When they got to the TV studio to shoot the segment in late February, they had fully rehearsed their own songs, and had little trouble pulling off "Street Missions" and "Life on a Distant Planet."

In a subsequent visit to RTE, a performance of "The Fool" was also shot and aired on a separate program called *Our Times*. By the time both of these performances were broadcast, the group had already changed its name to U2.

"Tomorrow"

On May 30, 1981, the day before wrapping its three-month North American tour at the Fast Lane in Asbury Park, New Jersey, U2 taped its debut U.S. television appearance for *The Tomorrow Show with Tom Snyder* at ABC Studios in New York. The band performed "I Will Follow" and "Twilight" and answered questions from the host, who ignorantly called them "the U2."

The band quickly corrected him. And when Snyder, who was prone to finger-pointing, remarked about The Edge's "funny" name, the guitarist replied, "Well, we wanted to call me Johnny Carson, but somebody else had thought of that."

TV Gaga

On January 30, 1986, U2 unexpectedly turned up on *TV Gaga*, an Irish television program recorded at Dublin's RTE Studios. Dismissing plans to just lay low and work on new material, Bono and Larry provided an interview before Edge and Adam joined them for performances of three songs.

The first was "Womanfish," which Bono told viewers was "about this mermaid we met in America." It was the only time the song was ever performed in public. Another song, introduced as "I Trip Through Your Wires," did wind up on the group's next studio album, but here got a primitive treatment. Finally, they rounded out the show with a rendition of Bob Dylan's "Knockin' on Heaven's Door."

Following the performance, in which Bono seemed a little tipsy, U2 resumed work on material for its upcoming album. The camp remained silent for the next few months.

Outside It's America

On April 2, U2 launched its 110-date world tour in support of *The Joshua Tree*, with former-Horslips-member-turned-director Barry Devlin along for the start of the trek. Devlin filmed the band and traced its early-spring tour activities for an MTV special named *Outside It's America* that would air later in the year.

Taking its title from a line in "Bullet the Blue Sky," the film balances light-hearted footage of U2's members with unreleased videos for "In God's Country" and the forthcoming B-side "Spanish Eyes."

The Simpsons

On April 26, 1998, U2 guest starred on the U.S. animated comedy series *The Simpsons*. It was the beloved show's two hundredth episode, and found U2 assisting Homer Simpson in his aspiration to become Springfield's Director of Sanitation.

In the episode, titled "Trash of the Titans," Bono and the boys brought their PopMart Tour to Springfield for "Homerpalooza" and invited Homer onstage as they performed the song "The Garbage Man Can" to the tune "The Candy Man."

According to Executive Producer Mike Scully, the legendary adult cartoon had heard that U2 was interested in doing the show. The episode—which also guest starred Steve Martin—won an Emmy later in the year for Outstanding Animated Program.

Cash

On April 6, 1999, U2 recorded a tribute to country legend and fallen friend Johnny Cash with a performance of "Don't Take Your Guns to Town," which it submitted for broadcast during the made-for-TV concert special. Airing on April 18 in the U.S. on TNT, it was filmed at their Hanover Quay facility in Dublin.

Top of the Pops

Atop U2's own Clarence Hotel in Dublin on September 27, 2000, the band shot its first live performance for BBC-TV's *Top of the Pops* since 1983. Several thousand fans got word of the performance, which could only be heard and not seen on the street.

The group filmed several renditions of "Beautiful Day," its lead single from *All That You Can't Leave Behind*, and "Elevation." Both aired on October 6.

The Super Bowl

On February 2, 2002, U2 performed in New Orleans during the halftime performance of Super Bowl XXXVI. During rehearsals in the Superdome, the band decided to use a large screen that will list all of the names of those that died during the terrorist attacks on September 11, 2001.

Beginning with "Beautiful Day," which had become U2's biggest hit in years, the band appeared on a larger version of the heart-shaped stage it had been using for the *Elevation* Tour. From there, as the group broke into its pensive "MLK," the names scrolled behind the band. It was a chilling moment that gave way to a powerful version of "Where the Streets Have No Name." It was arguably the best halftime performance ever.

Later, Bono revealed that the whole time he was performing, he was worried about the vulnerability of his earplugs, which caused him to panic during the gig. Looking back at his performance later, Bono was critical of his bothersome smirk and uncomfortable strut, describing himself as a 'prat.'"

"The Saints Are Coming"

In a unique collaboration but not entirely a side project, U2 teamed with Green Day on a cover of the Skids' song "The Saints Are Coming," which was produced by Rick Rubin and recorded at Abbey Road Studios in London. Released as a benefit single for The Edge's Music Rising charity in 2006, the digital download of the song—which also appeared on a new best-of compilation *U218*—included a shot of both bands walking across the street in homage to the Beatles' classic *Abbey Road* album cover. The photographer was, of course, Anton Corbijn.

Later in the month, both bands headed to New Orleans' Superdome to perform a ten-minute set in advance of the New Orleans Saints' and Atlanta Falcons' *Monday Night Football* game. It was the first football game held at the Superdome since Hurricane Katrina had struck in August 2005. Green Day opened the show—which aired on ABC—with its apropos number "Wake Me Up When September Ends"; and then U2 joined them onstage for a medley of "House of the Rising Sun" and "The Saints Are Coming" before Bono, Edge, Larry, and Adam took over for an uplifting rendition of "Beautiful Day."

Music Rising was the charity that Edge co-founded after Hurricane Katrina with producer Bob Ezrin and Gibson Guitar CEO Henry Juskiewicz in November 2005. Its aim was to provide for the purchase of new instruments for New Orleans musicians after the disaster.

American Idol

Bono appeared on Fox Television's *American Idol* broadcast in April 2007 as part of the program's special charity episode. For the show, he spent time educating the half dozen finalists about the poverty in Africa and telling them about his relief efforts to date.

The mega-popular show arguably allowed U2's singer to raise awareness to a much larger demographic than his band's fan base or the political world were capable of reaching.

The Cleveland Show

U2 drummer Larry Mullen, Jr. announced in early 2010 that he had landed two guest-starring roles on the second season of Fox-TV's *Family Guy* spin-off, *The Cleveland Show*. According to the BBC, Mullen got in touch with producers through a mutual friend and was cast as a mobster in one episode and an Elvis impersonator in another.

"He came in and we hung out for a couple of hours," Mike Henry, who voices the show's principal character, Cleveland Brown, told BBC.com. "We just recorded him doing a couple of different parts and he was very funny. It's a thrill for me to do all this. U2 is my favorite band of all time. . . . He's got his own studio so we just record it from Dublin. You don't have to record at a certain time. It's an easy gig and one that people like to do."

7

There's a Photograph

U2's Studio Album Sleeves

Boy

When *Boy* was released in the United States in March 1981, Island Records' American distributor at the time—Warner Brothers Records—pressured the band to release the album with a different sleeve. First, the U.K. sleeve's depiction of a shirtless Peter Rowen (a.k.a. Radar to Lypton Village members) didn't clearly mention the band's name or the album title unless you were able to see the back cover. While this was a marketing challenge, there was another serious concern.

Some at Warner Brothers and in the label's distribution chain felt that the image of a shirtless young boy might be construed as U2 pandering to pedophiles. The success of the disc as an import in San Francisco's gay clubs in late 1980 somehow sustained this notion. Oddly, no one in England, Ireland, or the rest of Europe made this suggestion in the months since its release.

Just the same, label bosses were worried about a controversy and went forward with an entirely different image for the U.S. market. The label supplanted Guggi's brother with a distorted photo of the band, which was put through a photocopier and stretched.

October

The album sleeve for *October* featured the four men of U2 at the Dublin Docklands, near the Windmill Lane Studio. Because Island Records deemed the artwork as unspectacular, label representatives from London came to Dublin told the band quite matter-of-factly, "Your cover stinks."

Citing artistic control, which was a clause in their Island contract, the cover remained. The sleeve—which was reminiscent of 1960s covers where a band photograph was surrounded by a white border and a track listing—was unusual for the time.

Bono remained particularly fond of that cover, which symbolized a period in time that the band spent around the Grand Canal dock. There was something extraordinary and inspirational about the area's industrial scenery. In today's renovated Dublin, it's the city's center and home to U2's own studios.

War

Peter Rowen—who had previously appeared on the U.K. version of *Boy* and on U2's debut EP *Three*—was again photographed for the band's third studio album. The band elected to use a child's face, as opposed the traditional images of war, like machine guns and tanks.

U2 recognized the emotional and mental ramifications of *War*. It didn't necessarily have to be a physical thing. Replete with a soldier's helmet taken at the same photo sessions, Rowen again surfaced on U2's *The Best of 1980–1990* compilation.

The Unforgettable Fire

With *The Unforgettable Fire* finalized, U2 began to focus in on the album art and promotional photos, and journeyed into the Irish countryside in early August 1984 with Anton Corbijn. The photo shoots surrounded castle ruins, with the cover shot coming from a session at Moydrum Castle.

Other pictures shot at Carrickgogunnel Castle were used for the back cover and the vinyl labels. But the shot on the front sleeve looks almost identical to a photo on the cover of the book *In Ruins: The Once Great Houses of Ireland*. As a result, U2—who claimed to have no knowledge of the other picture—paid a small fee as an apology to the book's publisher.

The Joshua Tree

With the recording of *The Joshua Tree* complete, U2 traveled to the California desert with photographer Anton Corbijn for three days in mid-December 1986 with plans to shoot the album cover. With the desolate landscape behind them, Corbijn snapped the photo at Zabriskie Point in Death Valley, California. Other photos of the band and the actual Joshua Tree were snapped near Death Valley National Park.

The images were inspired by the notion of the desert as a transitional place where there is no right or wrong. It was a journey to nonaligned ground—to places called Truth or Consequences, Hawkmoon, Telluride (short for "To hell you ride"), Whiskey Town, and Death Valley Junction. During the journey, the members of U2 saw firsthand the terrain travelled by people struggling as they headed west in covered wagons, in pursuit of gold and unconquered land.

Rattle and Hum

The cover to 1988's *Rattle and Hum* was shot by Anton Corbijn. It is a black-and-white shot of Bono holding a spotlight on The Edge playing his guitar. It features "U2" in small white block letters in the top right-hand corner, and much bigger brown "block" letters of the disc's title to the middle left.

Achtung Baby

After working with Steve Averill—the man who named their band in 1978—on a number of U2's album covers in the 1980s, U2 continued that relationship with Averill for *Achtung Baby*. But Averill had a weighty task for the group's new effort, which needed to reflect their artistic shift.

In November 1990, U2 participated in a photo shoot near its Berlin hotel, with Anton Corbijn capturing the band in black and white. But after reassessing the idea, they decided it wasn't suggestive of the new project's style and attitude and flew to Tenerife, one of Spain's Canary Islands, with Corbijn in February 1991 while their Dogtown Studio was being finalized at Elsinore.

In Spain, U2 was shot by Corbijn during the Carnival of Santa Cruz de Tenerife. Here, the band was shot in drag, with a subsequent session in Morocco in July 1991, also shot with the four men in women's clothes. A month prior to that session, Adam Clayton was shot naked in Dublin at Bono's suggestion when the group considered naming the album, *Adam*. Other photos that had been in consideration included a cow captured in County Kildare, and the band driving in brightly painted Trabants, the East German automobile that represented the winds of change they experienced working in Berlin.

When Averill, Corbijn, and the members of U2 found themselves disagreeing over which image to use, they decided to go for a cover with multiple images in a grid system that would balance the cold feel of the Berlin

When the members of U2 found themselves disagreeing over which of the many images shot by Anton Corbijn to use for the cover of *Achtung Baby*, the band compromised. A cover with multiple images in a grid system balanced the cold feel of pictures shot in Berlin with the warmth of photos snapped in Tenerife and Morocco.

Author's collection

pictures with the warmth of those from Tenerife and Morocco. The end result was what Bono has since described as his "favorite U2 artwork."

The nude picture of Clayton taken by Anton Corbijn was also included on the back cover, but the U.S. cassette and CD sleeves were censored with either a black X or a four-leaf clover over his genitals to avoid retailer complaints. The vinyl-edition album left Clayton's private parts unaltered.

Zooropa

Perhaps U2's most bizarre cover art, *Zooropa*'s background is purple and red in color with a hand drawn image of a face in a space helmet in its center surrounded by a total of twelve stars. A copy of the European Union flag can also be detected if you look hard enough. Hands down, this is the band's worst album cover.

Pop

U2's 1997 album *Pop* features four individual pictures of the group's four members, photographed individually by Anton Corbijn. Designed to be as direct as the music contained within it, each picture was touched with a different color.

Clockwise from its top left: Adam's photo has a blue hue, Bono's is yellow, Edge's is red, and Larry's is green. In the center of the cover, two stars surround the band's name with the disc's title in an italicized version of the same font.

While the contents of the album definitely don't hold up, it's too bad because the sleeve for the record is the band's third best, after *Achtung Baby* and *The Joshua Tree.*

All That You Can't Leave Behind

The photographs used for the album cover and inside artwork of U2's tenth studio album were taken by longtime collaborator Anton Corbijn in the Roissy Hall of the Charles de Gaulle International Airport in Paris, France. The band's music video for "Beautiful Day" was also filmed here in the second week of August 2000.

The album's cover picture reveals a clever biblical reference, "J33-3," in the departure gate sign that Bono had changed at the last minute. Early press advertisements used the original "F21-36" as it was at the Paris airport.

"It was done like a piece of graffiti," Bono explained to *Rolling Stone* in January 2001, describing the religious message which directs the curious to the book of Jeremiah, Chapter 33, Verse 3. It is here that the passage, often referred to by Christians as "God's phone number," reads: "Call to me and I will answer you and will tell you great and hidden things which you have not known."

How to Dismantle an Atomic Bomb

The album cover for *How to Dismantle an Atomic Bomb* features a black-and-white photo of the band taken by Anton Corbijn. Matted by a red and black colored frame and block lettering, it's unique and eye catching artwork.

No Line on the Horizon

The cover art for U2's twelfth album is a photograph of Lake Constance, located in the Swiss Alps, that was taken by Japanese photographer Hiroshi Sugimoto. One of two hundred pictures in his *Seascapes* collection, it is called "Boden Sea."

The image inspired Bono's lyrics for the title track, and the artist and the group agreed that the band could use his photograph as long as Sugimoto could use the track "No Line on the Horizon" in future projects.

Original copies of the album had an equal sign in the middle of the cover, but in keeping with their deal, no text could be placed on top of his image. The equal sign was eliminated from future releases.

Beauty may be in the eye of the beholder, but *Zooropa* is universally regarded as U2's least appealing album cover.   *Author's collection*

8

Do You Feel in Me Anything Redeeming?

U2 Develops Its Sound

Another Demo

U2 launched 1979 with a sellout show at McGonagle's on January 3, as its profile continued to rise in and around Dublin. In an effort to capitalize on its ability to draw in decent-sized crowds, the band again sought the interest of record labels, and got to work on a new studio demo that February. Heading into Eamon Andrews's studio, a location usually used to track radio spots, the band tracked five tunes, including "Twilight," "Alone in the Light" "Another Time, Another Place," "The Magic Carpet" (otherwise known as "Life on a Distant Planet"), and "I Realize." With these tracks, U2 made significant strides toward the development of its highly championed early sound.

Dark Space

On January 16, 1979, U2 headlined a twenty-four-hour "Dark Space" multimedia event. RTE DJ and sometime *Hot Press* music journalist Dave Fanning described it as a poorly attended event. During the hours of midnight until 6 AM, most attendees were watching a movie in an adjacent room. With their amps all the way up, U2 was trying to drown out the sound of the film. Meanwhile just six people were actually watching as they played.

Hot Press

Speaking of *Hot Press*, U2 came up short to the Bogey Boys in the paper's 1978 year-end poll in the "Most Promising" category. Later, in the March 8, 1979, issue, Bill Graham extolled U2's virtues while making an unusual prediction as he wrote, "I don't believe U2's future will be among the more predictable. They have the originality and vivacity to make their special contribution to Irish rock. But that lack of derivativeness means they could have translation problems in Britain. . . . Strangely, they may be more accessible to American ears."

Memory Man

Around this time, U2 rented a condemned cottage on Malahide Road, which it used as its rehearsal space. It was here, with Edge's newly acquired echo unit—called a "Memory Man"—that the "U2 Sound" later heard on *Boy* began to take shape during 1979 and 1980.

A low-tech analog-delay unit, which was already being used by the Cure, the Memory Man changed everything, as evidenced by the sound effect being used to craft several of U2's most memorable early songs.

The echo device took U2 into the rock and roll galaxy and rendered what Bono called "punk rock with a symphony," in *U2 by U2*.

Chas de Whalley

In March 1979, Paul McGuinness traveled to London to try to get the interest of some A&R folks. Chas de Whalley of CBS listened to the group's new demo and said he would come to Dublin to see the band in action.

Later, Chas would explain that although he wasn't too impressed with the tapes he did like Paul's pitch. "Obviously the fact that they'd won a CBS Ireland talent competition added to that story," de Whalley told McGee. "I just felt there was a bit of a vibe. He also showed me some photos, some

A signed set list from U2's December 7, 1980, performance at the Bayou in Washington, D.C.   *Suzy Sputnik* pop-art black-and-white photos, and it just felt that there was something happening with them, more than there was great music being made. And I think that's what I responded to."

Bono Heads to London

Frustrated with Paul McGuinness's inability to get U2 signed, let alone come up with a van for the band, Bono went to London in April 1979 to try to make things happen. Girlfriend Ali financed the journey and Andrew Whiteway, a friend of the singer's, went with them. Feeling pressure from his dad to make things happen, Bono tried on his own out a feeling of desperation to get a deal for the group.

Although McGuinness warned the singer that the demos weren't good enough to land a London deal, he didn't listen. Pressure at home from Bob Hewson, reminding him that his free year at home was nearly up, forced him to do something.

With the guidance of London-based former Radiators from Space member Phil Chevron—later of the Pogues—Bono did manage to talk to some record-label executives; and although he came home without a contract, his ability to schmooze music journalists like Dave McCullough of *Sounds* and Chris Westwood of *Record Mirror* did pay future dividends.

Checkerboard Pants and an Explorer

Save for Larry, the band's fashion sense at the time was a little bit brave. In photo shoots and onstage, Bono would wear polo shirts with one nipple cut out alongside Checkerboard pants, while Adam sported a two-tone orange-and-black wool jumper knitted by his then-girlfriend, Donna.

Meanwhile, the bushy-haired Edge had acquired a Gibson Explorer guitar, which was unique for its zigzag shape. It was remarkably different from the Les Pauls and Rickenbackers so common on the music scene at the time.

Rejected

On his nineteenth birthday, Bono received a letter of rejection from Alexander Sinclair of RSO Records. Home to the Bee Gees, Andy Gibb, and others, U2's placement on the label probably would have been an ill fit. Luckily, Sinclair had the forethought to recognize this in a note to the singer, calling the band's demo unsuitable for the label founded by Robert Stigwood.

9

There's a Radio and I Will Go

U2's First Official CBS Eire Releases

Chas de Whalley Lives Up to His Promise

By late June 1979, Chas de Whalley brought a CBS colleague, Howard Thompson, to one of the band's McGonagle's "Jingle Balls" shows. Soon after, the label offered U2 an Ireland-only contract that gave the band the option of looking outside of its homeland for other label deals.

Although disappointed that they were still without an album deal, the singles contract allowed the band to get an actual record in the shops by the fourth quarter of 1979.

Late at night on August 4, after its final Dandelion gig, U2 headed to Windmill Lane Studios, home to many future recording projects, to work with de Whalley in the producer's chair. The group recorded all night long.

Despite some tensions between Bono and the A&R executive—who was critical of Adam and Larry's performances during the session but was himself inexperienced behind the boards—the band came out of the studio with three finished tracks: "Out of Control," "Boy-Girl," and "Stories for Boys."

"Duff Windbag"

Listening back to the results of its session with de Whalley, A&R executive Muff Winwood—brother of musician Steve—was kind of impressed. In fact, he promised to sign U2 to CBS in the U.K. on one condition: The band would need to fire Larry.

Winwood supposedly felt the band was great but that its drummer was crap and should be dropped. Upon hearing the news, the group thought Muff's point was quite funny considering Larry was the only formally trained member of the band.

Of course, U2 dismissed the suggestion, and moved forward cautiously with its Ireland-only deal with CBS. But not before telling "Duff Windbag," as the lads would come to call him behind his back, to "stuff it."

Dave Fanning

On the strength of their live shows, U2 was already receiving support from RTE radio, but the news of a debut single on CBS increased the support. The band was invited to appear on legendary host Dave Fanning's show over four nights, with a different band member getting a turn behind the microphone. During the appearances, the three tracks that would comprise the band's then-forthcoming *Three* EP were played, and listeners were given the opportunity to select the A-side. Nearly all of Fanning's audience picked "Out of Control."

Sounds Support

In a July 1979 demo tape round-up, *Sounds* scribe Garry Bushell called U2 "another great undiscovered Irish band." A month later, the publication's Dave McCullough, the writer Bono first met in his April trip to London, gave the band its first real press outside of Ireland, writing in an August issue:

"Their set is quite brilliant. It's an often disarming experience traveling out of London and seeing relatively unknown bands taking on the prima donnas of the Hammersmith Odeon, Marquee, and Nashville and wiping the floor with them."

In the sizable review, McCullough closed out the piece by writing, "U2 are unashamedly didactic; they attack their audience and hope maybe to leave them at the end of the night feeling shifted or moved in their attitudes."

McCullough—who like Bill Graham became one of U2's most important early media allies—continued to plug the band, writing the feature, "Coming Up for Eire," on the band in advance of its debut three-track single.

Edge Goes to College, Sort Of

Although his heart wasn't exactly in it with the release of a single looming, in September 1979, Edge lived up to the promise he made to his parents in 1978 and resumed his educational pursuits after a year off. The guitarist began studying the Natural Sciences at the College of Technology in Dublin, but his commitment was iffy from the outset. He even skipped buying textbooks, instead borrowing those of his classmates when it was absolutely necessary.

He wasn't that great of a note taker in class, either. In fact, Paul McGuinness used to poke fun at the guitarist for filling up his chemistry notebook with ideas about the band.

Three

U2 released its first official single, *Three*, in September 1979. Produced as both twelve-inch and seven-inch singles, with an initial run limited to a 1,000 individually numbered copies respectively, the discs were an immediate sellout. Propelling "Out of Control" to #19 on the Irish singles chart, the three-song EP also creeps into the hands of U.K. tastemakers.

For The Edge, it was a remarkable feeling to hear U2's music on the radio for the first time. Despite the strong reception the single received on RTE and Radio Dublin, the guitarist also felt frustration in the belief that the group could do much better.

Cover Stars

Hot Press put U2 on the cover of its October 26 issue, easily one of the group's highlights of 1979. In a feature titled "Boys in Control," which was written by Niall Stokes, the entire band fielded questions about the serious and sometimes moralistic nature of its music.

"We might lack a bit of humor but we have enough humor in ourselves," Edge told Stokes. "We're aware that we're not going to change the world or anything."

Two weeks later, the band pulled down its first cover story outside of Ireland, gracing the cover of the November 10 issue of *Record Mirror*. Bono used the Chris Westwood penned feature to let readers in London and its outlying areas that he wants people in the U.K. to hear U2. He also said, "I want to replace the bands in the charts now, because I think we're better."

In the piece, Bono talked astutely of his stage presence. "I'm like the clown, calling people to look at the stage," he explained. "It's like putting a magnet to iron fillings, drawing them in. And once they're in that position, you can feed them, give them what you have. We give—and people look, and we give all—and that can affect people's emotions; so we get a sensitive audience, people who are aware. You see, I might be a hero onstage, but offstage I'm an anti-hero—you've seen me, I lose my bag . . . I louse up phone calls to John Peel . . . so you've got this hero image, which is rock and roll, and the reality, where I meet the fans afterward and I can't talk because I get embarrassed."

Bryan Morrison

In the third week of November 1979, one time Pink Floyd–manager-turned-music-publisher Bryan Morrison approached U2 and made a verbal agreement to pay a £3,000 advance for its song publishing rights. A week later, on the verge of a trip to try and conquer the U.K. for the first time, Morrison unexpectedly and inexplicably cut the offer in half.

Despite being desperately in need of the money to finance the trip, the group told Morrison to forget his proposition. Somehow the quartet managed to reach out to friends and relatives, who aided them in financing the trip.

London Calling

On November 29, a day prior to the journey by ferry to Liverpool, England, Adam and Edge were in an accident in Adam's parents' car. On the way to rehearsal at the Stardust in Artane, Edge put his left hand through the window and wound up needing a plaster hand cast.

The following day, on the ferry, Edge attempted to soothe his injury by sticking his hand in a bucket of ice. Upon arrival in England, U2 headed to Liverpool Hospital, where the guitarist was given a prescription for pain pills. Settling into their rented apartment in Kensington's Collingham Gardens, Edge worried how he would handle U2's first U.K. gig with his injuries. Cheaper than hotel rooms, the band made the two-bedroom apartment its base of operations for its two-week stay.

Over the series of the next few weeks, the group had its share of hit-and-miss gigs, but the tour opener at the Moonlight Club in West Hampstead was a success, despite the fact the band was mistakenly billed as "Capital U2." *Sounds* scribe Dave McCullough again raved about the group, calling them "the most refreshing new pop music I've heard all year," and added, "the effect is, three or four times in twenty minutes, having the hairs on the back of your neck stand on end."

Midway through the tour, on December 7 and 8, the band opened for rising international stars Talking Heads during a two-night stint at Camden's Electric Ballroom. Up-and-coming new-wave band Orchestral Manoeuvres in the Dark were also on the bill.

Despite that high profile slot, and on the heels of a bevy of press coverage, the label people in attendance neglected to sign the band. Although U2 returned to Dublin before Christmas 1979 without an album deal, the group—recognizing perception is everything—turned its disappointment into something positive. U2 took its glowing reviews and plotted a new approach.

Stiff Little Fingers Praise U2

On their way home to Dublin, U2 were waiting in line to board the ferry in Fishguard, Wales, when they managed to tune into Dave Fanning's show on RTE's Radio Two. Speaking to Jake Burns, frontman of prominent Belfast punks, Stiff Little Fingers, Fanning asked him what bands he liked at the moment.

Burns complained about the lack of exciting new groups, but when pressed for a new favorite, he said that he thought a new Dublin band called U2 might someday be the best band of all time. Tired and a little frustrated after its U.K. journey, that glowing remark gave the band a reason to be cheerful.

Focusing on the Positive

For Christmas 1979, U2 returned to Dublin, touting its journey to London as a success. Sidestepping the topic of sparsely attended gigs, they focused

An ad to promote U2's gig supporting Echo & the Bunnymen at the Lyceum in London, which ran in the *NME*. Lesser-known bands like Delta 5, the Au Pairs, and the Books were also on the bill.   *Courtesy of Angelo Deodato*

on their triumphs. With the band's recent cover stories and press clippings under his arm, McGuinness was determined to make the group stars early in the new decade. As part of his plan for 1980, he booked a sellout tour of Ireland. The trek concluded with a career-making gig at National Stadium.

"Another Day"

Prior to their London trip the previous December, Paul McGuinness went to CBS Ireland and asked the label to release another single. The company agreed and during U2's stay in England, the group again went into the studio with A&R man and sometime producer Chas de Whalley.

A non-album single, "Another Day"—which Adam Clayton later described as "choppy" and "modern" with a "New Wave feel"—was backed by a February 1979 demo of "Twilight," which was later re-recorded for the group's debut album. Its sleeve was drawn by Bono.

"Another Day" was released in Ireland only on February 26, 1980, but it was hardly a favorite of the band's and only stayed in the U2 set list until the summer of 1980. The recorded version was hard to come by for nearly thirty years, until it was appended to *Boy* in 2008 for its expanded CD reissue.

The Boys and Girls Collide

Essential Gigs and Tours (1979–1989)

Dandelion Market

In May 1979, U2 began a run of six shows at the Dandelion Market's subterranean car park that Bono would later call its "Beatles-in-the-Cavern-Club" moment. These all-ages Saturday afternoon gigs—which ran periodically through to August 4—pulled in strong attendance, which improved with each successive event.

Writing of the final show in *Hot Press*, journalist Declan Lynch heralded the band, writing, "obstacles mean nothing to these boys now, or so it seems. They're making everything into momentum, turning it into gravy . . . U2 have frankly gigged their butts off to be as tight and effective as their excellent set continues to indicate."

If the ambience was dingy, the gigs were legendary. Using a backdrop featuring an early U2 logo, the band would lug in its own P.A. and lights, but it was worth it. This was their crowd: their loyal and ever-growing followers. The Dublin music hoi polloi was out in force, celebrating their hometown band running on all cylinders.

The Jingle Balls

As part of four consecutive Thursday night shows at McGonagle's in Dublin that began on June 7, 1979, U2 hyped the run of gigs as "Christmas in June—The Jingle Balls." With the venue covered in holiday decorations, the band drew noticeable crowds.

The Christmas-in-June-themed events offered U2 an opportunity to be surreal while still operating as a modern rock group. Tom Nolan, an executive of EMI Records loved the band and the gigs. So he drew up a contract with Paul McGuinness in response to the reception U2 earned at the Jingle Balls.

While it looked like U2 might have gotten its big break, it wasn't meant to be. Nolan could not get the approval of his bosses when he returned to London and the deal was called off.

It wasn't their first label disappointment. U2 already had the attention of record companies like A&M and Arista, but their interest never amounted to an offer. The nights they played great gigs, the record company folks would be absent. When they'd show up, they'd play a shit show. The band was inconsistent.

Stage Antics

Around this time, Bono created a cigarette routine for the shows, even though he didn't yet smoke. In a trick he would do repeatedly over the next couple of years, he would bum a cigarette from an audience member and try to light it, using a lighter as a revolver. In homage to Jesse James, the singer was somehow capable of making the lighter "flash like a six-gun cracking."

Meanwhile, for "the Jingle Balls" only, the singer and Edge's sister Gill would undress behind a screen at the side of the stage during "Boy-Girl." As the two silhouettes danced their clothes off, the band helped create a memorable visual experience for U2's burgeoning Dublin following.

Leixlip Castle

On July 27, 1980, U2 performed its first open-air festival, playing to 15,000 attendees of the "Dublin Festival '80." It was the biggest crowd the band had played in front of to date.

U.K. Tour Spring 1980

In support of "11 O'Clock Tick Tock," its first U.K. release, U2 started an extensive tour of England with Fashion on May 23 at London's Moonlight Club. The two-week trek, which covered locales like Sheffield, Brighton, Bristol, Birmingham, Manchester, and Leeds, wrapped up back in London on June 8 at the Half Moon.

Of the show, a *Hot Press* correspondent wrote, "U2 are like an imminent thunderstorm, inducing an electrostatic breathlessness, the prickling of the skin, the uncomfortable gnawing on the soles of the feet."

Mondays at the Marquee

Much like its Dandelion Market gigs in Dublin the year before, Paul McGuinness wanted to implement a similar philosophy in an effort to expand its following in London in advance of U2's debut album, *Boy*.

Selecting Mondays, because it was an easy night to get a club booking, the band played four consecutive weeks at the venue first made famous by the Who in 1965. Beginning on September 8, 1980, the gimmick worked remarkably well. The first night the venue was half capacity. The second week it was packed. The third show the lines were down the street. And the fourth night the street was blocked off.

The Ritz

U2's debut show at the notorious New York venue was instrumental in several ways. It was the group's first introduction to Ellen Darst, an employee of Warner Bros., which distributed *Boy* for Island Records in the U.S. at the time. Darst, an early champion of the band, would eventually be hired as a member of U2's Principle Management team.

The Ritz performance—for which the band were paid $2,300—also counted the attendance of U.S. journalist Jim Henke, who would cover the band for its first *Rolling Stone* feature in early 1981. But perhaps most importantly, it marked the first meeting with Premier Talent's Frank Barsalona, one of the most powerful men in American rock music. Barsalona booked U2 sight unseen and would help the band conquer America's stages in the next five years.

Bono worked hard to win over the crowd. Barsalona was understandably nervous about the new Irish band he'd booked. The Ritz audience wasn't pre-sold. In fact the crowd was somewhat hostile at first, but U2 won them over, little by little, with each successive song. By the time the band reached the apex of its set, it had triumphed. It was an affirmation of the power and conviction of the foursome from Malahide.

Boston and Beyond

The band's Boston show eight days after the Ritz debut was even more encouraging as U2 played the Paradise to an unexpectedly ecstatic crowd. The audience was already hooked on the group thanks to the advance exposure WBCN and other local college radio outlets had given them. U2 was booked as the opening act for a Detroit band called Barooga Bandit, but the crowd had mostly dispersed before the headliners could take the stage.

This Valentine's Day 1982 ticket stub gave early Houston-based U2 fans the opportunity to see the group for just four dollars! It wasn't the band's first time playing the venue. Ten months earlier, the band had been the opening act for a wet T-shirt contest.

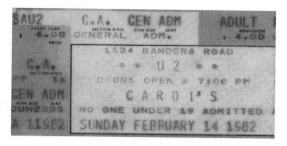

Courtesy of Angelo Deodato

Traveling up and down the East Coast in a small van with the band, a lighting guy, and a sound engineer, the group stayed in cheap hotels and ate at cheap roadside restaurants, finding themselves exposed to a unique side of American culture in their first short tour of the U.S. On the cusp of winter, U2 traveled in vans and station wagons, looking out at the stark American landscapes. Truck stop lunches meant time for video games like Pac Man and trying on cowboy boots.

U2 Back in the U.S.A.

On March 3, 1981, *Boy* was released in North America. The first week it entered the U.S. album survey at 135 and peaked at 94. The band celebrated the album's debut by launching its first significant tour of the United States at the Bayou Club in Washington, D.C. The three-month trek would take U2 around the country before wrapping up on May 31 at the Fast Lane in Asbury Park, New Jersey.

Paul McGuinness had put a lot of time into carving out a tour of the U.S. with Chris Blackwell and Frank Barsalona, in the hopes of making a significant impact. Having moved up to a tour bus, U2 had the energy of youth on its side, three months set aside and a determination to triumph over America.

At the time, before the advent of MTV—which was still several months off from its launch—a new rock band in a relatively unfamiliar land was reliant on the radio. For U2's brand of edgy rock at the time, some programmers were more accepting than others. In the markets where the support was there, so were the crowds.

With Pod—Bono's friend from the Lypton Village—in tow as its roadie—U2 spent a lot of time in the van. Listening to Top Forty AM radio of the time, the few cassettes it had along for the ride, including the Byrds' *Greatest Hits*, and the FM rock radio of the era, it knew a change was needed.

"We've taken quite a serious commitment," Adam was quoted telling a Chicago DJ in an April 1981 issue of *Hot Press*. "We're here for three months, which is very unusual for a non-American band."

Adam spoke of the encouraging audience responses in North America and predicted a musical shift was long overdue in the States. "I don't think it's going to continue much longer with very strict radio programming and very, like, middle of the road, and R.E.O. Speedwagon—very bland type of music."

Get Up, Stand Up

On March 7, 1981, U2 returned to The Ritz in New York, and this time, the club was packed with its own audience, plus a who's-who of music industry executives and stars from Blondie, the Ramones, and Talking Heads sitting at the tables in the balcony. Bono took exception to these "special" folks sitting in their chairs while everyone else in the venue was on their feet jumping up and down.

Bono stopped the band's set and made these luminaries stand up. Although they complied, McGuinness cautioned Bono afterward about his ballsy move. If they hadn't stood up, the show could have been an embarrassment.

The Gig of 1981

After wrapping its final U.S. show of 1981 on December 13 at the Malibu Night Club, Lido Beach, New York, U2 flew home to Dublin. The following week it traveled to London for a pair of sold-out shows at the Lyceum with support from the Alarm, an up and coming Welsh band that featured frontman Mike Peters, a former member of the punk band Seventeen. The Alarm were riding high on a new single "Unsafe Buildings/Up for Murder."

The Lyceum shows earned U2 tremendous critical praise, with *Record Mirror* calling the first concert the "Gig of 1981." After the December 20 show, Neil Storey of Island Records presents the band with a Gold Disc for U.K. sales of 100,000 for *October.*

J. Geils Tour

With U2's continued success, Paul McGuinness began 1982 by establishing Principle Management, a more structured organization. After playing three shows in Ireland in late January, the band—with the help of Frank Barsalona—was asked to support the J. Geils band on a lengthy U.S. arena tour. At the time, this Boston collective had a chart topping single, "Centerfold," and a #1 album, *Freeze Frame.*

An opportunity to get a feel for large arenas, give *October* a much needed push, and pick up a nice payday, U2 kicked off the first of fourteen gigs opening for the J. Geils Band at the Lee County Arena on March 3, 1982, in Fort Meyers, Florida. The tour gave U2 exposure to much of America's heartland, playing in locales like Tampa, Tallahassee, Knoxville, Memphis, and Indianapolis.

Frontman Peter Wolf, who would forge a friendship with Bono, was hospitable, kind, and supportive to the Irish band. Just the same, the gigs were tough. Few in the J. Geils crowd had ever heard of U2. This meant taking a creative approach to winning them over.

After watching the J. Geils Band play, U2 had a feel for what its headliner's audience responded to. The group conspired to make a dramatic entrance, with the hopes of, as Bono put it, "finagling" its way into the hearts of their fans.

Instead of just walking out and taking their instruments—which their promoters had warned them led to a previous opener, Tom Petty, getting a bottle to the head, they waited for the curtain to lift, which would trick the crowd—which would assume the headliner was coming—to stand and cheer.

Accepting the applause as their own, Bono and the band would emerge from behind the large amplifiers and greet attendees with a grateful "Thank you." It was cunning way of engaging the audience, but it worked.

After a run of solo dates in the Northeast, U2 resumed its second leg of the J. Geils tour, on March 25, 1982, in Phoenix. Days later, the foursome got a taste of the L.A. life before its gig at the Sports Arena. Staying at the Sunset Marquis, the Dublin band had its first real Hollywood experience. Lounging by the pool as the famous strolled behind yucca trees, it was a surreal glimpse at what the future would behold.

Bono the Acrobat

With U2 slated to play a handful of large music festivals in July and August 1982 leading up to the recording of its next studio album, Bono pondered how he might sustain the interest of his audiences. At a performance in Torhout on July 3, he got the idea of climbing to the top of the stage scaffolding, so that fans far away could see him. He also unveiled a large white flag during this gig, which he would use as a stage prop with much success over the next year and a half.

Waging *War*

With *War* complete, but still three months away from official release, U2 began a four-week "Pre-*War*" tour of Europe to road test songs from its upcoming album. Beginning in Glasgow on December 1, the group premiered "Sunday Bloody Sunday" and "New Year's Day."

After shows in locales like London and Copenhagen—where Steve Wickham joins the band onstage on December 14—the band took the stage with a mission at the Maysfield Leisure Center in Belfast, Northern Ireland on December 20. U2 ended 1982 with three nights of hometown gigs in the SFX Hall, finishing on Christmas Eve.

"Sunday Bloody Sunday" Belfast Premiere

With a nervous energy, U2 took the stage in Belfast with a little apprehension about the live debut of "Sunday Bloody Sunday." Bono introduced the song to the audience at a time when there was recharged hostility in Northern Ireland. Explaining it was "not a rebel song," the singer recited verses from the song to ensure the crowd understood the intent of his anthem-to-be.

Bono told the 3,000-strong audience that if it disapproved, U2 will never play the song in Belfast again. Luckily, with the exception of a couple of attendees who walked out of the show, the Maysfield crowd roared with overwhelming appreciation.

Because it was the first time the band ever really made a statement on the situation, and the fact that the group had decided it was morally wrong to continue to leave the subject unaddressed, U2 was relieved to have its audience's approval of the song.

This ticket dates back to U2's Spring 1983 *War* tour.
Courtesy of Tracy Sigler

War Tour Launches

Two days before the European release of *War*, U2 launched a tour in the record's honor with a sold-out gig at Dundee's Caird Hall. The band played "Seconds," allowing Edge to give his first lead vocal performance ever.

Meanwhile, Bono revived the stage antics he displayed during shows the previous summer, climbing to up to the balcony and venturing along a questionably thin railing to the back of the venue. The group closed its gig with "40," a ritual that will carry over for a number of years.

I Can't Stop to Dance

On April 23, 1983, U2 launched its North American run in support of *War* at Kenan Stadium in Chapel Hill, North Carolina. Appearing as the third of four acts on a bill dubbed "Carolina Concert for Children," the benefit—which also included Grand Master Flash and Todd Rundgren—found Bono working hard to engage the rain-drenched crowd.

With a walkway from the stage into the first section of seats, Bono wanted to get close to the crowd. He also hoped to make a visual impact. So with the white flag—used in previous shows as a means to express the group's position of "militant pacifism"—now a routine stage prop, he carried it with him as he ventured up the stage's slippery scaffolding. Some thirty feet in the air, he delighted the crowd and scared the shit out of his handlers and his bandmates. Bono's philosophy was to get his audience engaged by any means necessary.

US Festival

On Memorial Day Weekend 1983, U2 took the stage at the US Festival, held in Glen Helen Regional Park in Devore, California, and promoted by Apple Computers' own Steve Jobs. U2 performed on the third day of this gigantic outdoor festival, sharing the stage with Little Steven and the Disciples of Soul, Berlin, Missing Persons, the Pretenders, and headliner David Bowie in front of an estimated crowd of 250,000.

"I think when you're faced with 200,000 people there's no hiding," Bono laughed, when asked by KZEW's George Gimarc about the US Festival's massive crowd. "You can't hide behind your haircut, you have to deliver."

During "The Electric Co." Bono took his white flag, the infamous *War* tour prop, and carried it with him to the top of a one-hundred-foot-high scaffolding, singing the song as he moved across the top of the structure and down the other side. As the canopy began to tear under the singer's weight, the crew feared the worst. Later, after the gig, the band's tour manager Dennis Sheehan—who performed the same duties for Led Zeppelin a decade before—confronted the singer to put a stop to the potentially deadly Iggy Pop–inspired stage maneuvers that he feared would end in tragedy.

Although U2 audiences loved this circus act, Bono's daring stage antics were a risk that the rest of the group and crew no longer approved of. Of course, when asked about the gig two weeks later, the singer made no mention of the dangers.

Red Rocks Amphitheatre, Denver, Colorado, June 5, 1983

On the heels of *War*, which had elevated U2 to amphitheaters in North America, the band decided to shoot its very first concert video and record its first-ever concert album. During its spring 1981 trek through the U.S. the group discovered the venue and thought it would be the perfect, dramatic backdrop for a film.

Paul McGuinness flew in the film crew from the British TV show *The Tube* to capture the gig, and he tapped a Boston outfit, Effanel Music, to do the audio. Affirming the band's newfound popularity in America, NBC Radio picked up the broadcast rights, with Showtime and MTV opting for the U.S. television rights. The only problem was the freakishly inclement weather for June. Freezing rain jeopardized the safety of the show.

With the gig seriously in doubt, the band promised a free indoor show the next night in Denver for those who couldn't make it to the outdoor gig. When it finally got assurances late in the afternoon of June 5 that the show could go on, Bono, Edge, and Adam dialed into local radio stations to let their fans know that the gig would proceed.

With 5,000 fans in attendance, the audience was told to come closer to the stage, regardless of what seat number might appear on their ticket stub. The end result was one of U2's most memorable gigs, airing in its radio form as "War Is Declared" and its video form on cable television and later on VHS home video. Contrary to popular belief, a mini-LP, *Live—Under a Blood Red Sky*, produced by Jimmy Iovine and released on November 21, 1983, featured just two tracks from the gig: "Gloria" and "Party Girl." Other material, recorded during the *War* Tour in Boston and West Germany, rounds out the disc.

The Centrum, Worcester, Massachusetts, June 28, 1983

This was U2's first official arena gig and with the Alarm in tow as openers, the band nearly sold out the 11,000-capacity venue. Despite the Centrum's cavernous feel, Bono told the crowd early in the set, "Tonight we're going to turn this large complex into a living room," and over the course of the next eighty minutes the band does its best to bring intimacy to the roaring audience.

While there were few surprises during the gig, the four song encore was unique as Bono—now a rock and roll heartthrob—found himself mobbed by a dozen or so women, one of whom evidently tried to handcuff herself to his leg, according to a report in the band's own *U2 Magazine*.

"In any other city, there would have been a riot by now," the singer told the audience somewhat pompously. Later, the Boston-area crowd respectfully exited the Worcester arena.

"A Day at the Races" Festival, Phoenix Park, Dublin, August 14, 1983

U2 played a massive homecoming show to 25,000 friends and fans at this Dublin Racecourse. The band—supported by Steel Pulse, Big Country, Eurythmics, and Simple Minds—earned a rapturous reception when the event's MC introduces them this way: *"Are you happy? Do you want to hear the best in live music? Last December was the last time Bono, The Edge, Adam, and Larry played in Ireland. In six short months U2 have conquered the world."*

Those true words soon gave way to an explosive gig, during which Bono made an emotional dedication of "I Fall Down" to former Stiff Little Fingers and then-current Red Rockers drummer Jim Reilly, whose brother Thomas was shot in the back in Belfast the week before by British Army paratrooper Ian Thain. The event also marked the first onstage appearance of Bono's father, Bob, when his son pulled him onstage.

Steve Wickham, who performed on *War*, and will later join the Waterboys, played the fiddle with the band on "Sunday Bloody Sunday" and "The Electric Co." During the show's closing number, Eurythmics singer Annie Lennox joined Dublin's hometown heroes—who have now surpassed the popularity of other world famous Irish rock bands like Thin Lizzy and the Boomtown Rats—to sing "40."

Big in Japan

In November 1983, after a performance in Hawaii, U2 played its first live shows in Japan, in cities like Osaka, Nagoya, and Tokyo. The band's scheduled performance of "New Year's Day" was done with just percussion and piano when Edge's guitar malfunctioned.

Despite being treated like a teen-pop act and experiencing its first taste of Beatlemania-like frenzy, with Larry and Bono being chased from a train station to a taxi, the band used the trip to expand its learning.

Building on its Chicago Peace Museum visit earlier in the year, the group's interest in the nuclear bombings that took place in Japan in 1945 was heightened. They meet Tatsui Nagashima, a man who lived through the experience with his wife, but saw the rest of his family killed. It had a lasting impact on the group.

Electing to steer clear of Western-influenced hotels, U2 experienced the traditions of Japan from food to accommodations. The upshot of the visit was visible within a year, when the group lent Oriental touches to its next record in the form of calligraphy and album art.

New Zealand and Australia

In advance of *The Unforgettable Fire*'s release date, U2 embarked on its very first tour of New Zealand and Australia, playing in Christchurch on August 29, 1984. And because of its success in other parts of the world leading up to the trek, U2 were an instant sell-out, prompting the group to extend its visit to four weeks to meet demand. The tour finally wrapped on September 24 in Perth.

But Australia was also a calamity for U2. Sure the band pulled in record crowds, performing to 60,000 people over five nights in Sydney, with half as many attending shows in Melbourne, but there were serious problems when it came time to perform the new material in concert.

Much of the group's efforts with Eno and Lanois—like the heavily orchestrated title track, the meandering "A Sort of Homecoming" and the heavily tracked guitar number "Wire" couldn't be executed. The band retreated to its proven material and thought long and hard about how it was going to pull off a world tour in support of an album it had a hard time recreating for audiences.

Touring the world with a newborn baby was a challenge of its own, as The Edge would quickly learn when wife Aislinn, daughter Hollie, just four months at the time, and a nanny, joined him on the road.

The rest of the band, who had yet to experience parenthood, had no idea about the pressure and worry that The Edge, just twenty-three, was going through. Life had become more than guitar lines. The simultaneously amazing and startling gift of first time fatherhood prompted panicked thoughts of responsibility and whether he would be a good dad and provider.

A pair of companion advertisements that ran in the March 14, 1985, issue of *Rolling Stone* and marked the band's first cover story for the U.S. music bible. The first featured critical snippets from the likes of *Newsweek*, the *New York Times*, the *Los Angeles Times*, and the *Village Voice*. The second highlighted the band's first extensive North American arena run.   *Author's collection*

Madison Square Garden

On April Fool's Day 1985, U2 played New York's Madison Square Garden. Reserving most of the best seats for family like Bob Hewson, Jo Clayton, Garvin Evans, Cecilia Mullen, and friends like Dave Fanning and Bill

Graham, they had all been flown in first-class from Dublin at the band's expense for the occasion.

Joined at this point on the trek by California band Lone Justice as support, the MSG show—located right in the heart of Manhattan—was significant. The band's heroes, such as Led Zeppelin, David Bowie, Bob Dylan, and the Who, had all played the Garden. U2 had arrived.

During the gig, Bono injected a snippet of "Amazing Grace" into "The Electric Co.," inserted parts of the Rolling Stones' "Ruby Tuesday" and "Sympathy for the Devil" into "Bad." As part of the encore, U2 covered Bob Dylan's iconic "Knockin' on Heaven's Door" before closing with "40," which the singer personalized with lines from the recent all-star charity singles "We Are the World" and "Do They Know It's Christmas?"

Croke Park, Dublin

Billed as its "Homecoming" concert, U2 returned to Dublin to play in front of 57,000 people in Croke Park on June 29, 1985. Held at the location of 1920's Bloody Sunday tragedy, a day of violence during the Irish War of Independence that resulted in the death of fourteen British at the hands of the Irish Republican Army (IRA), fourteen Irish civilians who the British forces retaliated against when they opened fire at a Gaelic football match, and three Irish Republican prisoners beaten and killed while being held in Dublin Castle.

The day before U2's first headlining show in a football stadium, the band was asked to stop rehearsals for the gig when noise complaints over the band's volume were received from students taking final exams at the Rosmini Community School a half-mile away.

As encores, U2 delivered its first and only performance ever of Bruce Springsteen's "My Hometown" in tribute to its local fans. After the show, the crowd's excitement turned to trouble when two hundred people were injured, including six police officers. Local shops were looted during the riotous behavior, but the band made amends by donating proceeds from the show to the building of a music rehearsal center for young bands. Named the City Centre, it opened in Dublin in June 1989.

Live Aid

In April 1985, Bob Geldof had asked U2 if it would perform at Live Aid, a daylong charity concert he had been planning for July 13. The band agreed and was put on the bill for London's Wembley Stadium that memorable day in 1985.

Named for a line in the *Unforgettable Fire* song "Indian Summer Sky," U2's "The Longest Day" festival—held at the Milton Keynes Bowl on June 22, 1985—included support from the Faith Brothers, Spear of Destiny, Billy Bragg, the Ramones, and R.E.M.
                                                                                                    Chris Raisin

After Jack Nicholson introduced U2 live by satellite from JFK Stadium in Philadelphia, the band took the stage at "Live Aid," the day-long concert event held on two continents to raise money for famine relief in Ethiopia. Reportedly watched by over a billion people around the globe, U2 walked into the world's living rooms at approximately 5:20 PM London time for an allotted twenty-minute set.

With plans for three songs, the band launched its performance with "Sunday Bloody Sunday," but was forced to forgo its best-known song, "Pride (In the Name of Love)" to the dismay of Bono's bandmates after the singer elected to extend *The Unforgettable Fire*–extracted "Bad" to fourteen minutes.

"We're from Dublin," Bono told the Wembley crowd, introducing the song. "Like all cities, it has its good and it's bad." Defying organizer Bob Geldof's orders not to leave the stage, Bono went down to ground level where he danced with a young woman in front of the crowd. He was in search of a moment that would make people remember U2, and although he deviated from the plan, he was overwhelmingly successful in his mission during "Bad."

Bono's bandmates were angered at him for his antics—leaving the stage for what felt like hours. His shame even prompted him to consider leaving U2. But when he met a sculptor at work on a statue days after the gig, who was inspired by his dance with the woman at Live Aid, Bono reconsidered how he felt about the show. Meanwhile, journalists around the globe were citing U2's appearance as the top performance of the event.

When pressed for a comment on its involvement with the charity event, the camp issued the following official statement:

"U2 are involved in Live Aid Because it's more than money, it's music . . . but it is also a demonstration to the politicians and the policy-makers that men, women, and children will not walk by other men, women, and children as they lie, bellies swollen, starving to death for the sake of a cup of grain and water. For the price of *Star Wars*, the MX missile offensive-defense budgets, the desert of Africa could be turned into fertile lands. The technology is with us. The technocrats are not. Are we part of a civilization that protects itself by investing in life . . . or investing in death?"

Despite the awareness U2 helped raise globally for the cause and the profile boost it ultimately received for its involvement in Live Aid, it's a little-known fact that the band actually phoned Geldof the night before and told him they didn't want to play because they were concerned they wouldn't get a soundcheck. Geldof ignored the request, and a historic performance was achieved.

Self Aid

Although Ireland's music bible, *Hot Press* proclaimed U2's appearance at RDS Stadium in Dublin on May 17, 1986, "the blackest and most ferocious set of their entire career," U2 was scrutinized for its involvement in this concert, subtitled "A Festival of Hope." Organized by Tony Boland, a producer at the RTE (Radio Telefis Eireann) and inspired by Live Aid, the message of the day was "Don't wait for the government to help you, help yourself."

Performing alongside other great Irish acts like the Boomtown Rats and Van Morrison, U2 agreed to headline and lend its organizational resources to the event. This assistance was mistakenly perceived by *In Dublin* magazine, who believed the band was a driving force behind the concert. The anti-establishment publication's opinionated headline announced THE GREAT SELF-AID FARCE, ROCK *AGAINST* THE PEOPLE.

Thirty thousand fans turned out for the band's first show in ten months, during which the band served up a rare cover of Eddie Cochran's "C'mon Everybody" as their opener, and also tackled Bob Dylan's "Maggie's Farm."

In doing so, the band hit out at British Prime Minister Margaret Thatcher and later hit back at *In Dublin* for suggesting it was aligned with left-wing radicals, when it only wanted to help with the country's massive unemployment problem.

Later in the year, Edge acknowledged to *Hot Press* that U2 got involved because "we concurred with the sentiment behind it," adding "it was a gestural thing that was all about hopes and aspirations and very little about real answers." Just the same, the daylong event—which aired live on RTE Television and Radio—raised £500,000 toward unemployment relief through viewer donations, with some 1,200 jobs pledged to the cause.

Conspiracy of Hope

In August 1985, Jack Healy—the American Director of Amnesty International—was en route to a meeting in Finland when he elected to touch down in Dublin to visit Paul McGuinness. Healy was hoping to get a commitment from U2 to participate in an event that would celebrate Amnesty's twenty-fifth anniversary in 1986.

Instead, McGuinness—who it turns out was a friend of Tiernan McBride, son of Amnesty founder Sean McBride—offered at least one week of U2's time in the next year.

With a letter of commitment from U2's manager, Jack Healy was able to lure other major acts to a proposed two-week tour.

By the time the two-week trek, which was arranged to run from San Francisco to New York and would be known as the "Conspiracy of Hope" Tour, was announced in the spring of 1986, superstars like Sting, Peter Gabriel, Joan Baez, Bryan Adams, the Neville Brothers, Jackson Browne, and Lou Reed had all signed on for the cause.

The day before the June 4 launch of the Amnesty International Conspiracy of Hope Tour at San Francisco's Cow Palace, U2 participated in a press conference. "We're here," Bono explained in a *Rolling Stone* report, "because we very much want to be and because Jack Healey is a hard man to argue with."

To put some levity into an otherwise serious interaction with the media, Bono joked that U2 would be performing "Yummy, Yummy, Yummy"

The Final "Conspiracy of Hope" Concert

The last date in a two-week North American tour that saw U2 share the stage with Lou Reed, Peter Gabriel, and others while raising awareness of the human-rights organization Amnesty International and driving up membership counted an epic 55,000 attendees at New Jersey's Giants Stadium on June 15, 1986. The eleven-hour farewell "Conspiracy of Hope" concert also aired live on MTV and radio, and was also notable as U2's first stadium performance in the U.S.

U2's poignant set included "Pride," "Sunday Bloody Sunday," and a spirited rendition of Bob Dylan's "Maggie's Farm" before the band made way for the newly reunited Police, who headlined the event. Later, Bono joined the band for "Invisible Sun," a song inspired by the violence in Northern Ireland. Midway through the song, the members of U2 took the stage with The Edge taking Andy Summers's guitar, Larry taking over Stewart Copeland's drum duties, and Adam picking up Sting's bass.

After this symbolic gesture, by which rock's biggest band passed the baton to rock's next biggest band, U2 launched into "I Shall Be Released," which found all of the tour's performers and prisoners freed through Amnesty International's efforts singing in unison.

"I think we're more aware, due to our situation in Ireland," The Edge added in the press conference of U2's willingness to help Amnesty's Jack Healy by signing on for the tour, which launched on June 4 at the Cow Palace in San Francisco. "The civil rights in our area of the country could be improved upon. Ireland has been struggling for some time to extricate itself from a system of colonialism that is less than ideal. And that is something that America hasn't really experienced, so the profile of an organization like Amnesty is lower as a result."

But that all changed by the time the tallies were in: the tour raised more than $3 million for the cause and tripled the organization's U.S. membership.

U2 Versus Governor Mecham

While in Arizona to launch *The Joshua Tree* Tour, U2 spoke out against Arizona Governor Evan Mecham in protest of his state's decision to rescind Martin Luther King Day as a holiday. After listening to the concerns of fans, the band made what it called "a sizable financial" contribution to the Mecham Watchdog Committee, which was at the heart of an initiative to have the Governor recalled.

Prior to the group's April 2, 1987, show, the band sent promoter Barry Fey to the stage to announce why U2 has chosen to perform in Arizona, despite its objections about the state's handling of the holiday.

"We were outraged when we arrived in Arizona last weekend and discovered the climate created by Governor Mecham's rescission of the holiday honoring Dr. Martin Luther King, Jr.," the statement read. "Governor

Mecham is an embarrassment to the people of Arizona. We condemn his actions and views as an insult to a great spiritual leader. We urge all forward-thinking Arizonans to support the campaign to recall Governor Mecham."

According to Bono, this position resulted in a death threat when the group returned to Arizona State University in December 1987 to play its football stadium. Although authorities never found hard evidence of a threat against the band in Arizona, the frontman was aware of the threat made by an armed gunman with a ticket, who had warned he would shoot him during "Pride" as retribution for the group's position on the MLK holiday.

Bono closed his eyes and put mind over matter until he reached the song's third verse, where he describes shots ringing out at the time of King's Memphis murder in April 1968. When he opened his eyes, Adam Clayton was standing in front of him, serving as his comrade and protector.

A Stadium Band

Although U2 launched its fifty-date North American fall tour of the United States at the Nassau Coliseum in Uniondale, New York on September 10, the Long Island gig was one of just a few shows on the next leg of *The Joshua Tree* Tour that didn't take place in a stadium. For the trek, the band brought opening acts Little Steven and the Disciples of Soul and its Island labelmates the Pogues along.

In some of U2's most loyal cities, such as Boston, the band was able to play two shows at Massachusetts Foxboro Stadium. Although there were a few glitches, including the failure of the band's lighting system that prompted the band to play an entire hour with the venue's house lights on, the crowd wasn't bothered the first night. During the encore, Bono returned to the stage in a Celtics jersey, causing the audience to go crazy.

Dalton Brothers

At the Hoosier Dome in Indianapolis on November 1, 1987, U2 supported itself as it took the stage in between opening acts the BoDeans and Los

A ticket stub from U2's 1987 *Joshua Tree* tour from a gig at the University of Illinois Assembly Hall.

Courtesy of Angelo Deodato

Lobos. Performing as the Dalton Brothers, the group came out in Western outfits and wigs.

Speaking in a Southern drawl, Bono introduced the songs "Lucille" and "Lost Highway." The crowd doesn't recognize them as U2 until later in the show when they reprise "Lucille" before the show's closer "40."

Later, on November 18 at the Coliseum in Los Angeles, the Dalton Brothers again take the stage. For the record the group's aliases were as follows: Alton (Bono), Luke (The Edge), Betty (Clayton), and Duke (Mullen).

Stop the Madness

On the morning of November 11, 1987, U2 told a few San Francisco radio stations that it was planning on performing a free concert later that day at the Embarcadero Center in the city's Justin Herman Plaza. Because its gear and crew had already been shipped up to Vancouver for a forthcoming performance, the band borrowed gear from local residents the Grateful Dead.

Dubbed a "Save the Yuppies" benefit as a means of making light of the highly publicized stock market crash the day before, the band made headlines of its own for the show when, during "Pride," Bono spray-painted ROCK AND ROLL and STOP THE TRAFFIC on a sculpture created by Canadian artist Armand Vaillancourt. In reaction, the city issued a warrant for his arrest on a charge of vandalizing city property.

Bono promptly issued a letter of apology to local officials and arranged to have the sculpture scrubbed clean. In his letter, printed by the *San Francisco Chronicle*, he wrote, "I hope that the real street artists of San Francisco will not suffer because of a scrawler like me."

Three days later in British Columbia at U2's invitation, Vaillancourt—who flew in to the show from Quebec—was invited to spray paint graffiti on the band's equipment. He wrote STOP THE MADNESS!

At a press conference in San Francisco five days after the incident, Bono explained, "It's not really worth defending my action. I did it in the spirit

This ticket is memorabilia from Miami's Orange Bowl show on December 3, 1987.

Courtesy of Angelo Deodato

of the concert, and I thought I did it in the spirit of the artist's work—he agreed; but in fact he didn't own his work anymore, as us artists are prone to do, he'd sold it, and the city of San Francisco owned it and they didn't like what I did at all."

Broken Nose to the Floor

Edge's Disco Moves

In early 1978, U2 played a set during a gig in the basement of an old school building. Because of the heat from the large crowd and the poor ventilation, condensation built up on the wall. Edge, caught in a rock and roll moment, tried to run up the wall. He landed on his ass, to the amusement of those at the show.

Ladies and Gentlemen, the U2's

On December 4, 1979, while trying to make a name for itself during a two-week stay in the U.K., the band was mistakenly billed as the U2's at the Hope & Anchor in Islington. There were only nine people in the audience, plus a couple of record-company scouts.

To add to the embarrassment, Edge's guitar string snapped in the midst of the show. Out of frustration and shame, he walked offstage. Bono, Larry, and Adam followed him.

A Pant Splitter

On September 7, 1980, U2 opened for Echo & the Bunnymen at the Lyceum in London in what turned out to be quite a humiliation. In addition to being trashed by the *NME*'s Chris Salewicz, who compared Bono to Rod Stewart and wrote, "U2 are really quite awful," Bono had a terrible wardrobe malfunction.

In the middle of "The Electric Co.," the singer jumped off of a loud-speaker, and his pants split open in front of a room full of record company and media people. Trying to make the best of a bad situation, he started tearing his clothes off, and ranting at the crowd, "I'm wearing these for you! I'm wearing these for you!"

Ups and Downs

U2's first headlining tour of North America had its ups and downs. For every successful show, like their March 15 gig at the Reseda Country Club in Reseda, California, there would be a setback, like its show the following night at Woodstock, in Anaheim.

At U2's first Los Angeles–area show, they played to sellout audience of six hundred on the strength of KROQ-FM, which had been playing "I Will Follow" in heavy rotation for several weeks. Unfortunately, U2's Anaheim gig suffered from minimal promotion and only twelve people showed up.

At Cardi's on April 1, 1981, in Houston, the band was in the support slot for a non-musical headlining event. At the venue, located in a shopping mall, U2 had the unfortunate experience of being the opening act for a wet T-shirt contest. The band was quickly learning that America was far different from the Emerald Isle.

Bono's Briefcase

After U2's gig at the Foghorn in Portland on March 22, 1981, Bono left his briefcase—which had $300 and the lyrics he had supposedly written for the group's upcoming album—behind. For the next twenty-three years, he believed that two female fans had come into his dressing room to greet him and absconded with the case.

It turned out that a local soundman, Denny Livingston, who worked the gig, and his friend Steve Graeff found the case and had hoped to return it to the band before they left the Northwest. Attempting to contact the local promoter, Livingston's calls went unreturned. Graeff—with no way to get in touch with the singer—held onto the briefcase until October 2004, when he managed to get it back to Bono.

Perhaps more embarrassing than the fact that the case was forgotten and not stolen is what was inside. Not much. After ballyhooing for years about the valuable lyrics he had lost, Bono admitted in *U2 by U2* that the contents of the case were—"obscure hieroglyphics"—hardly the essential documents he remembered.

Panic in Detroit

Although U2's gig in Detroit would be a considerable success—drawing 1,400 fans despite the lack of radio support—it almost didn't happen. Bono just escaped getting his ass kicked en route to the gig.

"Did you call that car of mine a cab?" a local, clearly intoxicated, denim- and boots-sporting Cadillac enthusiast asked the singer as he exited the Detroit Holiday Inn after taping a cable-TV interview. "Did you call that car of mine a cab, you muthafucker?" he asked again, according to a *Hot Press* piece from 1981.

Undaunted by the nearby police station, the local man goofed on Bono's white shoes and tartan pants, calling him a "fucking faggot," which sparked the singer to stick his head into the Cadillac and reach for his throat.

"I realized he was a six-hundred-pound gorilla with two big dogs a shotgun in the back," Bono told the Dublin music publication. "He was a monster of a man, and he just pushed open the door and came running for me." Thankfully, the singer and his accomplices were able to calm down the irate man.

Opening for Thin Lizzy

On August 16, 1981, just as U2 had been finalizing *October*, the band was offered the opening slot on a bill with Thin Lizzy at Slane Castle, just outside of Dublin. It marked the group's only performance in Ireland in 1981, and allowed them the opportunity to play alongside one of their heroes, Phil Lynott.

Although it was later seen as a misguided decision, the band opened its set by playing some of the new songs at the biggest open-air show in the country that year. They bombed miserably, or as Bono would simply explain, "We were shite."

With little if any time to rehearse the new songs for preparation in a live setting, it wound up being one of the worst shows they ever played. Technical troubles with their guitars only added to the debacle.

October November

After flying into New York for a month-long North American tour, the members of U2—as guests of Frank Barsalona—were invited to watch the Rolling Stones' November 12 performance at Madison Square Garden. Despite the excitement surrounding that band's *Tattoo You* Tour, a jet-lagged Bono fell asleep during the Stones' set.

Two nights later in Boston, U2's *October* campaign got underway at the Orpheum, where its show aired live on WBCN and was recorded for the syndicated concert program *The King Biscuit Flower Hour*. But things got complicated fast on the Connecticut stop the next night.

With tensions running high in the band for personal and professional reasons during the campaign to support the newly released *October*, Bono lost his cool when Larry's snare stand broke at Toad's Place in New Haven, Connecticut, on November 15, 1981. The singer—enraged that his drummer had stopped playing—turned to see Larry laughing about the mishap.

In front of the audience, the twenty-one-year-old Bono charged Mullen and proceeded to take his frustration out on his drum set, kicking it over to the delight of the audience, who believed this was all part of the show. It became evident it wasn't once the singer chased after Larry. Luckily, Edge intervened, grabbing the frontman by his mop of hair.

After storming out, Bono—sore from a right hook also delivered by Edge—contemplated leaving the band that very night. Blaming the argument on too many miles on the same bus, being homesick, and having a sore throat, he came to his senses after what was likely U2's only-ever visible onstage fracas.

The band—clearly feeling the pressure that was coming with bigger venues and a higher profile—made up the following morning when an apologetic Bono showed up to rejoin the group for breakfast. Bono referred to the event this way during U2's Rock and Roll Hall of Fame Induction in 2005:

"A fight breaks out. It's between the band. It's very, very messy. Now you look at this guitar genius, you look at this Zen-like master that is The Edge, and you hear those brittle icy notes, and you might be forgiven for forgetting that you cannot play like that unless you have a rage inside you. In fact, I had forgotten that on that particular night, and he tried to break my nose."

Rooftop Rock

As part of Dublin's "Inner City Looking On" Festival, U2 performed a free gig from a Sheriff Street rooftop in July 1982. It was a dicey, crime-addled neighborhood, but the presence of attendees on the streets below meant it shouldn't have been a dangerous gig. However, approximately three dozen people climbed the building's only stepladder to join U2 onstage.

Most were just enthusiastic fans, but one frightening older man grabbed Bono's microphone to sing "Let's twist again, like we did last summer." Recalling the incident, Bono told *Musician* in 1983, "This guy who looked six feet wide, a docker, just walked onstage and stood in front of me." Citing the Chubby Checker classic, he ordered U2 to "play it."

"The whole crowd quieted—this was the confrontation: 'Were we chicken or not?'" Bono continued. "I must admit, I was chicken. I just stopped the show and started to sing, no accompaniment, 'Let's twist again, like we did last summer . . .' And I looked at the crowd, and all the kids, the mothers, fathers, the wine and whiskey bottles in their hands, started singing and dancing. And the guy smiled."

Bono Retires His High-Wire Act

At the Los Angeles Sports Arena, June 17, 1983, despite the heated exchange between Bono and tour manager Dennis Sheehan at the US Festival, Bono got caught up in the moment one last time. Again during "The Electric Co." the singer turned acrobat, going up the stairs behind the stage and around the balcony with a white flag and his microphone in tow.

Once Bono was opposite the stage, a fight between attendees broke out next to him. Someone grabbed his flag, prompting to singer to climb to the edge of the balcony, promising to jump if the brawl didn't end. When it continued, U2's singer jumped twenty feet, landing on top of the crowd below. Sheehan—serving as Bono's spotter—did the same and landed safely.

Seconds later, when members of the crowd—inspired by their rock and roll conqueror—also jumped, no one was there to catch them. As the bodies piled up, the singer felt trapped and hit back at fans with his fists clenched until security got him back to the stage. Despite his proclamations about the importance of pacifism and peace, the scrappy kid from Cedarwood Road lost his shit for a moment and hit back in rage.

After the show, with a shredded white flag and ripped shirt coupled with the scornful looks of his bandmates to remind him that he had gone too far, Bono pledged to put his concert circus act to bed forever. Reviewing the show, *Los Angeles Times* critic Robert Hilburn said it was one of the most exciting moments at a rock show he'd ever seen and one of the dumbest.

Ironically, Bono would also reveal that he was in fact afraid of heights unless he was lost in the music. It was then, during "The Electric Co." that he would turn to his suspenseful moves. But God forbid he might fall and sustain an injury, become paralyzed or kill himself. Luckily the singer came to his senses and stopped the foolish behavior.

The Forgettable Guitarist

With U2's tour commitments carrying them well into 1985, the band started rehearsals for the world trek in August 1984. But there was a problem.

The Edge had forgotten how to play the songs in the band's back catalog. He sent a Principle Management employee to buy him all of the group's albums so he could re-learn the tunes.

Performing Songs from *The Unforgettable Fire* Proves Challenging

Returning to Dublin in late September 1984, U2 knew it had to focus on how it might deliver its complex new material in a live setting. The band stalled its European leg of *The Unforgettable Fire* Tour for several weeks and held emergency rehearsals to determine how it would deliver its expanding musical approach to fans.

With the tour set to get underway on October 18 in Lyon, France, The Edge mastered a relatively new technology. Using sequencers, he could program all of his keyboard parts, add a click track for Larry, and play his guitar parts live. "We suddenly had a keyboard player in a small black box," he joked to Bill Flanagan a decade later. "Magic!"

"The Most Boring Band in the World"

The *NME*, which had long supported the U2 cause, was not impressed with its pair of London shows at the Brixton Academy. It took aim at the group and fired away, calling the foursome, "The most boring band in the world."

"There may be groups equally as dull, but I fail to see how any of them can be worse," the U.K. music weekly said. Ouch.

Scalpers and Violence in the States

After joining U2 on a series of U.K. dates the month prior, the Waterboys joined the band for a two-week run of American dates intended to sustain interest and sales until the group could return for a full arena tour in early 1985.

A testament to its bulging popularity, U2's Philadelphia-area gig at the Tower Theatre in Upper Darby, Pennsylvania, sold out, with scalpers commanding $150 for a single ticket.

Two nights later, U2 participated in an Amnesty International fundraiser at New York's Radio City Music Hall. Intended to support the organization's "Stop Torture Week," the show was marred by violence.

With fans clashing with security, the band stopped the show twice, once while The Edge threw his guitar to make a point. When the show continued, the tension built, with fans climbing onto the stage to avoid being injured by the force of the pushing crowd.

Fan with a Gun

U2 kicked off the second run of U.S. dates behind *The Unforgettable Fire* at the Reunion Arena in Dallas. But the concert left the band completely freaked out by what may have been its scariest fan interaction yet.

An audience member in the front row screamed at Bono and pointed an object at the singer that turned out to be a gun. Security apprehended the individual and the show resumed. Just the same, all of the U2 camp—which prided itself on messages of peace, love, and tolerance—was understandably angry and confused by the incident.

Around this time, Bono came to the realization that U2's increasing fame might mean that it would no longer be able to sustain the closeness to its fans. People could no longer relate to him as a person, but as a pop star. He found the emptiness of a sterile hotel room similar in notion to a prison cell. Although he explained at the time that he had too much to keep him from falling victim to drug abuse, Bono said he understood how others in his position might dabble.

Hands Across America

After a successful run of shows in Phoenix and Los Angeles, U2 took a two-night residency at the infamous Cow Palace in Daly City, California, on March 7 and 8, 1985. But the band had the scare of its life when Larry Mullen found himself rushed to a San Francisco hospital before the second show with excruciating pain in his left hand.

Because rest was not possible midway through the extensive tour, the drummer received painkillers and a plaster cast for his hand that he removed before each gig and reapplied after. The injury continued to cause concern for U2 in later years.

When the band's U.S. tour wrapped in Fort Lauderdale, Larry returned to Dublin to seek medical treatment from a top hand doctor in Ireland, who

This ticket to the Reunion Arena in Dallas, Texas, marked admittance to what had to be the most frightening show of U2's Spring 1985 tour. A crazed fan was witnessed pointing a gun at Bono. Security apprehended the attendee, and the show went on.

Courtesy of Angelo Deodato

prescribed an anti-inflammatory to help control the pain and discomfort in his hand. Reducing the swelling, the drummer was forced to learn to use his hand in moderation, care for it, bathe it in cold water, and rest it whenever possible.

Don't Fuck with the Fire Officials

Having been warned not to encourage fans to leave their seats and crowd the stage—a lesson one would have though U2 might have learned after its Radio City Music Hall gig the previous December ended so abysmally—Bono defied the request. Instead the singer invited attendees at U2's April 8, 1985, show at Landover, Maryland's Capitol Centre down to the stage.

As a result, the show was brought to a halt until a sense of order could be established—but the matter was hardly over. After the show, local police showed up to arrest Bono, manager Paul McGuinness, and production manager Steve Iredale.

Iredale—whose signature was on the Fire Official's order—was cuffed and stuffed before he could be released on $500 bail. Later, U2's U.S. attorney negotiated to have the charges dropped.

Near Miss

On April 16, 1985, during the first of three gigs at the Centrum in Worcester, Massachusetts, Adam Clayton looked up at the ceiling to notice that one of the group's lighting rigs above the crowd appeared to be slipping. He gave Bono the heads-up, and they stopped playing.

The singer asked the audience down in front to move back from the lighting assembly so the crew could repair it. Within minutes, the show was underway, and a crisis was averted.

Nice Mullet!

Although Bono first began cultivating his mullet—a hairstyle that is short at the front and sides, and long in the back—during the group's *War* campaign in 1983, by the time the band played "Live Aid" in 1985, his coif was remarkably distinct for its length. By the time the singer surfaced for performances in 1986, he had abandoned the style for a more traditional approach to long hair.

Now cringe-worthy, this photo from *The Unforgettable Fire* Tour circa 1985 captures
Bono with his mullet in full effect.   *Photofest*

"Forget about a bad-hair day; I was having a bad-hair life," the singer
joked of his mullet to McCormick, admitting that there were still people
who dislike U2 based solely on his hair-do during that era.

Bono in Stitches

In its final rehearsal before the start of *The Joshua Tree* Tour at the University
Activity Center at Arizona State University in Tempe, U2 worked through
the Curtis Mayfield classic "People Get Ready" and a medley of the Johnny
Cash songs "I Walk the Line" and "Folsom Prison Blues." But in doing so,
Bono fell walking up a ramp while carrying a spotlight and cut open his chin
requiring a trip to the hospital for stitches.

A Falling Rain

In September 1987 during a show at Robert F. Kennedy Stadium in
Washington, Bono slipped on the stage in a pouring rain and sprained his

shoulder, forcing the band to continue the tour with the singer in a sling and a nurse in tow. A video screen the band had brought with it for stadium gigs and had placed behind its lighting tower captured the injury for the many thousands of attendees to see.

Because of his injury, a roadie must step in and carry Bono's spotlight for him during the dramatic performances of "Bullet the Blue Sky" until his shoulder heals.

The Lovetown Tour

Named for the collaboration with B. B. King, it was a fitting moniker for the trek that brought the blues fixture together with U2 for three months of live dates. Although U2's experiment with B. B.'s brass section was invigorating, it was also an idea that was going nowhere. Audiences were clapping, but the band's perception was that attendees were puzzled by the direction.

Meanwhile Larry was starting to loathe the tour. It felt joyless—U2 was going through the motions. The band had worked steadily from late 1985 until late 1989 with very little downtime along the way. Although accolades continued—the group won an MTV Video Music Award for "When Love Comes to Town" in the Best Video from a Film category—they were running out of gas.

After bomb threats that caused the band to clear the Sydney Entertainment Center of its 12,500 fans in November, exhaustion that sent the band—save for Bono—to bed early in Osaka, leaving an *NME* journalist in limbo, and a terrifying mishap at Paris' Palais Omnisports De Paris-Bercy where part of the band's lighting rig fell forty feet causing a fractured pelvis to a crew member, it was clear it was time for a break.

Shows in Germany and Amsterdam were cut short by a strain to Bono's voice, with additional dates in Rotterdam canceled on doctor's orders and rescheduled for January 1990.

Finally back in Ireland and with an end of the road in sight, U2 played the first of four shows at the Point in Dublin on December 26 and wrapped the Lovetown Tour for good on New Year's Eve. Staring down the crowd at the end of "Love Rescue Me," Bono advised his fans that they were attending a going away party. This was the end of an era. U2's members were tired and emotional.

"We've had a lot of fun over the last few months, just getting to know some of the music which we didn't know so much about—and still don't know very much about, but it was fun!" Bono told the audience. "This is just the end of something for U2. And that's why we're playing these concerts—and we're throwing a party for ourselves and you. It's no big deal, it's just—we have to go away and . . . and dream it all up again."

Rotterdam

The four Rotterdam dates, held at Sportpaleis Ahoy on January 5, 6, 9, and 10 signified the end of the line for *The Joshua Tree* and *Rattle and Hum* campaigns. The break couldn't have come at a better time for Mullen, who told his mates in advance of the shows that he didn't want to carry on with the band with the way things had become. It was becoming joyless and tedious and unless things changed in the group's approach in the 1990s, he might in fact exit U2.

Trashcan Bootleg

In April 1991, news broke that bootleggers managed to get their hands on digital audio tapes of U2's recording sessions in Berlin. With anticipation of the band's forthcoming album, due later in the year, copies were traded among fans and a vinyl bootleg surfaced.

Reports alleged that the tapes were taken from a trashcan in one of the band's hotel rooms, which a U2 spokesperson quickly shot down. "It's impossible to fathom the band leaving these tapes in the hotel trash," the group officially responded. "They would always be under lock and key."

Bono called the bootlegs "gobbledygook" in the statement and, despite fronting one of the biggest bands in the world, had the audacity to add, "I don't know why anyone would be interested in them."

In a tandem statement, Paul McGuinness addressed the controversy. "There is always a strong demand for U2 material, but these tapes are very early recordings and I don't like to see people being ripped off."

Island Records stepped in, placing advertisements in the music weeklies the following month warning record retailers that legal action would be pursued with any stores selling the stolen studio tapes. But the leak had created what Lanois described as "a bad scene for a few weeks," shaking the band's confidence.

In the months after a three-and-a-half-hour CD box-set bootleg titled *Salome: The Axtung Beibi Outtakes* emerged, the band felt violated by the fact that fans were listening to their incomplete musical thoughts. "Most of it is just mumbo-jumbo crap," Edge said to Flanagan, "but it's made significant by becoming a U2 artifact."

Negativland

Electronic band Negativland would have been better off leaving "U2" alone. Although that was the name of the band's 1991 single on SST Records—the label founded by Black Flag's Greg Ginn that was home to seminal releases by Hüsker Dü, the Minutemen, Dinosaur Jr., and others—the song's title and much of its content had been built around unauthorized samples of U2's "I Still Haven't Found What I'm Looking For." Coupled with snippets of *American Top 40* host Casey Kasem trying to introduce the song, this idea for a collage was a bad one.

It's a possibility that Negativland might have never have caught the attention of Island Records, had it been a little less obvious about its album art. With "U2" in large letters on the disc's cover, and its own band name in small print toward the bottom of the sleeve, the packaging was misleading to fans.

In September, two weeks after "U2" was released, Island and Warner-Chappell Music jointly sued SST and Negativland for copyright infringement and obtained an injunction. A month later, the parties settled with SST. The company agreed to halt production, recall the 13,000 copies in existence, and hand them over to Island.

Meanwhile, Island picked up the copyright ownership of "U2," and SST was required to fork over $29,292.25 plus $15,000 in future payments.

In 1994, after months of requests from Negativland, Paul McGuinness allowed the return of the "U2" parody single back to the group. They were given permission to re-release the single provided that it had new artwork and got the agreement of Casey Kasem to release the track. Polygram and Island Records also signed similar contracts.

Take It Off

During an interview with writer Sean O'Hagan at Nikita's Restaurant in March 1992, Bono unexpectedly undressed. Explaining his peculiar behavior to the scribe later, Bono said, "I did it to try and snip in the bud any possibility of another serious, in-depth U2 inquisition."

Bono's spokesperson offered this explanation: "The writer was so unimaginative, so frozen, so unloose that Bono thought it would be a good idea to take his clothes off . . . and there wasn't much of a reaction."

As for the restaurant owner, he was okay with the singer's behavior. "He was very nice and very civilized," Nikita's owner Sylvain Borsi explained to *Newsday*. "I think he just felt more comfortable with nothing on."

Bomb Japan Now

Following a ZooTV gig in Atlanta in March 1992, a review in the *Atlanta Journal-Constitution* claimed that at one point during "The Fly," the words BOMB JAPAN NOW came across the screen. When it became newsworthy, U2 did damage control.

"At no time do the words 'bomb Japan now' appear together," the band said in an official statement. "U2 have no wish to offend the people of Japan, where they have many fans."

You're Fired

Days after the European leg of the ZooTV trek got underway, U2 ran into trouble in Milan, when a crowd of 12,500 showed up but was sent away after the show was forced to be postponed. One of the trucks carrying U2's equipment broke down while en route from Barcelona, but in the days before cell phones were common, the driver neglected to tell the band about the problem in a prompt manner.

Pop Fizzles

On April 26, 1997, ABC Television aired an hour-long U2 special about the band and its ongoing PopMart Tour. Narrated by actor Dennis Hopper, *U2: A Year in Pop* was a documentary of the band working on the disc in the studio and plugging it out on the road during the Las Vegas tour opener.

A remnant of U2's Auckland, New Zealand, performance at Western Springs on November 10, 1989, this show included snippets of the Rolling Stones' "Ruby Tuesday" during "Bad," and a couplet from Joy Division's "Love Will Tear Us Apart" during "With or Without You." As was relatively common during this era, the band also performed Curtis Mayfield's "People Get Ready" during its encore.

Hugh Lynn Collection

The broadcast was an overwhelming flop, however, ranking 101 out of 107 network programs that aired that week. Making matters worse, its low ratings meant that *U2: A Year in Pop* was the worst rated non-political documentary in the history of the U.S. network.

Smoking Ban

During a stop on their world tour, the Red Hot Chili Peppers hung out with Bono at U2's Clarence Hotel in Dublin on June 12, 2004. The next day, Bono made headlines for violating the city's smoking ban by lighting up in the building.

"It was the wee small hours," he told *Reuters*. "I was in the company of people from out of town who didn't know about the ban, and for a moment nor did I. I was quickly reminded by the staff and a few friends. I apologized then, and I apologize now."

Bono's Back Injury

In May 2010, Bono injured his back during concert rehearsals in Munich, Germany, which resulted in U2 being forced to postpone the sixteen North American dates on the band's summer American tour until sometime in 2011. Its highly anticipated Glastonbury music festival debut appearance— which would have celebrated the U.K. event's fortieth anniversary—was also forced to be shelved.

"Our biggest and I believe best tour has been interrupted, and we're all devastated," Paul McGuiness said in a statement on U2.com. "For a performer who lives to be on stage, this is more than a blow. Bono feels robbed of the chance to do what he does best and feel like he has badly let down the band and their audience. Which is, of course, nonsense. His concerns about more than a million ticket buyers whose plans have been turned upside down, we all share, but the most important thing right now is that Bono make a full recovery. We're working as fast as we can with Live Nation to reschedule these dates."

On May 21, Bono underwent emergency surgery on Friday. According to Bono's doctor, Muller Wohlfahrt, the U2 frontman had suffered severe compression of the sciatic nerve. On review of his MRI scan, Wohlfahrt realized there was a serious tear in the ligament and a herniated disc. He urged Bono—who was experiencing partial paralysis in his lower leg—to have emergency spine surgery with Professor Jörg-Christian Tonn at Munich's LMU University Hospital.

During the surgery, Tonn determined that fragments of Bono's disc had traveled into his spinal canal. Full recovery of his motor deficit was expected following an extensive period of rehabilitation.

In July 2010, U2 announced that Bono had fully recovered. "I can sit, I can stand, I can move around a bit. Feeling strong. Feeling confident," the singer said in a video on the band's website. "I'm going to be fighting fit next summer in the U.S."

12

Boy Meets Man

U2 Signs to Island

Annie Roseberry

During a Belfast gig in February 1980, Annie Roseberry from Island Records watched the band play Queens University. Roseberry was blown away by the performance and approached Paul McGuinness back at U2's hotel to express her interest in the band and inform him of her intentions to notify her bosses at the record company.

"They just had something unique," Roseberry told Matt McGee. "Bono was already a star. He was running around and climbing on speaker stacks even then, like he was playing in a stadium. There was absolutely no doubt that he had something really special."

National Stadium

National Stadium was a boxing venue that usually featured established touring acts. Booking the band into the facility was a ballsy move for a group at U2's level. For Paul McGuinness and the members of U2, the notion they might fill the stadium was a stretch, but it was a risk worth taking.

The fact that the group triumphed in five categories of the annual *Hot Press* reader's poll seemed promising. Coupled with a January appearance performing "Stories for Boys" on RTE's *The Late Late Show with Gay Byrne*, and plans to release "Another Day" to coincide with its February 26 appearance in the venue, they hoped the activity would put people in the seats.

Although the group only wound up drawing 1,000 fans, friends, and family members to the 2,500-capacity stadium, the turnout was celebratory and ultimately triumphant. In the crowd—on the glowing recommendation of Roseberry—was Nick Stewart, an A&R executive from Island Records.

Nick Stewart

Backstage after the show at National Stadium, A&R man Nick Stewart offered U2 a contract with Island Records. Stewart, who went by the name "the Captain," was especially impressed by the captivating performance and thrilled with the audience reaction to the group's hometown gig.

"I knew I was watching something special," Stewart said in *U2: A Diary*. "Musically, I found them a little naïve, but the way they got their own crowd going, the way Bono handled it . . . I just thought, 'I've got to have this band.'"

But Stewart still needed Island Records founder Chris Blackwell—who was at his mansion in the Bahamas—to sign off on the deal. Nick eagerly traveled to the Caribbean commonwealth to convince Blackwell to okay the signing. It would take four weeks before the deal was official.

Truth be known, Island needed a band like U2 as much as U2 needed it. Save for quickly defunct punks Eddie and the Hot Rods, the label didn't have much in the way of edgy rock bands. Bob Marley and the Wailers, Robert Palmer, and newly signed former Traffic member Steve Winwood were already elder statesmen of the genre.

So on March 23, while U2 was in London to perform at the "Sense of Ireland Festival," Stewart caught up with Paul McGuinness and the rest of U2 while they were hanging out at the Lyceum. They finalized their recording contract in the ladies room.

Released on February 26, 1980, "Another Day" was a non-LP A-side backed with a demo rendition of "Twilight." The back cover features hand-drawn art by Bono.

eil.com

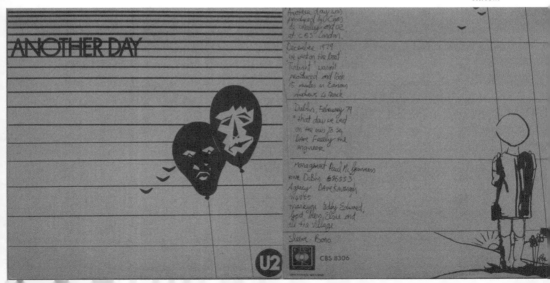

It was a four-year, four-album deal with a £50,000 advance plus an additional £50,000 in tour support. Island's intentions were to release three singles in the first year.

First *NME* Cover

U2 graced the cover of the *NME* on March 22, a day before the group's Island deal was finalized. Journalist Paul Morley had traveled to Ireland to interview Bono over breakfast on March 2, 1980. In a piece called "U2 Can Make It in the Rock Business," Bono was incorrectly listed as Paul Houston, a mistake the *NME* will again make in a subsequent 1981 feature, but the publicity was significant for a band with just two Irish-only singles in its discography.

The article found Bono singing the praises of U.K.'s mod-movement heroes the Jam, criticizing the Boomtown Rats for abandoning Ireland for London, and taking aim at the gimmickry of pop music in early 1980.

Comparing his band's development to a child working with Legos, Bono said, "Onstage I look exuberant because I feel exuberant. I don't pretend. U2 never pretend. It's not that we've planned a compromise—it's what has come naturally within the group. U2 is like learning, it's like a child learning. We've been given Lego, and we're learning to put things together in new ways. This is a stage that we've got to that I'm not ashamed of, but I believe we will get much stronger."

"11 O'Clock Tick Tock"

At Nick Stewart's suggestion, U2 recorded "11 O'Clock Tick Tock" with Joy Division producer Martin Hannett at Dublin's Windmill Lane Studio on April 5 and 6, 1980. The band first met Hannett weeks earlier in London while he was recording what would become that band's swansong single, "Love Will Tear Us Apart."

U2's first Island single was released on May 23 but failed to chart in the U.K. The A-side was once known as "Silver Lining" until Bono rewrote the lyrics after finding inspiration while supposedly standing on the balcony at the Electric Ballroom watching the Cramps perform. Its flipside was a track called "Touch."

Bono called Hannett a "genius" in *U2 by U2* and praised him for helping to properly establish Edge's guitar sound. By putting a harmony guitar part on the single, the producer made it sound "otherworldly," according to the singer. Hannett took cues from his studio tenure with Joy Division, and helped U2 elevate its sonic suburban sentiments into a new realm. Martin, as Bono explained, made the band sound as if it came from the "furthest edges of the Milky Way."

While Hannett was also slated to produce U2's debut album for Island Records, he cancelled at the last minute. Devastated by the May 18, 1980, suicide of Joy Division's frontman Ian Curtis, Hannett wasn't in the proper frame of mind to take on the task.

Finally, a Van!

After the release of "11 O'Clock Tick Tock," U2 was able to buy a van, which was outfitted with a bulkhead, a bench seat, and a brown carpet that the members often slept on. Suitable enough to carry the group, its equipment, and one or two others, it wasn't exactly comfortable, but it got the lads around England, Ireland, and parts of Europe for a couple of years.

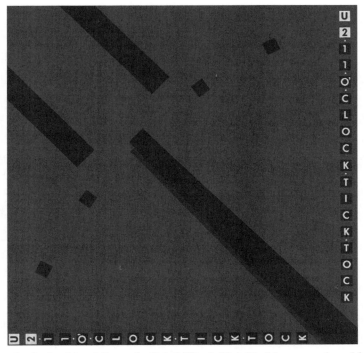

U2's first single for Island Records, "11 O'Clock Tick Tock" was produced by Joy Division veteran Martin Hannett and released in the U.K. on May 23, 1980. *991.com*

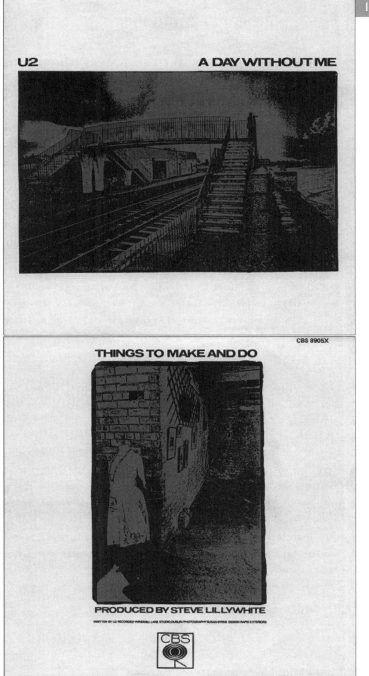

The front and back covers of the Irish pressing of "A Day Without Me"—U2's first recorded effort with Steve Lillywhite—which was released in August 1980. Issued by CBS Eire, it—like its U.K. counterpart for Island—has distinct artwork. *eil.com*

13

I Am Found

Boy

"A Day Without Me"

U p-and-coming producer Steve Lillywhite was a veteran of recordings by the likes of Siouxsie & the Banshees and XTC, groups that the members of U2 had admired. To get a feel of how things might work with Lillywhite, the band brought him onboard for its second Island Records single, "A Day Without Me."

Serving as the lead single for what would become *Boy*, U2's debut long-player, "A Day Without Me" was released in August 1980. Although it wasn't an obvious single, Lillywhite helped build the song into a commanding piece of music, with Edge's unique, echo-soaked guitar—courtesy of his Memory Man effects pedal—a fine forum for Bono's ruminations.

As for its black and white artwork, it displayed the footbridge across Princess Road in Hulme, outside of Manchester, England. A photo session with Joy Division was supposedly held on the same bridge by photographer Kevin Cummins in early 1979. The single was backed by the instrumental track "Things to Make and Do."

Although it failed to chart, the single somehow found its way into the hands of Boston DJ Carter Alan, who began to play the song on his weekend specialty radio show on WBCN.

Steve Lillywhite Sticks Around

Pleased by the outcome of "A Day Without Me," Steve Lillywhite was indeed selected to produce U2's debut album. Capable of pulling the best out of everybody, Lillywhite was as encouraging as he was sensible.

Recording Larry's drums in the stairwell, Lillywhite helped to make *Boy* an album that would stand out. He wasn't one for wasting time and encouraged the band to work quickly, recording all of the material it had brought to the session promptly and then dedicating just a few hours to overdubs before it moved along to the next track.

The Songs of *Boy*

Bono had decided that U2's debut album would be titled *Boy* well in advance of its recording. The singer proudly referred to the Steve Lillywhite–produced debut as "autobiographical" upon its release. A deeply emotional record, *Boy*—recorded in the summer of 1980 and released in Europe on October 20 of that year—tackles subjects very close to Bono's 1970s adolescence, including the loss of his mother, anger, faith, love, and confusion.

1. "I Will Follow" has been described by Bono as the unconditional love a mother has for a child. Released as a proper single on October 6, just slightly ahead of *Boy*, the song—which counts a glockenspiel and boasts sound affects derived by Bono breaking bottles on the floor while Lillywhite ran knives through the spokes of a bicycle wheel—was the first song many early U2 fans were introduced to. It continues to retain its contagious allure thirty years later. The singer once said it was written in about ten minutes.

Balancing rage and a sense of longing, much of the song's power comes from Bono's emotional delivery. Adam's thundering bass, Larry's taut drumming, and Edge's minimalist but declarative playing cannot be denied, making it one of the most important and enduring songs in the history of modern rock.

2. "Twilight," which is about the grey area of adolescence—first appeared as the flipside of the group's "Another Day" single, which was released through CBS in early 1980. Rerecorded for *Boy*, the song was misinterpreted by early champions of the band in the gay community, who felt the song was written for them. Despite the fact that Bono insisted he "never had any homosexual experiences," he told *Hot Press* in late 1980 that it was about "that twilight zone where the boy that was confronts the man to be in the shadows." Lyrics like *"The old man tried to walk me home, I thought he should have known"* lent themselves to be misunderstood by listeners who thought they were a gay band.

That community strongly supported the band on its first U.S. tours. Although the members of U2 weren't exactly sure why their shows were heavily attended by guys dressed in leather, they eventually found out. These weren't well to do punk rockers, they were homosexual fans who misunderstood much of the lyrical content of *Boy* and the cover imagery found on the album's import version.

3. "An Cat Dubh," which ultimately meshes with "Into the Heart" on *Boy*—is Gaelic for "the black cat." The song is purportedly about a young woman Bono had an affair with during the time he and his longtime girlfriend Ali Stewart, who he would eventually marry in 1982, had briefly broken up. It also explores the guilt he felt afterward.

"The image is of a cat and a bird," he was quoted in *U2: Into the Heart*. "The cat kills the bird and shakes it—you know the way they do, they play with the dead prey—and then sleeps beside it. It's like someone has taken you, thrown you around the place and then you sleep beside them. I think for the sake of the song I switched things around, but in reality I think I was the cat. I was the one who did the dirty."

4. "Into the Heart" is bridged to "An Cat Dubh" by a musical passage that highlights The Edge's innovative and refreshing guitar playing approach. Fused together for U2's live shows, the same presentation of the songs on *Boy* made sense to the band and Lillywhite.

With its sheer musical beauty and poignancy—in which Bono mourns the lost innocence chronicled in the previous track—the song's simple yet directly sincere lyrics made it a high point of the quartet's debut. Emoting *"Into the heart of a child, I can go back, I can stay awhile"* against the glistening, ethereal tone of Edge's guitar, U2 brought its listeners on a shimmering, powerful, and above all else, honest journey with its first long player.

5. Although it surfaced more than a year earlier in its original state as part of the Eire-only *Three* EP, the version of "Out of Control" that appeared on *Boy* was miles ahead of its predecessor in terms of power, energy, and vast presentation. An exuberant blast of rock and roll, it explored the notion that the eighteen-year-old frontman—and anyone for that matter—had no control over the decisions of being born or dying.

When the song was translated for the lyric sheet of the Japanese pressing of *Boy*, the opening lines translated back into English as *"Monday morning/ Knitting years of gold."* Bono would later admit that the misinterpretation was actually a better fit.

6. While U2's manager thought "Stories for Boys" was a song about masturbation, Bono told *Hot Press* at the time it first surfaced on the *Three* EP that it was a reaction to advertising imagery. "I remember seeing heroes on television—people like James Bond and so on—and thinking 'I'm not very good looking—I'm not going to get things like that,' and being unhappy about it," he said in 1979. "We feel that we're qualified to comment on things like that because we're teenagers."

When the muscular version heard on *Boy* first earned the attention of the gay community, much like "Twilight," it too gave homosexuals a song they felt they could identify with. "For the gays in our audience, this was definitely a love song to a man," Bono said in *The U2 File.* "I thought of it as just simple escapism. And it's not really. We were very conscious on one level but there was a whole subconscious thing going on too. There really is a sense in which the songs write themselves."

7. Speaking of the lilting, reflective song "The Ocean" in 1981, Bono described it as "a complete teenage thought," in an explanation cited by Stokes in *The U2 File.* "It is the thought of every teenager. It is the thought of everybody in a band who thinks he can change the world."

Looking back on the song some years later, discussing the verse, *"A picture in grey, Dorian Gray / Just me by the sea, and I felt like a star,"* the singer laughed about his youthful confidence. "That takes some fucking neck," Bono marveled in the 1986 book *U2—In the Name of Love: A History from Ireland's Hot Press Magazine.* "On the record it doesn't sound funny, but we used to open the show with that. We used to walk out and go straight into that. In a way it was so audacious."

8. Released as a single ahead of the album in August 1980, "A Day Without Me"—which sports Edge's surging and memorable guitar line—was the result of a trial arrangement between U2 and Steve Lillywhite, then a veteran of sessions with XTC and Siouxsie & the Banshees, to see if the up and coming producer would be a good fit for their debut album on Island Records. The guitar part—which Edge helped craft on his cheap Memory Man echo unit—was a jarring accompaniment to the song's suicide-inspired lyrics.

Written after the suicide attempt of Sean D'Angelo, an acquaintance of Bono's, the singer ultimately suggested that he was captivated by this consideration: "Would it make any difference if you did commit suicide?" There has also been speculation that Joy Division vocalist Ian Curtis, who killed himself on May 18, 1980, was the inspiration for the song, although no one in the U2 camp has ever made the suggestion.

9. Bono once confessed that the title for "Another Time, Another Place" came before the actual lyrics. Little attention was paid to lyrics at the outset of a song in those days—the music took precedent. Perhaps this explains why the musical punch of this album track is much stronger than its cryptic lyrical matter. Vague romantic imagery—perhaps written with his future wife,

Ali, in mind—is conveyed on lines like *"I'll be with you now/We lie on a cloud,"* rendering it one of the disc's underdeveloped ideas.

10. "The Electric Co." makes reference to Electro Convulsive Therapy, the Electric shock treatment given to the mentally unstable in the 1970s. Bono, along with his friends in the Lypton Village, was in ardent opposition to the practice, which he condemned in 1980. "ECT is nothing more than witchcraft," he opined of the anger-driven number.

A catharsis onstage, the song embodied the belief that rock and roll could be a form of therapy and a way of exacting vengeance on the naysayers in the music community and in the adult world in general. For Bono, the song would also become notorious in U2's early career as an opportunity for him to take off running, climbing up scaffolding and venue structures and even occasionally for jumping off balconies.

11. Taking its name from the fourth chapter of William Golding's *Lord of the Flies*, "Shadows and Tall Trees" was one of U2's very first songs, originating on the group's very first demo tape, which was recorded with and produced by Barry Devlin of Horslips. Within Lypton Village, Bono's surrealistic gang of friends that rejected adulthood, the book sparked the short-lived idea of refusing to grow up.

"I remember thinking about that comparison between Lord of the Flies and where we were [on] Cedarwood [Road], between Ballymun and Finglas," Bono explained in *The U2 File*. "It was a quiet little street in one sense but my memory of it, growing up, is of being stuck between cowboys and Indians, and so on. That's the way it was. And I remember thinking the shadows and tall trees are different here—but it's the same story, isn't it? It's all about war."

NME Writer Trashes U2

On September 7, 1980, U2 returned to London's Lyceum, the same place where it had signed its Island Records contract earlier in the year. This time the band was one of four on a bill headlined by hot U.K. band Echo & the Bunnymen. Unfortunately, Bono was having trouble engaging the audience, and he let his dissatisfaction show.

NME scribe Chris Salewicz took the opportunity to give the band a good thrashing. "U2 are basically little more than nonsense, or perhaps the new Boomtown Rats—one of the two, and they both amount to the same thing, anyway . . . U2 are really quite awful, though the young people—particularly the mutant punks—at the concert seemed to enjoy their tired old fakery." Ouch.

Less than a week later, the band redeemed itself in the press when its September 13 show at Leeds' Queen's Hall earned the band a glowing review in *Melody Maker*. Performing as part of the Futurama Festival, scribe Lynden Barber wrote, "U2 play truly great rock music which inspires the heart. They make Echo & the Bunnymen sound as stupid as their name."

Three Committed Christians

In a letter home to his father which he later shared with fans, Bono wrote the following to Bob Hewson from his hotel room in Birmingham, England: "The band are getting tighter and tighter. The nights at the Marquee are very successful. Each Monday the crowd gets bigger and bigger, a situation that hasn't occurred at the Marquee on a Monday night for a long time. We did three encores last week. The single sold a thousand copies and for the first time we are getting daytime radio play on Radio One. We have four DJs behind us now. It's only a matter of time."

Aside for his enthusiasm for the band, Bono told his dad proudly of his devotion to God, in the note, which Bob Hewson shared with Dunphy. "You should be aware that at the moment three of the group are committed Christians. That means offering each day up to God, meeting in the morning for prayers, readings, and letting God work in our lives. This gives us our strength and joy that does not depend on drink or drugs. This strength will, I believe be the quality that will take us to the top of the charts."

Boy Is Released

With its austere black-and-white cover featuring Guggi's little brother Peter Rowen, *Boy* projected a message of seriousness that matched the disc's musical force and naivety. Propelled by the urgent and memorable single "I Will Follow" as its signature anthem, the album managed to reach number 52 in the British charts.

It was praised by Paul Morley in *NME*, who called it "touching, precocious, with archaic flourishes and modernist conviction." Critical response to *Boy* was even stronger in *Melody Maker*. "U2's live performances have raised their audiences' expectations to what must have seemed like an impossible height," it wrote. "But not only have they reached that peak with their first album, they've risen above it."

As expected, *Boy* also captured the heart of Dublin's music bible, *Hot Press*. Giving it an 11 out of 12 rating, the paper said, "It rushes your senses,

U2's music, like it's been lying under the tree all year, and at Christmas it's taken out of its box and shown to everybody, open-mouthed."

In Bono's assessment with a year of hindsight, he described *Boy* as an exposition of U2 as it closed the book on its adolescence. Chronicling innocence as it was about to spoil, the disc was unique because rock and roll had never taken on this subject outside of a romantic-love context.

Boy Tour

With an active tour through the U.K. in the third quarter of 1980, U2 was putting a lot of miles on its van. But its commitment to the road, and the strong publicity that *Boy* had earned in the few weeks since its release helped the band land its first television appearance outside of Ireland. During the second week of November, Bono, Edge, Larry, and Adam performed "I Will Follow" on London's ITV.

Coming to America

In advance of U2's debut U.S. tour, Paul McGuinness had the forethought to service import copies of *Boy*—which wouldn't see Stateside release until March 1981—to certain college radio outlets. The move helped the band

Unlike the U.K. and Ireland pressings of "A Day Without Me"—which have divergent artwork—the debut U2 single in the Netherlands and German markets has art similar to that on the *Boy* cover. The German version—released in August 1980 and featured here—counted the same flip side, the non-LP instrumental "Things to Make and Do." *U2 Wanderer.org*

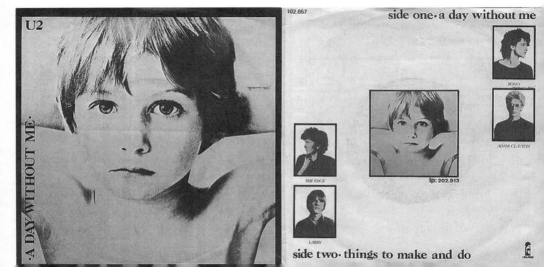

earn some early followers on the East Coast, where the group was testing the market and getting its feel for North America.

In early December 1980, U2 landed at New York's John F. Kennedy Airport and was transported into Manhattan, where they were dropped off at the Gramercy Park Hotel. But the band quickly learned to reassess its trusting nature when it got out of its limousine and walked into the lobby of the building, leaving two guitars behind on the sidewalk.

Turning around, Edge witnessed two men about to grab them when he intervened. Soon after, Bono—sporting his black, fake fur coat—was approached by a man in a car offering to have sex with him. This was a far cry from Dublin.

U2's first American gig was held at the NYC venue the Ritz on December 6, 1980. It was triumphant in the sense that Bono managed to use his charms as a performer to earn the attention of a mostly disinterested crowd of 1,200, who—save for maybe one hundred fans who were turned onto *Boy* as an import—were in the venue expecting a dance party.

14

Can't Find My Way

U2's Growing Pains

Bono, Edge, and Larry Attend a Christian Retreat

The third weekend of January 1981, the members of U2—minus Adam Clayton, of course—attended a weekend retreat for Christian musicians in Worcester, England. During a lengthy presentation, Bono and Edge talked about their faith, the future of their group and the challenges that existed for Christians in a rock band.

After citing Psalm 40—which will surface, in part, in the future on the song "40"—Edge passed the microphone to Bono, who shared his thoughts with those at the Gaines Christian Center.

"I see our position as Christians as to make way," Bono said during the retreat, according to speeches that surfaced in 2006 as a recording known as *U2's Vision*. "Make straight a path for the Lord for a second time. In that sense we have to make the rough smooth and get involved in making the rough smooth. But before the Lord can use the band, he has to sort of make our rough ends smooth and that's what the Lord had to do."

Chris Rowe

By 1981, Bono, Edge, and Larry were more active than ever in the Shalom, the group they befriended back in 1978. Following the group's leader, Chris Rowe, and his wife Lilian, they—along with others in the congregation—lived communally without possessions. Sharing the little money they had, the band still wasn't earning much and as they put it, relied on the Lord to provide for them.

But Rowe, who was a teacher of the scriptures serving as pastor of the church, was really only tolerating the members of U2. When Bono told him that someday he would be able to provide the group with plenty of money,

Rowe laughed at the singer and told him he wouldn't want money earned by a rock group.

It was at this moment that the singer realized Rowe couldn't fathom U2's mission. They were serving God through their music, and if even if their songs weren't overtly religious, the group's next album would surely change that stance.

Merch Control

In late January, Paul McGuinness learned of a shady businessman named Chris Parkes, who made his living selling band merchandise—including U2's—without authorization. Unexpectedly, McGuinness agreed to allow Parkes to license U2 merchandise, and he did such a fine job with it that Chris was later hired to handle official band products.

Your Bono Valentine

By early 1981, Bono had become more comfortable with his rock star image, sporting a fur coat as he spoke to Gavin Martin for the aforementioned *NME* piece "Kings of the Celtic Fringe," which ran on February 14, 1981. In the lengthy article, U2's members also stunned the reporter in the cover story as they used profanities and imbibed alcohol (save for Larry).

Bono and The Edge served up a refreshing critique of Spandau Ballet and Adam & the Ants, two of its chart peers of the moment. Speaking out against the former, Bono called the U.K. pop band's approach boring. "You see it all in one go," he snapped. "Clothes, fashion, hair, and that's it. There's nothing to discover, no mystique, no charm and no personality." As for Adam & the Ants' gimmick of using escapism, the singer explained, "He's using the imagery of a warrior to achieve it, but you might as well go to a drive-in-movie."

U2's genuine stance wasn't just unique, it was challenging at the time. According to the singer, U2's biggest obstacle for the time was its authentic approach to music. They didn't wear make-up, they didn't wear outfits, they didn't play ska, which hurt them in the U.K. In the U.S. they were unfairly lumped in with the new-wave scene. If they wouldn't be easily pigeonholed, they had what the others on the charts sorely lacked—heart.

Trouble at the Border

On February 17, 1981, U2 ran into some trouble while attempting to play its first dates in Germany. Still split into the East and the West, the band needed to travel through a stretch of the Eastern part of the country in order to get to its gig in West Berlin and then turn around quickly to make a performance the next day in Munich.

The band's van was pulled over and detained by border guards with guns and dogs who rousted members from their sleep. It seemed that the East German guards thought U2, McGuinness, and their meager road crew were smuggling people out of the country.

Awoken by noise and shouting, the border guards were extremely suspicious of the van's occupants, forcing them to exit the vehicle so that they could do an extensive search. And if it at first seemed like a hassle, the unpleasant experience with the young German officials—who were the same age as the guys in U2 but eons away from them in terms of outlook—left a lasting impression on Bono. The occurrence gave the singer the inspiration for "Stranger in a Strange Land," one of the songs on U2's next album.

The Sugar Shack

The next night at the Sugar Shack in Munich, U2's members were overserved Bavarian Schnapps, which inhibited their ability to stay awake for the night's 1 AM performance. The foursome passed out after in their dressing room before the show, but Paul McGuinness had the good sense to raise them from their sleep, and the show took place.

More Border Problems

Was U2's luck with border guards cursed? The band's February 19, 1981, Geneva show was nearly cancelled when Swiss custom officers refused to let the band bring most of its instruments and equipment into the country. With the exception of one guitar and one bass, the rest of their gear was banned. Luckily, with the help of gear from the opening act and the promoter—who had a drum set Larry would borrow—they managed to perform and avoided disappointing fans.

15

And I Felt Like a Star

U2 Goes International

"I Will Follow" Goes #1 in New Zealand

In advance of *Boy*, which had a staggered release in certain parts of the world, "I Will Follow" was distributed in Australasia and North America. Although the U.S. pressing of the song failed to chart, the band was stunned to learn it pulled down its very first chart-topper outside of Ireland. The future classic reached number one in the New Zealand singles survey.

Rolling Stone, February 19, 1981

Rolling Stone journalist Jim Henke's profile of U2—which was its first significant piece of American press coverage—ran in the magazine. Boasting the Police on the cover, the piece stemmed from the band's U.K. club gigging three months prior, where Henke hung out with the band in London and Coventry.

The piece found Bono giving one memorable, if not utterly haughty quote to the scribe: "I don't mean to sound arrogant, but even at this stage, I do feel that we are meant to be one of the great groups. There's a certain spark, a certain chemistry, that was special about the Stones, the Who and the Beatles, and I think it's also special about U2."

Adam on the Outside

At a time when his bandmates in U2 could have been partying it up with him, Adam Clayton often found himself alone in his chemical pursuits. Bono, Edge, Larry, and roadie Pod held prayer meetings in the back of the tour bus that they had graduated to, or in their rooms. Meanwhile Adam would either hang out and cut loose with Paul McGuinness or be left to his own devices.

Released in October 1980, this original "I Will Follow" sleeve was the second single released from *Boy* in the U.K. and Ireland, and became its signature song. The song has been in the band's set list for thirty years.   *U2Wanderer.org*

Clayton and McGuinness would likely be found in the front part of the bus, listening to music, cracking a few beers and maybe partaking in a joint or two. This was the unique dichotomy of U2, where the others found comfort in their Bibles. Bewildered and a bit let down by his bandmates, Adam didn't let it keep him from having his fun—he just wished the others would partner up with him for some mischief.

Gay Following

Boy first found its way—via import—into America's gay clubs in late 1980. Based on its album cover, which was misunderstood as suggestive by those with an alternative lifestyle, plus the lyrical slant of "Twilight," U2 had a built in homosexual following by the start of its U.S. tour in March 1981.

One of the band's early advocates was a gay activist and U2 fan who wrote for a subversive San Francisco publication. He reported that among the homosexual community it was believed that the boy on the cover had a gay connotation. It was also incorrectly reported that the boy was Larry, which made him the object of some fans' desires when the band made it to San Francisco that spring.

Although he was at first freaked out by the unwanted interest, Mullen— who had briefly found himself something of a gay symbol—later realized there was no reason to be pissed about the attention. He ultimately recognized he should instead be flattered.

It's Better in the Bahamas

Midway through the tour, on April 22, 1981, U2 and their entourage— including girlfriends who were flown in from Ireland for the trip—headed off to Nassau in the Bahamas for a working holiday. The band participated in a recording session with Steve Lillywhite at Compass Point studios, tracking an upcoming single known as "Fire."

The song had been introduced to the band's live set in the weeks prior, but was still without permanent lyrics until the actual session.

Because of the beautiful weather and the luxuries to be had at Chris Blackwell's island home, the band only spent one day in the studio. The rest of the time was spent in the sun and in the turquoise-colored sea. As their first real warm weather vacation, it was not without its share of incidents. Bono, for one, got a waterskiing boat stuck on a reef.

16

Raise Me Up

U2's Mentors, Friends, and Business Partners

Gerry Cott

A dam Clayton was determined to make it in rock and roll. Inspired by other Irish bands who had done well, he took the initiative to hunt down the Boomtown Rats' guitarist, Gerry Cott, by pretending to be from CBS Records in London and calling his sister at home. After successfully tracking him down after the Rats' Dublin gig in the spring of 1978, Cott kingly gave the bassist valuable and encouraging advice.

Phil Lynott

Upping his game, the Clayton next sought the advice of Thin Lizzy's iconic frontman Phil Lynott. Catching Philo off guard by phone in his Clarence Hotel room the morning after his band's Dublin gig, the frontman for what was then Ireland's biggest band was also quite nice. The man behind "Whiskey in the Jar" and "The Boys Are Back in Town" told Adam to get a good demo, send it to all the labels in London and get a manager.

A Radiator from Space Christens the Band "U2"

Steve Averill, who was better known as Steve Rapid, the frontman in the short-lived Radiators from Space, received a phone call one day in March 1978 from Adam. The bassist explained he had once attended school with his brother, reminded him that his and Averill's parents were friends and said he was looking for advice.

Averill, who had a day job working at Arrow, a Dublin ad agency, as a designer, told Clayton point blank: "Your name suggests a certain contempt for the rock and roll business." Offering to mull it over, Steve got back to Adam a few days later with a few suggestions: the Blazers, Flying Tigers, and U2.

That last one had a ring to it. Discussions ensued. An American spy plane had previously held the name, as did a submarine, and a line of Eveready batteries. Nobody knew what it meant, but it was memorable. U2 it would be.

The band played as the Hype for the last time in late March 1978 at the Presbyterian Church Hall in Howth. It was the final performance with Dick Evans—who was being forced out of the band.

After playing a set of covers with Dick, the new quartet known as U2 took the stage for a set of originals.

Bill Graham

With the *Evening Press* Harp Lager contest win in their back pocket, the members of U2 were looking for more advice on how to elevate their band. Adam—who had since printed up cards that read ADAM CLAYTON, MANAGER OF U2—contacted Bill Graham, a *Hot Press* writer that the group respected. U2 asked to meet with him at Dublin's Green Dolphin bar, so that they could pick his brain. During the meeting, Graham agreed to witness the band's upcoming recording session.

Determined to make it, Adam, Bono, Edge, and Larry listened intently to Graham, who was ten years their senior, talk about the music business. The most important bit of advice Graham offered was for U2 get a manager.

Having already suspected the need for representation, they previously solicited Jackie Hayden of CBS Ireland for the task, but he declined. The boys pressed Graham for a name, and he recommended Paul McGuiness, who was then managing a fledgling band called Spud.

Kindly, Graham also left the meeting with a copy of a photo taken of the band during a shoot it financed with part of its £500 Harp Lager Contest winnings. Impressed enough with what he saw, he gave the band a short write up in Ireland's music weekly, *Hot Press*. He went on to become one of U2's biggest media allies.

Upon his death of an unexpected heart attack in 1996, Bono wrote a tribute for *Hot Press* about the publication's fallen comrade. "From the beginning there were four or five in there who were like a band—losing Bill, for them, must be like how I'd feel if something happened to Edge or Adam or Larry," Bono wrote. "He was like a brother to his colleagues and a cousin to us."

Paul McGuinness

Born in an army hospital in Rinteln, West Germany on June 16, 1951, Paul McGuinness was the son of a Liverpool-bred Englishman. His father was stationed with the Royal Air Force on an RAF base at the time.

By the age of ten, McGuinness was sent to a Jesuit boarding school in Ireland known as Clongowes Wood College. A stranger to Ireland when he arrived, by the time he graduated and went on to attend Trinity College in Dublin, U2's future manager began to think of himself as Irish.

But McGuinness was eventually booted from Trinity—despite having been involved with the Trinity Players, the college theatre group, and serving as an editor on the school's magazine. By his third year, Paul's active social life had kept him from missing most of his lectures, and he was asked to leave.

He ended up moving on to the University of Southampton, which was near to his parents' home in Bournemouth. But after just two weeks, he left the school and went to work odd jobs in London. McGuinness set his heart on either working as a film producer or becoming the manager of a rock and roll band. Within a year, he landed a job as a location manager on a movie, John Boorman's *Zardoz*, after befriending the production manager.

Inspired by famous managers like Brian Epstein and Andrew Oldham, who managed the Beatles and the Rolling Stones, respectively, Paul befriended Michael Deeny, who was managing the Irish rock band Horslips. McGuinness observed how the band handled itself with record labels and filling out customs forms. Meanwhile, a friend from Trinity College named Don Knox had formed a folk rock outfit known as Spud. Already signed to Polydor, they hired Paul to book them and handle their affairs.

Once, while hanging out in the pubs with Bill Graham, a friend of his, McGuinness and the *Hot Press* scribe spoke of finding a baby band of young, Irish musicians and building them into one of the biggest acts in the world. Not long after, on Graham's recommendation, Adam Clayton came knocking with a demo tape.

On May 25, 1978, the members of U2 met Paul McGuinness at the Project Arts Centre. Ten years older than the band, the twenty-seven-year-old looked like a true adult, albeit a cool one with his leather jacket and jeans.

Opening for the Gamblers, a band managed by McGuinness's younger sister, U2 may have been the support act but they were, in Paul's estimation, considerably better. Bono looked his audience in the eyes, Larry and Adam exuded a certain confidence and Edge had a unique approach to the guitar, focusing on notes over chords.

After the show, Paul guided the band into the Granary Bar next door. He bought the lads a round and spoke of his enthusiasm for the band—especially Bono's stage presence. Still, McGuinness wasn't entirely sure that he wanted to manage U2 just yet. He needed to mull it over.

The band conveyed to Paul that it wanted to make a demo and get a record deal and needed someone like him to make it happen. They needed an authoritative figure of his ilk to help work through the financial concerns, assist with acquiring a reliable van and some quality gear. However, McGuinness wasn't exactly sure they were ready.

If U2 felt rejected at first, the band was determined to team with McGuinness. Eventually, after a number of weeks of pestering by the band as he considered the idea, Paul finally committed himself to them. For the band, it was a relief to know that McGuinness—with his experience in media, working with film and music folks in the past—was worldly wise and capable of dealing with talent bookers and record company A&R folks.

In taking on the job, Paul—who was married and feeling some pressure and uncertainty from his wife over the decision—made it clear that he didn't want to be friends. It would be a business relationship. While this didn't endear him to the other members of Lypton Village, who nicknamed him "The Goose," Paul needed to keep things professional. U2 were his clients.

Into the summer of 1978, McGuinness would regularly meet with his "baby band"—which he'd later describe as "ingenious and ambitious and very bright" at his flat on Waterloo Road. It was here that they would plot their first step toward global domination.

When pursuing Paul McGuinness to take on U2's management duties in the late spring of 1978, its devout members—Bono and Edge—kept their religious beliefs concealed for fear of scaring off the potential manager. Much later, in 2006, McGuinness admitted that had he known the group's creative axis was a pair of bible thumpers, he indeed might have told the foursome to get lost.

Chris Blackwell

Returning to London in July 1980, the members of U2 finally met Chris Blackwell, Island Records' owner and music business legend. Blackwell had made his mark by signing landmark reggae artists Bob Marley and the Wailers and had since worked hard to establish the independent label Island as a company open to a variety of genres.

Born in England, Blackwell was the product of an Anglo-Irish father and a Costa Rican raised, Portuguese-Jewish mother. Raised in Jamaica, his father was in the army while his mother's family produced rum.

Sent to boarding school in England at the age of ten, Blackwell returned to his homeland in his early twenties. Blackwell tried a number of tourist-tailored business ventures, including a car rental agency and a water skiing school at a local hotel. Here, he discovered a local band and offered to record them.

At the time, popular music outside of calypso was nonexistent, and Blackwell worked hard to fill that gap. Blackwell began exporting records from the island to New York and later, took advantage of a growing interest in reggae in the U.K. by importing titles from Jamaica to immigrant areas of London like Brixton and Lewisham. When "My Boy Lollipop," a single by a Jamaican girl named Millie Small that Chris had shipped into the U.K. topped the charts, Blackwell quickly had the resources to properly launch Island Records.

Legend has it that Bob Marley and the Wailers walked in off the London streets one day, seeking out Blackwell. They were heroes in Jamaica with a cult following in U.K. ghettos, but mainstream record labels were hesitant to take a chance with them.

Blackwell was impressed by Marley's talent and conviction. Although others in the business suggested Marley was "unreliable," Chris felt he could trust the Wailers and decided to back them. He put up the £4,000 needed to have the reggae stars on his label. Together, Bob Marley and the Wailers became global music legends while Blackwell established what was—at one time—the most successful independent record company in the world.

Ian Flooks

When U2's first agent, Ian Wilson, left to manage a band in early 1980, Paul McGuinness began working directly with his boss, Ian Flooks. Flooks was the man behind Wasted Talent, which handled tours for the coolest bands of the time, including the Police, the Pretenders, the Clash, and Talking Heads.

Flooks saw real potential in U2, and gave the band the same care he lent to his more established acts. With the belief that selling out a small venue was infinitely better than leaving a bigger venue partially filled, Flooks and McGuinness put U2 into clubs and halls that were slightly smaller than ones that they could likely fill.

They would also avoid booking U2 for a second night in the same venue if they didn't anticipate filling them to at least near-capacity. This philosophy established the perception that U2 gigs were always a sell-out.

Steve Lillywhite

Producer Steve Lillywhite has been involved in the studio success of the world's biggest band since it inked its recording deal with Island Records in 1980. But before Lillywhite helmed the band's first three albums, he was already an established studio hand. Beginning as a tape operator for PolyGram in 1972, he produced the 1977 demo that led to Ultravox signing with Island Records. Hired as a staff producer he built his name by working with New Wave acts like Siouxsie & the Banshees (he produced "Hong Kong Garden").

In 1980, he worked with former Genesis frontman Peter Gabriel on his landmark eponymous third album and produced the Psychedelic Furs' debut before joining U2 in the studio for *Boy*. Lillywhite kept busy in these early years, working again with the Furs on *Talk, Talk, Talk*. In between his work with U2 on *October* and *War*, he continued producing albums by Simple Minds, Big Country, XTC, and the Chameleons. With his career on the rise, his status rose, and he was given assignments with Talking Heads and the Rolling Stones.

Lillywhite has since worked with the Pogues, Travis, Phish, the Dave Matthews Band, and Guster. He returned to work with U2 on *All That You Can't Leave Behind* and was also on board for *How to Dismantle an Atomic Bomb*. In 2002, he accepted a post at Mercury Records as Managing Director, where he signed Darius Danesh and Razorlight. He also produced Jason Mraz's *Mr. A-Z* in 2004 before moving to Columbia Records in September 2005 as a Senior Vice President of A&R. Although he was only with the company for eighteen months, he signed platinum modern rock duo MGMT.

Frank Barsalona

Paul McGuinness had worked hard to establish a relationship with Frank Barsalona. And he was wise to do it. Barsalona, the man behind Premier Talent, was a legend in the business, having booked tours by the Beatles, the Who, and Led Zeppelin, among countless others.

While working at General Artists Corporation in the 1960s, Frank was the first person to bring the British Invasion bands to the United States. With a network of promoters in cities around America, Frank's proven track record gave him influence, which meant he could get a lesser known act into a venue. Barsalona's big thing was loyalty. Promoters who started with U2 on the *Boy* tour, reaped big dividends by the time of *The Joshua Tree* and ZooTV Tours.

Anton Corbijn

A month before U2's 1982 support dates with J. Geils were to begin, the band got a run of headlining shows underway in New Orleans on February 11 by playing a unique venue, the *USS President* riverboat. *NME* reporter Richard Cook was there to chronicle the start of the second U.S. leg supporting *October* and with him was a tall Dutch photographer named Anton Corbijn, who would become a career-long collaborator of the band's.

Corbijn, who had previously worked with Joy Division, impressed the band with his phenomenal work and his personality. A nearly immediate friendship and creative alliance was forged upon their meeting in New Orleans.

In a 2000 exhibit of Corbijn's photography, Bono told attendees, "When I first met Anton, I had one request. 'Make me look tall, skinny, intelligent, with a sense of humor.' He said, 'So you want to look like me?'"

Anton went on to become the group's official photographer and a close friend of Bono's who would help shape U2's image. In the past three decades, he has pushed the band to take incalculable risks. They've gotten naked, stood for hours in snow drifts, and—in a 1991 shoot in Morocco—even agreed to put on designer gowns and don make-up for one of its funniest and most memorable photo sessions.

Willie Williams

Before he was an acclaimed stage and lighting designer, Willie Williams was a punk-rock enthusiast who began doing lights for the likes of Stiff Little Fingers and Deaf School. Raised in Sheffield, England, Williams was instantly excited by *Boy*, and contacted U2's manager to see if he could work with the group. Paul McGuinness hired him.

Williams began working on the design and lighting of U2 tours beginning with 1982's "Pre-*War*" jaunt. Although the minimalist production of that tour soon gave way to more extravagant presentations like the mind-blowing ZooTV Tour, the *Vertigo* trek, and the spellbinding 360° Tour, Williams was nothing short of a visionary. His reputation also earned him the employ of other major acts like R.E.M., David Bowie, and the Rolling Stones.

Jimmy Iovine

Jimmy Iovine has a long history in the music business. The current chairman of Interscope-Geffen-A&M Records got his start as a recording engineer, working with the likes of John Lennon and Bruce Springsteen in the

Before he established a long-lasting artist/producer relationship with U2, Brian Eno had been a production collaborator and confidant who worked with the likes of the Talking Heads. Eno—seen above with the latter's frontman David Byrne—has gone on to oversee albums by acts like Coldplay, Dido, and cult favorites James. *Photofest*

1970s, before assuming production roles on releases by Tom Petty and the Heartbreakers, Stevie Nicks, Dire Straits, Patti Smith, and U2.

Iovine was persistent when it came to U2, and began expressing an interest in working with the band on a project as early as 1982. His determined approach kept him in the back of U2's mind. When U2 decided to make a live album, Iovine was asked to take the reins for *Live—Under a Blood Red Sky*. The album was a massive success. Four years later, when the band took on its *Rattle and Hum* project, they again brought Jimmy in, and the results were equally lucrative.

In addition to his talent in the studio, Iovine also had business savvy. In 1990, he co-founded Interscope Records, which was acquired by Universal Music in its acquisition of PolyGram in the late 1990s. At the time, Iovine had been co-chairman of PolyGram, and by 2001 he was named chairman of the IGA corporation. As a result of this position, he continues to work alongside U2, whose contract is currently with Interscope in North America.

Brian Eno

Brian Eno had a long run as a performer, musician, and record producer—becoming one of the initial developers of ambient music—long before U2 sought him out to work on *The Unforgettable Fire*. Twelve to fourteen years older than the members he'd work with to his widest acclaim, Eno was studying painting in art school when he was invited to play keyboards and synthesizers with Roxy Music in 1970.

Eno had little musical experience, but he managed to stick with the band during its early glam rock ascent. He eventually left the band after 1973's *For Your Pleasure* because he didn't care for touring or frontman Bryan Ferry. After forays into acclaimed art rock on his 1974 solo album *Here Come the Warm Jets*, Eno abandoned rock on releases like 1978's *Ambient 1/Music for Airports*.

As a producer, Eno worked with David Bowie on his acclaimed "Berlin Trilogy" of albums, *Low*, *Heroes*, and *Lodger*. Eno also produced Ultravox's 1977 self-titled debut, Devo's 1978 breakthrough, *Q: Are We Not Men? A: We Are Devo!* and Talking Heads' albums *More Songs About Buildings and Food* (1977), *Fear of Music* (1979), and *Remain in Light* (1980).

When U2 approached him to help with its fourth album, the producer was hesitant. "I had never worked with that kind of music before," he told *Pitchfork* in 2009. "I was not completely convinced that I would be the right person for it."

"I had this phone call with Bono," Eno continued. "He is the greatest salesman of all time, you have to bear that in mind—where I said to him, 'Look, what I'm worried about is that I might change things rather unrecognizably. People might not particularly like the new you that comes out of this.' And he said, 'Well, actually we want to be changed unrecognizably. We don't want to just keep repeating what we've done before.'"

The rest is history.

Daniel Lanois

Daniel Lanois—who has been affiliated with U2 since 1984—was born in Quebec in 1951 and raised in Ontario. He got his start producing and engineering bands like Martha and the Muffins (which featured his bassist sister Jocelyne) and Parachute Club at his Hamilton-based Grant Avenue Studios.

Earning the attention of Brian Eno, Lanois helped the infamous producer on the soundtrack to David Lynch's film *Dune*, and when Eno accepted a job working with U2 on its fourth studio album in 1984 it was on the condition that Lanois could assist him.

After the success of *The Unforgettable Fire*, Lanois and Eno were asked to helm *The Joshua Tree* and few could argue that Lanois has been instrumental in the artistic direction of U2's most essential material during a twenty five-plus-year association.

At the recommendation of Bono back in the late 1980s, Lanois began working regularly with Bob Dylan, producing his 1989 album *Oh Mercy* and 1997's *Time Out of Mind*, the latter of which earned a Grammy for Album of the Year. In between those efforts, Lanois produced Emmylou Harris's *Wrecking Ball*, which pulled down a Grammy in 1996 for Best Contemporary Folk Album.

Greg Carroll

Before U2's September 1984 performance in Auckland, the group was introduced to a Maori named Greg Carroll. Carroll had approached U2's production manager Steve Iredale in the street. Iredale was wearing a distinct jacket with a U2 logo emblazoned on it, and Carroll asked if he could have it.

While Iredale declined, Carroll—who was working as a local stage manager with one of the opening acts—managed to charm Bono right quick. They had an instant rapport, and before the band left New Zealand for Australia, he was hired as Bono's roadie/assistant.

Sadly, Carroll's time in the U2 organization was short lived. He would die in a motorcycle accident in Dublin in 1986, but not before he became the singer's confidant and one of his best friends. Greg's endearing personality made him a favorite to everyone in the U2 organization.

Flood

Born Mark Ellis in 1960, London native Flood got his start in 1980 working as a runner at that city's Morgan Studios. After playing guitar in the band Seven Herz—who had one cassette release called Forbidden Frequency—he got his first major assignment the following year, when he was hired as an assistant engineer on New Order's post-Joy Division debut *Movement.* That led to similar work with Soft Cell and Cabaret Voltaire.

By 1983, Ellis was credited as the engineer on Ministry's new wave classic *With Sympathy,* and the following year, he assumed a producer's credit on *From Her to Eternity,* the first of five discs he would work on with Nick Cave and the Bad Seeds. In 1987, Flood was picked to engineer U2's album *The Joshua Tree* but also kept busy producing and engineering albums by the Silencers, Nine Inch Nails, Depeche Mode, the Jesus & Mary Chain, the Smashing Pumpkins, the Cure, Erasure, Curve, Nitzer Ebb, the Killers, PJ Harvey, and others in the years in between U2 assignments.

Flood continued to work with U2 alongside Brian Eno and Daniel Lanois on U2's *Achtung Baby* and has been an active presence in the studio with the band in the years that have followed. In 2006, he shared the Grammy Award for Album of the Year honors bestowed to *How to Dismantle an Atomic Bomb.*

Phil Joanou

During a three-night run of gigs in Hartford, Connecticut, in early May 1987, U2 was approached by a twenty-five-year-old up-and-coming film director named Phil Joanou, who presented an unsolicited pitch to the band. Joanou was asking to direct a feature-length documentary about *The Joshua Tree* Tour.

Joanou's brazen approach worked, as U2 asked the young filmmaker to visit them in Dublin during an upcoming break in their tour. Wrapping up the first leg of the trek with a five-night stay at the Brendan Byrne Arena in East Rutherford, New Jersey, U2 went home for a break before embarking on a two-month tour of Europe.

Hitting it off immediately, the band asked Joanou to spend the summer of 1987 fleshing out the idea. The fact that Phil knew so much about the band and had an unbridled enthusiasm about the project made up for his lack of experience.

17

The Trees Are Stripped Bare

October

onths before U2 got to work on its second album—eventually to be titled *October*—the band was thinking out loud about what kind of record it might be. Tentative song titles that were revealed to a New York journalist but never came to fruition included "Assaulted by Underpants" and a number about Bono's dad called "Father Is an Elephant."

In interviews, the singer predicted the next album would be about battles. It was a battle not to conform to the pressures of the music business at just twenty years old. U2 were committed to be true to themselves, their music, and their freedom of expression.

Steve Lillywhite spent some time on the road with the band in advance of its "Fire" session in the Bahamas, helping to hone the songs. Joining Adam Clayton for a radio interview, Lillywhite told a Chicago DJ, "I don't think they will be as shaped as the first album at the start."

Prepping its new material, the group rented a space at their Dublin alma mater, Mount Temple, in an effort to save money. Working on the cheap, and surviving nearly exclusively on Chinese take-out, the sessions were a bit of comedown from the excitement of the *Boy* Tour.

Pressure

U2 was feeling an almost insurmountable level of pressure to build on the success of *Boy*. Having had a couple of years to work through the material for its debut album, and just a few weeks to tackle the songs for its follow up, resulted in tension.

Save for the already completed "Fire," the new tunes were still being tweaked as the sessions for the album approached. Bono was experiencing writer's block, which may have been exacerbated by the criticism he, Edge, and Larry were experiencing at the time from the other members of their Christian group, the Shalom, for their career choices.

State of Mind

In July 1981, U2 began recording its second album, working again at Dublin's Windmill Lane Studios, where it tracked *Boy* a year earlier. Working with a tentative title of *Scarlet*, and in spite of what they told reporters, the band entered the studio largely unprepared.

"I think we have to own up to the fact that we really weren't that interested in being in a band after *Boy*," Bono told *Rolling Stone*'s Anthony DeCurtis in May 1987, of the spiritual searching they were experiencing at the time. "We were going through a stage where we thought, 'Rock and roll is just full of shit, do we want to spend our lives doing it?'"

U2: God's Work

With the exception of Adam Clayton, the members of U2 were deep into Bible studies and discussions of all things spiritual. At the same time, the band had long held the belief that they didn't want to be the band that talks about God. When it finally felt it could lift that restriction and follow in the footsteps of Patti Smith, Bob Marley, and Bob Dylan—who had dealt with the subject of their beliefs in rock songs—the album that would be known as *October* began to take shape.

With the belief that the spiritual facet of one's life can be as complicated as the other aspects, Bono embraced his imperfections and susceptibility in the lyrics on *October*. And although Adam Clayton wasn't in line with his bandmates' religious philosophies, he was okay with its lyrical course—after all rock and roll came from soul music, which itself emerged from spirituals—even if he wasn't sure that a New Wave band could pull it off.

"Fire"

In July 1981, U2 released the single "Fire." Backed in various formats with tracks like "J. Swallow," "11 O'Clock Tick Tock/The Ocean (Live)" and "Cry/The Electric Co. (Live)," the A-side cracked the U.K. Top Forty in August, peaking at #35. Soon after the song hit the shops and the airwaves, the band was asked to appear on the long running BBC program *Top of the Pops*.

Sadly, the added exposure for the single—which would also find a permanent home on *October*—had the opposite effect of what Island Records anticipated—it slid down and ultimately off the charts. Perhaps it was due to their iffy miming, Bono's questionable mop of a haircut or the Beeb's obvious flame imagery.

With its apocalyptic feel, "Fire" was the band's deliberate attempt at a single. Despite suggestions that it had its roots in the Book of Revelations or was steeped in notions of nuclear Armageddon, the band never conceded the track stemmed from either topic. Perhaps that vagueness was part of its allure.

Pushing Through Writer's Block

Much of *October* would ultimately be improvised, where a guitar riff or a rhythmic line would be used as the basis to build a song. With Bono working feverishly to find melodies and lyrics to fit the music, the group went into panic mode when it realized it had a problem—their singer still had very little to draw from.

Bono sought refuge in an upstairs room at Windmill Lane where he came extremely close to deadline trying to get his words straight. Running short on patience, producer Steve Lillywhite became extremely frustrated with the frontman. After all, there were only eleven songs that averaged around three-and-a-half minutes.

Finally, the band came to the resolution that whatever came closest to the spiritual feel of the music would have to suffice. The time constraints left no room for any kind of unnatural lyrics. As a result, the singer's desperation fueled a resounding honesty and directness that yielded some extremely powerful and emotive performances.

The Songs of *October*

After first considering the title *Scarlet*, Bono petitioned to call the album *October*. The title came before the song and signified the idea that U2's members and most of its fan base were born in the sunny, materialistic 1960s. But by the early 1980s, the world was a dark, somber place, where unemployment and hunger were prevalent. Mad money was being spent hand over fist on technology that was being used to create bombs. *"Kingdoms rise and kingdoms fall,"* indeed.

But despite that angle, thematically *October* was a deeply Christian album, with lyrics that seek out and question God. It cannot be understated just how difficult it was for the band to complete. A struggle from start to finish, the album was crafted in the face of time constraints U2 had never faced before.

Not to mention the fact that Bono, Edge, and Larry were thinking of throwing away all that they had achieved to date during the disc's creation in pursuit of a more meaningful calling. In what Edge would describe to McCormick decades later as U2's "most out-there phase, spiritually," the band's singer, guitarist, and drummer had each developed and nurtured a very intense personal relationship with not just God, but the other members of the Shalom.

This, in turn, had Adam—who considered his bandmates' concentrated religious focus disruptive to the path U2 had travelled along—contemplating his next move without U2.

For a period of six months during and after the creation of *October*, the future of the band was very wobbly. Its sophomore album—which magically sidestepped what could have been an artistic slump—became a sonic chronicle of how U2 overcame complicated times. Instead of abandoning rock and roll, the group delivered a poignant triumph.

This is the limited edition "Gloria" seven-inch picture sleeve. It was released in Australia in 1981 through a distribution deal Island Records had made with Festival Records.
991.com

1. "Gloria": In an attempt to connect with Bono on a spiritual level, Paul McGuinness gave the twenty-one-year-old singer an album of Gregorian chants. The album opened up horizons for the frontman, giving him the idea of singing the chorus to one of U2's new standout songs in Latin.

Bono approached Gary Jermyn, a mutual friend of his and Gavin Friday's, who had studied Latin at Dublin's Trinity College, to translate his lyrics so that his vocal part made sense. Afterward, Bono took the lyrics to Albert Bradshaw, a teacher at his alma mater, Mount Temple, to ensure they were on point.

Using the song as a vehicle to unlock himself creatively and spiritually, the frontman was able to open the floodgates with a song that was part Gregorian chant and part psalm.

"It is a love song," Bono said in John Waters's 1994 book *Race of Angels: The Genesis of U2*. "In a sense it's an attempt to write about a woman in a spiritual sense and about God in a sexual sense. But there certainly is a strong sexual pulse in there."

When translated, the song's chorus *"Gloria in te Domine/Gloria exultate"* means "Glory in you, Lord/Glory, exalt [him]," which references the Bible's Psalm 30:2 (*in te Domine, speravi*). "Gloria" also contains links to Colossians 2:9–10 ("Only in You I'm complete") and James 5:7–9 ("The door is open/ You're standing there").

Released as the band's next single on October 5, 1981—a week ahead of its parent album—"Gloria" backed with "I Will Follow (Live)"—peaked at #55 in the U.K. charts. Import copies of the single reached U.S. shores, where it climbed as high as #81.

2. "I Fall Down": A successful experiment that tells the story of Julie and John—a song supposedly based on the romance of roadie Pod and an American girl involved in the Shalom—this song sees Bono taking the band in a new lyrical direction.

Still very much spiritual, "I Fall Down" is propelled by Bono's powerful vocal delivery and Edge's glistening piano work. Easily one of U2's warmest early numbers, the song was and is an overlooked piece of the group's 1980's canon.

3. "I Threw a Brick Through a Window": The third song on *October* is built around Larry Mullen's drum hook. For the lyrics, Bono looked back on the anger that was simmering in the Hewson home in the years after his mother's passing.

"Brick" was based on a specific incident in the previous decade when Bono and his brother Norman went after each other and the singer threw a carving knife at his sibling. Thankfully he missed. The song's lyrics also reflected the self-loathing and shame he felt after his violent eruption.

4. "Rejoice": Using the same image as "I Will Follow," in which a house tumbles down, Bono was struck later by the unusual likelihood that he would write two songs using the same image.

Launched by Edge's sparking guitar lines and maintained by the bedrock rhythms of Adam and Larry, Bono's delivery sounded downright furious. Spewing into the mic and seeking guidance from God, some of the lyrics for the track came to the singer live on the spot in the studio. Discouraged and desperate for guidance, Bono asked his savior, "*And what am I to do? / Just tell me what am I supposed to say.*"

5. "Fire": [see previous entry]

6. "Tomorrow": One of Bono's and Edge's favorite U2 songs of all time, the lyrics to "Tomorrow" began as unconscious rambling. Built as a tribute to the Irish traditional music of its heritage, the dramatic song was sustained by the power of Vinnie Kilduff's Uileann pipes and the band's own restrained performance.

If Bono's words were stream of conscious, they were also plaintive and meaningful. Soon after its release, the singer spoke of the song as a depiction of the senseless violence in Northern Ireland at the time.

Later, upon his realization that it was a narrative account of his mother's funeral—with its imagery of a black hearse parked by the side of the road and fear in answering the door, Bono acknowledged the song was therapeutic and stated that if life's tragedies aren't faced, they eventually "find holes."

7. "October": Although he hadn't played piano since he gave it up around his twelfth birthday, Edge managed to craft one of U2's most enduring and meditative keyboard-steered numbers with the title track to U2's second album.

The band was just as amazed as its guitarist to find out that Edge not only had some remaining keyboard ability, but that he could craft such a lasting piece of music on the keys. Sitting at a piano, the chords came to life albeit in a stark, somber manner that was reflective of the guitarist's recent travels under Europe's grey skies during U2's 1981 winter tour.

8. "With a Shout": The musical power of "With a Shout" makes it arguably the most edgy number on *October*, while the inclusion of trumpets courtesy

Recorded in the Bahamas in the spring of 1981, "Fire" was released that July, months in advance of its still-in-progress parent album *October*. It was backed by the fan-cherished B-side "J. Swallow." *Ninnee from Norwich*

of Some Kind of Wonderful—a Dublin-based soul band of the time—makes it decidedly unique.

Add to it Bono's lyrics about the crucifixion, and the song becomes one of the most innovative of its day. With its illustration of blood being spilled at the side of the hill in Jerusalem, the singer's words came straight from the Psalms of David, which he was avidly reading at the time.

Brave enough to dismiss any fear of those who might criticize him for being so forward about his Christianity, Bono had come to the decision that if he was to serve God, there was no need to disguise who he was.

9. "Stranger in a Strange Land": Stemming from U2's interaction with a young East German border guard en route to Berlin, Bono described the song as "a little portrait of him." He was their age, but instead of holding a guitar, he had a gun. Instead of a leather jacket, he had a uniform.

Although Bono's performances on *October* were heavily improvised, this was a true story of their interaction, where they took the guard's picture, gave him a cigarette and thanked God that their fortunes were different from his. And unlike the bulk of the material on the album, it wasn't delivered impromptu. It was sharp, direct, and effective.

10. "Scarlet": Commonly mistaken as "Rejoice"—because the lilting, ethereal song's lone refrain is that word—"Scarlet" has been called a precursor to the *War* track "40." Another song derived from the Gregorian chant album McGuinness gave the band in advance of the sessions for *October*, the piece evokes thoughts of calm and kindness.

11. "Is That All?": Built from a guitar riff that originally surfaced on "The Cry"—a quickly abandoned song that was fused to "The Electric Co." in a live setting—"Is That All?" came together quickly in the studio. While some critics dismissed the song as a failure, specifically because of Bono's lazy lyric *"Is that all that you want from me?,"* the closing number on *October* packs a wallop and has held up over time.

Don't Quit Your Day Job

In the weeks leading up to recording *October*, Bono, The Edge, and Larry were living out in Portrane, on the northern coast of Dublin where they were still actively involved as members of the Shalom group. Living in a caravan in a field beside the beach, they were fasting and praying. Bono was even baptized in the sea during this time.

Reading and studying scriptures, Edge found himself wondering if he—as a Christian—could continue to play in a rock band. Was rock music the right form of expression? Removed from the culture of rock, U2 was just a day job. Their primary focus was its evening prayer. At least that's how Edge, Bono, and Larry approached it.

But none of it was sitting well with Adam Clayton. The bassist disdained the exclusive, holier-than-thou attitude of the Shalom's other members, who looked down at him for his hedonistic, rock and roll lifestyle.

Reaction from Fans and Critics to October

Upon its release, *October* made a decent debut, placing at #11 in the British album charts. In the United States, the disc debuted at #181 on November 7 and climbed to #104. If the band's luck on the album survey wasn't quite what they had hoped, the record received overwhelming critical praise.

In *Hot Press*, Neil McCormick wrote, "*October* is a musical and spiritual growth for U2, a passionate and moving LP for me. U2 have evolved

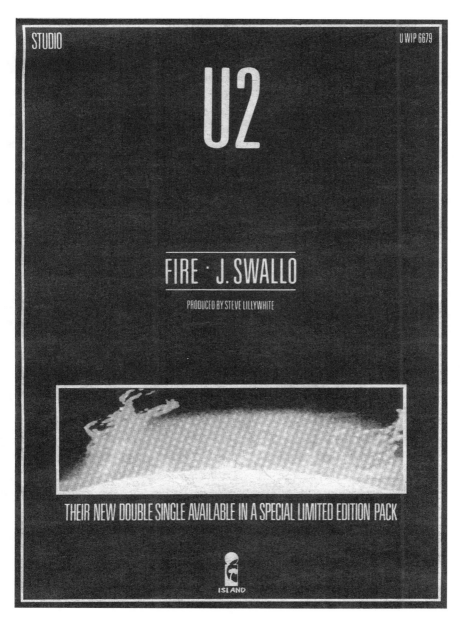

This ad from the August 1, 1981, issue of the *NME* announces U2's single "Fire," recorded with Steve Lillywhite in the Bahamas during a break in the band's spring tour supporting the J. Geils Band.   *Author's collection*

constantly, songs changing and growing over a period of time." Elsewhere he said, "It's a Christian LP that avoids the pedantic Puritanism associated with most Christian rock [and] avoids the old-world, emotional fascism of organized religion."

Meanwhile, *Melody Maker* said, "Their whole musical sensibility is shaped by a strong emotional bond to their homeland. It gives them a completely different frame of reference from most groups. . . . And on *October* it's given them the strength to assimilate a barrage of disorientation and to turn that into a cohesive body of music."

Sounds added, "It all breathes, from the pair of standouts appearing at the start of each side—'Gloria' being possibly their finest moment and 'Tomorrow,' low and muted, gently oozing emotion. This *October* will last forever."

Rolling Stone writer Jon Pareles wasn't so kind. He called the album "barely coherent" and opined ". . . the way to enjoy U2 is to consider the vocals as sound effects and concentrate, as the band does, on the sound of the guitar."

October Philosophy

Looking back on U2's sophomore offering, Bono thought of it as a game changer for the group. Honesty and clarity were the priority on *October* as U2 pledged to shun whatever notions it had about what was cool or hip in its pursuit of sincerity and spirituality. Describing its credo during this era in *U2 by U2*, the frontman said, "We will be as raw emotionally as we have to be."

After its release, the singer would confess to *U2 Magazine*, "A lot of people went 'What the hell is going on here?'—especially in England, where people wouldn't be aware of how much religion is part of everyday life here in Ireland. They're not aware of how deep that runs."

18

I Can Change the World in Me

U2 Nearly Shatters

European Tour

On October 1, U2 started a European tour, in advance of the release of its new disc, sharing stages with up and coming bands Wall of Voodoo and the Comsat Angels. Having already recorded a series of BBC sessions—and with another one set for the fourteenth that would mark its first and last-ever performance of "Scarlet" on Kid Jensen's radio show, the group traveled across the U.K. and Europe, winding up at the Metropol in Berlin. Its final show was recorded for the German TV series *Rockpalast*, which aired the performance in 1982. It also came close to being the last U2 show ever played.

The Village Crumbles

With the Shalom group occupying the private lives of most of U2's members, Bono's connection to the Lypton Village began to crumble in 1981. First, Guggi exited the prayer group, claiming he felt evil vibes from the meetings, which had become as much about the scrutiny of its members' lives—specifically if rock and roll had any valid relationship to Christ—as it had been on the Scriptures.

The Shalom had called for the surrender of ego, but as performers in the public eye, it questioned how those in U2 and the Prunes complied with that tenet? As for Gavin Friday—who was prone to wearing earrings and had a flamboyant stage presence—he, specifically, was being judged. When it was suggested that certain members might have to choose between a career in rock music and God, Gavin left the group. He would not be manipulated

Bono and Gavin Friday have been friends since their early teens. As members of Lypton Village, and later as participants in the Shalom, it was Gavin who first recoiled against that organization's founder Chris Rowe—calling him a hypocrite for using U2's rising popularity as a way to draw new members to his prayer group. Friday—seen here with Bono promoting their collaboration on *Peter and the Wolf*—remains one of the singer's oldest and dearest mates.   *© Harry Line/Allactiondigital.com/Retna Ltd.*

and did not go quietly over the suggestion, either. In his opinion, *the Shalom group could fuck off.*

Although Bono, Edge, and Larry couldn't see it at the time, in Gavin's estimation, the Shalom was using the members of U2 to promote their organization. Around Dublin, music fans had learned that the band was involved with the religious group and this had drawn a lot of younger folks to the meetings.

In Gavin's mind, Chris Rowe was a hypocrite. He was happy to have the boost in membership that U2's presence undoubtedly brought, but at the same time, Rowe and his followers were increasingly critical of the music and culture that came with their famous members.

Edge and Bono Try to Quit the Band

Bono and Edge were beginning to feel increasingly uncomfortable with the criticism of their rock and roll careers by their supposed friends and neighbors in the Shalom. But the suggestion that someone couldn't have a spiritual life and play in a rock and roll band seemed like nonsense to Larry, whose bullshit detector was starting to function.

"I got out before anybody else. I'd just had enough," Larry said of his exit from the Shalom in the 2007 book *U2: An Irish Phenomenon.* "It was like joining the Moonies." Like Gavin and Guggi before him, Mullen decided to stop attending the meetings.

Edge—young and impressionable—took the opposite point of view and became the first to succumb to the "support" of his peers in the Shalom. He told Bono that he couldn't serve both God and man. He was planning on leaving the band to fully develop himself spiritually and to find God's purpose for his life. Bono decided that Edge might have a valid point and elected to follow suit. Besides, he had no desire to continue playing in U2 without the guitarist.

Bono and Edge approached Paul McGuinness at Windmill Lane to inform him that they were quitting the music business. They were struggling with the idea of being devoted Christians and members of a rock band. There would be no tour of North America in support of *October.* There would be no more U2. A shocked McGuinness needed to process the information and asked the musicians to come back in a few hours.

McGuinness Stands Up for U2

Paul McGuinness took a walk around the block that Windmill Lane Studios was a part of, trying to absorb the notion U2 would be coming to an end if he didn't do something. After all he worked for with the band in the past three years, he couldn't let them throw it all away without first putting his own beliefs on the table.

McGuinness explained to Bono and Edge that the group had made a commitment to the crew, the venues and the fans awaiting them in the U.S. Despite whatever religious feelings they were having, these obligations needed to be honored. Hewson and Evans knew Paul was right. They agreed to move forward with the tour. If McGuinness hadn't completely talked Edge and Bono out of leaving the band, he at least made them realize what they would be throwing away. As time elapsed, Bono and Edge came to embrace the belief that they could indeed serve God *and* devote their lives to music.

U2 and Shalom Grow Apart

With their increasing philosophical differences about where rock music fit in with their Christian lives, and U2's renewed commitment to soldier on, Bono and Edge began to part ways with the Shalom. The first signs of a separation occurred when Bono told the group's leader Chris Rowe that it wouldn't have to worry about money because U2 would be able to support the group with its earnings.

"I remember he [Rowe] said to me: 'I wouldn't want money earned that way,'" Bono told Michka Assayas. "Even though he had known we were serious about being musicians, and being in a rock group, he was only really tolerating it. He didn't really believe that our music was an integral part of who we were as religious people unless we used the music to evangelize. I knew then that he didn't really get it, and that indeed he was missing out on our blessing."

19

Rock as Hard as You Can Tonight

Ten Bands That Opened for U2

Our Daughter's Wedding

Accarding to Our Daughter's Wedding's one-time frontman Scott Simon, his band's gig at the Ritz in New York City with U2 on March 7, 1981, was a co-bill, but as the Irish band's star rose, that got lost in translation. ODW, who had a significant new wave favorite with "Lawnchairs," which was riding a six-week run at #1 on the College Radio charts at the time, was arguably more popular.

"We knew who U2 was and liked their music," Simon remembered in 2010. "However, among people at the show there was a question as to why the band wore their religion on their sleeve. The light show consisted of a giant crucifix, constructed from aircraft landing lights. The show was sold out and it felt great. U2 was spectacular. Anyone listening knew they were destined for greatness. The *New York Post* reviewed our performances calling them flawless."

The Alarm

The Alarm had just released a five-song, eponymous EP on California independent label I.R.S. Records in June of 1983, when U2 plucked them from obscurity and put them out in front of its bulging U.S. audiences. At the time, the band—Mike Peters, Dave Sharp, Eddie MacDonald, and Twist—balanced an acoustic-punk approach with high hairstyles to take a unique musical stance. Its first significant single "The Stand" grew to the level of a cult hit in the summer of 1983, thanks to exposure on the *War* Tour and respective support from college radio.

"The people who do like us, really like us, really love us—it's not a kind of passing trend with this band, I think that's true. I think it's true of the Alarm as well, and I'd also like to say it's our privilege to have a band like the Alarm guesting with us," Bono said in the aforementioned June 1983 interview with George Gimarc.

Of course, within two years, the Alarm would gravitate toward a more electric style on radio hits like "Strength" and by 1987, "Rain in the Summertime." While alluring, these songs were remarkably similar to the style of guitar rock made famous by U2.

The BoDeans

In 1987, Wisconsin's own BoDeans were supporting their second album *Outside Looking In* when they were tapped to open a run of U.S. dates on *The Joshua Tree* Tour. The acclaimed roots rock group—which remained active and released the album *Mr. Sad Clown* in 2010—looked back fondly at the experience in 2008.

"They were fantastic to us, really nice people," the BoDeans' co-founder Kurt Neumann said to *Modern Guitars* in 2008. "I loved it! It was a great experience, and it taught us a lot about real big-time music."

Neumann—who along with Sam Llanas had a smash hit of their own in 1993 with "Closer to Free" (U.S. #6)—described the band as great people and remembered the "big machine" that drives a group at that level of success. "There's almost a whole different pressure around you of what you kind of have to do or what's expected," Kurt told Skip Daly. "And, maybe, not so much where they're at now, but certainly around the time of *The Joshua Tree* years there was. And I think U2 wanted that. I think they wanted to be a huge, huge band that ruled the world, and that's what they strived for and worked for, and I can respect that."

The Pixies

Beloved Boston band the Pixies were a major influence on Nirvana, Weezer, and many other bands during its original six-year tenure. Founded in 1986, the band—frontman Black Francis, bassist Kim Deal, guitarist Joey Santiago, and drummer David Lovering—had just released its fourth album, *Trompe Le Monde,* when U2 tapped the band to open all thirty-two dates on its first leg of the ZooTV trek.

Interestingly enough, the members of the Pixies had never met the members of Ireland's biggest-ever musical export. "They came to see us in Dublin two years ago, but we have never formally met them," Lovering told the *Boston Globe* in advance of the tour. "They sent us a note backstage, saying they liked the show. But that was it."

U2 was apparently fond of sending notes to the band behind such classics as "Here Comes Your Man" and "Monkey Gone to Heaven." When it got word that the Pixies were struggling to keep things together on tour, U2 reportedly sent them another note that said, "Keep digging for fire. We love you."

Pearl Jam

In 1993, Pearl Jam was the support act on several dates of the ZooTV Tour, including one date in Verona. Trying to connect with the massive Italian audience, who—unlike the band's millions of U.S. fans—didn't know who the Eddie Vedder–fronted quintet were, Vedder explained, "This is a big place for such a little thing like music. I can't wait 'til we can come back and play in a place where we can see you."

Although he seemed a little odd, Bono liked this Vedder guy—even though he wore a mask in public at times. If Eddie wasn't prone to embrace the trimmings that most rock stars—including Bono—held dear, he respected the Pearl Jam frontman's need to protect himself as he got acclimated to life in the limelight.

Oasis

Britpop favorites Oasis were asked to open for U2 on select dates of its PopMart Tour, including a two-night June 1997 stand in the Bay Area at Oakland-Alameda County Stadium. On the first night, U2's members donned disguises in order to watch Oasis' performance without being identified.

With both bands prone to partying at this stage in their respective careers, U2 and Oasis whooped it up backstage, singing along to the latter's upcoming *Be Here Now* album. Afterward, en route to a late-night dinner at Tosca Café, the radio played "One," which purportedly inspired Oasis' principal songwriter Noel Gallagher to call it "the greatest song ever written." Together they partied into the San Francisco night before watching the sun rise near the Golden Gate Bridge.

Rage Against the Machine

Many of the PopMart shows featured explosive, punk- and metal-influenced band Rage Against the Machine supporting U2. It was an opportunity that helped the politically charged group expose its second album, 1996's *Evil Empire*, to a wider audience. But for guitarist Tom Morello, it was also a chance to perform with one of his favorite groups.

"I'm a big fan of U2. I've been a fan for about ten years," Morello told MTV.com at the time. "When I first moved out to Los Angeles I had this really horrible job. I was a filing clerk—I alphabetized eight hours a day all by myself and the bosses were very cruel and I was super poor, making sub-minimum wage, and I had one tape, and it was *The Unforgettable Fire*. I was listening to that for hours and hours, day after day, month after month to really help me get through that time. In that music there's so much hope and so much passion, it helped me transcend that mundane, grim, crappy experience, and I've been a fan since then."

Smash Mouth

Best known for songs like "Walking on the Sun" and "All Star," Smash Mouth were tapped to open for U2 on its PopMart Tour's third leg. But when the pop band's bassist Paul DeLisle was asked how they were picked to open for the Irish giants in late 1997, he wasn't exactly sure how they were selected for the honor.

"I have no idea," DeLisle told *Drop-d* at the time. "We still don't know. . . . They want to take different, new, up-and-coming bands." Opening just a

Tennessee rockers Kings of Leon known for the massive hits "Sex on Fire" and "Use Somebody," supported U2 on its *Vertigo* trek.   *Photofest*

handful of dates, including one Halloween show where Smash Mouth's members dressed up like old ladies, U2 was so impressed with their fun spirit and good-natured approach, they got the group a case of Guinness.

As for the audience's reaction to the band—which wasn't widely known in 1997, DeLisle said, "They were nice, polite. Though they weren't jumping up and down for us or anything like that! You know it's funny, we weren't nervous at all. And the whole tour is very well run, incredibly smooth and efficient."

Kings of Leon

Before they became rock giants in their own right, Tennessee's Kings of Leon were given an opening stint on U2's North American *Vertigo* Tour. "We did a show called *Court Down: United Kingdom* in London," drummer Nathan Followill told MTV.com in 2005, "and U2 were on the show too."

"We played and they played, and then we're getting ready to leave and their publicist said, 'Hey. Bono wants you guys to stay. He wants to meet you guys,'" Nathan added. "So we had some drinks, and he was pretty cool and complimentary of our [then-current] record [*Aha Shake Heartbreak*], but just like a normal down to earth guy. Like a month later, our manager was like, we just got the U2 offer."

"I still can't believe we're going to be opening for U2," he continued. "Since the news first came out, we've had calls and emails from about three hundred of our friends and family asking us for tickets."

Muse

U.K. trio Muse was asked to open dates on U2's massive 360° Tour. The band, already hugely successful, was happy to promote its 2009 album *The Resistance* by warming up for its mentors in U2.

"The U2 tour was amazing because we didn't know what to expect being a support band again," drummer Dominic Howard told *Spinner*'s Dan Reilly. "It's very different playing to a bunch of people that's not your crowd, especially if there are 50,000 of them like in those stadiums."

Howard said that it gave them the opportunity to win over new fans in the U.S. and hang out with the Dublin-based superstars. "They're all really sweet and nice people," the drummer said. "We had a few drinks here and there. They're nice, enthusiastic, and very complimentary about our band. They seemed to know the music, know the album and they spent a bit of time drawing parallels between what they've been doing for the last twenty-five years and where we're at now."

20

A New Heart Is What I Need

October Flops

D espite getting its first real exposure on *MTV*, U2's second album was a resounding flop in the United States. Less successful than its predecessor, the disc's failure had U2 fearful lit might be dropped by the label. With that perspective, Paul McGuinness and the band knew they had to take things to another level the next time out. Their lives were depending on it.

With the uncertainty of their future lifted by Chris Blackwell's commitment to let the band move forward and make another record, U2's members made a resolution to come out swinging.

Out of cash—things had gotten so bad that American Express stripped McGuinness of his credit card when he was delinquent on the bill—the band was indeed on the ropes financially.

Sandy Pearlman

After *October*, Steve Lillywhite had informed U2 that he had a rule—he would only produce two albums with them, or any band for that matter. Therefore the group was in a quandary to find another collaborator for its third disc.

U2 seriously considered Sandy Pearlman. When they headlined New York's infamous Ritz for a three-night run beginning November 20, 1981, U2 visited with Pearlman, a veteran of records by the Clash and Blue Oyster Cult, at a Long Island recording studio to see if he might be a good fit for their next album.

While the Ritz shows were a sellout, as were the band's shows at Hitsville North in Passaic, New Jersey and Hitsville South in Asbury Park, the sessions at Kingdom Sound studios weren't as fruitful as they had hoped.

At the time, Bono described a song they were working on to an interviewer with *Trouser Press* as "a psychotic rockabilly song with a drum figure that runs beginning to end." The results were never released.

Lillywhite's Third

U2 had also tried testing the waters with potential producers like Blondie's Jimmy Destri and had been pondering Roxy Music's Rhett Davies and American Jimmy Iovine, who had engineered albums by Bruce Springsteen and manned the boards for Tom Petty and the Heartbreakers' classic *Damn the Torpedoes*.

Iovine was persistent and called the band multiple times, but U2 had still decided it still wasn't ready to cut the cord with Steve Lillywhite. Steve had a similar feeling and elected to sidestep his own work rule. He would produce *War*.

A Slap in the Face

In U2's Ireland, things had gotten dangerous. The Republican Movement had gotten out of hand, or as Bono would put it, "Nationalism was turning ugly." When fans would throw the Irish flag onstage, the singer would tear off the green and orange pieces and fly the remaining white cloth. The white flag—which would go on to be synonymous with U2's *War* performances—made a powerful statement.

Thinking about where they stood as Irish citizens in 1982, the men of U2 believed in nonviolence, to an extent. At the time, war was prevalent around the globe, from the Falklands and South Africa, to the Middle East and in U2's own backyards. The title of the album was a wakeup call to the music world. If *War* was designed to shake people from their apathy, it would also change the public's perception of the group.

Howth

In preparation for the album, the band returned from its North American tour behind *Boy* and rented a bungalow on Dublin's north side, in Howth, to write and rehearse the songs that would comprise *War*. The three-room beach house—which doubled as Bono and Ali's place of residence—was a converted stable, where the group could hear the waves splashing on the edge of the structure.

Ready for *War*

With Bono and Ali away from the cottage in Howth on their honeymoon, Edge had two weeks to throw himself into his work. With Larry and Adam also on vacation, the guitarist came up with the nuts and bolts of three songs, the future classic "Sunday Bloody Sunday," the acoustic winner "Drowning Man" and the fiery anthem "Seconds." Another memorable song, "New Year's Day"—which was built around a bass line of Clayton's, took shape.

Working alone with a four-track recorder, Edge—who had caught hell from Aislinn for working while the rest of the band had time off—put his frustration with his future wife to good use and made significant progress as a songwriter during this time. Picking up his guitar, he drafted an anti-terrorist missive that became "Sunday Bloody Sunday."

Upon his return from Jamaica, Bono took the political direction of Edge's song sketch and heightened it. With the idea of contrasting Easter—a holiday observed by both Catholics and Protestants—with the historical Irish event known as Bloody Sunday, where innocent protestors were shot by paratroopers from the British Army, the singer's idea was brilliant and poignant.

The Trenches Dug with Our Hearts

If the theme of *War* was a risk for U2, it was the step forward that the foursome had to take. Society had become numb to violence by 1982. Television-scripted rage and the brutal realities of the six o'clock news were becoming indistinguishable.

If *Boy* and *October* were topically intangible, *War* was purposely specific. With it, the band hoped to drive home the point that the emotional consequences of war were as important and in some cases far more lasting than the physical effects.

"It's a heavy title," The Edge told Adrian Thrills in the *NME*. "It's blunt. It's not something that's safe, so it could backfire. It's the sort of subject matter that people can really take a dislike to. But we wanted to take a more dangerous course, fly a bit closer to the wind, so I think the title is appropriate."

Steve Wickham

Electric violinist and future Waterboys member Steve Wickham found his way onto *War* in quite an unusual way. He met The Edge at the bus stop. Unlike most rising rock stars, Mr. David Evans had little issue with waiting for the bus in 1982. Standing there with his guitar in hand, the outgoing and enthusiastic Wickham approached him toting his violin case.

Just nineteen, a brazen Wickham asked the budding guitar hero if he ever thought about having violin on U2's albums. He gave Edge his number. Three days later, Steve Wickham participated in his first-ever recording session, joining the band at Windmill Lane to contribute to two tracks.

The Songs of *War*

This was the album on which the recognizable "U2 sound" coalesced. Bono's supple tenor, The Edge's jangly guitar work, and the formidable rhythm-section offerings of Larry and Adam were now unmistakable. What *Boy* originated and *October* further suggested, *War* delivered via ten solid tracks, many of which remain critical and fan favorites.

1. "Sunday Bloody Sunday": With the chords and lyrics to this future U2 classic still in rough form, the band went into Windmill Lane with Steve Lillywhite and tracked the song as a work in progress. With Larry's drumming experience in the Post Office Worker's Band paying big dividends as evidenced by the song's defining percussion hook, his military drum beat collided with Edge's vibrant, charging guitar and the declarative violin of guest performer Steve Wickham. As Adam's bass part underpinned the song, Bono's furious delivery of thought-provoking sentiments—about what Clayton would call "the human carnage of families being wrecked"—were equally alarming, abrasive, and necessary.

"I originally wanted to contrast the day, Bloody Sunday, when thirteen innocent people were shot dead in Derry by the British army, with Easter Sunday," Bono explained in Timothy White's *Rock Lives, Profiles and Interviews*. "I wanted to make this contrast because I thought that it pointed out the awful irony of the fact that these two warring faiths share the same belief in the one God. And I thought how . . . it's so absurd, really, this Catholic and Protestant rivalry. So that's what I wanted to do. In the end, I'm not sure I did that successfully with the words. But we certainly did it with the music. The spirit of the song speaks louder than the flesh of it."

Released in January 1983 throughout Europe, this rare seven-inch pressing was available in France and was unique because its use of red block lettering. Other pressings included lettering in various shades of gray and black.   *eil.com*

When U2 began performing the song in concert, Bono would announce to audiences, "This is not a rebel song!" Instead it was announcing to the world that U2 was sick of the troubles in Ireland and Northern Ireland. "There is no right or wrong, there can never be a right or wrong when it comes down to somebody putting a gun to somebody else's head," Bono told KZEW's George Gimarc. "And as an Irishman I feel I can make that statement."

For those who would argue that because U2 came from the southern end of Ireland and the band had no right to talk about the bombs going off in the North, Bono would counter that the bombs may not explode in Dublin, but they were being made there. It was that very reason that he felt he had the right to sing the volatile, controversial, and thought-provoking song.

2. "Seconds": Marking the first time Edge sang lead in U2, the spry, acoustic-driven "Seconds" was written about the notion of someone building a suitcase bomb out of nuclear material in a Times Square apartment. Fusing the guitarist's voice with Bono's—who picked up the second verse—the bandmates at times sound indistinguishable in a song that ranks among one of the more underrated in its songbook.

Innovative for the time, "Seconds" incorporated a sample from the 1982 film, "Soldier Girls," a documentary about women training for war. According to Bono, Oasis frontman Liam Gallagher once called it "brilliant."

The band suggested at the time that the song's intent was to raise questions about the bomb and motivate people to question blind acceptance while using a touch of black humor. In an era where the threat of nuclear terrorism was real, the idea behind the song—of holding a large number of people for ransom—may have been fiction, but it was a believable plot.

3. "New Year's Day": The origins of "New Year's Day" started during sound-checks on U2's 1982 tour. Adam Clayton had become obsessed with the New Romantic classic "Fade to Grey" by Visage and was trying to play it. Instead of paying homage to that outfit's Steve Strange, Clayton stumbled on his own amazing bass line, which gave birth to U2's global breakthrough.

Meanwhile, Edge worked diligently to link a piano part he had come up with to the song, which became the lead-off single on *War.* Elsewhere, the guitarist's fiery guitar riff helped define the song musically.

As for the lyrics, Bono was inspired by the thought of Polish Solidarity leader Lech Walesa being kept away from his wife during his prison sentence. Using snow as a metaphor to *"begin again,"* the group was stunned to learn after recording the song that martial law in Poland would be lifted on New Year's Day.

Amazingly, Bono improvised five or six verses to the song live in the studio without a lyric book. Made up on the spot, producer Steve Lillywhite cherry picked the lines he liked best for the final cut.

4. "Like a Song": This blistering rock number thumbed its nose at the cooler-than-thou music community that was quick to dismiss U2 at the time for its assertions of faith and ambition. Not content to be a punk or new-wave footnote like the many naysayers of this era, Bono urged music fans to come together in his lyrics, rather than be so divisive.

However, a look at the lyric sheet and the seriousness in which his message is delivered, coupled with war-inclined lines about the song's subject wanting to fly a flag and wear a badge or uniform, suggests that there may be a double meaning to the track. Either way, "Like a Song"—which was for many was fans of *War* one of its explosive high points—was only ever played live once.

5. "Drowning Man": Built from The Edge's strumming acoustic guitar line and Adam Clayton's supportive bass part, "Drowning Man" is bolstered by

Bono's uplifting vocal and lyrics that pledge his devotion to his wife, Ali. Rhythmically augmented by Larry Mullen's careful tapping, the fifth song on *War*—which also thrives on the guest violin work of Steve Wickham—is counted among the band's favorite early achievements. Speaking of the track to Carter Alan in *Outside Is America*, Edge said, "With 'Drowning Man,' it's perfection for that song. It's one of the most successful pieces of recording we've ever done."

6. "Refugee": Produced by Irishman Bill Whelan before Steve Lillywhite committed to tackle U2's third LP, the percussion-heavy "Refugee" is a unique presence on *War*, with its thumping, tribal-like drums and chanting voices. Despite its upbeat tack, the song never made it to the live setting.

"For me a performance is kind of a total thing, and the songs have to fit the mood," Bono explained to KZEW in 1983 as to why it hadn't made their live set. "We're looking for a certain feeling for onstage, and there is an ebb and a flow, and we leave songs out if we feel that they're going to interrupt

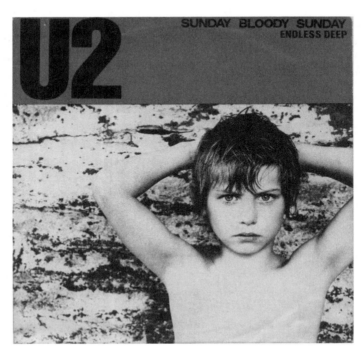

The German seven-inch sleeve for "Sunday Bloody Sunday," which, like the *War* cover, features young Peter Rowen, the only non-U2 band member to ever to appear on the group's record jackets until 1997's "Please." It was released in March 1983.
Author's collection

that flow, and though 'Refugee' is a song I'm very proud of, I'm not sure it would fit in with what we're doing on this [tour]."

7. "Two Hearts Beat as One": Another *War* track based around a distinct and unmistakable Adam Clayton bass line, "Two Hearts Beat as One" was one of U2's four singles [see below] released from the album. A worldwide hit, it was one of two songs Bono worked on during his honeymoon. It became a staple of U2's live set for two-and-a-half years until the band abandoned it in mid-1985.

8. "Red Light": A U2 trip to Amsterdam gave Bono the inspiration to pen "Red Light," where he observed legal prostitutes under dark lighting in the city's storefront windows. Speaking about the song in the year it was released the singer revealed that he had a brief fascination with the world's oldest profession. And in spite of his religious perspective at the time, Bono announced he was non-judgmental about prostitution.

As for the actual song—which marked the band's desire to broaden its artistic scope—it had a catchy percussive feel heightened by the trumpet stylings of Kid Creole's Kenny Fradley. It also had the unmistakable female backing vocals of Cheryl Poirier, Adriana Kaegi, and Taryn Hagey—who were Kid Creole's Coconuts—providing the memorable "da-da-da's."

Working in Windmill Lane in the heat of the summer, and with the air conditioner evidently on the fritz, the session got quite heated. In search of relief, one of the brazen, New York–based Coconuts took her top off for the rest of the session, much to the amazement of the men in the room.

9. "Surrender": Launched by Edge's clanging guitar, the haunting "Surrender" is Bono's tale of Sadie, a woman who tried to raise a family and be a good wife but fell victim to the lure of the streets. Drawn into drug use and abuse, as a means to feed her habit she fell into a life of prostitution. Sadly, the guilty conscience of the song's character leads her up to the forty-eighth floor of a building to find out—in the words of the song— *"what she's living for."* While Bono leaves the song open-ended, offering no conclusions on Sadie's fate, one hopes she made the right choice.

10. "40": After working through the night on *War*, U2's very last day of studio time was wrapping up and it needed to exit Windmill Lane so that the next band, Minor Detail—who were about to record their debut album with Bill Whelan—could start their session. With just two hours to go and nine songs completed, the band took a stab at a bass-driven number that it had attempted but left somewhat incomplete.

With no time for lyrics, Bono reached for his bible and found Psalm 40 and used it as the basis for the song. With Steve Lillywhite quickly editing the song together, part of its brilliance was the band's efficiency. The song came together in just forty minutes, morphing from a sketch to the final product, replete with the vocals and the mixing. As U2 left the studio, another band was waiting to get to work.

For years to come, the song—a modification of the bible entry—would be sung by U2 audiences as they exited venues around the world. Speaking to a Chicago crowd in April 1987, Bono joked, "We wrote this song in about ten minutes, we recorded it in about ten minutes, we mixed it in about ten minutes and we played it, then, for another ten minutes and that's nothing to do with why it's called '40.'"

Chart Success

In January 1983, "New Year's Day" was released as a single in Europe. Peaking at #10 in the U.K. charts, the song marked U2's first visit to the Top Ten, which was propelled by a pre-recorded song on the BBC chart show *Top of the Pops*. In advance of *War*, the group also released the song to radio in North America where it reached #2 on the *Radio and Records* Album-Oriented Rock chart. Meanwhile, *MTV* began heavy rotation of the song's video, which elevated "New Year's Day" to #53 in the *Billboard* singles survey.

When questioned about the single's breakthrough on the eve of the release of U2's third album, Bono contended in the press that music fans were disenchanted with the existing pop-music climate. People wanted music with substance. U2 was a meaningful alternative to the mindless, synth-driven music on the U.K. charts.

War Is Declared

On February 28, 1983, U2 released *War* to a tremendous reception from music critics and fans, who pushed the album to debut at #1 in the U.K. charts. While it only entered the U.S. survey at 91, by mid-year, the disc would reach #12.

"It is a major leap forward," Liam Mackey wrote in *Hot Press*. "Conceptually and technically, to the view that it totally eclipses their previous two albums. I'll even go a step further and proclaim *War*, among the major albums of the last few years."

Elsewhere, *Rolling Stone* scribe J. D. Considine gave the album four stars, writing "U2 may not be great intellectuals and *War* may sound more profound than it really is. But the songs here stand up against anything on the Clash's *London Calling* in terms of sheer impact, and the fact that U2 can sweep the listener up in the same sort of enthusiastic romanticism that fuels the band's grand gestures is an impressive feat."

As for the album art, U2 opted against using guns, tanks, and other violent imagery on the cover of *War*. Instead, the band returned to the maturing face of *Boy* sleeve-star Peter Rowen to drive home the message that the disc could be as much about the story of a broken home as it was about opposing nations or opposing religions.

Released on vinyl with a gatefold sleeve, fans were treated to lyrics to some, but not all, of the tracks. By April 5 it was certified Gold in the U.K. with sales of more than 100,000. Another Gold milestone followed on July 12, when the Recording Industry Association of America awarded U2 for 500,000 U.S. sales.

Two Hearts

In a unique marketing move, U2 issued two singles internationally in March 1983. "Sunday Bloody Sunday" was released in Germany, Japan, and the

This distinct and somewhat rare Japanese seven-inch pressing of "Sunday Bloody Sunday" was released in March of 1983. Its B-side, "Red Light"—which is also found on the *War* album, is different from the non-LP flip side, "Endless Deep," that appeared on pressings issued in Germany, the Netherlands, Spain, and Brazil.   *991.com*

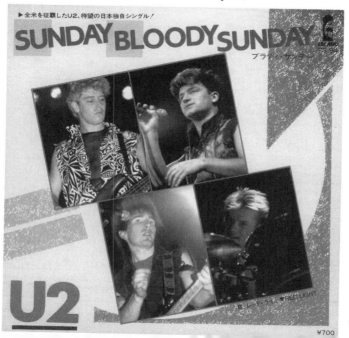

Netherlands, where it made #3. Meanwhile "Two Hearts Beat as One" hit the shops in the United Kingdom, France, Australia, and the United States.

On March 30, the band appeared on BBC's *Top of the Pops* as the single peaked at #18 in the U.K. survey. To support the single's chances in North America, where MTV had become increasingly important in breaking bands, the foursome shot a video for it in Paris. Working again with Meiert Avis, it was lensed in the Sacre Coeur Basilica in Montmartre, where the gothic scenery was given levity by scenes of an acrobat in action, and footage of the band's cover boy, Peter Rowen.

In France to perform at Festival de Printemps in Bourges, the band also participated in a photo shoot with Anton Corbijn. Around this time, Bono was at the height of his memorable albeit awful mullet-hairstyle stage, as evidenced by a photograph from these sessions, which was used some eighteen months later for the cover of the "Pride (In the Name of Love)" single.

"Two Hearts" was also remixed for the club scene by twelve-inch dance specialist Francois Kevorkian. Introduced to the band by Island's Chris Blackwell, Kevorkian took the song's master tapes and reworked the sounds that were already in place to give the song a unique presence for dance venues.

At the time, U2 were one of just a few rock bands willing to experiment beyond rock's traditional confines. The group took risks and avoided rock's clichés at a time when such approaches were well out of fashion. The last

The respective A- and B-side labels of Polystar's "Two Hearts Beat as One" 45 release. Note that the tree from the Island Records logo of the time could have been an influence on *The Joshua Tree* imagery that surfaced in 1987.   *Author's collection*

thing they wanted was to be considered "a nice safe band." *War*—which sounded original, artful, and inspired—affirmed that such needn't be a concern.

Five Facts About *War*

1. War knocked Michael Jackson's landmark album *Thriller* from the top of the charts, becoming the band's first #1 album in the U.K.

2. Producer Steve Lillywhite encouraged Larry Mullen, Jr. to use a click track to keep in time, but the drummer was a purist and refused until he met Sly and the Family Stone drummer Andy Newmark. Newmark—who swore by a click track in the studio—got Mullen to change his outlook.

3. The studio version of "40" was recorded without Adam Clayton, who left the studio with the belief the track was finished. As a result, Edge recorded the bass part Adam would play onstage for many years after.

The inner sleeve of U2's Japanese single "Two Hearts Beat as One"—released via Polystar—boasts the lyrics for the A-side which were left off the *War* album's gatefold sleeve, plus advertisements for the song's parent disc and other recent singles.

Author's collection

4. In 1989, *War* was ranked #40 on *Rolling Stone*'s list of "The 100 Greatest Albums of the 1980s."

5. In 2003, the album again found its way onto another *Rolling Stone* list, where it ranked at number 221 out of "The 500 Greatest Albums of All Time."

The Chicago Peace Museum

At its Chicago tour stop in May 1983, U2 was invited to meet with Marianne Philbin and Terri Hemmert, representatives of the Chicago Peace Museum. The facility's contents were inspirational for Bono, who was awestruck by its exhibition of paintings and drawings created by Hiroshima and Nagasaki nuclear-bomb survivors.

The presentation was called "The Unforgettable Fire," and the members of U2 were drawn to its lesson in nonviolence. Bono also agreed to donate handwritten lyrics for "New Year's Day" and pieces of its stage backdrop and a white flag from the *War* trek to an upcoming display it intended to call the "Give Peace a Chance" exhibit.

U2 Versus the Clash

As U2's ascent continued in the summer of 1983, its punk-rock heroes in the Clash were crumbling. The US Festival marked guitarist Mick Jones's last-ever performance with that band. He was unceremoniously sacked by the group's other co-founders, Paul Simonon and Joe Strummer— soon after the show for both "punctuality" and creative differences.

An interviewer suggested that year that a U2 gig and a Clash concert felt the same in terms of audience reaction. "I think they're worlds apart," Bono said to *Hot Press* in July 1983, shooting down the comparison. "I like the Clash and I like Joe Strummer. I think he's an honest man and I don't want to be hard on them. But sometimes people go to a concert, any concert, and they're nervous. A U2 concert seems to be different, and that's the healing thing, the washing thing. I really believe that rock and roll is very powerful."

Live—Under a Blood Red Sky

In the throes of a number of European gigs, U2 played the Lorelei Festival in Germany, which was broadcast live on German radio and television on August 20, 1983. The performance was rapturously received, prompting

Island to put out a double A-sided single of "40"/"Two Hearts Beat as One," which cited the group as "the discovery of Lorelei '83."

With plans for a live U2 album to round out 1983, five songs the band played at the event were included on the recording *Live—Under a Blood Red Sky*. Although it boasted a cover photo of Bono taken at the Red Rocks gig, merely two of the mini-album's eight tracks were culled from that gig. Coupled with the Lorelei tunes—which were produced by Jimmy Iovine—and a song from the group's May show in Boston, the aim of the disc was to exhibit the kind of excitement one could experience at a U2 gig.

It debuted at #9 in the U.K. album survey and peaked at #2, also climbing to #28 in the United States and ultimately selling three million copies there. But the album and video suffered a bit of a setback from Stephen Sondheim's camp. Bono's rendition of "The Electric Co." on *Live—Under a Blood Red Sky* included a piece of that songwriter's legendary "Send in the Clowns," which was used without permission. As a result, the band agreed to pay $50,000 to Sondheim and conceded to pull that section from the song on all future pressings.

A copy of *Live—Under a Blood Red Sky*, U2's tremendously successful mini-LP, signed by all members.   *Chris Raisin*

21

Set Your Spirit Free

They Shine as Silver and Gold

In February, just as *Live—Under a Blood Red Sky* earned a gold certification in the U.S. for a half-million in sales, Bono spoke out to fans in the group's own *U2 Magazine* about the direction of its next album.

"I can't tell you where we're about to go but I know that I can't sleep at night with the thought of it all," he explained. "I'm so excited about this idea that we've just begun—the way I feel is that we're undertaking a real departure. I can't stop talking about it. It would take about ten men to hold me down at the moment."

Confidence and Innovation

U2 knew if it continued on the same path it forged with *War*, it would soon occupy the void left after the initial demise of stadium bands like the Who, which parted in 1982, and Led Zeppelin, which crumbled after the death of its drummer John Bonham in 1980. But the band wanted to change direction.

Instead the foursome elected to add another aspect to its sound, and pursued the ethereal feel that ultimately surfaced on *The Unforgettable Fire*. The band shunned a standard rock approach, in pursuit of a different kind of feeling. They found it with ambient music pioneer Brian Eno.

Enter Eno

After considering German producer Conny Plank, who manned the boards for discs by Kraftwerk and Echo & the Bunnymen, and mulling the possibility of working with Jimmy Iovine after the success of *Under a Blood Red Sky*, U2

This 1984 U2 single for "Pride (In the Name of Love)" was autographed by all four
members.   *Chris Raisin*

declared that Brian Eno would produce its next album. The news was
a surprise to fans and the media alike, who wondered how Eno, once a
keyboardist in Roxy Music and a veteran of experimental and atmospheric
projects for the likes of David Bowie and Talking Heads, would impact the
group's sound.

   When word reached Chris Blackwell, he attempted to talk the band out
of the decision, but U2 believed Brian—who would go on to help shape
many of the band's future albums—was their man. For the record, Eno
did not agree instantly. U2 first approached Eno sometime in 1983, but he
rejected the offer, explaining he was tired of working in traditional studios
and was about to retire from production. But Bono was persistent and
somehow talked him into it.

   After Eno met Bono, he was intrigued. He wanted to give U2 a shot.
Impressed with the singer's attitude, he found the group's atmosphere—
where everyone contributed—to the development of its material downright
refreshing in an era where such an approach had become increasingly
uncommon.

Daniel Lanois

When Brian Eno came to Dublin for a lunch meeting, he brought along his Canadian engineer Daniel Lanois. At the time, the producer, according to Paul McGuinness, had conspired to land the gig and then hand the reigns over to Danny.

Eno was unimpressed when the band showed him the video of *Live—Under a Blood Red Sky*, but the band's desire to record in unorthodox places and its overall fortitude swayed him over lunch. In the end, Eno and Lanois agreed to work together on the assignment with U2.

The plan was to find a remarkable space with outstanding acoustics that would help to augment the feel of the project.

Slane Castle

Eno and Lanois relocated to Dublin, where they stayed with Paul McGuinness in Monkstown in the two weeks leading up to the actual recording. With plans for the band to rehearse at a church hall in Ranelagh at a premium cost, McGuinness somehow spoke of the matter with Lord Henry

This seven-inch picture disc for "Pride," released by Island in the U.K., boasts a picture taken by Anton Corbijn during the photo sessions for *The Unforgettable Fire*.

991.com

Mountcharies who lived at Slane Castle, where U2 once played with Thin Lizzy.

Mountcharies—who had become a friend of Adam Clayton's—offered the group his facility in County Meath at half the price. With a restaurant on site, and sleeping accommodations when necessary, U2 quickly decided it could make its album in the castle's Gothic Ballroom. Recording equipment was promptly brought over from New York and the band got to work in March 1984.

Working in the facility for two months, the band came to discover that the ballroom was too big for their needs, so they shifted into a library in the castle, which offered improved sound quality. U2 also suffered some creative setbacks from the generator that was powering the session's studio equipment and prone to fail from time to time.

The Songs of *The Unforgettable Fire*

Approaching the follow up to *War*, U2 was looking to make music that felt more serious, artful, and adventurous. Acknowledging it was time for a change, the band's recruitment of Brian Eno and Daniel Lanois was in keeping with their desire to make a more "European" and experimental sounding album.

While all of the band was appreciative of Eno's work in Roxy Music and his production efforts with Bowie and Talking Heads, the producer's own ambient solo efforts like "Before and After Science" had really sparked The Edge's desire to collaborate with him.

When work got underway on what would become *The Unforgettable Fire*, U2's fourth album, in March 1984, the band already had three substantial songs in place to anchor the disc—"A Sort of Homecoming," "Pride (In the Name of Love)," and "The Unforgettable Fire." The music for these songs was crafted at Bono's home in Bray.

Working with a new production team, the band quickly learned to strike a balance between Eno's unconventional mindset and the more traditional approaches that Lanois brought forth. Eno, for instance, was disinterested in an overt pop song like "Pride," but Lanois had little trouble with the band's more accessible side.

Despite the acoustics in Slane Castle, the band wasn't nearly as productive as it had hoped during the two months it worked there. Ultimately, U2 decided to move into Windmill Lane Studios on May 6, where it continued to work until August 5, 1984. Bono was still struggling to finish the lyrics to many songs, and later said that two of the disc's most enduring songs, "Pride" and "Bad" were incomplete "sketches."

By late July, U2 was under the gun to wrap up work on the project. It was putting in twenty-hour days. The hard work would definitely pay off. While the end result tempered atmospherics and orchestration with spirit and somberness, *The Unforgettable Fire*—in the words of Bono—indeed "proved how elastic a rock band can be."

1. "A Sort of Homecoming" is an aural sculpture of a song inspired lyrically by the work of Paul Celan, a Jewish poet of German and Romanian background that Bono had discovered after receiving a collection of his work as

Unlike the first two *4 U2 Play* singles packs, which featured the original artwork and, in some cases, colored vinyl, *U2 Pac 3* consisted of packaging that was noticeably different from what could be found on the individual singles. Boasting a simple white background, respective red, green, blue, and yellow color accents made it popular among collectors.   *Author's collection*

a gift from *Hot Press* scribe Bill Graham. "Poetry is a sort of homecoming," wrote Celan, and Bono identified with the phrase.

Downright jarring on the first listen for any fan that discovered the band during campaigns for any of its previous three albums, "A Sort of Homecoming" is starkly subdued. With tribal rhythms, a murkier mix than anything U2 had ever recorded before, and Bono's images of city walls coming down the track seemed to identify directly with the "Unforgettable Fire" exhibit, from which the disc took its name. Meanwhile, it sustains the hope and faith of a spirit that is—as the song puts it—"coming home."

Late in 1984, because of difficulties performing the song live—due to its experimental studio presentation and high vocal range—the band drastically reworked the song while on tour. The revised version surfaced on the four-song EP *Wide Awake in America* the following spring.

2. "Pride (In the Name of Love)": The lead single from *The Unforgettable Fire* first took shape during a sound check in Hawaii in late 1983 on one of the very last performances behind *War.* The band almost always had its sound-man Joe O'Herlihy tape its warm-ups because these sessions were where ideas would often develop.

With the melody and chords in place, the lyrics for the song—which became one of U2's most significant anthems ever—were at first steeped in the pride that American President Ronald Reagan had in the country's military strength. But upon reading the book *Let the Trumpet Sound: A Life of Martin Luther King, Jr.* by Stephen B. Oates, Bono shifted gears.

Inspired by King's nonviolent side of the U.S. civil rights campaign of the 1960s, and having explored the movement's more violent leanings chronicled in a biography of Malcolm X, Bono elected to pay homage to the fallen hero, who was murdered in 1968.

The song took a long time to perfect, and after two months of attempting the song at Slane Castle from countless speeds and perspectives, the group trashed it and re-recorded it at Windmill Lane. Visiting the foursome—who was worried about the change in direction at the time—in the studio, Steve Lillywhite supposedly told the band, "As long as you've got 'Pride,' you'll be all right."

"Pride" counts backing vocals from the Pretenders' Chrissie Hynde, who visited the Windmill Lane sessions in the late spring of 1984. At the time, she was married to Simple Minds' singer Jim Kerr, and is credited as Christine Kerr.

For the record, the song is factually incorrect, as it refers to Martin Luther King, Jr.'s shooting death as having occurred on "Early morning, April 4." King was actually murdered just after 6 PM on that horrific day in 1968.

An opportunity for U2 to release its string-laden second single, showcase the live audio track to its music video for "A Sort of Homecoming," and unveil a pair of new songs, this double-A-sided twelve-inch U.K. single was only available stateside in import form in early 1985. But its popularity prompted the release of the EP *Wide Awake in America*, which traded out "The Unforgettable Fire" for the live version of "Bad." *Author's collection*

3. "Wire": With the unique guitar opus, "Wire," Edge served up a mesmerizing six-string delivery that Adam and Larry bolstered with their crushing rhythms. An ideal forum for Bono's observations on the growing heroin problem in Dublin, the singer had known friends who had become addicted to smack.

With lyrics about throwing one's life away, Bono—who would later admit to having an addictive personality of his own—sounded scornful of the wasted potential that personified young addicts. Atop the chugging rock track, Bono improvised much of the song, before seething, *"Here's the rope/ Now . . . swing away."*

4. "The Unforgettable Fire": Inspired by the band's 1983 visit to the Chicago Peace Museum, in which the band learned about the 67,000 people of Japan that died from the atomic bombings on Hiroshima and Nagasaki, Bono knew it was just a matter of time until he would write a song based on the experience.

The title song to *The Unforgettable Fire* took its musical origins from a soundtrack piece The Edge had been working out on the piano months prior. Although he loved the music and appreciated its beauty, the struggle to make it fit around a melody prompted him to shelve it. During writing sessions for the album at his house, he re-discovered it on a cassette and with Bono's help, it finally took shape.

Working on a Yamaha DX7 keyboard, the pair—with Bono on bass—had written a verse section. The song came together in roughly an hour. The lyrics took a lot more time, and like the other, more prominent songs on the record, was also what the singer described as "a sketch."

Reciting the lyrics, Bono said, *"Carnival, the wheels fly and colors spin face to face in a dry and waterless place,"* adding, "It builds up a picture, but it's only a sketch . . . doesn't tell you anything," according to the 1986 book *U2—In the Name of Love: A History.* Purportedly about traveling to Tokyo, elsewhere the singer called it an "emotional travelogue" with a "heartfelt sense of yearning."

Glistening with Edge's ambient guitar and strengthened by a string arrangement, courtesy of Noel Kelehan, the lush song—which became a Top Ten U.K. hit—was among U2's most accomplished at the time.

5. "Promenade": A pensive tone steers the intimate lyrics that Bono wrote for the fifth track on *The Unforgettable Fire.* A song of devotion to Ali that also expresses his sexual desires, it is reflective of the time they shared in the Martello Tower, located in Bray, a seaside resort to the south of Dublin. Bono sings of the structure's spiral staircase which leads from the living room up to the bedroom. A glass roof above the bed opens to reveal a stunning view of the night sky.

A memorable, ethereal moment on *The Unforgettable Fire,* "Promenade" is arguably representative of Bono at his most vulnerable.

6. "4th of July": Less a song than an instrumental vignette, "4th of July" was an impromptu piece of music played by Adam Clayton and The Edge that Brian Eno captured without telling either of them he was recording it. In no way an acknowledgement of Independence Day in the U.S., the piece was a moment in time from July 4, 1984.

Significant because it commemorated the birthday of Edge's daughter, Hollie, Bono's godchild—who came into the world on that day—it was an inventive and experimental link to U2's epic "Bad."

7. "Bad": As with "Wire," this sprawling and uplifting song was penned about a friend of Bono's who got hooked on heroin. The drug had become an epidemic in Dublin in the late 1970s and early 1980s because it had become so plentiful that it was cheaper than marijuana.

His acquaintance—like so many—smoked it once a month, then once a week, and then daily. Ultimately Bono's friend had injected enough heroin on his twenty-first birthday to kill him. He had become a slave to the high, forgoing everything else in his life in the pursuit of smack.

As for the music to the song, which became a staple of the band's live show for many years to come, it stemmed from a jam session at Slane Castle. Aside from Bono's unforgettable vocals, the song is bolstered by the production efforts of Eno and Lanois, who took Edge's subtle, atmospheric guitar treatment and helped the group construct what is easily the most affecting U2 song on its fourth album.

"Those arpeggiating sequences you hear in 'Bad,' they're [Eno]," Bono was quoted by McGee. "He catalyzed our songwriting, allowed us to get away from the primary colors of rock into another world where we could really describe ourselves in what was going on around us. It was monumental."

8. "Indian Summer Sky": On the last stop of the *War* Tour in June 1983, Bono wrote the bulk of the lyrics for "Indian Summer Sky" quickly in New York City. Topically, the song expressed a desire to leave the concrete jungle for the vast expanse of the country.

The chugging rock song also was a lyrical precursor to its future smash "With or Without You" with the line, *"You give yourself to this the longest day/ You give yourself you give it all away."*

9. "Elvis Presley and America": This improvisation came together when Brian Eno and Daniel Lanois hatched the idea to slow down the musical bed to "A Sort of Homecoming." After they played it for Bono—who didn't recognize the music—they encouraged him to sing over it.

But Bono, who had success improvising in the studio on "Like a Song" from *War*, was used to Steve Lillywhite's approach, where he would string his best improvisations from a number of takes into one final song. Eno, had a different idea. He instead took the raw performance and went with it, telling the singer and the rest of the band it was finished.

Upon its release, critics who usually supported U2, called the stream of consciousness approach to it incomplete. Responding to those allegations, Bono later defended it to *Record* magazine in 1985, saying "I think that it does evoke that decline, the stupor, the [Elvis] period when—if you've seen the clips of him—he forgets his words and fumbles."

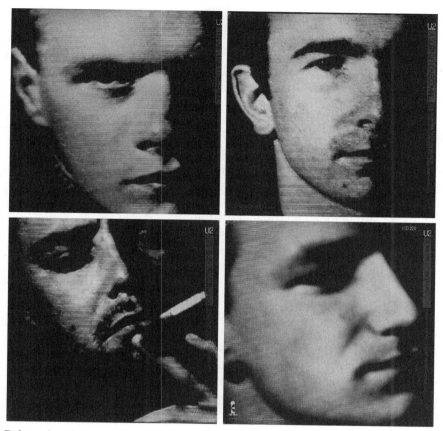

Released to the ever-growing number of U2 collectors, this 1985 double seven-inch U.K. single came in a gatefold sleeve with Larry on the cover, Adam and Edge on the inside sleeves, and Bono on the back of the package. The A-side, "The Unforgettable Fire," peaked at U.K. #6.   *U2Wanderer.org*

10. "MLK": Written as an elegy to Martin Luther King, Jr. this song—along with "Pride (In the Name of Love)"—earned Bono the highest honor from the King Center, an organization founded by Coretta Scott King. Pensive and ambient, it was a lullaby of sorts that worked to keep the civil rights activist's memory alive.

The U2 singer later admitted that he was upset when he learned that the city of Memphis had plans to tear down the Lorraine Motel outside of which King was murdered. At the time, Bono was bothered that the city had yet to produce a monument for King, while Graceland—the former home of Elvis Presley—thrived as a tourist attraction. The building—perhaps in part because of Bono's complaints—was kept standing and in 1991 became home to the National Civil Rights Museum.

Adam on Eno

On the verge of finally completing *The Unforgettable Fire* after five months of concentrated work, Adam Clayton spoke on July 29 about how Brian Eno reacted to being solicited by a rock band like U2.

Talking with Neil Storey for the Autumn 1984 edition of *U2 Magazine*, Adam said, "I don't think he was surprised by us. I think some of the other people who approach him are the ones that surprise him—like Whitesnake, or whatever. He said he gets two or three requests a week, and most of them are fairly normal, but he said the odd time when he gets metal bands approaching him, he finds that very odd. Mind you, it's probably the next thing he'd do, knowing the way he thinks."

"Pride"

Released in September 1984, three weeks in advance of *The Unforgettable Fire*, U2's rock anthem "Pride" reached #3 in the U.K. and offered the band its very first U.S. Top Forty hit, making it to #33. A chart topper in New Zealand, a country that was loyal to Bono and the boys from the outset when "I Will Follow" peaked at #1, the song was the band's biggest international breakthrough to date, climbing to #2 on *Billboard*'s album oriented rock airplay chart.

"Pride" went into heavy rotation on MTV and was produced in three versions. The first two are identical performance clips lensed by director Donald Cammell in a Dublin school auditorium, except that one is black and white and the other is color. A third clip contains footage of the band working on the album at Slane Castle, and intersperses studio performance footage with shots of the band interacting with Brian Eno and Daniel Lanois. Another video that was attempted by Anton Corbijn that features close ups of the bands faces, was deemed unsuitable for release.

Rolling Stone writer Kurt Loder had a mixed take on the song, writing "'Pride' gets over only on the strength of its resounding beat and big, droning bass line, not on the nobility of its lyrics, which are unremarkable," in his review of the album. But most reviews were positive, and the *Village Voice*'s 1984 "Pazz & Jop" poll of some 240 music journalists ranked the song as the twelfth best of the year.

Mixed Reaction

On October 1, 1984, U2 released *The Unforgettable Fire* globally. And if the record received a variety of critical reactions, its fourth album still managed to have an impressive commercial reach.

At first, journalists and loyal fans seemed surprised by the group's often subdued and ambient take on rock. But U2's intentional departure from its then-patented sound had enough immediate moments to land it at #1 on the U.K. album survey. In the United States, the build was less instantaneous, but *The Unforgettable Fire* eventually reached #12 on the *Billboard* album survey.

Rolling Stone called the album "formless and uninhabited," citing "occasional interludes of soggy, songless self-indulgence." Meanwhile *Hot Press* rated it a 12 out of 12 and called it "the beginning of the new chapter of U2." As for the *NME*, it fell somewhere in between by describing *The Unforgettable Fire* as "music worth spending some months getting to know."

But the band's desire to take a radical artistic step forward guaranteed it would have a future. Opening itself up to new influences, taking new approaches to creativity, and exploring new methods, U2 had reinvented itself. It wouldn't be the last time.

Five Facts About *The Unforgettable Fire*

1. Many of Edge's guitar parts recorded at Slane Castle were recorded with his amplifier outside on a balcony with a plastic sheet over it to keep it from rain damage.
2. Describing U2's fourth album to journalist David Breskin, Bono said, "*The Unforgettable Fire* was a beautifully out-of-focus record, blurred like an impressionist painting, very unlike a billboard or an advertising slogan."
3. The Edge's guitar parts for "Pride (In the Name of Love)" vary throughout the song. Each verse, chorus, and melody has its own, slightly distinct guitar line.
4. "MLK" was director Richard Kelly's original choice for the soundtrack to the final sequence of *Donnie Darko*. When he was unsuccessful in licensing the song, Gary Jules's take on the Tears for Fears song "Mad World" was selected.
5. Brian Eno actually left the studio sessions before U2 had finished the album *The Unforgettable Fire*. Daniel Lanois stayed behind to tie the project together and oversee completion of the final mixes.

MCP, CAMOUFLAGE CONCERTS & REGULAR MUSIC presents

U2

THE WATERBOYS

November 2nd & 3rd London Academy Theatre, Brixton.
November 5th Edinburgh Playhouse.
November 6th Barrowlands.
November 10th Manchester Apollo.
November 12th Birmingham N.E.C.
November 14th & 15th London Wembley Arena.

The Unforgettable Fire

In celebration of U2's sold-out U.K. tour in support of *The Unforgettable Fire*, with opening act the Waterboys, manager Paul McGuinness placed this ad in the November 3, 1984, issue of *Sounds*.   *Author's collection*

B.A.D. on "Bad"

In October 1984, Big Audio Dynamite—the new project of ousted Clash guitarist Mick Jones—was chosen as U2's support act for its European tour. Watching the band soundcheck in Mantes, France, Jones and his bandmates couldn't help but wonder why the fuck U2 kept playing the same song over and over.

The reality was that the band was still struggling to figure out how to present "Bad" to its audiences. The adjustment to working with programmed musical parts and a bassist and singer who were prone to improvise, was not an easy task.

Tony Visconti

Following U2's Eno effort, the band tapped another proven David Bowie producer, Tony Visconti, to rework a pair of tracks from *The Unforgettable Fire* on the road. Bono called Visconti and asked him to work with the group, explaining that hopes for Eno and Lanois to edit "A Sort of Homecoming" for release as a single had been unsuccessful.

After meeting with Visconti at a London rehearsal studio in late 1984 and talking it over with the producer, U2 elected to record a live version of the song, dropping it into a lower key so that Bono could sing it nightly.

Joining the band on tour for shows in Manchester and Birmingham, they recorded on a mobile studio with engineer Kevin Killen in tow. Days later, during a pair of shows at Wembley Arena, the group managed to record the new version—which was also heard on a forthcoming music video of the song. It and another track, a reworked version of "Bad," surfaced in the spring of 1985 on the EP *Wide Awake in America*.

As for his help in reshaping the song, Visconti revealed via his website, "We rehearsed it for a day or so before the tour began and the band loved it and played it night after night in its new form. However, we were not able to get a suitable version on tape due to over-excitement on the gigs—it was always played too fast or some serious mistakes were made. So we recorded it on the stage of Wembley arena, at an afternoon sound check, then we took the tape back to my Good Earth Studio in Soho, London and overdubbed some more guitars and vocals. We also took the applause from that night and dubbed that onto the track.

"It was wonderful to work with this amazing band and I think the world of Edge," added Visconti, who recorded the band for a live album that never came to light. "Unfortunately, I never got to work with them again."

Newsweek

The final issue of *Newsweek* for 1984 found writer Jim Miller giving U2 some weighty praise.

He wrote in the December 31 issue: "From the outset, the group's atmospheric style—one of the few truly original styles to appear in the '80s—represented an odd but effective fusion of two rival rock archetypes: the didactic grandeur of the Who playing *Tommy* and the sleekly modernist David Bowie of *Heroes*."

The band was rumored to be secretly thrilled to be compared to the watermark achievements of two of its biggest influences.

Going Platinum

Two weeks in advance of an extensive North American tour, the Recording Industry Association of America awarded U2 a platinum album for one million in U.S. sales of *The Unforgettable Fire* on February 7, 1985. On the twenty-fifth, the day of the tour's launch in Dallas with opening act the Red

Rockers—who were supporting their album *Schizophrenic Circus*—U2 received the same distinction for sales of *War.*

Rolling Stone: Our Choice

On March 14, 1985, a *Rolling Stone* magazine cover story on U2 was released. In an article written by Christopher Connelly after he visited the band in Germany and Dublin in late 1984, the magazine subtitled the feature: "Our Choice: Band of the '80s."

In addition to traveling with the band on its tour bus, Connelly returned to Dublin with the group, where he was given a car tour of the city and its outlying area by Bono. During the interview, the singer told Connelly that he'd just finished writing a song called "I Don't Live in Irishtown" which was "about a man who isn't Protestant or Catholic, English or Irish." The song was never released.

Of the honor, which gave U2 its biggest publicity yet in the States, Bono marveled in *U2 by U2* about the journalistic ethics of the magazine, which actually took the time to fact-check and spell-check. U2 wasn't used to reporters that would check its quotes. "In fact," as Bono explained, "we were used to people making them up."

Extra Tracks

A second proper single and video for "The Unforgettable Fire" was released in Europe and Japan on April 22. The song peaked at #6 in the U.K. and topped the Irish singles survey but never saw a proper release in the United States. The twelve-inch version of the single boasted unreleased tracks, including the Tony Visconti–produced "A Sort of Homecoming (Live)" and two new vocal tracks, "The Three Sunrises" and "Love Comes Tumbling." These songs surfaced the following month, on a four-song, U.S.-only EP.

Wide Awake in America

In May 1985, U2 released the four-track *Wide Awake in America* EP. A deceiving title, it included two live songs, "A Sort of Homecoming" and "Bad"—both of which were actually recorded on tour in England in December 1984. The two non-album B-sides that rounded out "The Unforgettable Fire" single are repeated here. The first, "The Three Sunrises," was produced by Brian Eno and Daniel Lanois, while "Love Comes Tumbling" was produced by U2 themselves.

Although the title wasn't actually released in the U.K., the EP was quite popular as an import and made it all the way to number 11 on the album survey there. It was eventually released to European record buyers on October 19, 1987.

As for the U.S. reception, the EP reached #37 on the strength of "Bad," which in its new form—and at eight-plus minutes in length—made it a favorite of AOR DJs looking to play a cool tune while having a cigarette or using the restroom. After "Bad" was performed during Live Aid later in 1985, sales of *WAIA* spiked.

As for the EP itself, reviews were largely positive. Having made them cover stars two months earlier, *Rolling Stone* did some backtracking on Kurt Loder's original review of "Bad," which he called unfocused in his survey of *The Unforgettable Fire*. The publication now dubbed the song, which was only slightly different in its revised version, "a showstopper."

Best Band

U2 won Best Band and Best Live Aid Performance honors in *Rolling Stone*'s 1985 Reader's poll when results surfaced in the February 27, 1986 issue. U2 dominated the voting in the 1985 Music Awards issue of *Rolling Stone*. Fans also named Edge as Best Guitarist, Adam as Best Bassist, Larry as Best Drummer and Bono as Best Male Vocalist.

A Canadian promotional item released in 1986 and unique to that market, *U2 Cassette Sampler* featured music from all of the band's releases up to and including *Wide Awake in America.*

U2Wanderer.org

22

I Don't Believe in Painted Roses

The Joshua Tree

Back to Work

U2 resumed work on new material on Monday November 11, 1985, at Larry's newly bought home in Howth. In the months the band had been apart, Edge and Aislinn had parented another daughter, Arran, who was born October 15. Meanwhile, Bono had also found time to produce three songs for Cactus World News, who were just releasing their single, "The Bridge," on Mother Records.

Setting up in Mullen's living room, the band was happy to be back together. With eyes on a new studio album for the fall of 1986, and plenty of creative freedom, the foursome allowed for ample time to write and perfect the follow up to *The Joshua Tree.*

Starting with soundcheck tapes, U2 intended to spend six months on the creative process before bringing the production team of Brian Eno and Daniel Lanois back into the fold. Rough versions of "With or Without You," "Red Hill Mining Town," and "Trip Through Your Wires" stemmed from these efforts.

Danesmoate

By January 1986, U2 had moved from Larry's home by the sea to Danesmoate, a large neglected manor house in Rathfarnham some six miles outside of Dublin. Here, the band set a four-day work schedule, beginning at noon and working until 8 PM, and hoped to be inspired by the building's architecture and atmosphere.

Edge had come across the estate that fall while he and Aislinn had been house-hunting for their growing family. Although it wasn't a fit for his family, he suggested that the band rent the old Georgian home in the foothills of the Wicklow Mountains.

Here, they set up a studio with an enigmatic engineer and producer named Mark Ellis, who had worked on records by New Order, Soft Cell, and Nick Cave and the Bad Seeds. Also known as Flood, he became an integral part of the U2 studio team.

As for the house, bassist Adam Clayton eventually wound up purchasing it. It was located just a half a mile from Columba's College, where Adam had spent a large part of his youth until he was asked to leave in 1975.

By late spring, the band—which had already left Danesmoate behind for STS Studios where it continued to demo new material—took a break from the project to embark on the "Conspiracy of Hope" Tour.

Greg Carroll Dies

On July 3, 1986, Bono landed in Texas from Dublin after a thirteen-hour flight to perform at Farm Aid II. But an hour after he arrived in his hotel room, he got a call informing him that his beloved friend and personal assistant Greg Carroll died in a motorcycle accident. Devastated—as was the entire U2 organization—the singer returned to the airport and caught the next plane home.

Carroll—who Bono had considered one of his best friends—had been on Bono's Harley Davidson and was relocating it for the singer in the rain when a car pulled out in front of him and killed him instantly.

Out of respect, Bono, Ali Hewson, Larry Mullen, and others from the U2 camp flew to Wanganui, New Zealand, on July 9 for the three-day funeral of Carroll. During the main ceremony the following day, Bono read a poem and delivered a short eulogy. Later, during a dinner reception, he sang the Beatles' "Let It Be" and Bob Dylan's "Knockin' on Heaven's Door." In homage to Carroll, Bono eventually penned the song "One Tree Hill," about the volcanic hills that overlook the city where they first met.

Central America

Following the Hewsons trip to New Zealand, where they paid respects to Greg Carroll and his family, Bono and his wife Ali flew directly to Managua, Nicaragua as part of a planned excursion to meet with Central American Mission Partners, an organization that promotes human rights and economic

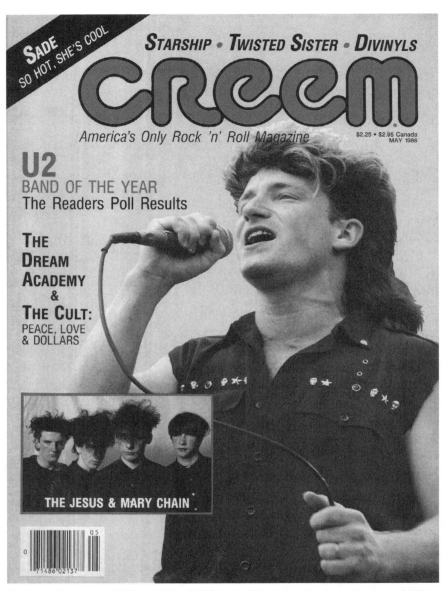

Bono on the cover of *Creem*'s May 1986 issue. The magazine's readers voted U2 as their choice for Band of the Year. *Author's collection*

development in Latin America. The trip would heavily inform the material on U2's next album, *The Joshua Tree*.

Along with CAMP members, the couple spent a week in Nicaragua where they met with Ernesto Cardenal, a Roman Catholic priest who doubled as the Minister of Culture in the Sandinista regime. During their journey, the Hewsons visited the run down palace of former president Anastasio Somoza, and later listened as President Daniel Ortega gave a speech on the country's Revolution Day on July 19.

On one of his final days in Nicaragua, Bono went to a church mass where he witnessed attendees stand up to yell out the names of loved ones that were killed fighting the Contras. This experience had a lasting effect on the singer.

On to El Salvador, where the Hewsons continued to travel with the three members of CAMP, they visited the U.S. Embassy where Bono encountered a group known as COMADRES. An acronym translated as "the Mothers of the Disappeared," it's an outspoken collective of women whose children have vanished or been killed by representatives of the El Salvadorian government.

One day, Bono, Ali, and CAMP's Harold Hoyle set out to deliver aid to farmers at a cooperative that Bono had been supporting financially. As they walked in a remote area of the country, ninety minutes north of San Salvador, government-backed troops shot bullets toward them.

Although the gunmen missed on purpose, Bono and Ali were given the scare of their lives. As they stood still on the road, the troops began laughing at them, sending a frightening message to the singer and his wife that they didn't care for their intrusion and they could kill them if they felt compelled.

Return to Windmill Lane

In August 1986, U2 embarked on four months of proper studio work at Windmill Lane with producers Brian Eno and Daniel Lanois. In advance of these sessions, the band had cultivated the roaring hard-rock tune "Bullet the Blue Sky" and continued to explore the potential of "With or Without You" at STS Studios in Dublin with producer Paul Barnett.

With additional time needed to hone the material, the targeted month of release was bumped from November 1986 to March 1987. If the Amnesty International Tour seemed like a disruption to the creativity of the band, suspending work on the album actually worked to the project's advantage. U2 went on to cite the tour for lending lyrical focus and musical power to what would become *The Joshua Tree*.

Drawing musically from influences like Patti Smith and Bob Dylan and elements of the American blues that Bono pursued after his experiences with the Rolling Stones in late 1985—as evidenced on the track "Running to Stand Still"—the album to be was lyrically informed by the singer's travels to Ethiopia and Central America, plus the sudden loss of Greg Carroll.

Tabloid Tales

Although U2 was hard at work on its fifth studio album in September 1986, the U.K. newspaper the *Daily Mirror* suggested otherwise when it reported that Larry Mullen was Stateside in a Manhattan hospital to have hand surgery. When a Dublin disc jockey announced the story on RTE's Radio 2, more reputable papers like the *Irish Independent* and *Evening Herald* picked up on the tabloid's report without confirming the validity of the story with U2's management.

Finally, *Hot Press* had the wherewithal to make an inquiry of Principle Management, who ultimately tracked down Mullen. Still in London and indeed hard at work in the studio, Larry gave the publication reassuring news. "I'm having very few problems with my hand," explained Mullen.

Up Against the Clock

Well into the fall of 1986, U2 continued developing *The Joshua Tree*. Despite the abundance of creative energy, Brian Eno reminded the band that the album could experience further delays if an end point for the project was not determined soon.

By late November, U2 had completed recording its fifth album. The following month, the band brought in Steve Lillywhite to remix a few of the songs. By early 1987, the band had also tracked a series of non-album numbers—including "Walk to the Water," "Luminous Times," and "Spanish Eyes"—that would surface as B-sides.

Another song from this period, called "Birdland," was considered a keeper, and the band decided to hold it for possible use as a future album track. It would remain unreleased for twenty years, eventually surfacing on the 2007 expanded reissue of *The Joshua Tree*.

Mrs. Lillywhite

Kirsty MacColl, the late singer behind songs like "They Don't Know," a pop-charting cover of Billy Bragg's "A New England" and the female vocal on the Pogues' legendary "A Fairytale of New York," joined her husband Steve Lillywhite in Dublin as he mixed tracks for *The Joshua Tree* in late 1986.

Desperate for something to do, she decided to see if she could help U2 with a track sequence for the project. Because she was a passive U2 fan at best, her insight turned out to be downright valuable.

The only instruction U2's members gave Kirsty was to put the song "Where the Streets Have No Name" first and "Mothers of the Disappeared" last. Although her selections were based on her own personal preferences and put together pretty hastily, when the group listened back to the running order she had picked, it worked.

Sadly, MacColl—who divorced Lillywhite in the early 1990s and was the daughter of folksinger Ewan MacColl—died on December 18, 2000. Only forty-one, she was killed when a powerboat had erroneously entered a diving area where boats were prohibited while she was vacationing in Cozumel, Mexico. At the time she was struck, she had been pushing one of her sons out of the way of the speeding boat's path.

The Songs of *The Joshua Tree*

The Joshua Tree in its finished version was heavily informed, as Bono put it, by "America—the continent as opposed to the country." And as much as the singer loved and admired parts of the Western World, there were parts of it that he needed to come to grips with on a political level. The album projects U2's feelings as Irishmen on the outside looking in.

The group sought to balance the darkness it had experienced in the aftermath of *The Unforgettable Fire* and its triumphant reception at Live Aid. In the U2 camp, 1986 was marred by loss and general frustration with the inhumanities of the world, some of which Bono experienced firsthand.

If 1986 was a year of growth, pain, loss, and deep association with human frailty, Bono's headspace helped him to write some of his strongest lyrics yet. Not surprisingly, the album was dedicated to twenty-six-year-old Greg Carroll, who had died the previous July.

As for influences during the album's creation, the band's exposure to and support of likeminded acts like the Waterboys and Hothouse Flowers along with the encouragement of Bob Dylan, Van Morrison, and Keith Richards to explore its Irish roots, began to subtly infiltrate U2's work.

1. "Where the Streets Have No Name": The lead-off song on *The Joshua Tree* came late in the germination of the record when The Edge became concerned that the album was short of a high energy rock song. With Bono away on a lyric writing excursion with Ali, the guitarist set about penning one while working alone in an upstairs bedroom at his still-empty, newly acquired home, Melbeach.

The guitarist was so elated over both the guitar part and the song he had written on his own, working with a keyboard, a drum machine, a bass and some sequencers, he later admitted to punching the air with glee. Unfortunately he had no one to share in his delight, so he packed up and headed home.

Putting such exuberance to the side, U2 discovered that transferring the song from its demo form to the version heard on the album was not an easy task, because of the song's frequent chord changes and timing shifts. According to reports, Brian Eno became so exasperated that he conspired to erase the song with the hopes he might prompt the band to start recording it all over again. The final rendition was crafted by weaving a few different takes together.

With lyrics written about Bono's desire to break out of a city after feelings of claustrophobia, he told *Propaganda* in May 1987 he had "a feeling of wanting to go somewhere where the values of the city and the values of our society don't hold you down."

Elsewhere in that interview, the frontman said that the lyrics were "based on the notion that it is possible to identify a person's religion and income based on the street on which they lived, particularly in Belfast."

Edge's intention when he started writing the tune was to create an ideal new guitar rock song for U2's shows. He definitely succeeded. The end result would become the thinking person's rock anthem of 1987; one that only got better in a concert setting.

2. "I Still Haven't Found What I'm Looking For": Originating with the titles "The Weather Girls" and "Under the Weather," the second song on U2's fifth album began with a different melody than what was presented in its final form. The rhythm-steeped number had a theme of spiritual doubt Bono had developed around the final title, which Edge thought up and wrote on a piece of paper while Bono was trying out different vocal parts for the tune.

The song—which Edge once equated to Survivor's "Eye of the Tiger" if it were performed by a reggae outfit—stemmed from a jam session at Danesmoate that was furthered along by Bono's soulful, gospel-inspired vocal line. Having recently been turned on to a tape of gospel and blues music that *Hot Press* writer Dermot Stokes had made for him, U2's singer wrote the anthem with said styles in mind.

As with many of the songs on its predecessor, *The Unforgettable Fire*, Bono started his lyrics as a sketch, writing them on the microphone. Musically, it stemmed from a simple groove and a strong drum part, and upon completion it marked an exhilarating new direction for the band that wound up becoming one of its biggest hits.

3. "With or Without You": At first structured around a chord sequence that Bono thought up, the song's traditional feel ultimately gave way to unique guitar lines and an inventive presentation. Having decided that the loose

Released in 1987 by Polystar to help promote *The Joshua Tree*, this compilation includes songs from each of the group's previous releases.   *U2Wanderer.org*

approach to U2's fourth album had created its share of dilemmas for the band, the quartet placed restrictions on itself for album number five.

"We thought: let's actually write songs," The Edge explained to *Musician* in May 1987. "We wanted the record to be less vague, open-ended, atmospheric, and impressionistic." The goal was to be more direct, more intentional. Of all the songs that it came up with in 1986, "With or Without You"—with its fat-bottomed bass, weeping guitar lines and Bono's emotive, memorable vocal—was the most immediate.

At one point early on, The Edge deemed the song—which was fleshed out with Clayton's bass playing and a Yamaha drum machine—"awful" until Eno and Lanois encouraged them to "fuck it up" by adding a more ambient guitar part.

Coincidentally, Edge had been experimenting with a prototype of the Infinite guitar that developer Michael Brook had sent him. Although it was a challenge to work with, and its homemade technology could electrocute the user if he wasn't careful, Edge loved the fact that it gave him unbounded sustain, similar to that of a violin.

When Gavin Friday, who had been in the control room with his old friend Bono, overheard Edge playing the Infinite through an open door, he insisted the singer reconsider keeping the song, which was close to being pushed to the side over frustrations about its structure.

It was Gavin who not only salvaged the song, but organized it, helped arrange it and finally pushed for it to be a big hit. Coupled with Eno's sequencing talents—which helped create its keyboard arpeggio, Friday spotted the song's greatness.

Taking it a step further, Gavin believed it was destined to be a chart-topper and he fought vehemently with Paul McGuinness about releasing it as a single. After convincing Bono and the band to go along with the idea, it became the biggest song of U2's career. Fittingly, the band's manager wound up apologizing to Bono's dear friend for his lack of faith in the tune.

From a topical standpoint, Bono's lyrics explored the difficult balance between the temptations of being a rock star on the road and his need to be devoted to his wife. A multifaceted love song, "With or Without You" also spoke of Bono's dedication to and reliance on his bandmates for support and encouragement.

4. "Bullet the Blue Sky": Upon Bono's return from Central America in August 1986, he shared his experiences with his bandmates and told Edge to "put El Salvador through your amplifier." At the height of Ronald Reagan's America, "Bullet the Blue Sky" was Bono's will, as he put it in the May 7, 1987, issue of *Rolling Stone*, to "dismantle the mythology of America."

Deeply bothered by the United States' military intervention in El Salvador's civil war of the mid-1980s, and heartbroken by the poverty he witnessed in Nicaragua, where food and supplies were absent, the song was Bono's angry reaction to it all. Bolstered by Edge's blistering, Hendrix-inspired response and the explosive rhythms of Adam and Larry, "Bullet the Blue Sky" was a message of disgust aimed at "shameful" American policy makers who had helped finance the bullying of peasant farmers by Nicaraguan government soldiers.

Although Bono still loved the United States, he no longer had the "utter stars" in his eyes that he once did. By the second half of the 1980s, he could see it as a "broken country." In U2's estimation, America was a representation of all that was right and all that was wrong with the world. Those contradictions were what inspired "Bullet the Blue Sky."

5. "Running to Stand Still": While waiting to play piano on another song during the sessions for *The Joshua Tree*, The Edge began playing the chords that would become "Running to Stand Still." With the assistance of

Daniel Lanois on guitar, the haunting, blues-inflected ballad came almost effortlessly.

Bono's lyrics to the song were built on the chronic heroin problem he first touched on with "Bad." The ongoing smack epidemic in the seven towers of Ballymun built near to where he grew up on Cedarwood Road was still very much on his mind.

He had also been taken aback by the drug-related death of Thin Lizzy's Phil Lynott in January 1986. Sure, the band had heard the rumors of Lynott's smack-fueled demise, but they dismissed them instead, thinking of the Irish rock legend tearing through classics like "Whiskey in the Jar" and "The Boys Are Back in Town," as he had at Slane in 1981.

With his brother to thank for the song's title, Bono had never heard the phrase "It's like running to stand still" until he asked his older sibling Norman about the status of his failing business. Bono felt the phrase-turned-title summed up perfectly the toll heroin addiction can take on the human body. A monologue from the 1984 Wim Wenders movie *Paris, Texas* also supposedly helped to inspire the song.

6. "Red Hill Mining Town": Considered by Larry Mullen to be one of the band's lost songs, Bono wrote it about the National Union of Miners fighting the pit closures in England during Margaret Thatcher's regime, but the band's uncertainty about the song and its message was what Mullen said kept it from being truly great.

In addition to the actual strike itself, the heartfelt tune was designed to take a look at the emotional ramifications of the fight, which caused families to buckle. Although Bono felt enraged by the strike itself, he felt far more qualified to comment on the relationship aspect of it than the stresses of working in a mine.

7. "In God's Country": *"We need new dreams tonight,"* Bono sang on one of *The Joshua Tree*'s most direct numbers, a tune he eventually dedicated to the Statue of Liberty. Written about the American Dream, he had wondered who might rise up to the challenge and shoot holes in the political system of the time.

Bono had grown increasingly sickened by both Republicans and Democrats, right-wingers and liberals and the political system in America. As he sung of sad eyes and crooked crosses, he was hopeful that U2 might continue to help give its fans a turnaround in the way they thought about things. Perhaps through the band, new visionaries with new ideologies would surface and thrive.

8. "Trip Through Your Wires": Beginning with Bono's swampy harmonica playing and Edge's blues-inflected guitar approach, "Trip Through Your Wires" was a loose, enigmatic piece of the *Joshua Tree* puzzle that first saw its public unveiling on RTE in January 1986.

If it seemed sloppy against the more perfect moments of the album, it was in fact exactly what U2 needed to keep the disc diverse and cohesive. Bono's communicative harmonica playing and its spontaneous feel were ideal augmentations to the song's nasty groove.

Describing the song's impetus years later, the singer said cryptically in U2's 2006 book, *U2 by U2*, "It was inspired by a series of phone conversations I had with somebody who might have meant well and who was fascinating in their own right, it's just they were pretending to be somebody else."

9. "One Tree Hill": Penned about Greg Carroll, for whom *The Joshua Tree* is dedicated, "One Tree Hill" was and still is one of the most heartfelt songs in U2's canon. In the months following the album, Bono said he had cut himself off from it completely, but by September 1987 the band began playing it onstage as a way of keeping Carroll's memory alive.

It also served as a reminder to U2 that its family, friends, and the band itself were more important than playing rock and roll. The possibility that today could be your last day with someone you love was driven home every time they decided to play the song.

After sixteen years out of the band's set, U2 resuscitated the song in November 2006 in memory of Carroll. Twenty years after the death of its friend and employee, the group performed "One Tree Hill" in Auckland during a pair of gigs there as part of the *Vertigo* Tour. It remains among the most poignant tunes in the group's canon.

10. "Exit": The intent of "Exit" was to convey the state of mind of someone driven to commit murder. Unlike most of the songs U2 had written up to this point, "Exit" lacked any optimism. After reading Norman Mailer's *The Executioner's Song*, which had been written about serial killer Gary Gilmore, Bono was said to have been given the creative push to head into such dark territory.

Answering for the song to *Musician* in 1987, Bono explained, "To be an optimist you mustn't be blind or deaf to the world around you." As bleak and evil as it might have felt, it was an exhilarating musical creation.

11. "Mothers of the Disappeared": Inspired by his trip with Ali to Central America, the album's commanding and evocative closer dealt with his experience with the COMADRES. Written on his mother-in-law's Spanish guitar in tribute to the women who lost their children and had only pictures of their sons and daughters, the "Disappeared" were in most cases students who opposed the military regimes and suffered for their beliefs.

For their divergent viewpoints these young adults were met with torture and murder at the hands of police and military personnel. Not only was this an ongoing practice in El Salvador at the time, but Bono had learned of similar horrors in Chile and Argentina. Perhaps even more disturbing, the governments of these countries had each received similar financial backing from the United States of America.

Most jarring for Bono was the one specific incident where he had been on a motorway in El Salvador when he saw a body on the road that had evidently been thrown out of a car. It was an image that would stay with him forever. Those who opposed the status quo would be terrorized and killed without mercy.

Minimalist Playing

By the time of *The Joshua Tree*, Edge had long since discovered how powerful guitar notes could be. In his mind they were expensive, and not to be carelessly tossed about. When it came to the guitar for The Edge, less was indeed more.

"With or Without You," the band's enduring hit was a perfect example. At the end of the song his instinct told him to go with something simple, something restrained. His collaborators balked but he ultimately won out.

Sure it could have had a much bigger climax, but the outcome of the song under Edge's vision couldn't be any more perfect. Because it was restrained, the song—in the guitarist's opinion—was more potent than it would have otherwise been.

You Give Yourself Away

On March 4, 1987, "With or Without You" was released for airplay as part of an Island Records campaign designed to saturate the marketplace and spread the word about *The Joshua Tree*'s imminent arrival. An instant global favorite, the song entered the U.S. *Billboard* charts at #64 and began its ascent to #1, which it reached in early May.

The song's video—which was shot in Dublin in February 1987—was an immediate smash on MTV. Starring a dancer who would be the future Mrs. Edge, Morleigh Steinberg, the clip was directed by Meiert Avis and Matt Mahurin and unveiled a new image for Bono, who went sleeveless under a leather vest and had his long hair slicked back. Meanwhile, a bespectacled

THE MUSIC THAT INSPIRED
✳ THE JOSHUA TREE ✳

IN GOD'S COUNTRY

Featuring: Elvis Presley ❧ Hank Williams ❧ Woody Guthrie
John Lee Hooker ❧ BB King ❧ Billie Holiday ❧ Blind Willie McTell
Patsy Cline ❧ The Staple Singers ❧ Ramblin' Jack Elliott
Johnnie Allan ❧ Bill Monroe ❧ Mose Allison and more...

To accompany *Uncut*'s 2003 cover story on U2's seminal 1987 album, the U.K. rock magazine released a compilation of signature tracks by the American artists that Bono had previously acknowledged as having an influence the project. Not only would the music of Elvis Presley, Woody Guthrie, John Lee Hooker, B. B. King, and Billie Holliday inform *The Joshua Tree*, but it also heavily inspired *Rattle and Hum*.

U2Wanderer.org

Adam's hair was cropped and its natural color restored, The Edge wore a brimmed hat to cover up his receding hairline, and Larry looked the same as ever with his trademarked spiked blond hair, white T-shirt, and jeans.

Fans who bought the "With or Without You" single were treated to a pair of top-notch non-album B-sides that had disciples wondering how songs this strong could have been left off of the new album. At the time Bono called the B-sides of the single extraordinary, opining that although they didn't fit within the confines of *The Joshua Tree*, "Walk to the Water" and "Luminous Times" were among the best songs in U2's catalog.

I Want to Reach Out

March 9, 1987, marked the official release of U2's artistic and commercial triumph, *The Joshua Tree*. The band's fifth studio offering was an instant smash that quickly topped charts around the world and made the group superstars.

A thematic record with poignant lyrics and some of the best songwriting of U2's career, it became the fastest-selling album in British music history, selling a staggering 300,000 copies in its first week. In the United States, the album debuted at #7 and jumped to the pole position by the week of April 14.

Touted by Island executives to the media as "the most complete merchandising effort ever assembled," the album was heavily marketed by the record label, which spent a whopping $100,000 on in-store displays. Shipped on vinyl, cassette, and CD simultaneously—a rarity in 1987—the album earned a double-platinum certification from the RIAA on May 13 and went on to sell more than ten million copies in the U.S. alone, earning a diamond certification on September 11, 1995.

If the commercial reception was tremendous, reviews were unanimously positive. *Los Angeles Times* critic Robert Hilburn perhaps said it best, writing, "*The Joshua Tree* finally confirms on record what this band has been slowly asserting for three years now onstage: U2 is what the Rolling Stones ceased being years ago—the greatest rock and roll band in the world. In this album, the band wears that mantle securely."

Meanwhile, Bill Graham wrote in *Hot Press*, "*The Joshua Tree* rescues rock from its decay, bravely and unashamedly basing itself in the mainstream before very cleverly lifting off into several higher dimensions." And the *NME* proclaimed it "a better and braver record than anything else that's likely to appear in 1987."

Time

On April 27, 1987, U2 graced the cover of *Time* next to the title, "Rock's Hottest Ticket." But in the lengthy feature that followed, longtime fans and people who were still unfamiliar with the group learned that the band from Dublin—then already in their eleventh year—were unlike the Bon Jovis and Depeche Modes that otherwise occupied the rock scene.

U2 was not about "partying down," the piece explained. Bono spoke of ducking mortar fire in the hills outside of San Salvador during his expedition to El Salvador the summer before. The article covered the band's conscience in its efforts with Amnesty International and it explored U2's deeply personal spiritual searches.

As for Adam Clayton—who blamed past journalists for taking the "easy angle" in discussing U2's beliefs—the bassist finally admitted to having a spiritual link to his bandmates. "We all believe in much the same things but don't express ourselves in the same way," he explained. "The spirituality contained within the band is equal to all the members."

But the magazine was quick to point out that U2 was, at its very heart, a rock and roll band. Or as Bono said, "I would hate to think everybody was into U2 for 'deep' and 'meaningful' reasons."

A Tin of Beans

Bono was secretly thrilled that "With or Without You" had such lasting power on Top Forty radio. In the 1970s he remembered how for every twenty or forty songs there might be one that he would like and by October 1987 he told David Breskin he believed U2 provided that same alternative to the competition, which he called "product-oriented."

In the singer's estimation, U2 filled a void with songs that were musically and topically provocative. They were the antidote to groups and record companies "who treat music like a tin of beans—a product to be sold."

"I Still Haven't Found What I'm Looking For"

In May 1987, after its remarkable chart success, "With or Without You" began its slide down the charts. But *The Joshua Tree* campaign got an immediate boost by the reception of its next single, "I Still Haven't Found What I'm Looking For." Its slow and steady climb to #1 in the United States by August followed its #6 peak in the United Kingdom the month after its release.

Backed with two more non-album winners, "Spanish Eyes" and "Deep in the Heart," the songs on the flip of U2's second single of 1987 lured fans who already owned the album back into the record shops for the stellar bonus material.

Another New Deal

By August 1987, U2 learned that Island Records was in serious financial trouble. Island was unable to pay the group the $5 million in royalties it had earned from sales of *The Joshua Tree*. Island's money woes stemmed from

The second of two stadium gigs in Rotterdam, this show—held on July 11, 1987—featured U2 with support from In Tua Nua, Big Audio Dynamite, and the Pretenders.

Author's collection

its expansion into the film business, which started out successfully with the release of *Kiss of the Spider Woman* and *The Trip to Bountiful*, but soon failed after a pair of duds had eaten up the group's royalties.

Quick to respond, Paul McGuinness negotiated for the label to forgo the money owed in exchange for a percentage of the company. When the deal was completed, U2 owned ten percent of Island Records.

"The Sweetest Thing"

The third single from *The Joshua Tree* emerged in August 1987, when Island dropped "Where the Streets Have No Name." As a twelve-inch single, the release counted the three additional tracks: "Silver and Gold," "The Sweetest Thing," and "Race Against Time."

The "Streets" single reached number four in the U.K. and went on to place at number 13 in the U.S. Meanwhile, with U2 fever in full effect in anticipation of its fall North American stadium gigs, modern rock radio stations like WLIR in New York, KROQ in Los Angeles, and 91X in San Diego began playing "The Sweetest Thing," a lilting pop nugget that the band eventually revised and released as a single more than a decade later.

U2 in the Americas

By early September 1987, Phil Joanou and U2 had finalized plans to move forward with a concert movie. It wasn't called *Rattle and Hum* yet; it's tentative title was *U2 in the Americas*.

Plans were to film the band in Chicago and Buenos Aires before the end of 1987; however, neither of those locales were ultimately used for the motion-picture project.

"Christmas" Comes Early

On October 12, U2's contribution to the charity album *A Very Special Christmas* was released. It was the first in a series of albums designed to raise funds for Special Olympics, an organization started in the 1960s by Eunice Kennedy Shriver.

The song, a cover of "Christmas (Baby, Please Come Home)" which was originally recorded by Darlene Love for the 1963 album, *A Christmas Gift for You From Phil Spector*, features Love on backing vocals. U2's version, which was produced by Jimmy Iovine, who produced *Under a Blood Red Sky*, was recorded at a Glasgow soundcheck earlier in the year.

23

But I Won't Wear It on My Sleeve

U2's Influences

The Beatles

Bono's exposure to music began with the Fab Four. He distinctly remembered hearing "I Want to Hold Your Hand" on the radio when he was four years old. Later, Bono recalled watching the Beatles movies *A Hard Day's Night, Help!,* and *Yellow Submarine* on television on St. Stephen's Day, the day after Christmas, one year with his brother Norman.

The Beatles had a gang-like presence, melodic fortitude, cool haircuts, and an underlying sexuality that may not have been apparent to the youngest Hewson at the time. Later, "Dear Prudence" would become one of the first songs that Bono learned on the guitar. Norman taught him to play using the Beatles' *Songbook*.

If that book opened his mind, exposure to the group's 1968 double album was life-altering. Bono—like his future U2 bandmates—was drawn to *The White Album*, citing it as his all-time favorite Beatles disc because of the combination of its songcraft and experimentalism. Also citing *Abbey Road* and *Let It Be* as touchstones, the members of U2 took its appreciation of really heavy and really soft sounds from John, Paul, George, and Ringo.

Tom Jones

In his eighth year, Bono spotted Tom Jones performing "It's Not Unusual" on a Saturday night variety show, and was transfixed. Jones was perspiring as he performed unencumbered. With a powerful black voice in a white body,

Jones was—in his prime—one of the sexiest men alive. "He's an animal," Bono has said of the Welshman.

Elvis Presley

Although he was late to the Elvis party, discovering him once the King had gone Las Vegas, Bono was a fan of a lot of his movies and cites his 1968 *Comeback Special* as "a work of God-like genius."

Bono found Presley's reckless abandon appealing. Going on to call Presley's comeback television broadcast "a pivotal moment," Bono explained his dress during the ZooTV trek was inspired by Elvis. He later contributed a solo recording of "Can't Help Falling in Love" to the soundtrack of the movie, *Honeymoon in Vegas.*

Middle of the Road

After watching this pop band perform "Chirpy Chirpy Cheep Cheep" on *Top of the Pops* in June 1971, Paul Hewson was mesmerized. A decade later, Bono told *NME*, "I must have been about eleven at the time, and I thought, "Wow! This is what pop music is all about. You just sing like that and you get paid for it."

John Lennon

When Bono first heard John Lennon's "Imagine" at twelve years old, it blew his mind. The album of the same name, released in 1971, was one of the first LPs he owned and it really stirred something inside of him. Lennon continued to show the young Paul Hewson a different way of looking at the world when he lost his mother in 1974. It was then that he rediscovered Lennon's debut solo offering, *Plastic Ono Band.*

In his room with his headphones on, it was an intimate experience for Bono, as if his hero was on the phone. "Oh My Love" was among his favorites by the former Beatle. "It's like a little hymn," Bono told U2.com. "It's certainly a prayer of some kind—even if he was an atheist."

In the 1980s, U2's frontman met Lennon's widow, Yoko Ono. She put her hand on the singer and complimented him, saying, "You are John's son." Years after, Bono would suggest, "I think if I'd gotten to know John, I would have got on really well with him."

In 2007, U2 paid tribute to one of its biggest inspirations by recording Lennon's classic "Instant Karma" for the all star compilation, *Instant Karma: The Amnesty International Campaign to Save Darfur.*

Paul McCartney

If Lennon was Bono's paramount hero, he would also explain, "Paul McCartney is somebody I'm in awe of." McCartney's penchant for hits during the years that the men of U2 came of age, not to mention his mind-blowing canon of tunes with the Beatles, plus his acquaintance and eventual live collaboration at "Live 8" was equally important.

During the 2005 concert, U2 backed Paul McCartney for a performance of "Sgt. Pepper's Lonely Hearts Club Band," with Bono singing John Lennon's part. The performance marked the first time McCartney had played the song—save for the coda version at the album of the song's parent album—live.

"We had a very easy kind of repartee between him and the band," *the Associated Press* quoted Bono telling reporters after the show on July 2. "He was probably waiting for us to have a lot of attitude, but we played students to the professor, not big rock band, which is correct pecking order."

Bob Dylan

Friends since their first meeting in the summer of 1984, U2's singer once said in *Bono in Conversation* of Bob Dylan, "No artist alive or dead has meant so much to me." Around the age of twelve, the singer started with Dylan's acoustic albums, but he was only a passive fan until their meeting prompted a period of rediscovery.

In fact, the first time U2's singer joined Dylan onstage at Slane Castle, he didn't know the words to "Blowin' in the Wind." As evidenced by their penchant to collaborate with one another live and in the studio, U2 has long since studied up on Dylan.

David Bowie

In 1972 Bono discovered a new folk duo called David Bowie/Hunky Dory. Although he felt foolish when he learned Bowie was the artist and *Hunky Dory* was the name of the album, it was one of his favorite reel to reels of this era. From the lilting haunt of "Life on Mars" to the pop of "Changes" and the riff roaring "Queen Bitch," which gave a cue to where the chameleon-like performer would go on *Ziggy Stardust and the Spiders from Mars*.

Bowie was one of the first artists Bono discovered on his own and his impact was immeasurable. Pictures of the "English Elvis," as Bono once dubbed him, hung on his bedroom walls at 10 Cedarwood Road. It was no accident that "Suffragette City" was in U2's set in the days before its own songs took precedent.

Lou Reed

When he was thirteen, Bono and his friend Guggi were obsessed with Lou Reed's *Transformer*. Having no clue that the title was about transsexuals, Guggi was eventually inspired enough to wear a frock when he was in the Virgin Prunes. With classics like "Walk on the Wild Side," the pensive "Perfect Day," and the soulful "Satellite of Love"—the last of which U2 performed live during its ZooTV trek with a prerecorded video accompaniment from Reed—this album was and still is perhaps the best of Reed's lengthy career.

Rory Gallagher

Adam Clayton's very first concert at the Carlton Cinema in Dublin in the fall of 1974 was a show by Irish blues-rock guitarist Rory Gallagher. Meanwhile, Edge was very into Taste, Gallagher's group, when U2 first came together at Mount Temple as Feedback. Gallagher—who played with everyone from Muddy Waters to Jerry Lee Lewis in the 1970s—was an inspiration to the band when it sought out the Sun Records sound in 1987.

Like most musicians who get started in their teen years, Edge first learned cover versions. "Knowing a few Rory Gallagher licks or whatever," he told Flanagan. "Then suddenly you're in this band and there's all this fantastic music coming at you that challenges everything that you believed about what the electric guitar was for."

Upon Gallagher's 1995 death at the age of forty-seven, Bono—in a statement—called him one of the top ten guitarists of all time, adding, "More importantly, he was one of the top ten good guys."

In 2006, at the unveiling of a guitar sculpture honoring Gallagher in Temple Bar, Dublin, Edge—according to the *Irish Independent*—told attendees, "Rory was an incredible influence on me as a guitar player. He laid the road on which we followed."

Horslips

Before he was christened The Edge, Dave Evans saw his first rock concert when the Irish rock outfit Horslips performed in Skerries, in North County Dublin sometime in 1975. Credited for creating Celtic Rock, the innovative band fused the power and electricity of rock and roll with traditional Irish folk.

Led Zeppelin

Although it wasn't cool to admit it in the early years of U2, Edge—who had since met Robert Plant and Jimmy Page on occasion—finally felt compelled to acknowledge the influence of Led Zeppelin in a 2007 BBC.com interview with Zane Lowe.

"At the time that punk rock happened, they were at the top of the list of bands that had to be seen off," he said. "But the dust has settled on their legacy, and listening back at this point it is clear that they've made an immense impact."

The Rolling Stones

Aside from "Satisfaction," "Brown Sugar," and "Miss You," the Rolling Stones taught U2 "swagger," according to Bono.

"Their body of work: I can only stare at in awe," he confessed to Jann Wenner in 2005. "He's a great lyricist. He described his world very well, with humor, with intelligence and, you know, the odd Polaroid."

Citing *Exile on Main Street*—which was made around the corner from Bono's estate in the south of France—the singer explained, "There's humidity on that record and a certain free-form that I relate to."

The Who

By the time he was fifteen, Bono was caught up in the power chords of "Won't Get Fooled Again," the vocal range and harmonies of Roger Daltrey and Pete Townshend on "Behind Blue Eyes" and the explosive feel of the Who taking him to the "teenage wasteland" that "Baba O'Reilly" chronicled. Simultaneously, The Edge had already discovered the band a year or two earlier thanks to the keen ears of his brother Dick.

When U2 came together, there was a mutual belief that the Who had, as Bono would say, "written the book." Sure the Beatles were important, as were the Stones, but if they had their pick, U2 wanted to be like the Who.

Edge, specifically, found himself drawn to Townshend because he wasn't just the Who's guitarist, but its songwriter. Because of his creative duality, Townshend was a cut above the doodling, solo-happy lead players that defined so much of rock music in the 1970s.

Van Morrison

Although Edge was never much of a fan, since meeting fellow Irishman Van Morrison in 1984, Bono has often contended there was a spiritual link between the two of them. While the singer suspected that Van wouldn't want to associate himself with the kind of music U2 created because of his long-standing affiliation with soul and roots music, it was something that Bono felt necessary to acknowledge.

The Beach Boys

Bono was heavily into the Beach Boys at the time the band came together. One of the very first pieces the band played live was a medley of classics Brian Wilson penned for the band.

The Beach Boys' catalog evoked a range of emotions, but most of them were positive. These were the songs of the late 1960s, when life was less complicated and his mom was still alive. Through songs like "Good Vibrations" and "California Girls," Bono would be transported to the time when his family would holiday at the Rankin's beach spot.

Peter Frampton

U2's first live performance counted a cover of Peter Frampton's "Show Me the Way" at Adam's suggestion. The band kept it in their repertoire for a while, because Bono was able to not only sing it, but make it his own.

In 2003, Bono finally met Peter Frampton at an AIDS event outside of Chicago. When he saw Frampton, he was there with his sleeves rolled up and willing to help in an unassuming manner. When Bono approached the guitarist behind the classic album *Frampton Comes Alive*, he got to tell him how he discovered his own voice on the song Peter had penned.

Thin Lizzy

This highly influential hard-rock band gave U2 the belief that an Irish rock band could make it. From "Whiskey in the Jar" to "The Boys Are Back in Town," Thin Lizzy was the biggest band to ever emerge from the Emerald Isle when U2 formed.

Sadly, Philip Lynott—the group's black frontman who once kindly gave Adam Clayton telephone advice from his Dublin hotel room—died of drug-related complications, as mentioned elsewhere, in early 1986.

As Bono once marveled of Lynott in *U2 by U2*, "[He was] the only black man in Ireland . . . and he joins a rock band! That's great." It was an inspiration and proof that adversity could be overcome, with international success reaped for a Dublin band.

The Radiators from Space

As Ireland's first punk band—featuring future Pogues member Philip Chevron—Bono felt inspired by their song "Television Screen." The single found Chevron singing about jamming his Telecaster into his TV. Coupled with its fuzzbox-fueled take on twelve-bar rock, it went straight to the young singer's heart.

Bono was not only confident that his band could play the urgent, forceful musical style that the Radiators were bashing out at forty-five rotations per minute—he loved the way it sounded. It was the kind of stuff he was dying to perform.

Iggy Pop

In 1977, Bono became fascinated with Iggy Pop's Bowie-produced album *The Idiot*. A student of the man born James Jewell Osterberg, Bono would later take inspiration from Iggy's onstage antics, implementing them during the *War* Tour, when he climbed scaffolding, jumped off balconies, and dived from the stage.

If Iggy had a "Lust for Life," his stage show was one that gave U2's singer some big ideas.

The Stranglers

Bono was a huge Stranglers fan and petitioned his bandmates in the fall of 1977 to take on "Go Buddy Go." He would change his point of view a year later when U2 opened for the band and ultimately describe its members as "arseholes."

The Stranglers, in fact, were influential in teaching U2 how not to treat their opening acts. The Hugh Cornwell–fronted group refused to share its dressing room, screwed U2 out of a soundcheck and wouldn't even let the foursome have one of their beers.

The Jam

When The Edge saw the Jam, the punk/pop trio of Paul Weller, Bruce Foxton, and Rick Buckler on TV for the first time in 1977, he called it "a watershed moment."

He said to U2.com, "[I realized] that not knowing how to play was not a problem, in that music was more about energy and trying to say something and not necessarily about musicianship."

Edge, who continued to follow the band—and was in the fourth row of the trio's concert at the Top Hat Ballroom in Dunleary in 1980—would add, "When Paul Weller hit that Rickenbacker twelve-string, it meant something."

The Clash

Still performing under the name the Hype, the future members of U2 attended a Clash gig at Dublin's Trinity College on October 21, 1977. Supporting their eponymous debut album on their "Get Out of Control" Tour, the British group's vitality and aggression had a significant impact on the young Dubliners.

"Can't remember much about the music, to be honest," Bono told the *Observer* in January 2007. "I just know that everything changed that night and I'm sure it was not just for me. . . . As I stared out the window the next day, it was very clear. The world is more malleable than you think; reality is what you can get away with."

On December 23, 2002, when co-founding Clash frontman Joe Strummer died unexpectedly of a heart attack at his home in England, Bono paid tribute in a statement, "The Clash was the greatest rock band. They wrote the rule book for U2."

Just before his death, Strummer and former Eurythmics guitarist Dave Stewart had been working together on a song called "American Prayer" for an upcoming Nelson Mandela charity event. In January 2006, Bono attended the Sundance Film Festival in Utah to support the new Julien Temple film *Joe Strummer: The Future Is Unwritten*. Bono appeared in the documentary about the Clash's lead singer, announcing that the aforementioned Trinity College gig was his favorite concert of all time.

The Ramones

On September 24, 1978, Bono got to see the Ramones live for the first time at the State Cinema in Dublin. Reflecting on the gig in a 2001 eulogy of Joey Ramone for *Time* after the singer's death from cancer, U2's singer wrote, "When I was standing in the State Cinema listening to Joey sing and realizing that there was nothing else [that] mattered to him, pretty soon nothing else mattered to me. If they remind me of anything now, it's that singular idea."

Unlike the gravelly voice of the Clash's Joe Strummer, Bono could identify with Joey's melodic pipes. "Joey Ramone sang like Dusty Springfield," he told *Rolling Stone* in 2005. "It was a melodic voice like mine."

"They kind of stopped the world long enough for bands like U2 and others to get on," Bono explained in his tribute. "The Ramones were actually the beginning of something new. They stood for the idea of making your limitations work for you. Everything added up. That takes an extraordinary intelligence to figure out."

In 2003, U2—who often performed *Leave Home*'s "I Remember You" live—contributed a cover of "Beat on the Brat" from the revered New York punk band's 1976 eponymous debut to the compilation album *We're a Happy Family—A Tribute to the Ramones.*

The Boomtown Rats

Although the Boomtown Rats weren't much of a musical inspiration, Bob Geldof was a muse for Bono. From Dublin, his influence on the singer was about attitude at first, and later, about political responsibility as an artist.

"I learned a lot of my lip from Bob," the singer said in *Bono in Conversation.* "I had a sense that the impossible was possible from him. Oddly enough, I didn't learn about social activism from him. In fact we used to argue about it. He used to tell me that pop and rock and roll should never stray from sex and fun. Leave revolution to politicians! Right up until he had his epiphany."

The Skids

Up until his suicide in December 2001, Stuart Adamson was best known as the frontman for Big Country, but before he played in that acclaimed rock band, he fronted the Skids, who Edge has cited as a big early influence.

"He was a great inspiration to me when U2 were starting out," Edge said in a statement following Adamson's death. "His first band the Skids made such a big noise and with songs like 'Into the Valley' and 'The Saints Are Coming' they made most of the other music of the time seem mundane and insignificant." U2 later collaborated with Green Day in 2006 on a cover of the latter.

Bruce Springsteen

The first time U2 observed Bruce Springsteen perform in an arena, it was a game changer for the band. The group realized performers could communicate with a large audience without weakening the power and the message of the music.

"We realized it could add to the experience: a bigger crowd, a bigger electrical charge," Bono was quoted as saying in Greg Garrett's *The Gospel According to U2*. Although they were stylistically different, U2 became friends with the Boss in 1981 and continued to sustain that relationship over the years.

From a songwriting perspective, Bruce taught Bono to look outside of himself for lyrical inspiration. But long before they were in communication

Nearly a quarter century after their first meeting, friend and mentor Bruce Springsteen joins U2 for a version of "People Get Ready" during the second of two shows at Philadelphia's Wachovia Center in October 2005.   *Photo by Mike Kurman*

with one another, Springsteen's records had made an impact when *Born to Run* made it to Ireland.

Still, for Bono, the early Van Morrison–influenced stuff like *The Wild, the Innocent and the E Street Shuffle* and *Darkness on the Edge of Town* were among his favorites.

Television

The Edge has long cited Television's Tom Verlaine as being an inspiration on his guitar playing. "*Marquee Moon* was a great album," he said to *Rolling Stone* in 1988, "but I think what I took from Verlaine was not really his style but the fact that he did something no one else had done. And I liked that; I thought that was valuable."

For the guitarist, his approach was minimal. He knew what he didn't want to sound like, more than how he didn't at first. So he played as few notes as possible while making those that were effective work in his favor. It was an alternative to the punk chords that were prevalent in the late 1970s.

"It became a whole way of working," he continued. "If I could play one note for a whole song, I would. 'I Will Follow' is almost that."

Patti Smith

The Edge became fascinated with Patti Smith's *Horses* album after Adam brought it back from London in September 1977. So much so that he went out and bought his own vinyl copy.

"Patti Smith's music had that confrontational aspect," he'd tell the *NME* in 1988. "What was different about it is that it's poetry. Punk had all of the anger, but none of the poetry."

In November 2005, Smith joined the band onstage at Madison Square Garden in New York to perform a cover of John Lennon's "Instant Karma."

Prince

Bono has proclaimed Prince "one of my favorite composers of the twentieth century," although he once suggested that the Purple One could use an editor.

"I really believe in him," the singer told Michka Assayas, citing albums like *1999* and *Purple Rain*. "But he needs an editor. He needs somebody in the studio to tell him to fuck off. 'And guess what? There's six great tracks and four of them are pretty average. I'm sorry, sir. Your genius was having a bad day.' Does he have that? No chance."

Johnny Cash

Bono had tremendous respect for Johnny Cash, who he first met in 1988. The Man in Black acted his age and grew old gracefully. Speaking about one of Cash's final recordings, his rendering of the Trent Reznor song "Hurt" and its respective, Mark Romanek–directed video, Bono once heralded it as one of the greatest things popular culture has ever offered, telling Bill Flanagan, "It's the end of rock and roll as juvenilia."

Upon Cash's passing in September 2003, Bono explained in a statement, "I considered myself a friend, he considered me a fan—he indulged me. He was more than wise. In a garden full of weeds—the oak tree."

Johnny Marr

Although the Smiths emerged in 1983 after U2 had already been established, The Edge found Johnny Marr's guitar playing very unique. While dozens of guitarists had been aping U2's sound by early 1988, Marr—whose Morrissey-fronted band broke up in August 1987—was an inspiration to him.

Edge was interested in innovation, and was excited to hear guitarists who were bringing something new to the table. Speaking to *Rolling Stone*'s James Henke in March 1988, he said, "Johnny Marr—I thought that was an interesting thing he was doing with the Smiths. That high-life-y quality was something I hadn't heard before."

R.E.M.

By the late 1980s, R.E.M. had become U2's American counterparts in the sense that they strived to create artful, thought-provoking records. The Edge cited the subtleties of the group's guitarist Peter Buck as an influence on his playing.

"Nothing he ever really does bowls you over—until you've heard it about twenty times," Edge told Henke. "I think that's a sign of music that really has longevity, when it grows on you like that."

The Pogues

In October 1997, Bono appeared in the BBC2 documentary, *The Great Hunger—The Life and Songs of Shane MacGowan*. During the show, Bono called the often-unintelligible former Pogues frontman—who eventually rejoined the group for live work—"the greatest songwriter Ireland has ever produced."

24

Where the Bright Lights and the Big City Meet

Rattle and Hum

B. B. King

P hil Joanou and his camera crew were hard at work on U2's motion picture when he filmed U2 and B. B. King in rehearsals and during a performance of the song "When Love Comes to Town" at the Tarrant County Convention Center in Fort Worth, Texas. Tour openers the BoDeans were asked to sit out the November 24 show so that the iconic bluesman could support the band and work through the new original collaboration.

Earlier in 1987, U2 had taken in a King gig and afterward, B. B. asked the boys to write him a song. This gave them the idea for a collaboration. In Dallas, King was waiting for the song to be presented, but Bono hadn't finished the lyrics.

When he finally delivered the song for the rehearsal, King was stunned by Bono's lyrics about soldiers rolling the dice for Christ's robes. Reacting to the singer's betrayal-laden lyrics, King wondered how a guy so young could write from such a dark place.

Sun Studios

On November 29, 1987, a day after the group's gig in Murfreesboro, Joanou accompanied U2 to Sun Studios in Memphis, where the band recorded in the same facility where influential rock and roll figures like Elvis Presley, Johnny Cash, Roy Orbison, and Jerry Lee Lewis had once tracked their most infamous hits.

Earlier in the day, the members of U2 had toured Graceland before making their way to the facility. But because the band was without instruments, studio owner Gary Hardy hurriedly tried to buy the best modern gear he could on very short notice to accommodate them. Sun had been closed for more than two decades until its re-launch earlier in 1987, and had only vintage instruments.

Humorously, it turned out that Edge, Adam, Larry, and Bono only really wanted to work with the older equipment. Dragging out gear that Edge later goofed "had been in mothballs since the Sixties," the acoustics of the room and the ambience—down to the microphones Elvis had used—were unlike any the band had ever experienced.

With producer/engineer Cowboy Jack Clement—who first worked with Presley—they tracked six songs between 7:30 PM and 3 AM the next morning: "Angel of Harlem," "Jesus Christ," "Love Rescue Me," "Can't Help Falling In Love," "When Love Comes to Town," and "She's a Mystery to Me."

Clement, who had relocated to Nashville decades earlier and worked largely with country-music artists, admitted that he had never heard of U2 when the band asked him to help with its album. But business associates who knew of the group's work and commercial reach advised him it was a good career move and encouraged Jack to take the job.

Absolut Angel

For "Angel of Harlem," the Memphis Horns joined the band and in an effort to try to lighten the mood Bono sent out for a case of Absolut Vodka. It was a misguided idea and Cowboy Jack let him know it.

After a decade in the business, Jack was surprised at the star's shitty judgment. The veteran engineer scolded Bono and apparently called him stupid for giving booze to the horn section. Cowboy was clearly concerned that the session musician's lips might no longer work. The horn-laden tracks on *Rattle and Hum* asserted that everything turned out okay in the end.

Sun Devil Stadium

In preparation for Joanou's plan to shoot the band's entire concerts at Sun Devil Stadium in Tempe on December 19 and 20 for *Rattle and Hum*, U2 performed a full dress rehearsal in the outdoor venue during a powerful thunderstorm on December 17. The next night, with cameras rolling, the band was filmed without an audience.

In between takes of the group taking the stage during "Where the Streets Have No Name"—which made the final cut—Edge screwed around by

A ticket stub from U2's 1987 *Joshua Tree* Tour, this show at the Tarrant County Convention Center in Fort Worth, Texas, occurred just days before the band would head to Memphis' fabled Sun Studios to record several of the tracks that would comprise *Rattle and Hum*.
Courtesy of Angelo Deodato

playing "Stairway to Heaven" on his guitar. Meanwhile Bono gave a live interview with a local radio station in order to keep from complete boredom while the director set up his shots.

During this activity, word spread to local fans, who showed up outside the venue a night early to listen to what was going on and hopefully catch a glimpse—but Tempe and Arizona State University Police dispersed the crowd.

For the actual gigs, tickets were sold for just five dollars, with fans informed that the show could be interrupted by film crews. The first night was a disaster with Bono struggling to feel at home with the rigidity of the shoot, which was also marred by rain.

On the second night—which was a make-it-or-break-it opportunity for both U2 and Joanou—both parties stuck to their guns, and the performance and film efforts wound up being a triumphant success. Everything that could go right both musically and visually did.

Keep Things Going

Returning home for Christmas in Dublin, U2 received word that *The Joshua Tree* was the third top-selling album of 1987 and had earned a distinction by the RIAA for four million in U.S. sales. The multiplatinum rockers were also amused to learn that their frontman was named one of *People* magazine's "Most Intriguing People of 1987."

Talking with longtime supporter and RTE host Dave Fanning, Bono spoke of his desire to keep things going in the world of U2. He explained that growing up he got excited when bands like the Who or the Rolling Stones released singles. He hoped that in the future U2 might have a few rock and roll 45s up its sleeve.

Without giving too much information away about what had occurred at Sun Studios the month prior, or the movie shoot, Bono spoke of the group's desire to continue writing songs and disclosed that they had already written a few new ones. "We'd like to put them out at the end of *The Joshua Tree* trail," he explained.

Sad Eyes, Crooked Crosses

With *The Joshua Tree* singles strategy beginning to run out of gas, after its fourth extract "In God's Country" stalled at #44 in the U.S. and #48 in the U.K. by mid January, U2 canceled its Australian tour commitments for the month. Instead the band decided to continue work on new material and tracked the tune, "Desire"—which it had earmarked for the soundtrack album of its upcoming film *Rattle and Hum*—at STS Studios in Dublin.

Meanwhile awards for *The Joshua Tree* began to mount, when U2 earned the International Group distinction at the seventh annual BRIT Awards.

Four Artists

Bono left his music pursuits to the side for one night to participate in an exhibition at Dublin's Hendricks Gallery on January 14. Alongside the work of his friends Charlie Whisker, Gavin Friday, and Guggi, who showed original paintings, the singer displayed a series of photographs he took during his 1985 work in Ethiopia.

Bono's photos were sold for a whopping £1,000 each. They were also compiled in a book he titled *A String of Pearls*. All proceeds from his photos and books sold benefited Ethiopia via Concern/World Vision, the organization that first made his work in Ethiopia possible.

Lost Angeles

With 1988 shaping up to be the year U2 would go Hollywood, the band moved to Los Angeles to record more new material while staying close to the final touches of *Rattle and Hum*. With the movie slated for a fall release, it was decided that the group would ready a companion album of the same name with not only the live tracks Joanou had captured but new studio material to sustain the project.

During their time in L.A., U2 worked on the new songs "Hawkmoon 269," "God Part II," and "All I Want Is You" with Jimmy Iovine at A&M Studios, Sunset Sound and Ocean Way Studios. Along the way, the band had sold the movie to Paramount Pictures for $5 million, the same amount it purportedly spent financing its Joanou-directed effort. Although that took some of the financial pressure off of the band, it added other stress, because

Bono during U2's *Rattle and Hum* period, embracing the style and influence of
Memphis' Sun Records.   *Photofest*

the expectations of the movie went from a limited release to plans for an
opening in hundreds of theatres around the world.

At the time Edge, Aislinn, and their children stayed in a rented house in
the Hollywood Hills, living a largely domestic existence. Truth be known,
the Evans' marriage had become rocky and would eventually crumble which
prompted the guitarist to throw himself into the completion of the album
and movie post-production. At one point, his marriage became so intoler-
able that Edge would come back from working with the band and sit in his
car pondering whether to go into his house or leave for good.

On the flipside, Bono, Ali, Adam, and Larry were having the time of
their lives, shacked up in an enormous Bel Air mansion that was built like
an army barracks with a swimming pool in the middle of it. Larry and Bono
rode Harley Davidson motorcycles, while the singer slurped whiskey and
tried to live an uninhibited existence, which was something he hadn't really
done in his adult life. Save for Larry, who was more reserved than the others
and was feeling a little homesick, U2's members were partying harder than
ever before.

Hitchin' a Ride

Sometime in the summer of 1988, Adam and Bono left Los Angeles with
plans to take a road trip into the heart of the United States by themselves.
In a rented Jeep Cherokee, they drove out into Arizona and New Mexico,

away from the madness of L.A. Over the course of two weeks, they travelled through Texas and again found themselves back in Tennessee.

At one point, their Jeep was either lost or became disabled, prompting the pair to use their thumbs. A young rock fan pulled up in a Corvette and offered them a ride. The new Def Leppard album, *Hysteria*, had been blasting at high volume. When they climbed in, the driver recognized his famous hitchhikers and turned off "Pour Some Sugar on Me" and put on *The Joshua Tree*. Bono and Adam were bummed to discover the inferior volume level of their final product and committed to make future recordings a better sonic experience.

In Bono's eyes, Def Leppard's anthem was one of the first industrial records. He couldn't help but feel jealous of the fact that a pop-metal band beat U2 to the punch with that musical style.

Blues Magoos

Back in Memphis during the same excursion, Bono and Adam tracked down *New York Times* writer Robert Palmer, who was a subject matter expert on blues music and the author of *Deep Blues*. Palmer offered to take the bandmates to see the genre performed in an authentic setting—a juke joint on the outskirts of the city.

Here the Irishmen were stunned to witness blues legend Junior Kimbrough, who was in his seventies at the time, perform the song "I'm Going to Rape You, Little Girl," among others.

The House of Cash

During their journey, Bono and Adam went to visit Cowboy Jack Clement—who had worked with them the previous November at Sun Studios—in Nashville. Clement brought them to have lunch with Johnny Cash. June Carter Cash, wife of the Man in Black, greeted them and brought them into a dining room where they all sat down.

Johnny—who would eventually work with U2 on 1993's *Zooropa* album—closed his eyes and said Grace in a moving manner. He then purportedly turned to Bono and said, "Sure miss the drugs, though!"

New Orleans

Travelling on to New Orleans, Bono and Adam visited Daniel Lanois, who had just wrapped up production on what would become Bob Dylan's comeback album *Oh Mercy*. The music legend and U2's producer/friend had been introduced by Bono.

The Canadian-born Lanois had made NOLA his home at the time and had owned a beautiful, baroque house in the city's French Quarter. It was here that Lanois had been working with the Neville Brothers on their album *Yellow Moon* at his Kingsway studio.

The final stop on their journey found the two bandmates mesmerized by the voice of Aaron Neville. Clayton and Bono were both struck by the fact that Neville could sing like an angel from heaven while looking like a mafia hitman.

Jesus Christ

In September 1988, the Woody Guthrie and Leadbelly tribute album *Folkways: A Vision Shared* was released. For the project—a benefit commissioned by the Smithsonian Institution—U2 lent its cover of Guthrie's "Jesus Christ," which it had recorded in Sun Studios in late 1987.

For Bono, the song was just as relevant as it was when Guthrie wrote it. With lines condemning bankers and the preachers, the singer cited morally bankrupt televangelists like Jimmy Swaggart and Jim and Tammy Faye Bakker that he would see on his hotel TV screens. These Christian preachers were asking the sick and elderly for money—and receiving it—to support their "ministries."

The Songs of *Rattle and Hum*

The original intent of the *Rattle and Hum* album was to have it serve as a memento of U2's mega-successful tour in support of *The Joshua Tree*. But the plan for new tracks, live material and a few odds and sods became a concern when the band and its handlers feared that the disc would be compared to all of the acclaimed studio records in its growing catalog.

With the realization that there was little the group could do about its presentation late in the game, the album—an exploration of roots rock with examples of blues, folk, country, and soul—was released as planned on October 10, 1988. In advance of the album, and the film—which was hit theatres in the United States on November 4—the group released a single for the song, "Desire."

1. "Helter Skelter": U2 launched *Rattle and Hum* with an explosive cover of the Paul McCartney–penned "Helter Skelter," which first surfaced on the Fab Four's eponymous 1968 double album, often referred to as The White

Album. Often cited for its "proto-metal" approach, the revved-up live version here—which was introduced as "a song Charles Manson stole from the Beatles"—is downright punk-sounding.

Recorded at McNichols Arena in Denver on November 8, 1987, the song was a reflection of what U2 had felt at the time. They were on top of the charts, but in their hearts there was plenty of drama, from Bono's stage injuries to the strain brought on by their rocket ride to superstardom.

2. "Van Diemen's Land": At the time of its release, this Edge-sung ballad was an appeal for nonviolent justice and what the guitarist called an "immigrant's song." It commented on the violence, suffering, and injustice that continued in Ireland.

But "Van Diemen's Land" was as much a song about the pain brought to lives in Ireland by the still-active Irish Republican Army as it was about Tasmania, the Australian region where Fenians led by John Boyle O'Reilly were banished in 1848 for uprising after the Great Famine.

Recorded at the Point Theater in Dublin and based on an old Irish folk song called "The River Is Wide," The Edge's composition shares its title with an altogether different Irish folk song.

3. "Desire": The riff for "Desire" was written by Edge at home in Rathgar and was based around a rhythm he nicked from Bo Diddley via *The Stooges* song "1969." An explosive rave-up of a song, it rocked like nothing else on the pop charts at the time of its release.

Although U2 had re-recorded "Desire" in the spring of 1988 at A&M Studios, it lacked the edge of the demo, which was tracked at STS in Dublin months before, so the first version won out. As for its lyrics, Bono used the song as a forum for his criticism of what he described as *"lunatic-fringe preachers,"* although almost every night he, too, was responsible for *"stealing hearts at a travelling show."*

The single became U2's first-ever U.K. #1, and it peaked at #3 in the United States. A nine-minute "Hollywood Remix" of the song became a favorite in night clubs and was notable for a sample of future President George H. W. Bush's 1980 speech in which he criticized the "Voodoo Economics" of Ronald Reagan, who soon became his running mate.

4. "Hawkmoon 269": Recorded at Sunset Sound, right in the heart of the Strip amid the drug busts, prostitution, temptation, and rock and roll, the song was written about a place in Rapid City, South Dakota, that the band travelled through during the 1986 Amnesty Tour. The 269 represents the number of mixes the band actually did for the song, which it spent three weeks working on.

Because of the amount of time spent working on the song, which was Edge's favorite going into *Rattle and Hum*, the guitarist could no longer listen to it.

5. "All Along the Watchtower": Written by Bob Dylan, reinvented by Jimi Hendrix, and resuscitated by U2 for its "Save the Yuppies" outdoor concert, the version in place is loose but powerful. There was one flaw in the live recording when the band's engineer failed to capture The Edge's thirty-second guitar intro, but the guitarist had little trouble dubbing it in later.

Fans of the versions of the song that emerged in the 1960s were quick to criticize Bono for his improvisation, *"All I've got is a red guitar, three chords, and the truth/All I've got is a red guitar, the rest is up to you."* Stacking them up against one another twenty-plus years after the fact, U2's rendition is acceptable if not disposable.

6. "I Still Haven't Found What I'm Looking For": The members of U2 were surprised and pleased to learn that their gospel-inspired pop song had been embraced by Harlem's own New Voices of Freedom. When the group submitted their version to Island Records, the band went up to the church with Gavin Friday to see the choir in action.

Next the band considered how to make a collaboration work, and the New Voices of Freedom were asked to join U2 for its 1987 performance at Madison Square Garden. Bono sounded in rare form on the resulting track,

This unique *Rattle and Hum* standee promoted U2's 1988 film in movie-theatre lobbies around the globe. *Author's collection*

which also boasted impressive work from the New Voices' soloists, George Pendergrass and Dorothy Tennell.

7. "Freedom for My People": Less a song than a musical vignette, this performance comes courtesy of vocalist Sterling Magee and harmonica player Adam Gussow, who were spotted by U2 on the streets of Harlem and filmed by Phil Joanou as the band was en route to meet the New Voices of Harlem.

8. "Silver and Gold": A song written by Bono that first surfaced on the 1985 *Sun City* charity album in an acoustic-blues rendition with guitar augmentation by Keith Richards and Ron Wood of the Rolling Stones, "Silver and Gold" had also been recorded by U2 in an electric form as a B-side of "Where the Streets Have No Name."

However, the version recorded live for *Rattle and Hum* wasn't just electric in presentation, it was electrifying. Taking a political slant in the song, Bono lashed out about apartheid, but fearing he had gone on too long and may have been trying the patience of those in the crowd who just wanted to rock, he kind of lost his cool.

"Am I buggin' you? I don't mean to bug ya," Bono told the crowd, before handing the reigns back to the band, as he added, "Okay, Edge, play the blues."

9. "Pride": The live rendition of "Pride" featured on *Rattle and Hum* was also culled from U2's impromptu free concert in San Francisco. In the movie of the same name, Bono can be seen spray-painting ROCK AND ROLL STOPS THE TRAFFIC during the song's performance.

10. "Angel of Harlem": This song was written about U2's trip to the United States in December 1980. During the band's first-ever limousine ride into New York from Long Island—which Paul McGuinness managed to coax Island Records to pay for—the group discovered WBLS, one of the urban radio stations at the time.

As the band came over the Fifty-Ninth Street Bridge in the limo to their destination at the Gramercy Park Hotel—where they would later discover the Clash and the Slits were also staying—Billie Holliday was singing. Holiday— a jazz singer who died of cirrhosis of the liver in 1959 when she was just forty-four—was also known as "Lady Day," a nickname Bono references in the song.

Recorded in Memphis with "Cowboy" Jack Clement at Sun Studios, the song features the legendary Memphis Horns, who appeared on a number of blues and soul tunes recorded in the city. Speaking of the song, Bono acknowledged it as one of U2's few "jukebox songs"—the kind of music people like to listen to in bars.

11. "Love Rescue Me": A song about a man people considered a savior, who was in need of his own salvation, Bono said that this song came to him in a dream. At first he thought it might have been an existing song by Bob Dylan, but when he approached his iconic friend he learned it wasn't, but felt it could be a song he would sing.

Together they finished it at Dylan's home on the Southern California coast, with the bard born Robert Zimmerman coming up with the line, *"I'm hanging by my thumbs, I'm ready for whatever comes."*

The idea came to the singer while he was crashing with The Edge in a rented Los Angeles home that would soon become occupied by the Menendez family. It was in this home that Erik and Lyle Menendez murdered their parents in 1989.

As mentioned earlier, Dylan had originally performed the vocal for the song, but declined to have it released because of contractual obligations to a forthcoming project at the time with the supergroup the Traveling Wilburys.

12. "When Love Comes to Town": A rare U2 duet, the band took advantage of an opportunity to collaborate with the American blues giant B. B. King after he asked the band to write a song for him. King was thrilled to learn that the members of the group—who attended a Dublin performance of his in 1987—were fans.

After rehearsing and performing the show in Fort Worth, Texas in November, 1987, King joined U2 for its recording session in Sun Studios just days later. During tracking, B. B. played his notorious Gibson guitar, which he had named "Lucille." In the movie *Rattle and Hum*, there is a scene where Bono and the blues great work through the tune for the first time.

The pairing with U2 wouldn't be King's last; he joined the band on their 1989 "Lovetown" Tour, supporting the band for dates in New Zealand, Japan, Germany, Holland, and Ireland. He joined the band each night during their set for a live rendition of "Love," and his affiliation with the band helped to widen his fan base.

13. "Heartland": Work on this song dated back to 1984 sessions for *The Unforgettable Fire*, and it resurfaced during the making of *The Joshua Tree*, but it was again left to the side when the group replaced it with "Trip Through Your Wires." Although the band at first had Ireland in mind, the lyrics were later inspired by the aforementioned road trip into America's heartland that Bono and Adam Clayton had taken earlier in 1988.

From that journey, which Bono later claimed he'd treasure for the rest of his life, came observations about Mississippi's "cotton wool" heat and the blacktop of Route 66. By its final incarnation, "Heartland" was essentially a travelogue set to music.

14. "God Part II": This tune was inspired by Albert Goldman's book about John Lennon. The book offended Bono, who felt it seemed unnecessary cash grab to rehash a lot of the flaws that the one-time Beatle had already revealed about himself. The song—which has a very contemporary approach compared to the rest of the album—is actually a clue to the direction the band wound up taking on its next studio album, *Achtung Baby*.

In the eleventh hour of making *Rattle and Hum* in the summer of 1988, Bono had decided that he was finished with nostalgia. In this answer song to Lennon's "God," Bono, too, had some things he didn't believe in, and biographer Goldman was at the top of his list.

One line from the song, *"Kick the darkness 'til it bleeds daylight"* was lifted from the 1984 Bruce Cockburn song "Lovers in a Dangerous Time." But the overwhelming angst was based on the group's disdain for Goldman's unflattering biographies of Lennon, from 1988, and Elvis Presley, from 1981.

"I think it has tainted a lot of people's views," The Edge told the *NME* in November 1988. "Sure, Elvis was fucked up. Sure, John Lennon was fucked up. I certainly knew that, but it doesn't take away from their music for me. People are interested in that kind of bullshit, but that's not to say that it's good."

15. "The Star-Spangled Banner": The musical accompaniment to Francis Scott Key's poem "Defence of Fort McHenry" was based on John Stafford Smith's British drinking song. But in its electrified version, which Jimi Hendrix first performed at Woodstock in 1969, the song blew the minds of rock fans around the world. A forty-three-second pre-recorded excerpt of that performance was a poignant lead in to the blistering live rendition of "Bullet the Blue Sky" that in many ways trumped the already brilliant studio version.

16. "Bullet the Blue Sky": As evidenced in the movie, during *The Joshua Tree* Tour, Bono would use a large spotlight and shine it into people's faces in the audience, perhaps as a way of waking them up to the religious and military-driven greed so prevalent in the 1980s. From Ronald Reagan's sanctioned "fighter planes" to the preacher Jerry Falwell's fall from grace, the world's formal and informal leaders were ostensibly peelin' off those dollar bills by the hundreds and thousands.

Despite the fact it was never released as a single, the always explosive and meaningful "Bullet the Blue Sky" has persevered through the years. Since it was debuted on the opening night of *The Joshua Tree* trek in April 1987, "BTBS" has almost always been a part of U2's live set.

17. "All I Want Is You": The swansong of *Rattle and Hum* is also the parting shot in the film, playing as credits roll in the documentary. Written for Bono's wife, Ali, the singer would describe the song and their relationship by saying, "She doesn't need me to be anything other than the person I am," he told Stokes in *Three Chords and the Truth.* "She's got that kind of belief in who I am at the essential level. It's an amazing thing."

A meditation on the Hewsons' commitment to one another, the singer's quiet delivery in the song's verses is supposedly Bono's dialogue to Ali, while his bold reiteration of the title in the song's refrain is evidently her response.

Bolstered by a haunting two-and-a-half-minute closing arrangement by Van Dyke Parks, the song just may be the highlight of an album that at times felt out of focus, but ultimately sold a whopping twelve million copies globally.

Do You, Don't You Want Me to Love You?

When the *Rattle and Hum* album was released on October 10, 1988, the reaction was decidedly mixed. U2's exploration of roots music at the encouragement of heroes like Bob Dylan was an intention to pay tribute to the music that it loved. Although the band's fans greeted the disc with open arms, critics like the *New York Times'* Jon Pareles were downright savage.

Pareles mauled U2 in an album review headline that read WHEN SELF IMPORTANCE INTERFERES WITH THE MUSIC. According to the critic, the album was a "mess."

"U2 insists that clumsy attempts at interpreting other people's music are as important as the real thing," Pareles opined. "What comes across in song after song is sincere egomania."

Robert Hilburn was kinder, giving it four out of five stars. The *Los Angeles Times* writer, who had been supportive of the band through much of its career, called it "a frequently remarkable album—a work that not only lives up to the standards of the Grammy-winning *The Joshua Tree*, but also places U2 more convincingly than ever among the five all-time greatest groups."

If the truth was somewhere in between those opposing viewpoints, the double album and single CD offering topped the U.K. charts just the same on October 22 and reached the same position in the U.S. on November 12.

The *Rattle and Hum* Movie Fizzles

A year and a half after it was conceived, U2's Philip Joanou-directed motion picture *Rattle and Hum* premiered on October 27, 1988, at the Savoy Cinema on O'Connell Street in Dublin, where fans packed into the theater's five screens. Before the film, the group played a short acoustic set and returned to perform another pair of tunes after the screening. The band donated box-office receipts from its debut to the "People in Need" fund.

The end product was a far cry from Joanou's original plan, which was to follow *The Joshua Tree* Tour and make a movie. When asked about what U2 might do if the movie bombed, The Edge suggested to reporters that it wouldn't really matter, pointing out that U2 was a rock band, not movie stars anyway. If he was acting like he didn't give a shit, the guitarist was just being guarded. After all, it was his band's name on Theater Marquees, the group was behind the film and fans—who had come to expect greatness from U2—had high hopes.

The film's U.S. premiere on November 1 was marred by rain, which prohibited the band from performing outside of New York's Astor Place Theater. Three days later, the movie opened around the world, and earned $3.8 million in its first weekend. Although its Friday turn out looked extremely positive, the project quickly lost steam. Three weeks later, with just $8.3 million earned, Paramount pulled the film from theaters.

In hindsight, the band acknowledged that although they felt Joanou did a great job with the movie, once Paramount's marketing machine went to work, it pretty much threw the idea of a U2 road movie off balance. "It was heralded as if it were the Ten Commandments," Edge remarked. But when it didn't catch on, the group was disappointed.

Paul McGuinness, who pushed for the film to be made, was especially bummed. It appeared that all of U2's devotees went to see the movie on its opening night. By Sunday, the receipts were way down. McGuinness—and the band, to a lesser extent—felt idiotic

Don't Look Back

"It lacked innovation," Edge said to McCormick of the music on *Rattle and Hum.* "It was our own fault. It wasn't really about experimenting and finding the next musical jumping-off point. It was more about expressing ourselves as fans . . . allowing ourselves to explore the roots of the form."

With that said, the movie wasn't crap, and most of the songs weren't crap. The project had some value. If the critical condemnation was hard to take, the accusations of egomania, portentousness, and superciliousness, ultimately prompted U2 to consider the artistic reinvention that arguably saved its career.

Take That, Sinead

On the rise with her single "Mandinka" and debut album, *The Lion and the Cobra*, Irish singer Sinead O'Connor—who had once been part of In Tua Nua, a band signed to U2's Mother Records—had accused Bono, Edge, Larry, and Adam of being villains. In O'Connor's estimation, U2 had become a Mafia running the music scene in Dublin.

Meanwhile, Fatchna O'Ceallaigh, O'Connor's manager and love interest at the time, had also been critical of the band and its label, Mother Records. Fatchna, interestingly enough, ran Mother until he trashed his employers in the final issue *of Hot Press* for 1987, publicly revealing he disliked the group, their music and their religious and political stances.

Sinead used the topic as a means to keep herself in the headlines, suggesting that Fatchna—who had essentially committed career suicide—was unfairly released by the U2 camp. When questioned on the topic in a two-part November 1988 *NME* piece, Larry Mullen and The Edge found the topic amusing, calling bullshit on O'Connor.

"I wouldn't believe anything that Sinead says, to be honest. Fatchna definitely sacked himself," Mullen insisted.

To which Edge added, "Sinead is not in the business of communicating facts, she's in the business of creating news for herself, that's the bottom line. I get on okay with Sinead and I just have to laugh when I read these things. I hate to think intelligent journalists are swallowing what she says. . . . She's just in a tradition of press manipulators that started with punk, with Johnny Rotten."

With a Red Guitar

Although movie tickets had stopped selling, U2 was still mining the hit-potential of *Rattle and Hum*, with "Desire" becoming U2's first gold-certified single in the United States. The band ultimately released three more singles from the disc, starting with the bright, warm "Angel of Harlem," which reached #9 in the U.K. in December and #14 in the U.S. in February 1989, while topping the *Radio and Records* AOR chart.

Late in January, U2 pumped out a series of covers: Patti Smith's "Dancing Barefoot," Creedence Clearwater Revival's "Fortunate Son," the Righteous Brothers' classic "Unchained Melody," Carl Carlton's "Everlasting Love," and Bruce Cockburn's "If I Had a Rocket Launcher." All but the latter would see official release on the flipsides of U2 singles released between 1989 and 1992.

The next month, as Roy Orbison's *Mystery Girl* with the Bono-penned song "She's a Mystery to Me" was posthumously released, U2 received word that the original songs from *Rattle and Hum* were ineligible for an Academy Award in the "Best Original Song" category. The explanation given was that the music did not contribute to the film's drama.

Despite that disappointment, U2 had a reason to be cheerful. The band was again victorious on February 22 when it received Grammy honors for the Best Rock Performance by a Duo or Group with Vocal for "Desire," and the Best Performance Music Video for "Where the Streets Have No Name."

The Road

For the fall of 1989, U2 decided it might be able to round out the decade in a refreshing and pressure free way if it toured for the sake of touring. Without a new album to promote, the band wanted to go back to Australia, New Zealand, and Japan, where it had never played *The Joshua Tree* songs. It also eyed some European dates to close out the year.

The second single from *Rattle and Hum*, "Angel of Harlem" was issued in late 1988 and featured a picture of bassist Adam Clayton taken during rehearsals.

Author's collection

This time out, however, the group planned to take B. B. King with them as a support act. It also offered the band the opportunity to share King's brass section and flesh out some of the horn-laden material it had tracked nearly two years earlier at Sun Studios. Rehearsals for the trek got underway, but there was a potential setback in the plans when Adam Clayton got busted for marijuana possession.

25

You're a Precious Stone

Prominent Fans, Friends, and Acquaintances

Ian Curtis

While being introduced to producer Martin Hannett—who would ultimately work with U2 on its debut single "11 O'Clock Tick Tock"—in March 1980, the band caught a glimpse of Joy Division tracking its last-ever single "Love Will Tear Us Apart."

According to the members of U2, there was an intense albeit magical vibe during the session, which would up being Joy Division's final studio effort.

Interacting with Ian Curtis just weeks before his suicide, Bono described the Joy Division frontman as having a "big, haunted, hunted voice." U2's members were amazed by the fact that these post-punk innovators had been listening to the likes of Wagner and Frank Sinatra. For Bono, such influences "blew it right open."

Bruce Springsteen and Pete Townshend

On June 9, 1981, U2 played the final show of its *Boy* trek at the Hammersmith Palais in London. The band launched the gig with a new song, "Carry Me Home," which it never played again. But perhaps the show was more significant because the band had two of its heroes in attendance, Bruce Springsteen and Pete Townshend from the Who.

At the suggestion of Frank Barsalona, Springsteen delayed his return trip to America by one day to catch U2's London gig. Probed by a journalist during the show for an opinion on the Irish group, the Boss declared, "I love 'em." After the gig, Bono, Edge, Larry, and Adam met Springsteen for the first time.

"Springsteen had filled my head with all kinds of images of America, and particularly New Jersey, the shoreline, Atlantic City . . . boardwalk America," Bono said in U2's 2006 book. "My brother had brought home *The Wild, the Innocent and the E Street Shuffle* and played it to me when I was fifteen. And I wasn't interested in brass-playing bands at that point, I really wasn't, but it just got under my skin."

As for meeting Townshend, Edge would later admit to telling his guitar hero about wanting to write a song as forceful as the Who's "My Generation."

Meanwhile, Townshend was supportive and complimentary. He was excited by what U2 was doing and he cared enough to meet the band and let them know that he felt the group was special. Considering the influence that the Who had had on the band, the group couldn't help feeling jubilant.

At U2's 2005 induction into the Rock and Roll Hall of Fame, Springsteen spoke of this very meeting. "I went with Pete Townshend, who always wanted to catch the first whiff of those about to unseat us, to a club in London," he told the audience at the Waldorf-Astoria in New York. "There they were: a young Bono—single-handedly pioneering the Irish mullet; The Edge—what kind of name was that?; Adam and Larry. I was listening to the last band of whom I would be able to name all of its members. They had an exciting show and a big, beautiful sound. They lifted the roof!"

Sting and John Entwistle

Midway through its *War* Tour, U2—which was supported by college radio favorites the Dream Syndicate—hung out backstage at the Capitol Theater in Passaic, New Jersey on May 12, 1983, with Sting of the Police and the Who's John Entwistle. Two nights later, at the Tower Theater in Philadelphia, Bono built on his budding friendship with Bruce Springsteen. During the gig, he dedicated a song to the memory of Steel Mill, one of Bruce's pre-fame bands of the early 1970s.

Bob Dylan (1984)

In July 1984, Bono met Bob Dylan when the legendary folk and rock performer was in Ireland to perform at Slane Castle. U2 had long pledged its love of Dylan with its many performances of "Knockin' on Heaven's Door" throughout 1983. The powers that be at *Hot Press* knew this and suggested that the singer interview him for the music paper.

Another music legend, Irishman Van Morrison, also participated in the discussion backstage at Slane that was documented for the publication. The experience put Bono in the room with two of his artistic mentors.

Dylan impressed both Bono and Van by reciting the eleven verses of "Banks of the Royal Canal," by Brendan Behan as they spoke about the history of Irish music. Later, U2's singer was flattered, if not stunned, when the American folk icon asked if he could have his picture taken with the twenty-four-year-old, mullet-sporting rocker.

Before Dylan took the stage, he asked Bono to sing his classic "Blowin' in the Wind" with him. U2's frontman didn't know the words. Too ashamed to tell his hero this—who he'd later call "the Picasso of pop music"—Bono made his own words up, only to apologize to Dylan later. Bob told him not to worry, admitting that from time to time he too would forget his lyrics and have to improvise on the spot.

The Rolling Stones

During his stay in New York in the fall of 1985, Bono expressed to Peter Wolf his interest in meeting Rolling Stones guitarist Keith Richards. Richards had been in Manhattan recording a new album with the Stones—soon to be known as *Dirty Work*—with U2 veteran producer Steve Lillywhite.

With Richards's bandmate Mick Jagger joining in, the Stones' creative axis played old country and blues numbers acoustically to the singer's delight. But when they asked Bono to reciprocate, he felt embarrassed that he couldn't pull off a song from his Irish heritage or elsewhere.

Depressed over the fact that he couldn't contribute because he had shunned most Irish music in favor of rock and roll, but inspired by a night spent listening to Delta blues tunes, Bono retreated to his hotel room, where he penned "Silver and Gold," a number that described the view from a South African prison cell. With the song in place, he asked Keith Richards and Ron Wood to quickly record it with him so that it could be added to the *Sun City* album at the last minute.

For the largely acoustic track, Wood reportedly used Keith's switchblade knife to play slide guitar. The song was eventually recorded in a more electrified form by U2 for use a B-side in 1987.

Speaking about Jagger to Assayas years after, Bono called his friend a conservative old school English man who thrives in a yacht-club setting and loves cricket. "I think he climbs into a character. Literally, you can see him, as he starts to sing, get into the skin of this other thing called Mick Jagger, which is this R&B singer."

In September 16, 2002, Bono joined the Rolling Stones onstage at the Aragon Ballroom in Chicago. Singing with Mick Jagger on "It's Only Rock and Roll," it affirmed the camaraderie that Bono and the Stones had built through the years has lasted.

Hotel Jam Sessions

During the Conspiracy of Hope Tour—which found rock stars on the trek staying in hotel chains like Ramada and Marriott as a cost-saving maneuver—bands and their crew members who were looking to cut loose after their performances began to infiltrate hotel lounges looking for a drink and some laughs.

Midway through the tour, after gigs in San Francisco, Los Angeles, and Denver, this cocktail contingency took over for a bar band playing in the lounge of their Atlanta hotel. Bono, Peter Gabriel's drummer Manu Katche, and Lou Reed's guitarist asked to borrow instruments for a turn, and ran through Reed's legendary "Sweet Jane," while the one-time Velvet Underground frontman Reed and U2 guitarist The Edge both slept upstairs. Joan Baez, Peter Gabriel, Bryan Adams, the Neville Brothers, and Larry and Adam all took turns performing until well into the morning. The Ramada hotel staff finally shut them down.

The next day—after hearing about the fun they had missed out on—Reed and The Edge made sure that should such shenanigans take place again on the tour, they wanted in. That night Reed was coaxed into performances of "Sweet Jane" and "Vicious."

Roy Orbison

Before U2's show at London's Wembley Arena on June 2, 1987, Bono couldn't sleep and put Roy Orbison's "In Dreams" on repeat as he eventually drifted off. When he arose the next day, he decided he would try to write Orbison a song. He came up with the track "She's a Mystery to Me."

In a completely unexpected surprise that night after the gig, Orbison arrived at U2's dressing room asking to meet the band. The group and its entourage were floored by the strange twist of fate. Bono sang the new composition, which Edge ultimately helped polish, for the rock and roll legend. Roy agreed to meet up again later in 1987 so that they could track the tune. The song would become the basis for the title of Orbison's final studio album, *Mystery Girl*, which was released after his death in February 1989.

Bruce Springsteen

On September 25, 1987, U2 set a U.S. attendance record at Philadelphia's John F. Kennedy Stadium, with more than 86,000 people in attendance. During the show, Bono asked the crowd, "Do you want to play my guitar?" and it roared. He then continued, "Does Bruce Springsteen want to play my guitar?"

Springsteen walked out onstage and together the band and the Boss performed Ben E. King's "Stand By Me." The audience was shocked and overjoyed.

Bob Dylan (1987)

During its aforementioned gig at the Los Angeles Memorial Coliseum, the Olympic Torch was ignited in advance of U2's encore. The symbolic gesture marked just the fourth time the torch had ever been lit, previously burning twice for the Olympics in 1984 and once for a visit by the Pope earlier in 1987.

During his stay in L.A., Bono and his good pal Bob Dylan teamed up to write a tune originally called "Prisoner of Love" that would surface the following year on *Rattle and Hum* when it became known as "Love Rescue Me."

The idea for the song came to Bono in a dream. He claimed to have been dreaming about Dylan and woke up wondering if it was a Dylan number. He decided to pick up the phone and call Dylan, who asked the singer to come to his home on the coast outside of the city. With trepidation, Bono told his hero about the song and Dylan asked him to play it. Although it wasn't one of Bob's songs, together they worked on it and finished it.

Although a version sung by Dylan was considered amazing by those in the U2 camp who had the opportunity to hear it, it was never released at the rock legend's request.

In 1988, Dylan was performing with Jeff Lynne, Tom Petty, George Harrison, and Roy Orbison as the Traveling Wilburys and asked U2 not to release the version with his lead vocal for fear it might interfere with that all-star initiative.

During this time in L.A., Bono and Edge also met up with Orbison and worked on the arrangement for "She's a Mystery to Me," which Roy intended to use on his next solo set.

Jane Fonda

While in Los Angeles, U2 was invited to the home of actress Jane Fonda and her husband Tom Hayden for a party thrown in their honor. Of the November 20, 1987, soiree, Hayden told the *Associated Press*, "We wanted to give them an opportunity to make some new friends and meet some new people."

High profile guests include rock guitarist Eddie Van Halen and his actress/wife Valerie Bertinelli, David Crosby, Graham Nash, Quincy Jones, and executives from the worlds of music and film industries.

Michael Jackson

While in town for the Grammy Awards in March 1988, U2 was asked by Michael Jackson to come see his performance at Madison Square Garden on the following night, March 3, and meet him afterward. U2 accepted the invitation, but when the King of Pop's people appeared backstage toting video cameras to record Jackson's interaction with the band, the lads got the creeps and quickly exited the venue.

It wasn't the first time Jackson expressed an interest in U2. Back in 1983 there was a big display for the *War* album cover at Tower Records in Hollywood. The band received word that the *Thriller* singer wanted to have it after the display—which, of course, featured a young, shirtless Peter Rowen—was no longer needed.

Robert Plant

U2's tour manager Dennis Sheehan—who performed the same function in the Led Zeppelin organization in the 1970s—once introduced Bono, Edge, Adam, and Larry to singer Robert Plant in an unorthodox manner. In the 1980s, Sheehan drove a car full of U2's members—who were dead asleep—to Plant's home in the very early morning.

Sheehan went to retrieve the voice behind Zeppelin's legendary catalog, who happily woke the dazed and confused Irish rockers. In homage to his iffy late 1980s solo track, Bono referred to Plant as the "Tall Cool One." The former Zeppelin singer wasn't as kind, dubbing Bono "the short, fat one."

David Bowie

On a visit to the United States which included visiting producer/engineer Flood at Giants Stadium in New Jersey, where he was assisting with Depeche Mode's live show in the summer of 1990, Bono and Adam flew out to Cleveland days later to join up with David Bowie. Bowie had hired U2's longtime lighting designer Peter "Willie" Williams, who encouraged members of the group to check out the thin video-screen technology that Bowie was using on tour in consideration for U2's next world trek.

Bono took the stage with Bowie for a rousing rendition of Them's "Gloria" while hanging out with the Thin White Duke.

The stars remained friends; and when Bowie married supermodel Iman in Florence, Italy on June 6, 1992, Bono happily attended.

Frank Sinatra

In the spring of 1987, after U2 attended a Sugar Ray Leonard prizefighting victory, the band was given free tickets to see Frank Sinatra and Don Rickles at a $25,000 table. After being introduced to the audience—which included the likes of Gregory Peck and Liz Taylor—by Frank, Bono and the legendary singer met and hung out.

In the months that followed, Bono became a devoted student of Sinatra, and in 1989 attended Frank's gig in Dublin. But since he hadn't seen the legend in almost two years, Bono worried Frank might have forgotten him and decided against going backstage. During the show, the Lord Mayor of Dublin tapped Bono on the shoulder and told him that Frank was wondering where he had been.

By the time of *Duets*, which boasted Bono and Frank on "I've Got You Under My Skin," they were old pals. As a way of saying thanks for his contribution, Sinatra sent the singer a lovely Christmas gift in 1993—a painting that he created called "Jazz" that Bono admired during his visit to the singer's home.

Phil Spector

On August 29 and 30, 1992, U2 took the stage at Yankee Stadium, becoming just the second rock act—following Billy Joel—to perform at the stadium. For Bono, the real milestone came after the show when he met iconic producer Phil Spector.

Spector paid Bono a huge compliment by telling the singer he was the only musician he'd ever met who compared to John Lennon.

ABBA

In June 1993, while playing in Stockholm, U2 invited Sweden's pop heroes Bjorn Ulvaeus and Benny Andersson of ABBA—who hadn't been onstage together for years—to come together at Bono's insistence in a performance that was one of ZooTV's highlights. Together with U2 they performed their smash 1977 hit "Dancing Queen," to the delight of ABBA'S hometown audience.

Salman Rushdie

During U2's ZooTV show at Wembley Stadium in August 1993, Bono came out as the devilish MacPhisto to make his nightly telephone call before

"One." On the phone was Salman Rushdie, the author of *The Satanic Verses*, who soon walked out onstage. It was a bold move for Rushdie, who had been on the run for several years since the Ayatollah Khomeini placed a death sentence on the writer for his book, which deeply offended Islam.

"I'm not afraid of you!" Rushdie told Bono's character during the show, according to *U2 Live: A Concert Documentary*. "Real devils don't wear horns!" Rushdie continued to maintain a friendship with the singer after the highly publicized event, although the media was critical of U2's frontman.

The *Sunday Independent* wrote: "Bono has made a holy joke of both Islamic affairs (of which he knows nothing) and the war in Bosnia (of which he seems to know even less)." But Rushdie had the final word later.

"Here's a rock group taking a fantastic risk of itself," he said. "I like when people go over the edge and invite you to go with them."

Michael Hutchence

When INXS frontman Michael Hutchence died of a suicide in November 1997, Bono was devastated. Hutchence had become one of the U2 singer's good friends. In an interview in 2005, Bono expressed remorse for not spending more time with the Australian-born rock star before his death, explaining that his wife Ali had seen him in advance of his passing and that "he looked a bit shaky to her."

On November 23, at the Alamodome in San Antonio, during the PopMart Tour, Bono revealed his sadness over losing the singer. "He was a good friend, and he was one of us. We're thinking about him today," Bono said, according to U2Station.com, introducing "I Still Haven't Found What I'm Looking For," as Hutchence's image appeared on the giant screen above. At the end of the show, as fans filtered out, the 1987 INXS smash "Never Tear Us Apart" was played.

Hutchence's eponymous solo album, released posthumously in 1999, included a duet with Bono on the song "Slide Away," which the U2 vocalist finished after his friend was gone.

Princess Diana

While playing "Miss Sarajevo" with Pavarotti during their 1995 Passengers performance for the world-famous annual charity event, Bono and Edge found themselves in the company of Princess Diana, who had been the guest of honor.

In 1997, during the PopMart Tour, the band got word that Diana had perished in a Paris car crash overnight. Having known her, Bono was clearly

INXS frontman Michael Hutchence (center) was one of Bono's closest friends. Hutchence, who was a superstar in his own right, committed suicide in November 1997.   *Photofest*

rattled during the group's performance the following night in Lansdowne Road Stadium in Dublin.

During "Gone" and "Last Night On Earth" Bono made reference to Diana; and later, he sang "MLK." As the *"sleep tonight"* lyric started, he was visibly weeping at the death of the Princess. An artful picture of her was shown on the screen above.

A week later, before the band's Paris show, members of the crew visited the site where Princess Diana died. In December, the band fittingly lent "Miss Sarajevo" to the *Diana: Princess of Wales* tribute album.

Willie Nelson

In April 1996, in advance of his Dublin concert, country legend Willie Nelson visited U2 in the studio to record a version of "Slow Dancing," a song Bono had written for him years before. The next night, Bono joined Nelson onstage at the Point Depot for a pair of tunes. "Slow Dancing" surfaced as a B-side to the song "If God Will Send His Angels" in March 1998.

Allen Ginsberg

To hype the release of *Pop*, U2 asked revered poet Allen Ginsberg to offer a thespian rendering of the lyrics to "Miami," as part of the band's ABC Television special. This was Ginsberg's last public experience—he died on April 5, 1997.

Bill Clinton

Bono had intended on wearing a blue cashmere coat when he went to visit President Clinton in the Oval Office to pitch the Jubilee 2000 "Drop the Debt" campaign. But because it was a much hotter day than he expected it would be, he wound up taking it off, revealing a T-shirt, combat pants, and boots.

Clinton and his staff burst out laughing at the unkempt rock star, but went on to welcome him with a cigar. It wasn't the first time Clinton had met up with the U2 frontman: the band once accepted a ride from his motorcade to a Chicago Bears football game.

Before that, U2 was active in Clinton's campaign in 1992, which ultimately brought the Little Rock, Arkansas–based governor to the White House. The story of Bono's drunken meeting with the future President in August of that year is chronicled in the "True Stories" section of *U2 FAQ*.

Another time, on June 5, 2002, Clinton and U2 hung out at the Spy club in Dublin, watching the Ireland-Germany World Cup match. A party was later held in the former president's honor at Bono's house, where Clinton spent the night as the singer's guest. The following day, both Bono and Clinton were inducted into the Washington-based Academy of

Achievement's Salute to Excellence at the Four Seasons Hotel in Dublin. Quincy Jones presented Bono with his gold-medal honor.

Pope John Paul II

Bono was in the company of both Bob Geldof and music impresario Quincy Jones when he met the heavenly father. Yet, despite the meeting, it wasn't heavily publicized, and there were no official photos taken of the interaction. Perhaps the Pope's handlers objected to Bono giving the Pontiff—who was fighting Parkinson's at the time—his sunglasses.

The Bishop of Rome seemed to be staring at the Fly. "Was it the fact that I was wearing my blue fly-shades?" Bono wondered, taking them off out of respect. Later, the singer gave them to Pope John Paul II, who not only accepted them graciously, he put them on. "He smiled the wickedest grin you could ever imagine," said Bono, relaying the story in *Bono in Conversation*. "He was a comedian."

Peter Buck

When R.E.M. guitarist Peter Buck's "air rage" trial took place in London in March 2002, Bono came to testify on behalf of his longtime friend. Buck apparently lost his cool during a trip from Seattle to London the previous April.

Bono reportedly told the court that Buck was "famously known for being a peaceable person. Of all the people in the music business, I couldn't believe my eyes when I read about this." With Bono's assistance and a weak case by the prosecution, Buck was acquitted of the charges.

26

Some Strange Music Drags Me In

Beneath the Covers

n the early days of U2, the band took an occasional stab at songs by other artists. But for either lack of confidence or interest, the group wasn't inclined to cover the material of other recording artists until 1987, after the release of its blockbuster fifth album *The Joshua Tree.*

While proof exists that Bono, The Edge, Larry, and Adam tried their hand at songs like Peter Frampton's "Show Me the Way," David Bowie's "Suffragette City," the Moody Blues' "Nights in White Satin," and the Sex Pistols' "Anarchy in the U.K.," in its infancy, U2 spent its first decade together honing its craft and recording and releasing original material.

The band's cover choices pay homage to their influences. Be it Bob Dylan, the Ramones, Elvis Presley, Patti Smith, the Beatles, Lou Reed, Creedence Clearwater Revival, or the Rolling Stones. That's not to say there aren't curiosities in their tribute pile, like M, Kraftwerk, and Cole Porter, but U2's selections were almost always well considered. Through the years, these official covers have nicely augmented their own songbook.

Darlene Love's "Christmas (Baby Please Come Home)" (1987)

Recorded during soundcheck before the band's July 30, 1987, gig at the Scottish Exhibition Center in Glasgow, Scotland, U2's rendition of Darlene Love's 1963 holiday staple has become a modern seasonal favorite in its own right. Originally released on the charity album *A Very Special Christmas*—which benefited the Special Olympics and also included tracks by Bruce Springsteen, Sting, and the Pretenders—the song also boasts backing vocals by Love.

The tune was later released on the *Unreleased & Rare* album as part of iTunes' *The Complete U2* digital box set in 2004. Speaking of Springsteen, he covered the song at many of his Christmas shows in New Jersey, although the Boss has yet to release a proper version of the tune.

The Beatles' "Helter Skelter" (1988)

Bono once named the "White Album" as his favorite in the Beatles' canon. Citing the strength of the songwriting and the adventurous studio craft, the influence was evident on what may be U2's most spirited cover version ever—a fiery, punk-like roar through Paul McCartney's "Helter Skelter."

The atomic blast of that song, recorded live at the McNichols Arena in Denver on November 8, 1987, wasn't Bono's only acknowledgement of the Fab Four on *Rattle and Hum*. In the song, "God Part II," Bono was timely enough to get in a lyrical dig at the then-new but controversial Lennon biography *The Lives of John Lennon*, written by Albert Goldman. *"I don't believe in Goldman, his type like a curse/Instant karma's gonna get him if I don't get him first,"* Bono seethed.

Bob Dylan's "All Along the Watchtower" (1988)

Written for Bob Dylan's 1967 album *John Wesley Harding* and made legendary by iconic guitarist Jimi Hendrix the following year, U2's cover was officially released on its 1988 album *Rattle and Hum*. Recorded live at the Embarcadero Center in San Francisco in October 1987, it launched what Bono called the "Save the Yuppie" concert, following the stock-market crash that had occurred the month before.

In the band's companion concert film, U2 is seen rehearsing the tune just prior to the show, which made headlines after Bono spray-painted STOP THE TRAFFIC—ROCK 'N' ROLL on a nearby fountain, a criminal offense in the city of San Francisco. Concert promoter Bill Graham paid to have it removed to avoid the singer's arrest.

A high-energy rendition of the Dylan classic, Bono adds the line "All I got is a red guitar, three chords, and the truth." Although the bulk of the song was captured live, The Edge's guitar introduction was not recorded during the show and had to be overdubbed later in the studio.

Clearly one of the band's key influences, Bono later wrote of his fascination with Bob Dylan in a *Rolling Stone* piece in which he called the folksinger "the voice of his generation." "Bob Dylan did what very, very few singers ever do," the singer wrote in 2008. "He changed popular singing. And we have been living in a world shaped by Dylan's singing ever since. Almost no one sings like Elvis Presley anymore. Hundreds try to sing like Dylan.

"I first heard Bob Dylan's voice in the dark, when I was thirteen years old, on my friend's record player. It was his greatest-hits album, the first one. The voice was at once modern, in all the things it was railing against, and very ancient. It felt strangely familiar to an Irishman. We thought America was full of superheroes, but it was a much humbler people in these songs—farmers, people who have had great injustices done to them."

Woody Guthrie's "Jesus Christ" (1988)

U2's contribution to *Folkways: A Vision Shared*, a compilation dedicated to the songs of Guthrie and Leadbelly, was recorded during the band's *Rattle and Hum* era and sounds downright jubilant. The number's celebratory delivery—juxtaposed by the lines, *"The bankers and the preachers/they nailed him on a cross"*—came quite easy to the band.

"We have to sing that song," Bono said in a 1990 promotional video to promote the project at the time of the song's release. "It's more relevant today than when [Guthrie] wrote it."

Produced by Jimmy Iovine—the future head of Interscope Records—the song is a respectful update of the original version, which dates to 1940 and had been captured on the collection *Library of Congress Recordings by Alan Lomax*.

Carl Carlton's "Everlasting Love" (1989)

Issued in June 1989 as a B-side to U2's "All I Want Is You" single, the band's rendition of the pop classic remains a radio favorite since it peaked at #11 on the U.S. Modern Rock survey in 1989. Written by Buzz Carson and Mac Gayden, the song was originally recorded by soul singer Robert Knight in 1967 and reached its primary notoriety with Carlton's 1974 rendition, when it became a Top Ten hit.

Despite its popularity, there is no evidence that the band ever played this cover live. It was produced by U2 and recorded at STS Studios in Dublin, with piano help by the session's mixer and engineer, Paul Barrett.

The Righteous Brothers' "Unchained Melody" (1989)

U2 covered this timeless classic as a B-side to "All I Want Is You," building on the July 1965 version by the Righteous Brothers that experienced a rebirth in the hit 1990 Demi Moore/Patrick Swayze film *Ghost*. Written by Alex North and Hy Zaret, it was first recorded by Todd Duncan for the prison film *Unchained*.

The rarely seen "clock face" sleeve for U2's 1990 promotional single "Night and Day" was released as a twelve-inch single in the U.K. A cover of the Cole Porter–penned song, it marked the first new recording from U2 since *Rattle and Hum*. An emphasis track on the *Red, Hot and Blue* compilation for AIDS research, this limited Island offering—which counts the "Twilight Mix" and "Steel String Mix"—was limited to just 5,000 copies. *991.com*

On Bono's suggestion, the band recorded the song in Dublin at STS Studios with Paul Barrett. The band played it live in the early 1990s, as evidenced by its presence in the concert film *Zoo TV: Live from Sydney*.

Patti Smith's "Dancing Barefoot" (1989)

Released as the B-side of "When Love Comes to Town" in April 1989, the song was co-written by Patti Smith and guitarist Ivan Kral and was originally the second single from the Patti Smith Group's 1979 album *Wave*. Although Bono's loyalty to the singer undoubtedly helped her financially, the influential Smith—who also counts R.E.M.'s Michael Stipe as a friend and devotee—hasn't always shown gratitude for the extra royalties she earned via U2 through the years.

In November 1997, Bono graciously provided a pre-recorded tribute to Smith at a music-magazine awards ceremony in London where she was to receive a lifetime achievement award. In his homage, U2's singer referred to Patti as a "sister, lover, and mother." This description upset Smith, who snapped, "I'm not your mother, Bono. Do your own dirty work. Fuck you," as she accepted the award.

Smith told *NME* that month, "I just thought it was presumptuous. I like to be considered a person; I'm not up for grabs." When asked about the incident, Bono told the U.K. music weekly that he expected "nothing less" from Smith, and that "she never lets you down." U2's spokesperson added, "It's not a lovers' tiff. He's still a fan."

Cole Porter's "Night and Day" (1990)

Popularized by both Porter and Fred Astaire, "Night and Day" was U2's contribution to *Red Hot + Blue*, a compilation for AIDS research. Notable as the first new material from the band in the 1990s, the song was recorded in The Edge's basement studio and found Bono assuming the previously unheard role of a cabaret singer.

Aside from the original version, the song would later surface in its "Steel String Remix" variation on the commercial release of "One." Although the song was released to radio, and was played on more adventurous modern rock outlets at the time, the song stalled commercially.

Creedence Clearwater Revival's "Fortunate Son" (1992)

This B-side to "Who's Gonna Ride Your Wild Horses"—which first emerged in its original state on CCR's 1969 album *Willy and the Poor Boys*—sounds as politically charged in U2's hands during its *Achtung Baby* era as it did at the dawn of the 1970s.

Originally popular during Vietnam, John Fogerty wrote the song to speak out against the war by symbolizing the thoughts of a young American man, who wasn't the son of a Senator, millionaire, or military leader, being drafted.

In U2's update on the tune, Bono—rather humorously—can be heard uttering "take it away, Bono" to himself before he breaks into his own harmonica solo. The song also features backing vocals from Maria McKee, formerly of Lone Justice.

Elvis Presley's "Can't Help Falling In Love" (1992)

Bono's take on the landmark Elvis Presley song was used to close nearly half of U2's 159 ZooTV concerts between 1992 and 1993. Bolstered by a rhythm machine and a strong keyboard presence, not to mention a falsetto flourish by Bono at the end, the group's rendition wasn't as successful as UB40's version—which was released the following year and topped the charts around the world—but was considerably more inventive.

In 1995, Bono penned a poem of devotion to the King, which he titled "Elvis: American David." In May 2009, BBC's Radio 4 aired the poem, which Bono recorded for broadcast.

Later, Bono admitted that he found the abandon that accompanied the first-ever Elvis Presley performance he witnessed mesmerizing. During Presley's 1968 *Comeback Special*, when Bono saw the undulating, leather-clad King do his thing, it left an ineradicable stamp on the future U2 frontman.

Lou Reed's "Satellite of Love" (1992)

U2 paid tribute to another of its musical heroes, Lou Reed, when it covered one of the New York legend's most enduring numbers for its "One" single in 1992. The band also gave "Satellite of Love" an added boost when it regularly performed the song during its 1992–1993 ZooTV Tour, with Bono singing it as a duet with a pre-recorded video image of Reed.

Released as the second single from Reed's 1972 album *Transformer*, the original boasted backing vocals from David Bowie, who produced the full length disc. The U2 camp also reworked the song when it appeared on the soundtrack to *The Million Dollar Hotel* in 2000, performed by MDH Band, Milla Jovovich, and Bono.

In the years since ZooTV, Bono has remained close to Reed. U2's singer joined Bowie in 2007 when Reed was honored by Syracuse University with the George Arents Pioneer Medal for Excellence in the Arts from his alma mater. Bono and Bowie were also witnessed leading the audience in a "Lou, Lou, Lou" chant as he accepted the award.

The Rolling Stones' "Paint It, Black" (1992)

Appearing as one of the B-sides to "Who's Gonna Ride Your Wild Horses," U2's rendition of the Rolling Stones' 1966 hit emerged in August 1992. While it was deemed "unremarkable" by some critics, the impact of Jagger/ Richards on the band had long been apparent, and elements of the song even crept into live renditions of their own iconic song, "Bad."

When asked what he learned as a student of Mick Jagger, Bono cited the Stones' frontman's cocksure strut, his ability to mesmerize an audience, and his willingness to create a spectacle while taking care of business. "It's not sexy to not know what's going on," Bono told Jann Wenner in 2005.

"I always respected Mick for that. He made those guys very wealthy and they made him cool. It's worth remembering."

The Beatles' "Happiness Is a Warm Gun" (1997)

The group's take on this Beatles classic was originally recorded as the theme song to ABC Television's six-part *Anthology* series, which aired in April 1997. U2's collaboration with the network at the time was part of a larger alliance to help promote the group's album during its May ratings sweep.

While it may have seemed like a good idea at the time, the marketing and promotional initiative, branded "ABC is POP," turned off many of the group's fans. The network's claim that it "embraced U2's attitude, style, and image to create a unique look for on-air promos, print, and radio advertising" reflected negatively on the band.

Unfortunately, U2's version of the Fab Four song—which was originally penned by John Lennon for *The White Album* and was a parody of Charles Schulz's 1962 Peanuts book *Happiness Is a Warm Puppy*—was pretty much overlooked when it was officially released on July 14, 1997, as one of two B-sides for "Last Night on Earth."

M's "Pop Musik" (1997)

M's 1979 chart smash "Pop Musik" was embraced by U2 during its 1997–98 PopMart Tour, with a reworked version of the new wave classic used to launch its shows each night. As the track played, the band would emerge from a small satellite stage located in the center of its stadium venues.

When it added the song to its "Last Night on Earth" single as a B-side in the summer of 1997, the group took the Robin Scott–penned track and owned it, thanks to a new vocal by Bono and slightly altered lyrics. Just as Scott's original successfully fused the various styles that emerged in the first twenty-five years of the rock era, the men of U2 gravitated to the song as they looked to explore what "pop" music had become, two decades down the line.

The Ramones' "Beat on the Brat" (2003)

U2's rendition of the classic Ramones track, "Beat on the Brat," was released on the 2003 compilation disc *We're a Happy Family: A Tribute to Ramones*. Reportedly written after frontman Joey Ramone witnessed a woman going after a kid with a bat in the lobby of his apartment building, the original version first surfaced on the New York punk innovators' 1976 debut album.

Writing about the Ramones in an April 2001 eulogy for the band's frontman Joey Ramone (born Jeffrey Hyman) for *Time*, Bono spoke of the group's influence on U2. "This was the best Punk Rock band ever, because they actually invented something," the singer wrote. "There were great bands like the Stooges and the MC5, but I think that they were still blues bands. The Ramones were actually the beginning of something new. They stood for the idea of making your limitations work for you."

"In film jargon, they would be 'a pure situation,'" Bono explained. "They talked like they walked like they sounded onstage. Everything added up. That takes an extraordinary intelligence to figure out."

Kraftwerk's "Neon Lights" (2004)

Released as the B-side to "Vertigo," U2's rendition of "Neon Lights," has only a passing resemblance to the original number, recorded by Kraftwerk for its 1978 album *The Man-Machine*. Bono described Kraftwerk, at the time of the group's emergence, as a "great soul band"; although some made fun of that proclamation, beneath Kraftwerk's "soulless" exterior and unusual presentation, there is some validity to the argument.

Kraftwerk "had a decisive influence" on Bono. As recently as 2009's *No Line on the Horizon*, the singer—according to a *Rolling Stone* report that January—was hoping to "allow our interest in electronic music, in Can, Neu!, and Kraftwerk to come out."

Leonard Cohen's "Tower of Song" (2006)

Recorded with Cohen—the man behind cult classics like "Suzanne," "Waiting for the Miracle," "Everybody Knows," and "Bird on a Wire"—at New York's the Slipper Room, and filmed for the concert film and documentary *Leonard Cohen: I'm Your Man*, the song is one of U2's least-publicized collaborations. Just the same, the band made its devotion to the seventy-something artist known in advance of the project's release.

"He's an extraordinary talent, and anyone who's interested in music has got to be interested in him," Bono told MTV.com that May. "He's the original rapper, you know, if you're interested in hip-hop. He's a sexy man who made sexy music, who made music asking questions about God and girls and everything.

"I first discovered Leonard Cohen's music back in 1978 when I was seventeen years old," The Edge added. "In those days we were listening to exclusively punk music. [Somehow] he managed to make his way under the radar into our circle of friends. He was different. He was welcomed, even though very few other artists were, and he stayed with me. And that's the thing about his work, it stays with you. If you become a Leonard Cohen fan, you never stop being a Leonard Cohen fan."

The Skids' "The Saints Are Coming" (2006)

Recorded in collaboration with punk-rock giants Green Day, "The Saints Are Coming"—which first appeared on the Skids' 1978 album *Scared to Dance*—was recorded for charitable purposes in the wake of Hurricane Katrina. Counting lyrics about storms and drowning, both bands performed the song on the *Monday Night Football* pregame show on September 26, 2006 in advance of the New Orleans Saints playing the Atlanta Falcons.

Tracked at Abbey Road Studios in London earlier that year, proceeds from the song went to Music Rising, a charity founded by The Edge that worked to help rebuild the musical heart and culture of New Orleans by replacing instruments that were lost during Hurricanes Katrina and Rita.

The song, which was included on the band's best-of disc *U218 Singles*, is still a fixture of New Orleans Saints home games and is often played over the loudspeaker as the team takes the field.

John Lennon and the Plastic Ono Band's "Instant Karma" (2007)

U2 recorded its rendition of "Instant Karma" for the all-star 2007 Amnesty International album which was designed to raise awareness for the humanitarian crisis in Darfur. In advance of its recorded appearance, the group road tested the song live during eight dates of its *Vertigo* Tour in November and December 2005.

Bono has previously said that Lennon's *Imagine* album and *Plastic Ono Band*—in which the late Beatle sings about his dead mother Julia—helped him deal with the sudden loss of his own mother in 1974 when he was just fourteen. "For me it was like he was talking about: the veil lifting off, the scales falling from the eyes," the U2 singer explained to Wenner. "Seeing out the window with a new clarity that love brings you. I remember that feeling."

27

Shine Like a Song

The Twenty Best Original U2 B-sides

1. "Boy-Girl": The flip side of U2's first single, "Boy-Girl" had a stuttered introduction and an exuberant musical punch. Inspired by the Buzzcocks, one of The Edge's favorites at the time of the recording, the song gives a nod to the punk movement that the band took inspiration from.

2. "Things to Make and Do": A magical instrumental with staying power, this flipside to "A Day Without Me" was actually recorded by Edge alone on a four-track when the rest of the band wasn't around.

3. "J. Swallow": The flip side to "Fire" was put together hurriedly in tribute to Johnny Swallow, the Lypton Village alias of Bono's longtime pal Reggie Manuel. Although they are difficult to pick out, Bono can be heard alluding to other old friends in the mostly unintelligible lyrics.

4. "Trash, Trampoline and the Party Girl": This flipside to "A Celebration" became far more popular with the band and its fans than the A-side ever was. A bona fide acoustic pop song with a lustful theme, it was rumored to have been written about Edge's future wife, Aislinn O'Sullivan.

5. "Treasure (Whatever Happened to Pete the Chop?)": Pete the Chop was a friend of U2's early management associate Andrew Whiteway, who happily joined the band on trips to its early gigs in London. He suggested to the band that they write a song about him and they complied. The result was a remarkably poppy song that both Paul McGuinness and Island Records wanted to release, but the band refused. Instead they—as Bono would say—"fucked it in the ear" and relegated it to the B-side of "New Year's Day."

6. "Luminous Times": With an abundance of leftovers, *The Joshua Tree*–era singles benefitted from some brilliant B-sides. The Edge fought hard to get this song, ultimately the flip side of "With or Without You," on the album, and although producer Brian Eno believed in it, it was left off because it wasn't finished in time.

7. "Walk to the Water": An amazing song that was time-barred, it also appeared on the twelve-inch single of "With or Without You." With a mood that band ally Bill Graham compared to Van Morrison's *Astral Weeks*, it is worth seeking out.

8. "Spanish Eyes": Another song of lust, in this case Bono's desire for Ali, "Spanish Eyes" found its way to the "I Still Haven't Found What I'm Looking For" single, and—with U2 mania in full effect in 1987—earned airplay on adventurous U.S. radio stations like New York's WLIR.

9. "Sweetest Thing": This song—which would ultimately find its way to A-side status in a revised form in 1998—is an irresistible love song Bono also wrote for Ali. "It's a soul-pop song," Edge described of Bono's piano-touched winner. In its original, unaltered form, it is simply majestic.

10. "Hallelujah (Here She Comes)": An uplifting rock song recorded during the same sessions as "Hawkmoon 269" and "Desire," it was perhaps foolishly omitted from *Rattle and Hum*. The band didn't feel it fit the album, but in hindsight that hodgepodge assortment of approaches could have benefitted from it.

11. "Lady with the Spinning Head": Released on the back of "One," this song gave birth to "The Fly" and "Light My Way"—two tracks that made it to the *Achtung Baby* album. While hints of both can be heard in this pulsing rock epic, it's just as alluring, albeit more adventurous, than the songs it spawned.

12. "Where Did It All Go Wrong?": A chugging guitar riff and the intertwining vocals of Bono and The Edge landed this song on the flipside of "Even Better Than the Real Thing." It isn't exactly amazing when compared with the tracks on *Achtung Baby*, but it's definitely a worthwhile listen.

13. "Slow Dancing": A song originally written for Willie Nelson, when Bono didn't get a response from the country performer, the group decided to keep it for its own. As a B-side to "Stay (Faraway, So Close)" it's warm and charming. Eventually, U2 did get Willie to join them in the studio and upped the song's strengths. It was released again in its new form nearly five years later on the flip of "If God Will Send His Angels."

14. **"North and South of the River":** A songwriting collaboration with Irish folk icon Christy Moore, the B-side to "Staring at the Sun" is heavy topically, using the River Liffey—Dublin's natural cultural divide—as a comment on the difficulties between the Nationalists and the Unionists in the North.

15. **"Two Shots of Happy One Shot of Sad":** Penned with Frank Sinatra in mind and produced by *Pop* collaborator Nellee Hooper, it's a spirited tribute thanks to Bono's informed delivery and obvious devotion to the Chairman of the Board. Sadly, Sinatra—who died in May 1998—never had the chance to take a crack at U2's original.

16. **"Summer Rain":** This swooning, acoustic pop nugget—found on the flipside of "Beautiful Day"—didn't quite measure up to the quality of the material that made its way to *All That You Can't Leave Behind*, but it was a great song just the same.

Released by CBS Ireland on cassette in 1985 under a new title, "Out of Control," in an effort to capitalize on the band's ever-growing success at the time, this recording boasts the same tracks that originally appeared on U2 *Three*, the band's 1979 three-song debut seven-inch single.

U2Wanderer.org

17.“Big Girls Are Best”: A holdover from the *Pop* sessions, this playful track has a great rock and roll feel and was never meant to be anything more than a throwaway, although it's a glorious one.

18.“Always”: This track, which stemmed from a jam session, was the purported source for what developed into “Beautiful Day.” It may not stand out the way the other tracks did during the creation of *All That You Can't Leave Behind*, but it's one that any U2 devotee is sure to appreciate.

19.“Are You Gonna Wait Forever?”: A leftover from the band's 2004 set *How to Dismantle an Atomic Bomb*, this B-side to “Vertigo” is immediate in its allure. A hard-rocking anthem, full of optimism and power—this is one the band should reclaim.

20.“Fast Cars”: A bonus track in some markets for *How to Dismantle an Atomic Bomb*, this pulsing tune has been compared to the band's 1992 single “Even Better Than the Real Thing” in content and presentation, but this time Bono's information overload comes from his Smartphone.

28

I'm Ready for What's Next

Achtung Baby

I'm Ready for the Laughing Gas

In mid-1990, when U2 began thinking about the follow up to *Rattle and Hum*, Bono began looking back on songs he had written a year earlier during the band's Lovetown trek through Australia. This material—which would ultimately comprise a good chunk of U2's next studio set—became the basis for new demos the band began recording that summer.

On the heels of *A Clockwork Orange*, Bono and Edge were anxious to reinvent the band's sound with something "forward-looking." The songs they were working with became "Who's Gonna Ride Your Wild Horses," "Until the End of the World," "Even Better Than the Real Thing," and "Mysterious Ways." The demos they recorded sounded promising.

With Daniel Lanois and Brian Eno again agreeing to produce the group, Eno assumed the role of overseer—coming and going during the course of the recording—while Lanois was the day-to-day producer and Mark "Flood" Ellis was the project's engineer. It was Eno's philosophy that he could keep an open mind about the material if he wasn't on top of the sessions. He would deliberately stay clear of the work in progress so he could offer a fresh perspective.

Berlin

In October 1990, U2 set up camp in Berlin, recording in the legendary Hansa Studios where Bowie had made *Low* and *Heroes* with the help of Brian Eno. In an effort to invent something new for its next studio album, the band wanted to use the city's "postmodern" European environs and influences and, in the process, lose the overstated, blues-inspired vibe of its predecessor.

The band wanted to go away to make an album and Berlin after the German reunification felt like as good a place as any to start. Although U2 wasn't entirely sure where it fit in among the "baggy" dance-rock movement that propelled the Stone Roses, the Happy Mondays, and Primal Scream at the time, its best course of action—at least as far as Bono was concerned— was to put the band together with its proven team in an unfamiliar city and wait for the magic. It wouldn't be that simple.

Sweeping for Bugs

Although the Berlin Wall had fallen in November 1989, the Germany U2 rolled into eleven months later wasn't exactly in celebration mode. The band caught the final British Airways flight into East Germany before the country ceased to exist. The streets were full of people, but they weren't partying. Before long, the band realized it wasn't at a party, but at a protest march held by the Communist Party.

For a time, the band stayed in a hotel that had formerly been occupied by the East German Parliament and where prostitutes roamed the lobby. The bellhops disconnected the KGB security cameras for guests and swept for bugs. Bono also briefly stayed in a guest house that had once been occupied by Leonid Brezhnev, the one-time president of the U.S.S.R. One night he woke up naked and looking for a glass of water and encountered a family of Germans led by a man who wanted to know what he was doing in their house. Bono realized that, after the fall of the Wall, the man had come over the border from the west to see the house where he had been born.

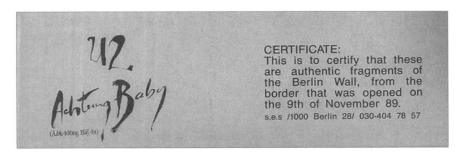

CERTIFICATE:
This is to certify that these are authentic fragments of the Berlin Wall, from the border that was opened on the 9th of November 89.
s.e.s /1000 Berlin 28/ 030-404 78 57

This collectible promotional certificate from the *Achtung Baby* era was accompanied by a small fragment of the Berlin Wall—which fell in November 1989—and a small Trabant toy car. Serviced to key radio, media, and industry people, the unique package came in a clear plastic case and signified U2's time spent working on the album at Hansa Studios in Berlin.   *U2Wanderer.org*

Trouble in Hansa

Maybe it was the fact that Hansa's Studio 2 was once an SS ballroom and felt like it—as Adam would say—"had been preserved in mothballs" or that Germany was just dark, gloomy, and depressing at the start of winter. Perhaps it was that the excitement that was experienced when the Wall fell had long since vanished. But the group's time in Berlin was plagued with arguments over direction, tension, resentment, and minimal progress.

As for the songs themselves, Bono and The Edge had pretty much left Larry and Adam out of the songwriting process, which was a complete change of direction for a band where everyone had creative input in the past. The quality of the material was also an issue as the worked long hours with on.

On one hand, Edge had become consumed with electronic and industrial music. Meanwhile Larry had delved into classic-rock records by Blind Faith, Cream, Led Zeppelin, and Jimi Hendrix. Edge wanted more drum machines, and Larry took that suggestion quite personally.

Adam was also leaning toward the band's fundamental approaches of yore. As for Lanois, he wanted to create something lasting and cinematic like U2 had crafted during its previous recordings in 1984 and 1986. Bono and Edge's songs felt disposable to the Canadian.

Communication Breakdown

Larry felt left out and understandably so. He knew U2 had to change, but there was a lack of communication between the change agents—Bono and Edge—and the rhythm section. Larry had spent his time off in 1990 studying drummers like Led Zeppelin's John Bonham and Cream's Ginger Baker, trying to up his game. Meanwhile, Edge was thinking of ways for him to split his duties with a beatbox.

In the past the songs evolved with the four members of U2 and there was accord. In Berlin, the nuts and bolts of the songs were already set by the technology that Edge had embraced—drum machines, loops, and synth pads. The rules had changed.

There were some awkward moments as the band found itself split into two camps. Adam and Larry thought the song ideas were shitty, but Bono and Edge were of the belief U2's rhythm section was close minded about the radical tactical shift. Things got bad enough that Larry actually thought about quitting U2 and nearly left when, after three weeks in Berlin, U2 had nothing to show for it. This was the first time there had been such dissension. But just as it looked like it was the end, there came a new beginning.

Elsinore

U2's decision to move the project to Elsinore, a seaside manor it reportedly paid £10,000 per month to occupy, was all part of Danny Lanois' tactic of bringing atmosphere to U2's records. Within walking distance of Bono's and Edge's Irish residences, the mansion's seaside location assisted in alleviating tension. Early on in its sessions at the manor, which it would nickname "Dogtown" because of the empty kennels adjacent to it, the group came up with a future B-side called "Lady With the Spinning Head," that wound up splintering off into three of *Achtung Baby*'s most notorious tracks, "The Fly," "Ultraviolet (Light My Way)," and "Zoo Station."

Another in a series of three-inch CD singles issued to support *Achtung Baby*, this Japanese single includes artwork and lettering distinct to this release.

The Songs of *Achtung Baby*

1. "Zoo Station": "Zoo Station" was the ideal proclamation that U2 was back, *"ready for the laughing gas,"* and *"ready for what's next."* With a newfound, self-deprecating sense of humor and a style drastically different from how people remembered them two years earlier, the opening number on *Achtung Baby* was a brilliant mindfuck.

A jarring experience for loyal fans hearing it the first time, the song was launched with heavy distortion on Larry's drums, distorted guitars and Bono's mutilated vocals. When some brought the disc home and put it on, they couldn't help but wonder if their CD players might be malfunctioning.

That in fact was the intention of "Zoo Station," which had an extended and somewhat out-there introduction. Sounding like a modern take on "glam-rock," the song—with its rumbling, distorted riff—was written with the aim of using it to open the album.

"When people put on the record, we wanted their first reaction to be either 'this record is broken' or 'this can't be the new U2 record, there's been a mistake,'" Adam Clayton told Flanagan. "Although it's the first song people hear when they put on *Achtung Baby*, it's one of the last ones to come together."

Crafted long after U2 exited Berlin, the history of the city made an impact on the band's members. Bono recalled the story of the city's zoo—which was bombed overnight during World War II—and its Zoologischer Garten subway, which stopped there. The tale of German people trying to regroup the following morning after the attack with, as Bono described it, "giraffes and lions and elephants roaming around," was a hard one for the singer to shake.

Elsewhere, Bono's lyrics reflected his new experiences of fatherhood, with the birth of his daughter Jordan in 1989 and Memphis Eve in 1991 in the lyrics, *"I'm ready to say I'm glad to be alive / I'm ready, I'm ready for the push."*

2. "Even Better Than the Real Thing": Beginning with a guitar riff that The Edge had developed back in 1988 during the *Rattle and Hum* sessions, the band first demoed a version of the song at STS Studios at the time "Desire" was tracked. Citing the Rolling Stones as a touchstone, the band toyed with the song—originally called "The Real Thing"—in Berlin but didn't get serious with it until U2's return to Elsinore.

Bolstered by the use of a Digitech Whammy pedal, The Edge's guitar effects brought U2 into the 1990s. As for its subject matter, Bono explained that "Even Better Than the Real Thing" was written about the world at the time, where the truth took a back seat to instant gratification.

The fourth single from *Achtung Baby* was released in June 1992 and peaked at #12 on the U.K. pop charts. It also did well on U.S. radio where it topped the Album Rock Tracks survey. It's a playful side of U2 that fans attending the ZooTV Tour had already seen.

Richard Branson was so fond of the title that he hoped to use it for his Virgin Cola launch. The band declined Branson's offer to take on Coca Cola, which had already been calling itself "the real thing" for years.

3. "One": Exhausted and frustrated, U2 finally had the breakthrough it needed in December 1990 when it wrote what became one of its most famous songs. Built from two guitar parts Edge had combined, the tune took shape with the encouragement of Daniel Lanois in about fifteen minutes.

This Island Records promotional cassette of *Achtung Baby* was submitted to the press and retail outlets on November 12, 1991, roughly two weeks in advance of the album's proper release.   *Author's collection*

"One" was a reassurance that U2 could pull through the most challenging period in its career. If the song was all that the group really had to show for two months at Hansa, it was plenty. "One" also reaffirmed the band's need to return to its "blank page" approach to writing and recording, where a consensus helped the band arrive at its best end product.

According to Adam Clayton, the song "fell into [U2's] laps." Bono once said the words were a gift that fell out of the sky, with lyrics of a more intimate approach. "One" was inspired all at once by the end of Edge's marriage, the German reunification, and a letter that the singer wrote to the Dalai Lama declining an invitation for U2 to perform at his "Oneness" festival. Ironically, when Brian Eno heard a tape of the song, he told the band that he despised it and felt they needed to deconstruct it.

Upon its return to Dublin for Christmas 1990, and with the satisfaction of what U2 had crafted with "One," the band decided to stay and work on the album in Ireland. Reconvening in February 1991 to record at the Elsinore mansion on the Dalkey coastline, Eno assisted the band by remixing "One" to minimize its beautiful vibe and toughen it up with a more aggressive "crying guitar" part. In September 1991, the song had to undergo additional mixes by Flood at Windmill Lane Studios when Bono changed a vocal line. Then one last and final mix was done when The Edge inserted an additional guitar line

Despite the fact that "One" is commonly misunderstood as a love song and has become a favorite at weddings, it is a bitter, painful ode to breaking up. Released as the third single from *Achtung Baby* in March 1992, "One" became a #10 hit in the U.S. and reached #7 in the U.K. Although it never got to number one, it was voted the greatest song of all time in a *Q* magazine critics poll of the top 1,001 songs.

4. "Until the End of the World": Structured around a guitar riff that Bono came up with during a brainstorming session at STS in 1990, it was first heard as part of "Fat Boy," which emerged on the *Berlin Trashcan* bootleg. Although Edge loved the guitar part, neither he nor the band was sure it would become part of anything solid until German filmmaker Wim Wenders approached the group to record a song for his upcoming movie, *Until the End of the World*.

Wenders had come to Berlin to shoot a video for U2's Cole Porter cover, "Night and Day," when he pitched the idea. When the band started up work at Elsinore in 1991, the riff came together with input from Adam and Larry, and music for the song took shape. From there, Bono came up with the lyrics one morning while he had been staying at his father-in-law's home in Wexford. It was a conversation he had imagined between Jesus Christ and his deceiver, Judas Iscariot.

Suddenly the band was in a quandary about whether to give the song, which became one of their favorites, to Wenders or keep it for their album. U2 decided on a compromise, which gave the song exposure on *Achtung Baby* and on Wenders's soundtrack, which also featured standout material by R.E.M., Depeche Mode, Talking Heads, Patti Smith, Elvis Costello, and Lou Reed and became one of the most acclaimed soundtracks of the 1990s.

5. "Who's Gonna Ride Your Wild Horses?": One of the earliest songs to surface for U2's seventh album, "Who's Gonna Ride Your Wild Horses" was a magical tune that Bono played in its original demo form for Jimmy Iovine in the summer of 1990. Iovine loved the melody. But once in Berlin, U2 couldn't get the song right, recording it and mixing it multiple times. Eventually, Steve Lillywhite was brought in to mix the version of the song that surfaced on the album. Lillywhite's mix is said to capture the spirit of the initial demo.

According to Lillywhite—who spent a month working on the tune—the band didn't care for the song, but American label executives, who were turned off by some of the disc's industrial touches, believed it was radio gold. The band's longtime friend and producer felt that the song was never completely realized.

A lover's quarrel was the original lyrical basis for the song, but Bono hastily and inexplicably revised it to reflect sexual jealousy. "It's been said to me that there's a lot of references to oral sex on the record," Bono told *Hot Press.* "It's a very equal position. But I hadn't thought about the cumulative effect. I guess there's something for everybody. Don't try this at home."

Speaking of not trying it at home, the band has never played the song live because, according to Edge, "it doesn't come alive." It was, however, released as the fifth and final single from the album in an alternately arranged "Temple Bar Remix." That version—the one the band preferred—made #14 in the U.K. and peaked at #2 on the U.S. Album Rock Tracks survey.

6. "So Cruel": Written mostly by Bono in Elsinore one late evening when he picked up a guitar and started singing, "So Cruel" began with the same kind of basic approach to songcraft that gave wings to "She's a Mystery to Me," which he gave to Roy Orbison a few years earlier. Steeped in themes of betrayal, obsession, and possessiveness, this pensive, crooned ballad was another piercing example of love breaking down in U2's world.

This unique three-inch CD format single for "The Fly" was released in the fall of 1991 to the Japanese market, in advance of *Achtung Baby.* It includes the non-LP B-side "Alex Descends into Hell for a Bottle of Milk/Korova I." *U2Wanderer.org*

Released in the fall of 1991 to club DJs, this rare twelve-inch single sleeve boasts the Stereo MCs' remix of "Mysterious Ways"—known as the Ultimatum mix. The flip side features a different reworking of the track by house-music icon Paul Oakenfold and Steve Osborne, who had worked with Manchester dance-rock band the Happy Mondays.

eil.com

Holistic in its original presentation, with acoustic guitar, bass, and an Irish drum called a bodhran, the song—which Bono revealed was also inspired by cabaret and cult singer/songwriter Scott Walker—was an ill stylistic fit for the album in its first incarnation. Reworking the song, Flood magically transformed it into the version heard on *Achtung Baby* through a series of studio manipulations and overdubs.

7. "The Fly": As the first single off of *Achtung Baby*, "The Fly" was an epic musical statement that gave the world its first taste of how the reborn U2 might sound. Written in character, Bono conceived the idea for "The Fly" persona after the foursome's wardrobe manager Fintan Fitzgerald gave the singer an oversized pair of black 1970s "blaxploitation" sunglasses to add some levity to the tension in the studio. With the launch of the album, Bono had embraced "The Fly" fully, with a full black leather outfit, slicked back, shorter hair, a sinister smile and an egotistical wink.

The tune's distorted guitar proclamation, assortment of dance-derived beats and Bono's prose—piled high with "single-line aphorisms"—was instantly received by radio upon its release on October 12, 1991. Lest there be any doubt, the song made it clear, the single was "the sound of four men chopping down *The Joshua Tree*."

Fans in the U.K. were clearly drawn to the song's sonic torrent and undeniably campy refrain, making it the group's second #1 single there. But because it was such a stylistic departure from the material on *Rattle and Hum*, it didn't fare too well at U.S. Top Forty radio, stalling at #61. Still, the burgeoning modern rock radio format played the hell out of it, asserting that U2's leap of artistic faith was in fact accepted by the bulk of the band's audience.

One high-profile friend and fan, David Bowie, didn't love it. According to Bono, when U2 and their teenage hero David Bowie were hanging out one night in 1991, they played the tune for him. When asked what he thought, the brainchild behind Ziggy Stardust told them they should re-record it.

Stemming from "The Lady with the Spinning Head," the song wasn't initially named for Bono's "bullshit philosopher" character or the shades he would don in the studio to lighten the mood, it stemmed from The Edge's energetic axe, which Bono compared to an amplified fly swirling around, buzzing inside one's brain.

8. "Mysterious Ways": Adam Clayton and Edge first came up with the bass line to U2's second single from *Achtung Baby*—which was released on November 25, 1991—in June 1990 when the band was working on its Cole Porter cover, "Night and Day." Built as Edge would say, "from the groove up" with the help of a drum machine, the song's funky guitar riff was the band's take on the Manchester dance-rock movement of the early 1990s.

Strengthened by Larry Mullen's real drumming, Bono took a long time to find the right melody for the song. Nearly titled "Fear of Women," the song at first had lyrics about a man living without romance, but they were soon swapped out for the singsong-y verses Bono scribed.

At one point while working on the track, producer Daniel Lanois and the singer had a severe disagreement over the direction of the tune that lasted two hours and made sound engineer Joe O'Herlihy worried that they would come to blows. In Bono's estimation, however, the incident was just a reflection of Lanois' dedication to the project.

In the end, the struggle was apparently worth it as "Mysterious Ways" was a massive success. Released as a single the week after its parent album, it topped the *Billboard* Modern Rock Tracks and Album Rock Tracks charts, eventually making #9 on the U.S. Hot 100.

9. "Trying to Throw Your Arms Around the World": Inspired by a night of alcohol consumption in Los Angeles, Bono dedicated this number to the drinking establishment that once overserved him, the Flaming Colossus. With lyrics describing a drunken walk home, he wrote them in Australia in 1989 after staying out all night and missing Ali, who was away for a time.

With its stumbling, staggered feel, "Trying to Throw Your Arms Around the World" has touches of Serge Gainsbourg, the French singer/songwriter that members of the band had been exploring leading up to sessions for *Achtung Baby*. It also has one of U2's funniest lyrics, *"A woman needs a man, like a fish needs a bicycle."*

As for the use of alcohol, Bono once explained that by his late twenties he was making up for lost time, after he had kept away from excessive drinking in his teen years. This was his ode to getting home in one piece.

10. "Ultraviolet (Light My Way)": A crumbling relationship also drives the lyrical approach of this song, which may be *Achtung Baby*'s most overlooked track. With its haunting, soulful chorus and deeply moving opening admission, *"Sometimes I feel like checkin' out,"* just one of its many winning disclosures, it's a bleak song with an amazing ethereal feel at first, until it achieves lift off.

This full-page June 1992 ad from the *NME* announced U2's fourth single from *Achtung Baby*. It peaked at #12 in the U.K. singles chart.   *Author's collection*

Fitting then, that Bono has cited it as one of his favorite songs from this era. "Ultraviolet"—one of three tunes that was spun off of "Lady with the Spinning Head"—also marked the first time that U2 incorporated the "baby, baby, baby" rock cliché.

As for its complexities, "Ultraviolet" is not one U2 has played too often. In fact, after it was last played in Dublin in August 1993, the band didn't perform the unwieldy song in its entirety until 2009's 360° Tour.

11. "Acrobat": Another deeply personal song, it's about the fight to persevere as evidenced by the line, *"Don't let the bastards grind you down."* For Bono, he has publicly proclaimed this musical manifesto as another of his favorites from the album.

Replete with the distorted guitar that was so prominent on *Achtung Baby*, "Acrobat" was long on piss and vinegar, as evidenced by its snarling, cynical approach. Despite being a favorite of U2, the group has never been performed it live.

12. "Love Is Blindness": After discovering the musical joys of Frank Sinatra and becoming acquainted with the Chairman of the Board after their 1987 introduction, the influence of Old Blue Eyes made its way onto the closing song of *Achtung Baby*.

The origins of "Love Is Blindness" date to both the sessions for *Rattle and Hum* and U2's 1989 Lovetown Tour of Australia. Bono wrote the song on the piano and first considered sending it to Nina Simone, but the band decided it was a keeper and, with the assistance of producer Brian Eno, it became the ideal ending to what many regard as U2's finest achievement. With lines like, *"Squeeze the handle/blow out the candle,"* Edge once called it "one of Bono's finest lyrics."

Attention Baby

Up until it was nearly complete, U2 wasn't certain what it might be called. Bono remembered U2's soundman Joe O'Herlihy was prone to using the expression "Achtung Baby." When the singer asked about it, O'Herlihy reminded him it was a line from the movie *The Producers*, which the band's crew often watched on tour buses as the band toured the United States.

Translated, it meant, "Attention, baby!" or "Watch out, baby!" By August 1991, Bono had convinced the band it was a superb title because it was memorable, made reference of Germany and suggested childbirth and romance, two of the album's most important themes.

At one point, U2 considered naming the album *Man*, a distinction from the group's 1980 debut *Boy*. The group also purportedly considered *Cruise Down Main Street*—a play on the Rolling Stones' *Exile on Main Street* that was based on the cruise missiles aimed at Baghdad during the Gulf War. *Fear of Women*, *69*, *Zoo Station*, and *Adam* were also in contention before the quartet finally decided on *Achtung Baby*.

Sex Themes

In addition to its abundant themes of heartbreak, *Achtung Baby* has a number of references to oral sex. Consider the lines, *"Surrounding me. Going down on me,"* *"You can swallow or you can spit,"* *"Here she comes, six and nine again,"* and *"Did I leave a bad taste in your mouth?"*

Five Facts About *Achtung Baby*

1. One month before the recording deadline for *Achtung Baby*, Brian Eno felt the band was in crisis and needed a break. He revealed that "everything seemed like a mess." U2 took a two-week break from the album, and when they returned to work at Dogtown, they had a renewed point of view and were more assertive in their decisions.

This auxiliary pressing of *Achtung Baby*'s final single had an orange and yellow color scheme and—unlike its more widely available blue-and-red-schemed counterpart—it features block white letters of the title.

eil.com

2. Contrary to typical promotion and publicity efforts at the time, U2 refused to make advance copies available for the media. Magazines—who typically have a three-month lead time to produce their issues—were out of luck. It was the decision of the group and Island Records to let the fans have the first listen.

3. *Achtung Baby* **was one of the first CDs released** without the cardboard longbox, in an "eco-friendly" cardboard Digipak format and a jewel case. It sold 295,000 copies in the U.S. in its first week of release.

4. When the covers to the "The Fly," and three of the album's four other singles, "Even Better Than the Real Thing," "Who's Gonna Ride Your Wild Horses," and "Mysterious Ways," are arranged, a picture of the band members driving a Trabant—a car produced for the East German market that the band used in its publicity and promotional campaign for the record and subsequent ZooTV Tour—is formed.

5. In 2003, The Edge was named *Rolling Stone*'s twenty-fourth greatest guitarist of all time. "The Fly" was named his essential recording.

November 18, 1991

Response to U2's seventh studio album was overwhelmingly positive after its release on November 18, 1991. But before it pulled down a Grammy Award in 1993 for Best Rock Performance by a Duo or Group with Vocal, it took a short while for fans to absorb, as most of the greatest albums ever made sometimes do. But within three months of release, *Achtung Baby* had sold seven million albums worldwide, eventually selling a staggering eighteen million.

The critical reception to the album was overwhelmingly strong, with *Spin* magazine one of the rare exceptions, calling it an "ambitious failure." But nearly every other significant publication called it a triumph. Jon Pareles of the *New York Times* was at the front of the line, citing U2's "noisy, vertiginous arrangements, mostly layers of guitar" and its ability to "maintain its pop skills" while "defying its old formulas."

Elysa Gardner of *Rolling Stone* gave *Achtung Baby* a rare four-and-a-half-star review, explaining that that U2 had "broaden[ed] its musical palette, but this time its ambitions are realized." In a five-star review, *Q* called it U2's "best" album yet, while *Entertainment Weekly* gave *Achtung Baby* an "A" and described it as a "pristinely produced and surprisingly unpretentious return by one of the most impressive bands in the world."

29

Don't Talk Out of Time

True U2 Stories

St. Columba's

Soon after they became bandmates, Bono agreed to accompany Adam to his former boarding school St. Columba's. Breaking into the school, by going over the wall, Bono met some of Clayton's posh pals. The singer was surprised to discover these wealthy WASP kids were total stoners.

After a brick of hashish made its way out of the breast pocket of a blue-blazered former classmate, Bono realized where Adam had picked up on his lingo. In a room covered with Hendrix and Zeppelin posters, Bono listened to guitars being strummed and hippies rambling on and discovered this was where Adam had picked up terms like "gig" and "jamming."

Bono didn't quite know what to say when he was asked if he had heard the new Jeff Beck album. But he was, just the same, stunned such an environment existed at a place like this.

This Is a Stickup

According to Bono, U2's first road manager Barry Mead, was anxiously carrying $10,000 in earnings in the back of a New York City cab in the spring of 1981 when he was nearly robbed. A burglar fleeing from a seventy-dollar stickup jumped into the taxi and put a gun to the driver's head, and shouted, "Take off!"

"We can't take off!" the driver told the gunman. "We're stuck in traffic!" Before the argument could continue the cops ran up and opened fire on the robber, killing him. Afterward, Mead had to explain why he was in possession of a paper bag filled with so much money.

Aliases

During the *Joshua Tree* Tour, Bono registered in hotels under the alias of "Tony Orlando," which worked perfectly until the night U2 wound up staying in the same spot as the genuine "Tie a Yellow Ribbon" bard. That caused some serious confusion at the front desk!

After that went awry, the man born Hewson began checking in as "Harry Bullocks," but wound up ditching it when his wife Ali objected to being "Mrs. Harry Bullocks." Adam and Larry's respective names weren't nearly as clever: "Maxwell House" and "Mr. T. Bag."

For the ZooTV Tour, Bono had hoped to get his bandmates to agree to adopting the names of the Monkees as hotel pseudonyms. Bono was anxious to be the 1960s TV band's singer, Davy Jones. Adam was fine in the role of Peter Tork, that group's hell raiser, and Edge was an ideal fit for Mike Nesmith, the Monkees' staid guitarist who was also prone to sport a wool hat. But Larry refused to assume the name of Mickey Dolenz, the group's inane drummer.

For the European leg of the tour the following year, hotel reservations were made under the names of Irish fashion models. Bono was Mr. Doody (after Alison Doody), while Edge took Mr. Rocca in honor of Van Morrison's then-girlfriend and future wife Michelle Rocca, the former Miss Ireland.

Van the Man

One evening in the early 1990s, Van Morrison and his collaborator Georgie Fame were visiting Bono's manse, when the former jokingly suggested that Bono had ripped off his breakthrough 1964 hit with Them for *Rattle and Hum*'s lead single.

"That song of yours, 'Desire,' was just 'Gloria' backward, wasn't it?" Morrison asked with a wink. Denying it, Bono chuckled, "I think it was Bo Diddley, actually."

When Van went on to suggest that U2 hadn't done such a fine job with the Bo Diddley beat, Bono asked Van how much of his "original" style was owed to Ray Charles.

Get Out of the Car

One time Bono and his lifelong friend Gavin Friday had been driving in the northern part of Ireland to visit their old buddy Guggi, who had been incarcerated for an undisclosed reason. Working on a play idea called *Melthead* as they drove, and drinking whiskey, they mistakenly found themselves heading into Northern Ireland.

British soldiers jumped out at them with rifles in hand, screaming at them to get out of the car. Soldiers approached the alcohol imbibing musicians, who hesitated getting out of the car. Suddenly they realized who it was.

"Good Lord, It's Bo-no!" they marveled quite elated. After an autograph session they were on their way.

Take Off Your Pants

On a Greenpeace ship en route to U2's early morning protest of the Sellafield 2 nuclear-power plant, a woman on board told Bono—who hadn't been to sleep after the night's concert in Manchester, England—about an empty cabin that was available if he wanted to go lie down for a while.

Appreciative for her assistance, he followed her to the room and then, as he lay down on the cot, she stood next to the exhausted rocker. A short time went by, and then she said to him, "Aren't you going to take off your pants?"

He declined, but the woman was persistent and climbed next to him on the cot. Bono told her that his wife was also on board the ship. The woman offered to get Ali for him while he breathed a sigh of relief.

A half-page advertisement for U2's twelve-inch single, "Desire—The Hollywood Remix." It ran in the October 1, 1988, issue of *Melody Maker*.   *Author's collection*

Ali entered the room and cuddled next to Bono for a few moments. But then the hostess returned and hopped onto the cot with them. In an awkward predicament, the Hewsons decided to skip naptime and rejoined the rest of their entourage on the ship deck.

The Breakfast Club

Bono, Edge, T Bone Burnett, and Kris Kristofferson were once thrown out of the coffee shop in the Beverly Hills Hotel because of their shabby clothes. Bono—who was in pursuit of breakfast on rock-star time—at two o'clock in the afternoon—wondered aloud if the restaurant staff might forgive the jeans if he and his friends ignored the inferior impressionist paintings. A minute or two later, the four of them were kicked to the curb.

Meeting Governor Clinton

In September 1992, after having already spoken to the Democratic Presidential nominee Bill Clinton when he called into U2's appearance on the syndicated radio show *Rockline*, the band and Clinton came face to face. But it was hardly a distinguished meeting when U2 arrived at its Chicago Hotel from a gig in Madison, Wisconsin at 3 AM. The lads were intoxicated and in their stage wear.

Informed that Governor Clinton was also staying at the Ritz-Carlton, Bono started demanding to see the Governor. "Go bring him here!" the singer ordered, but when a member of the U2 road crew attempted to track down the Presidential hopeful, Secret Service agents shut him down. The governor was sleeping.

The next morning, Bill Clinton was notified that U2 had summoned him at the wee hours of the morning. "Why didn't you wake me?" Clinton asked. With the rock stars now in slumberland, the Secret Service detail scurried to try and track down Bono and the boys, waking up manager Paul McGuinness. McGuinness rushed to wake the band.

McGuinness and Edge—who had barely gotten to brush his teeth—accompanied Clinton into Bono's suite, but the singer wasn't there. Within minutes, Edge tracked him down. "Get up," Edge told his smelly frontman, who was still drunk. "Bill Clinton is in your room."

Back in the suite, Bono—with his Fly shades and a small cigar—arrived, much to the amusement of Clinton, who laughed hysterically at the site of the blasted pop star. After an hour together, Larry asked Clinton, point blank, why he would want the job. He responded by saying that he knew the system was corrupt, and wanted to try to make a change.

Backbeat

With his movie-star looks, it's little surprise that U2 drummer Larry Mullen, Jr. was asked to audition for the role of Pete Best, the original Beatles drummer, in a movie called *Backbeat* about the Fab Fours' Hamburg era. Larry wound up turning down the opportunity because of the group's busy ZooTV Tour itinerary.

Focusing on the relationship of Stu Sutcliffe and John Lennon, the 1994 film's music was provided by some of the biggest names in alternative rock's heyday, including Soul Asylum's Dave Pirner, the Afghan Whigs' Greg Dulli, Sonic Youth's Thurston Moore, Gumball's Don Fleming, R.E.M.'s Mike Mills, and Nirvana's Dave Grohl.

Mrs. Charles Bukowski

One night, often-troubled actor and friend Sean Penn had come over to Bono's house. Cocktails and stories continued until 6 AM when U2's frontman told Penn that he was a fan of Charles Bukowski.

Penn quickly picked up the phone and called Los Angeles, and got the *Barfly* writer author on the line. Bukowski—who would die in 1994—was in good spirits, laughing and joking with the singer.

"I've got someone here wants to talk to you," he told the singer, who relayed the story to Flanagan. "It's my wife, Linda. And, by the way, she really wants to fuck you." Flattered but unwilling to take him up on the offer, it turned out she was a U2 fan who'd been to every concert the band had played in LA.

Bull's Blood

After the injuries to his hands that first began on *The Unforgettable Fire* Tour and a subsequent and serious back ailment, Larry Mullen began to take interest in the medical woes of others. For a while, Mullen even carried his own kit bag of pills, powders, and cures.

It's understandable that after the trouble with the tendons in his hands— which could have put an end to his drumming pursuits—Mullen would be this enthusiastic about medicine. Since his hands have been cured, however, he has suffered from brutal back pain stemming from a disk that protrudes from his spine. That was until he came across a miracle cure: bull's blood.

A German holistic healer introduced the idea of shooting bull's blood into his back, which eliminated the drummer's back pain. However, Larry's Dublin-area doctor—examining X-rays of his crooked spine—refused to accept the treatment as effective. But Mullen swore by it, and flew to Germany on a regular basis for his shots in the 1990s.

Paul Is Dead

A music writer once went shopping with Bono, who pulled out his credit card to pay for a gift. The scribe was surprised to learn that neither Bono nor his birth name Paul Hewson appeared on the plastic. The card displayed his initials.

"I don't want people in shops calling me Paul," he supposedly told the journalist. "It suggests an unwarranted familiarity."

When the journalist gave off a surprising look, Bono proudly declared, "Paul is dead."

Dave Grohl Has No Brains

Nirvana drummer Dave Grohl came to a U2 show during the first leg of the ZooTV Tour to visit his friends in the Pixies, the tour's opening act. At the time, Nirvana was on a meteoric rise to fame and Bono invited him in for a chat.

Grohl couldn't understand why the Pixies would want to try opening for U2 in arenas. Bono told him that he thought it was brave of them to give it a shot. The drummer conveyed to him that Nirvana would never play big venues. He insisted that they were just a punk band with a fluke success and felt that it probably wouldn't last. Bono contended that he shouldn't rule the idea out, arguing you never know what you'll want to do in five or ten years. Grohl dismissed the advice, reiterating that Nirvana was just a punk band.

Weeks later, Grohl took to the *NME* insisting that Bono tried to convince Nirvana to change, but they wouldn't do it. "Definitely not the brains of the group," Bono cracked to Flanagan during U2's 1992 tour.

Pavarotti Stalks U2

In the summer of 1995, opera star Luciano Pavarotti was calling Bono almost daily, but Bono ducked his calls. "Tell God to call me back!" the tenor apparently griped. Pavarotti was looking to have Bono write him a song and join him for a performance at his charity concert, slated for that September.

Bono refused the singer's requests, and paid for it with continued calls from the tenor. By July, he and Edge were considering the idea, but the others in the band were still against it.

Days later Pavarotti showed up with a camera crew at U2's Dublin studio. In front of his crew, Bono, Edge, and producer Brian Eno asked him if he would join them on "Miss Sarajevo," one of U2's creations that saw release under the Passengers moniker.

After agreeing to do the song, Bono, Edge, and Eno conceded to perform at Pavarotti's upcoming benefit gig.

Burning for You

When asked to attend the *Q* Awards in London to give a special Merit Award to Shane MacGowan from the Pogues in October 2004, Bono gladly agreed. But when it came time for the U2 singer to participate in a photo session with the hard drinking MacGowan, it almost ended terribly.

As the photographer snapped away backstage, MacGowan had his arm around Bono while carelessly clutching a cigarette. In doing so, he almost set the singer's perfectly coifed hair on fire.

30

Better by Design

Zooropa

Instead of taking a planned six-month break between the 1992 and 1993 legs of its ZooTV Tour, U2 set its sights on making a new EP with four or five tunes to accompany its European summer dates. Originally intended to close out some of the ideas that went unused on *Achtung Baby*, Edge—who had no home to come back to now that his marriage ended—threw himself into the project in an effort to sustain the psychological momentum of the past year and a half.

Bono, too, was anxious to keep working. With Brian Eno and Flood able to help out on relatively short notice at the Factory in Dublin, U2 created what became its eighth proper studio album during the first quarter of 1993. Driven by the enthusiastic reception of its predecessor, *Zooropa* continued the band's fusion of rock and roll and electronica, and marked the act's first studio disc without the help of Daniel Lanois—who was promoting his own solo album—since 1983's *War*.

Time constraints forced U2 to write and record efficiently, eliminating much of the studio improvisation of past works. Although the band worked very hard, the album was incomplete when the guys headed back out onto the road in May 1993 for the European leg of their ZooTV initiative. This forced the band to fly back to Dublin on its off days to continue working until it wrapped up the project at the end of that month. Speaking about it later, Adam Clayton described the grueling schedule in *U2 at the End of the World* as "about the craziest thing you could do to yourself."

Payday

In June 1992, U2 and Island Records announced an extension of the band's record deal, which gave the label rights to U2's next six albums in exchange for a $60 million pay out, or a $10 million advance per album.

The band—which was already pondering where its next recordings might go creatively—also scored an unheard-of twenty-five percent royalty rate on every album sold, making them the highest-paid rock act in recorded music history.

"Island Records and their owner Chris Blackwell have stood behind U2 since the second he heard them," Paul McGuinness said in a statement. "We are extremely pleased to stay with a company that believes in us. We couldn't be happier."

Rock Toss

Nearly named *Squeaky*, the disc that became *Zooropa* was very much an alternative to the angst-driven grunge rock that was at its heyday in 1993. This was by design, as the group unanimously decided to push all of the overtly guitar-driven rock and roll songs like "Wake Up Dead Man" and "If God Will Send His Angels" to the side in favor of an experimental pop album.

"Realizing, 'Oh, this is not a rock album,' is a big relief," Bono told Flanagan. "The world is sick of macho, sick of grunge. We need to get a female perspective in." The album took on a very European vibe, as its title indicated, that was bolstered by electronic touches.

1. "Zooropa": "Zooropa" was the outcome of combining two song ideas—one which was conceived in the studio and another which came from a soundcheck recording during the ZooTV Tour. With lyrics penned by Bono describing two characters in a brightly lit futurist European city—with a look similar to Tokyo—the song includes ad slogans taken from an array of advertisements.

"Vorsprung durch Technik" came from an Audi advertisement and translates as "Advancement through technology," while the U.S. Army and United Airlines were the source of the lines "Be all that you can be" and "Fly the friendly skies," respectively. Elsewhere, Colgate ("Ring of confidence"), Daz's "Bluey white" ("A bluer kind of white"), and Fairy's "Mild green Fairy liquid" ("We're mild and green and squeaky clean") round out the song. U2's own slogan "Dream out loud" was also incorporated into the tune, full of themes of commercialism and moral confusion.

Not only the album's title track, the futuristic feeling "Zooropa" was also the theme song of the fourth leg of the ZooTV Tour and the setting for the album's concept, which was based on an attractive and united Europe of the future.

The song itself is launched by a two-minute introduction the band dubbed "Babble," which was written and performed by Larry, who created it entirely separate from the rest of the tune. The album's closing song,

"The Wanderer" has been previously cited by the band as the antidote to the ultra-modern opening track.

2. "Babyface": "Babyface" finds Bono serenading a "cover girl with natural grace." A comment on the propensity for voyeurism among television junkies, it specifically chronicles a man who upholds his obsessive love for a celebrity by manipulating her image on a TV recording.

"It's about watching and not being in the picture," Bono told *Hot Press* in 1993. "About how people play with images, believing you know somebody through an image—and thinking that by manipulating a machine that in fact controls you, you can have some kind of power. It's about the illusion of being in control."

While there's no word on whether it's based on the lives of its supermodel friends like Christy Turlington, Helena Christensen, and Naomi Campbell, it's an eerie idea in any case.

According to The Edge, the initial idea behind the song was based on the 1991 Gulf War coverage on CNN, where the world became desensitized to the slaughter. "It had reduced a terrible human catastrophe to the level of a take-it-or-leave-it video game," he marveled in *U2 by U2*. "What's on television tonight? Shit, they're showing more bombs on Baghdad. Turn it off. Boooooring."

3. "Numb": An unusual choice for the album's first single, the industrial rock touched "Numb" is a rarity in the U2 camp because it boasts The Edge on lead vocals with backing vocals by Bono in his "Eartha Kitt" falsetto. Lyrically, it's a bombardment of monotone orders (*"Don't grab/don't clutch/don't hope for too much"*) sustained musically by a variety of samples, from arcade sounds to the noisy drumming of a young Hitler Youth in Leni Riefenstahl's 1936 Nazi propaganda film *Triumph of the Will*.

Based on an *Achtung Baby* demo called "Down All the Days," its instrumental backing is bolstered by a layer of keyboards courtesy of Brian Eno. With the quickly written lyrics delivered in an almost percussive manner and the first-ever backing vocals of Larry Mullen, Jr., "Numb" was unlike any song U2 had ever concocted. But the song was clearly a novelty, as evidenced by the fact it only made #39 on the U.S. Top Forty. Although it marks a moment in time, it hasn't endured with U2 fans.

4. "Lemon": Written late in the *Zooropa* sessions, "Lemon" originated with a rhythmic foundation The Edge conjured up with a bass guitar and drum machine. The musician struggled to find a traditional guitar part until he found a unique "gated" effect that worked.

As for Bono's part, he was hoping to deliver a vocal reminiscent of Prince. Lyrically it was written with his mother in mind after he had received early Super 8 footage of Iris Hewson, aged twenty-four, in the mail from a distant relative. At the time, she had been a maid of honor in a wedding and wore a lemon-yellow dress. The footage also inspired lines about using film to preserve the moments in one's life.

Stylistically, "Lemon" defies U2 of yore, and has been called "futuristic German disco." The second single from the album, it topped the Hot Dance Music Club Play survey after house music giant Paul Oakenfold remixed it. But as far as mainstream success goes, "Lemon" was far too adventurous for rock or pop audiences.

5. "Stay (Faraway, So Close!)": "Stay (Faraway, So Close!)" was supposedly inspired by the music of Frank Sinatra—so much so that the song's initial title was "Sinatra." With a verse melody dating back to the group's 1990 Berlin sessions, Edge came up with some "old-school chord progressions, trying to summon up the spirit of Sinatra" on the piano.

Finished at the urgency of Wim Wenders, who had a film of the same name, the version on the soundtrack is almost two minutes longer than the *Zooropa* version, and has an edgier guitar and drum performance.

Bono has cited "Stay" as one of his favorite U2 songs, and believes it to be one of its most underrated. The fifth track from *Zooropa* was stylistically similar to U2's *Achtung Baby* ballads, and was the disc's third single. Released on November 22, 1993, the song peaked at #4 in the U.K. but stalled at #61 in the U.S.

6. "Daddy's Gonna Pay for Your Crashed Car": Originally conceived as a blues song, Bono had hoped to have John Lee Hooker sing it one day. In its final version, "Daddy's Gonna Pay for Your Crashed Car" is what Bono called "industrial blues," with lyrics written about a heroin addict who is "protected from the consequences of her own actions by an indulgent sugar daddy."

Introduced by a pre-recorded fanfare sampled from the album *Lenin's Favorite Songs*, the track proudly samples "The City Sleeps" by electronica purveyor MC 900 Ft. Jesus.

A song about being strung out, it depicts an image of an area of Berlin, near Hansa Studios, where gypsies and homeless people live. "When we were there it was like a surreal junkyard," Bono told *Uncut*, describing parts of tanks and wrecked cars and stray dogs in the heart of what had once been one of the greatest cities in Europe. "That's where the crashed-car imagery came from."

7. "Some Days Are Better Than Others": "I think that's just one of those songs, it's like a summer song, it's just fun," Bono explained of the memorable, modern tack of "Some Days Are Better Than Others." The song is also something of a confessional.

"There's a bit of owning up too," he revealed, singing lines like *"Some days I feel like a bit of a baby."* If some of the lines seem like throwaways, Bono's lyric *"Some days you use more force than necessary"* is one that sticks.

8. "The First Time": A pensive song, "The First Time" is a confessional number initially inspired by the singing of Al Green. But when the tune arrived in its soul-baring and sparsely executed form, it was hardly the up song Bono had originally intended it to be.

Although Bono had insisted his faith was intact, the song was about losing it, if even for a moment. Recognizing that a lot of people had those feelings, at first U2 didn't think it was a good fit for the album and put it to the side. But the song—about a prodigal son who falls into a life of sin before asking for forgiveness—stuck around and made the final cut.

Listening to it now, "The First Time" definitely sounds out of place—it has the feel of a *Joshua Tree* B-side or something off of *Rattle and Hum*. Which could be why the typically eccentric Brian Eno loved the song, and when he insisted on keeping it on the album, U2 acquiesced.

9. "Dirty Day": Emerging from an in-studio jam, "Dirty Day" was written about a man who left his family only to return many years after and meet the child he abandoned.

Released as a VHS single in June 1993, "Numb," the U2 anomaly counting Edge on lead vocals was a unique move for the time, but one that didn't really catch on in the industry. The single also included a haunting video of the *Achtung Baby* track "Love Is Blindness." *U2Wanderer.org*

U2 NUMB

3 TRACK VIDEO

Based lyrically around phrases Bob Hewson used, including, *"I don't know you and you don't know the half of it,"* and *"It won't last kissing time,"* the title, too, came from one of Bono's dad's favorites: *"It's a dirty day."*

10. "The Wanderer": The final track on *Zooropa* counts Johnny Cash on lead vocals with harmony from The Edge. Contrary to popular belief, Bono is nowhere to be heard on the song. Tracked by Cash in Dublin during a February 1993 tour stop, it was Bono who imagined the country legend singing the song. Cash had previously worked on a tune with Bono called "Ellis Island."

Portraying a man searching for God after the Apocalypse, the uniquely arranged tune has no guitar. Adam Clayton's synthesized bass line and Larry Mullen's drumming underpin the song. Originally titled "Johnny Cash on the Moon," U2's producer Flood said the Man in Black's appearance on the album's closing number was ideal.

"If you imagine the album being set in this place: *Zooropa*," Flood said to Dave Urbanski in the 2003 book *The Man Comes Around: The Spiritual Journey of Johnny Cash*. "Just when you're expecting the norm to finish the album, you get somebody who's outside the whole thing, wandering through, discussing it. It's like the perfect full stop. It throws a whole different light on the conceptualization of the record."

Critical and Commercial Reception

Response to *Zooropa* was remarkably positive in the U.S., where critics were especially pleased with the disc. The *O.C. Register* called it the band's "best album since *The Joshua Tree*," but if that sounded like a stretch, the *Chicago Sun-Times* critic Jim DeRogatis wrote, "It's satisfying and surprising to hear a band of U2's status being so playful, experimental, and downright weird."

At home, the *Irish Independent* was less appreciative of the disc, writing, "The songs sound like they were knocked up in double-quick time and with about as much thought put into the lyrics as goes into a DJ's time check." Regardless, the album topped the U.S. and U.K. album surveys as fans turned out in record shops to pay their respects.

31

Ain't Love the Sweetest Thing?

U2's Personal Lives

Bono's Private Life

O n August 21, 1982, Bono married Alison Stewart at a ceremony at the Guinness Church of Ireland in Raheny, Dublin. Reverend Jack Heaslip—who first met Bono and Ali while serving as a guidance counselor at Mount Temple—officiated their nuptials; and the Shalom's Chris Rowe—who still retained a bond with the singer—provided the sermon.

Surprisingly, Bono selected Adam Clayton, and not his lifelong friend Guggi—with whom he had become distanced from—to be his best man. Bono made the decision after speaking to the bassist about marriage. Having found the woman he wanted to spend the rest of his life with, Adam advised him to go for it. Bono also admitted that he asked Adam—who behaved like a perfect gentleman—to stand up for him because he was looking to close a gap between the two of them. He wanted to be as close to the bassist as he was to the others in U2.

The reception was held at the Sutton House Hotel, with musical accompaniment by a local band known as the Cyclones. During the party, U2 assumed the wedding band's instruments for a cover of "Tutti Frutti." Later in the evening, all of the fuses in the building gave way to darkness.

For their honeymoon, the newlywed Hewsons spent two weeks in Jamaica at Chris Blackwell's "Goldeneye" estate, named for its former owner, James Bond brainchild Ian Fleming. Bono utilized part of his time in paradise writing lyrics to the songs for an album called *War*.

After seven years of marriage, Bono and Ali became parents for the first time, when Jordan, or Jo Jo as her daddy would come to call her, was born on May 10, 1989. She arrived on Bono's twenty-ninth birthday. At the time Ali went into labor, U2 had been working at STS studios. When she picked the singer up at the studio, he wasn't sure she should be driving, but Ali wanted to be in control of the situation. A model of preparedness, she packed her husband a flask of whiskey and something to read.

Before the baby's birth, which the frontman later called "really psyche-delic," Bono had noticed that the heartbeat monitor sounded as if it was slowing down. A doctor at Mount Carmel Hospital was called in and Jo Jo was born.

On July 7, 1991, Bono and Ali had a second daughter, Memphis Eve. Eight years later, on August 18, 1999, a son, Elijah Bob Patricius Guggi Q Hewson, was born. A second son, John Abraham, arrived on May 21, 2001.

Edge's Private Life

The Edge met his first wife Aislinn O'Sullivan at a Dublin gig headlined by the Buzzcocks, a punk band from Manchester, England, in 1978. Although he first saw Aislinn at his band's own show weeks earlier, it was took some time before he came up with enough courage to talk to her.

They dated for five years and were married in a Catholic mass held in Enniskerry on July 12, 1983, that took place when U2 a month off from roadwork in support of *War*. The guitarist picked U2's frontman Bono to be his best man.

Because Edge was Protestant, he was required to attend Catholic educa-tion classes and counseling from the Roman Catholic church before they could be married. Although the band had started to show a profit, little of the money had made its way back to the members yet. As a result, and in keeping with tradition, Aislinn's father financed the event.

Afterward the couple elected to honeymoon in Sri Lanka, but days into their trip a civil war broke out there. They perilously traveled back to their hotel after an exploratory car trip only to discover all foreign guests had been evacuated.

Later, after ten years of marriage ended in divorce, The Edge observed jokingly, "All of this was unfortunately portentous of how the marriage would go."

Edge and Aislinn first became parents to a daughter, Hollie, on July 4, 1984. A second daughter, Arran, arrived on October 15, 1985.

In 1989, despite hints in the press by Edge that theirs was a complicated union that had seen its share of struggles, the Evans became parents to a third child, Blue Angel, on June 26.

Around Easter 1991, The Edge and Aislinn—who had been having mari-tal difficulties for years—decided to split up for good. He wound up moving out of the family's home, leaving his three children with their mother. The split was quite hard on The Edge, and the U2 camp in general because Aislinn had long been part of the group's extended family.

They ceased functioning as a couple, prompting the guitarist to move in with Adam Clayton for a few weeks that spring. He wound up settling in a cottage up from the bassist's main house for several months. Facing the failure of his marriage after counseling didn't work, Edge threw himself into songwriting and learning technical aspects of record making as a means to distract him from the upheaval in his life.

The stress and anguish of the separation was felt by all in the U2 camp. The complicated issues of relationships would shape the tone of 1991's *Achtung Baby* and the lyrics Bono crafted for it. It was a side of Edge the others in U2 had never seen.

Due to Irish laws against divorce, which was illegal until 1995. The Edge and Aislinn remained betrothed until a divorce was granted in 1996. By this time, the guitarist was already long involved with Morleigh Steinberg, a professional dancer and choreographer hired by the band a belly dancer in 1992 for its ZooTV Tour. Steinberg had previously appeared in U2's "With or Without You" video.

In 1993, they began dating seriously and were a couple for several years, becoming parents to a daughter Sian, who was born on October 15, 1997, in Los Angeles while Edge was en route to the hospital by plane from Israel during the band's PopMart Tour. A son, Levi, was born on October 25, 1999.

In June 2002, Edge and Morleigh married in a civil service at a Dublin registry office, with Bono standing up for Edge as best man once again. A public wedding ceremony followed at the Garden of Eze in southern France. It was held at the ruins of a medieval castle near to where both Edge and Bono co-owned an estate. In addition to the band, R.E.M.'s Michael Stipe, Eurythmics guitarist Dave Stewart, Dennis Hopper, and supermodels Helena Christensen and Christy Turlington were among the one hundred or so guests.

Larry's Private Life

Although U2 drummer Larry Mullen, Jr. isn't married, he has been with the same partner since the mid-1970s, when he met Ann Acheson in their first year at Mount Temple school. "She was the popular girl, I was the moody kid holding up walls," he remembered in U2's official book.

Starting off as friends, they became serious; and once the band took off, Larry found himself missing her dearly. While Mullen tended to keep his private life private, this much is known: the couple became parents to a son, Aaron Elvis—named in honor of the legendary performer Elvis Aaron Presley—on October 4, 1995. A daughter Ava was born on December 28, 1998; and a daughter named Anya followed on February 8, 2001.

Larry is also fond of Yellow Labrador Retrievers and has acknowledged his dogs JJ and Missy on U2's albums.

Adam's Private Life

Adam Clayton has never married, remaining a bachelor for his thirty-plus-year career with U2. Clayton did date British-born supermodel Naomi Campbell after Bono introduced them in early 1993. Their relationship was tabloid fare for much of that year, becoming public knowledge when they were spotted out at a Duran Duran concert in Dublin. The couple hit it off instantly and wound up becoming engaged over the telephone in 1993 while he was in London and she was in New York.

That May, Adam told the media—who have tracked the couple down at his Dublin area home—"I just knew from the very first moment that this was it." They set a wedding date of September 14, 1993. When that date passed, Campbell told *Entertainment Weekly* in October, "It's safe to say [we'll marry] sometime in the New Year. We've not had time to think because Adam's on tour and I'm working." By May 1994, Clayton confirmed they had split up.

Fast forward to April 2006 and Adam and his girlfriend of a decade, Suzanne Smith, a one-time employee in U2's Principle Management, announced they would be married sometime in the year, after becoming engaged on Valentine's Day. By March 2007, however, he and Susie had revealed to the Irish media that they had split on amicable terms.

32

Space Junk Coming in for the Splash

Ten Totally Random U2 Facts

1. Bono has said that his favorite lyric in a country song is the Kris Kristofferson tune, "Help Me Make It Through the Night."

2. "Amazing Grace" is one of Bono's favorite religious songs.

3. Bono is mum on the topic of drugs. "If I ever had so much as a spliff, I would not talk about it, because it's too easy a headline: BONO DENIES SMOKING JOINT, BONO ADMITS SMOKING JOINT. It's an invitation to a debate that I'm not interested in."

4. On U2's Boy Tour, Larry always brought a sleeping bag. "We stayed in bed and breakfasts ranging from the sublime to the ridiculous," he explained on U2.com. "The final straw was the nylon sheets with little grime balls on them. It was time to buy a sleeping bag."

5. On that same tour, Edge got hooked on the video game Space Invaders. "We would call into the motorway service stations to have something to eat, spend ten minutes eating some dodgy sandwich then spend the rest of the time in the arcade playing Space Invaders."

6. During a May 1993 tour stop in Rotterdam, Gavin Friday surprised his friend Bono with a unique thirty-third birthday gift. On his hotel bed he placed an eight-foot-tall cross, painted blue, with HAIL BONO, KING OF THE ZOOS inscribed on the top. Bono had the cross blessed and flown back to Dublin.

7. Bono, Larry, and Edge all started smoking in their late twenties. Explaining it to *Rolling Stone* in 1993, Bono said, "When people are staring at you all the time, smoking a cigarette can give you something to do."

8. In September 1994, Bono paid £35,000 for Charlie Chaplin's uniform from the 1940 film *The Great Dictator* at a Sotheby's auction in London. He planned to display it at Mr. Pussy's Café Deluxe, a cabaret café in Dublin owned by the singer Gavin Friday and movie director Jim Sheridan.

9. After U2's widely heralded 2002 Super Bowl Half Time performance in New Orleans, U2 and some friends took in a dinner in the city's French Quarter to celebrate. For some reason, Bono—who is allergic to red wine—decided to have a glass anyway. As a result, he was eventually found passed out on the restaurant's bathroom floor.

10. Adam Clayton won't go on tour without his favorite brand of Irish tea bags. "Barry's decaffeinated tea bags," Adam announced during the band's 2009 tour. "I know it sounds crazy, but if you don't travel with your own tea, it never tastes the same."

33

Jesus Never Let Me Down

U2 and Religion

When Bono was fourteen he sought the comfort of God after he lost his mother. At Mount Temple School, he became involved in Bible study and then, later, found his calling with the band that would become U2. When the quartet took form, it gave him the idea of becoming a Christian to go into battle.

But if his calling, which would also fit into the lives of The Edge and Larry, left Adam—who rejected their Christian focus and was clearly in it for the fringe benefits—outside of their circle, the bassist respected the importance of religion as a source of inspiration.

The Early Years

Despite being a deeply committed Christian, the Presbyterian-raised singer shunned church-going in U2's early years. "I think the church is a big problem," Bono told Gavin Martin in 1981, sharing the belief that that Christianity was often grossly misinterpreted. At this time, he, Edge, and Larry were still involved with the Shalom, a religious group they had been active with since 1978.

"They were expectant of signs and wonders; lived a kind of early-church religion," Bono said of the Shalom in *U2: An Irish Phenomenon*. "It was a commune. People who had cash shared it. They were passionate, and they were funny, and they seemed to have no material desires."

But in the wake of the group's achievements behind the *Boy* album, the Shalom had been increasingly critical of their chosen profession and the music they created and listened to. Things got intense and it nearly divided the band, but U2's U.S. tour commitment in late 1981 gave the group an out.

By July 1983, however, the deeply spiritual Bono—back from an extensive tour of the televangelist-addled United States—continued to question organized religion. "I'm frightened by [it]," he told *Hot Press.* "I've seen what it's done to [Ireland]. I've seen what it's done to people around me," referencing the way religion was approached in his largely Roman Catholic homeland: as a means of power and a way of controlling people's lives.

"I go to America and I turn on my television set and I start sweating profusely because those guys have turned faith into an industry," he continued. "It's appalling. It's ugly." The raving lunatics who appeared on hotel TV screens—think Jerry Falwell and Jimmy Swaggart—scared U2. The words coming out of the mouths of hucksters looking to fatten their pockets with the money sent in by the elderly and destitute came from the same Scriptures the band was using onstage and in the press. This sickened U2, prompting the group to clam up in interviews when it came to the topic of spirituality.

Spirituality in the Music

If organized religion left Bono cold, even as a lad, he knew the power of hymns like "When I Survey the Wondrous Cross" and "Be Thou My Vision." In early U2 material—most noticeably on *October*—a spiritual intimacy could be heard and felt. Aged nineteen to twenty-one at the time, most rock bands would be writing about cars, bars, and women.

In U2's world, rock and roll—long branded as the devil's music—and God could be compatible. It wasn't an either/or scenario, as Bono's influences asserted. From Patti Smith's rendition of Them's "Gloria," where she inserts the line *"Jesus died for somebody's sins/But not mine,"* to Bob Dylan's born-again efforts *Slow Train Coming* and *Saved.*

Meanwhile, spiritual music like Bob Marley and the Wailers and Marvin Gaye taught the band just how uptight much of white rock music was. In 1985, Bono told *Rolling Stone* that "Sadomasochism is not taboo in rock and roll. Spirituality is."

In the years to follow, Bono's spiritual observations in song would become far more subtle than they had in 1981, with rare exception. 1997's "Wake Up Dead Man" from *Pop*, for instance finds the singer pleading with God to save us all: *"Jesus, Jesus help me, I'm alone in this world/and a fucked up world it is too."*

Christianity Today

By *Achtung Baby*, the band had long since gotten away from wearing its Christian beliefs on its sleeve. Looking back on U2's "out-there" spiritual phase, captured for posterity on *October*, the group's outlook had changed considerably.

Sure the band's faith was still in place, but the group had no time or interest for the rules of the religious world. Drinking, smoking, sexual relationships, or what you wore or how you looked didn't fit into U2's definition of what constituted a life of faith. The men of U2 still acknowledged that their musical abilities were gifts from God, and they respected and cherished what that meant.

Social Justice

As far back as 1987, Bono was expressing his frustration with Evangelicals who were removed from the wider world and the need for global social justice. Self-professed Christians who weren't doing their part to help the greater good by investing in AIDS treatment and research and helping starving children were empty in his eyes.

"Why, in the West, do we spend so much money on extending the arms race instead of wiping out malaria, which could be eradicated given ten minutes' worth of the world's arms budget?" he told David Breskin during *The Joshua Tree* era. "To me, we are living in the most un-Christian times. When I see these racketeers, the snake-oil salesmen on these right-wing television stations, asking for not your twenty dollars or your fifty dollars but your one hundred dollars in the name of Jesus Christ, I just want to throw up."

His commitment to the poor was stronger than ever nearly two decades later. Throughout his forties, Bono was leading the cause for AIDS relief and Dropping the Debt in Africa, acting on his faith.

Bono's Beliefs

Bono has said that he feels most relaxed and at home in the black church. He has a distrust of other believers—they make him uncomfortable. He finds solace in prayer and meditation, and makes time each day to do so. He also respects atheists for having the courage not to believe in God, and once revealed most of his friends were non-believers.

As for his concept of God, the singer told the *Dubliner* in 2005, "If I could put it simply, I would say that I believe there's a force of love and logic in the world, a force of love and logic behind the universe. And I believe in the poetic genius of a creator who would choose to express such unfathomable power as a child born in 'straw poverty'; i.e., the story of Christ makes sense to me." He has said that the Bible sustains him as both a belief and a source of creativity.

When asked in recent years who he admired most in this world, Bono responded, "The person I most admire is Jesus Christ."

Afterlife

Bono also told the *Dubliner* that he'd be disappointed "if this is all there is."

"I love the idea of hell as a flame that will burn away all the crap and only the precious stones will remain," he explained. "I think that's probably where things get evened out and I think that's probably what the idea of 'the first shall be last' means, that if you have spent your whole life accumulating material things and material ideas about yourself, you will be left with very little."

Foreword Thinker

In October 1998, Canongate Publishing announced that Bono had agreed to write an introduction to the Book of Psalms for its upcoming Bible series. According to the publishers, Bono earned just $1,440 for his 1,500-word essay. In 2002, Bono wrote another foreword for the Adam Harbinson book *They've Hijacked God*, which is a scathing examination of organized religion.

34

I See an Expression

U2's Essential Music Videos

"Gloria" Video

Although its album failed to crack *Billboard*'s Top 100 during the initial promotional run, U2 began to see its first real exposure on MTV, a new music video cable channel that launched on August 1, 1981, but was still only available in select markets.

Shot on a barge in the Dublin docks, U2's first official music video was directed by Meiert Avis. It was a significant element in the band's success at this stage, when radio support of "Gloria" in America was spotty.

With the advent of MTV, U2 had found an uneven concert draw. In cities where the network was carried on local cable systems, the band could book bigger venues and draw sellout crowds. In cities where "Gloria" couldn't be seen, U2 was strictly a club act.

The band was stunned when it played the Hollywood Palladium in Los Angeles on the tour, where it pulled in four thousand fans. It had MTV, which had twenty-four hours to fill and a small library of clips at the time, to thank for putting its clip in constant rotation. Of course, MTV in return had U2 to thank for one of the coolest music videos at the time.

"New Year's Day" Video

With the decision of U2 and Island Records to release "New Year's Day" as the lead single from *War*, and based on the increasing popularity of the music video medium, the band shot a video for the song in Konserthuset, Stockholm on December 15, 1982. Having flown by helicopter to the Salen ski resort, the group was shot standing in snow lip-synching the song under the grey Scandinavian skies.

The next day, shooting continued outside of Oslo, Norway, where female stand-ins were shot riding in the snow on horseback. This was done U2's insurance was limited and wouldn't cover any injuries the group might incur.

Interspersed with footage of tanks and other war imagery, plus aerial shots of the arctic forestry, Larry whacked a lone snare drum, while Edge and Adam mimed performances on their unplugged guitars. Because Bono refused to wear the extreme weather gear, such as the wool hats and long underwear that his bandmates opted for—he wanted to resemble himself—his mouth nearly froze up.

"Where the Streets Have No Name"

On March 27, 1987, U2 shot a promotional video for "Where the Streets Have No Name," the *Joshua Tree* album-opener which had been picking up steam on U.S. rock stations. While filming the clip atop a downtown Los Angeles rooftop, the quartet attracted thousands of fans to the streets below, because area radio stations and local newscasts erroneously announced a free, impromptu concert by the band.

As depicted in the video, the Chief of Police became concerned that morning when he heard these announcements on the way to the office. When the crowds became what the LAPD determined to be dangerous and excessive, the band received word that the plug was about to be pulled on the event. Hence Bono's infamous announcement at the start of the clip, "I think we're being shut down."

Often compared to the Beatles' Apple rooftop performance, U2 has always maintained that its similar approach wasn't intentional. It picked the city environment because it signified the song's message of, what Bono referred to as, "a feeling of escape from an urban situation."

Acknowledging that save for Hollywood and the Sunset Strip, very little of Los Angeles had been seen by the rest of the world, the group wanted to give this fascinating—if not crime-addled and rough—area of the city the exposure it felt it deserved. The result—which was an instant MTV favorite when it premiered several weeks later—may just be the band's most memorable video eve r.

Achtung Videos

A clip for "The Fly" was shot by Jon Klein and Ritchie Smyth in Dublin and on the streets of London in September 1991. The directors were ecstatic to be part of the band's new sound.

"What we want to do here is start a new chapter," Klein said to *Propaganda* at the time. "'The Fly' feels different to me."

Meanwhile, the following month, "Mysterious Ways" was filmed in Fez, Morocco in October 1991. The clip for U2's second single was directed by Stephane Sednaoui.

Three for "One"

U2 shot three videos for the song, "One," beginning with a shoot helmed by Anton Corbijn and filmed in Berlin in February 1992. The clip featured Bono's father Bob Hewson in a starring role, with the members of U2 appearing in drag as an extension of some of the photos the director had taken of the band for the *Achtung Baby* album art. Several Trabants, which would become a fixture of its ZooTV trek, were shot travelling through the city.

A second clip, directed by Mark Pellington, was designed to pay homage to David Wojnarowicz, a gay artist and friend of U2's that had died of AIDS. The clip, which features flowers in bloom and footage of buffaloes running over a hill—imagery that originates from a photo Wojnarowicz had taken—gave the song headline exposure but little airtime on MTV. On a related note, royalties for the "One" single were donated by the band to AIDS research.

Lastly, a third video of the song was shot by Phil Joanou, the director of the band's *Rattle and Hum* film. Lensed at Nell's, a Manhattan bar, in March 1992, the clip interspersed shots of Bono drinking beer and smoking a thin cigar while lip synching the tune. It also featured footage of the band in performance.

"Even Better"

Hoping to get most of its music video responsibilities out of the way before the ZooTV Tour launched at the end of February 1992, U2 joined up with one-time 10cc-member-turned-director Kevin Godley to shoot "Even Better Than the Real Thing" in the middle of the month.

The clip was shot in a Carnaby Street clothing store, with the band performing in the shop window while fans watched from the sidewalk. A U2 lookalike act, the Doppelgangers, were also on hand for the shoot, which intertwined footage of the real group with its imposters.

"Numb"

Kevin Godley was again called in on short notice to shoot a video for "Numb," the first single off of *Zooropa*. For the clip, Edge—the lead vocalist—was placed in front of the camera and began to lip-sync the words as Adam blew smoke in his face, his shoulders were massaged, his face was poked, he was kissed and licked by two beautiful women, and spoon-fed yogurt.

As the shoot continued, Edge was treated to a belly dance, feet on his face, pictures with fans, and slaps on the face by little kids.

"Beautiful Day"

Shot in August 2000 at Paris' Charles de Gaulle International Airport, the video for "Beautiful Day" was directed by Jonas Akerlund. Featuring U2's members performing on the runway, as planes took off and landed above them, the clip was a smash on VH1 in the United States, where it ranked at the top of its weekly video countdown.

Watching closely, jets belonging to Air France and Middle East Airlines were captured by Akerlund while the group—atop an Oriental rug—rocked out to the tune.

Boasting the photographic art of American David Wojnarowicz, this cover picture depicts how Indians would hunt buffalo, resulting in them running over cliffs. According to the inlay card on the CD single, Wojnarowicz identified with the buffalo and felt pushed into the unknown by forces beyond his control. The artist—who had been infected with the H.I.V. virus and ultimately died in July 1992—was outspoken on the AIDS crisis. Released in March of that year, U2 donated its royalties from "One" to AIDS research. The second of three music videos made for the song, which was directed by Mark Pellington, includes slow-motion footage of buffaloes running and also incorporates the "Falling Buffalo" photograph.

eil.com

35

I Never Bought
a Lotto Ticket

Pop

In October 1995, U2 and Brian Eno began thinking about a proper
follow up to *Zooropa*. Although Larry Mullen was about to undergo
back surgery in New York and would be recuperating until Christmas,
the group moved forward with early recording sessions in Dublin the following month. The plan was to continue its reinvention by continuing to
explore its modern rock- and dance-influenced approaches.

On the heels of the Passengers project, however, Eno stepped aside. *Pop*
would become the first U2 studio album since 1983's *War*—save for *Rattle
and Hum*—to be made without Eno's guidance.

An array of record producers were lined up, including Flood, Steve
Osborne, Howie B, and Nellee Hooper, and the band got to work on the
album at Hanover Quay, Windmill Lane, and the Works studios. However,
as work continued into 1996, the band found itself facing the pressures of a
self-imposed deadline after Paul McGuinness began booking a tour itinerary
before the record had been completed.

When its creativity stalled five months into the project, the band considered a trip to Cuba in April 1996, but instead settled on Miami. The following month, with the hope that the change of environment might help U2
develop some solid songs and possibly move the band in a new direction, it
left for Florida. By the end of May, however, the guys had just one new song
to show for their time at South Beach Studios.

Back in Dublin, the band worked through the summer but ultimately
conceded in late August 1996 that its ninth studio effort wouldn't be out
in November as fans and Island Records had hoped. Holed up at Hanover
Quay Studios, U2 felt under the gun to complete the album by the end of
the year, even if it meant it didn't believe completely in its final outcome.

To make matters worse, the band and its label weren't exactly communicating. When the *Los Angeles Times* reported that U2's next disc was bumped to 1997, an Island spokesperson told the paper, "As far as we're concerned, we still have a U2 record this year."

Polygram—Island's parent company—wasn't quiet about the fact that it was upset that it didn't have a new U2 album. For its stockholders, it meant the company was going to be millions of dollars short of its year-end projections.

But McGuinness wasn't quiet either, telling the *Guardian*, "I believe Polygram respects the creativity of the band. The problem with the delay in the album is that forecasts are made and expectations generated [but] the creative process is imprecise."

When the album, to be called *Pop*, was finally finished on November 20, the band got cracking on upcoming B-sides and decided to record the Beatles' "Happiness Is a Warm Gun" before it worked on plans for the PopMart Tour.

Fans visiting the group's official website were met with the image of its studio-cam fixed on a markerboard that claimed ELVIS HAS HACKED HIS WAY OUT OF THE BUILDING. The album was dedicated to its longtime fan, Bill Graham. The *Hot Press* writer/editor and co-founder died during the making of the disc.

Defending its title, Bono would tell U2.com, "I thought *Pop* was a term of abuse, it seemed sort of insulting and lightweight. I didn't realize how cool it was. Because some of the best music does have a lightweight quality, it has a kind of oxygen in it, which is not to say it's emotionally shallow. We've had to get the brightly colored wrapping paper right, because what's underneath is not so sweet."

Internet Leak

U2's *Pop*, as it would be known, became one of the first recordings ever to suffer from an internet leak when, on October 26, 1996, a U2 fan based in Hungary made clips of two new songs, "Discothèque" and "Wake Up Dead Man" available for fans to hear. But the buzz on the tracks built quickly across the World Wide Web, as radio stations played the snippets as a means to give listeners a taste of what the band had up its sleeve.

The clips on the Hungarian site were eventually traced back to Polygram. It turned out that an executive had shared a VHS tape with previews of the tracks to marketing managers worldwide. From there it got into the hands of a label employee's friend.

The Songs of *Pop*

Bono once told *Rolling Stone* magazine that, "In this age of celebrity, it's sensible to question the values of being a pop star." This theme underscores much of U2's end-of-the-millennium concept album, which—while maligned by some—also garnered respect for its musical audacity and technical prowess.

1. "Discothèque": "Discothèque" is often cited as U2's first experiment with electronica, because of its production assistance by disc jockey Howie B. A continuation of the experimentation the band had done on *Zooropa*, it distanced many of the band's rock fans. Edge once told Mani, the one-time Stone Roses bassist, that the song had structural similarities to that band's 1994 tune, "Begging You."

Released in advance of *Pop*, the single debuted at #1 in the U.K. in its first week of release, but the track fared worse in the U.S., stalling at #10 before it fell off the charts. While it was a favorite among club goers, and even peaked at #1 on the *Billboard* Modern Rock chart, the song's modest performance Stateside asserted the band's long-running American audience had a genuine lack of enthusiasm for U2's dance-oriented endeavors.

U2's video—directed by Stephane Sednaoui—pays tribute to the disco movement of the 1970s, with the band performing inside of a mirror ball. To further its commitment to the style, the foursome wore uniforms similar to those once worn by the Village People. Edge is dressed as a gay biker, Adam as a sailor, Larry as a cowboy, and Bono as a motorcycle cop.

2. "Do You Feel Loved": The second track on *Pop* was initially built from "Groove Sensation," a dance track by Naked Funk that Howie B had used to launch his DJ set one night when he was spinning in U2's club Kitchen. A celebratory jam, the pulse was extracted with the help of Howie to build the song's foundation.

Steve Osborne, who had worked on the Madchester classic *Pills 'n' Thrills 'n' Bellyaches* for the Happy Mondays and had previously worked with Paul Oakenfold remixing U2 songs like "Even Better Than the Real Thing" and "Lemon" for the dance floor, assisted the band with "Do You Feel Loved," which had been in consideration for a single release.

"It's quite a question," Bono once said, "but there's no question mark on it." The band took the grammatical symbol away for just that reason. It feared it would be perceived as too heavy with the question mark left in.

3. "Mofo": Continuing a trend that began with "I Will Follow," Bono wrote "Mofo" partially in memory of his mother, Iris, who died in 1974—specifically on the song's middle eight. "[It] just sends a chill down your spine" said Gavin Friday to *Hot Press,* who is credited as the band's "consultant poptician" on the album. "It's got real heart to it."

The song also mulls the meaning of the phrase "motherfucker," which had shifted from a nasty insult to—in some cultures—a praiseworthy term. Elsewhere, Bono has said it gives the lyrical nod to Salman Rushdie, William Butler Yeats, and Jack Kerouac.

Stylistically, the end product is way off from the blues feel that dominated the song in its infancy. A Motown-influenced bass line took over; and although "Mofo" was almost a no-go, in the end, Flood's suggestion to inflect it with a hip-hop element brought it back to life.

4. "If God Will Send His Angels": Originating during the *Zooropa* era, this song is a techno-tinged ballad that find's Bono looking for help from the Lord above. Lyrical depictions include domestic violence; and despite its bleak imagery, optimism and faith ultimately triumph over evil.

Written on an acoustic guitar, Bono and Edge crafted the song together during an creative excursion in France. When it was formed, the tune made Bono think of both the Fugees and U.K. pop outfit Boyzone. But as U2 was inclined to do at the time, he told U2's studio co-conspirators to fuck it up. "I thought, this is, like, pure," Bono admitted to Stokes in *Into the Heart.* "Now drop acid onto that."

The end result was a single that might not have been as popular as "One"—only reaching #14 in the U.K. and #11 in Ireland—but it certainly deserved the airwaves. It was the fifth single from *Pop,* and was released on December 8, 1997.

5. "Staring at the Sun"; The second single from *Pop,* "Staring at the Sun" was a rock-touched winner that peaked at #3 in the U.K. upon its release in April 1997. A testament to the increasing compartmentalization and formatting of music in the United States, it topped *Billboard*'s Modern Rock chart but only made it to #26 on the Hot 100.

"Staring" evolved out of another tune U2 had been working on in the studio, but when that song stalled, Larry began playing an altogether different but remarkably infectious drum part. Edge threw a riff on top of it, and they had the basis for the song. The guitarist perfected it later during tracking, playing through an organ speaker by Leslie—a practice first attempted by Eric Clapton and Jimmy Page in the 1960s.

Nicking a line from the title of the 1990 album *Stuck Together with God's Glue,* by another Dublin band at the time, Something Happens, the bulk of Bono's lyrics were written in an "everything but the kitchen sink" approach.

Headlines were an inspiration, as was the television, the European Cup, and even an abscess producer Howie B had developed in his ear.

6. "Last Night on Earth": A familiar but nerve-wracking way of completing tasks in the U2 organization is to continue working up to the last minute. Pressing its luck at deadline, the group was still missing lyrics and an entire chorus for the suitably titled "Last Night on Earth."

With Bono's voice shot, Edge had to up his vocal game on the tune. The chorus came into the U2 frontman's head at 4 AM; it was tracked by 7 AM on the final night. Surrounding the band in the eleventh hour were engineers who hadn't been to bed in a week.

Ultimately picked as the album's third single, it was released on July 14, 1997. But perhaps its rushed completion was detected by discerning listeners. "Last Night on Earth" barely made the U.K. Top Ten at #10, and didn't even crack the U.S. Top Forty, stopping at #57 before sliding away.

"Discothèque" was the first single from *Pop*. It peaked at #1 in the U.K. and in Canada. It reached #10 in the U.S. The sleeve is unique because it features one of the few commercial pictures of The Edge without a hat since he began balding in the mid-1980s.   *U2Wanderer.org*

7. "Gone": As a rock star, Bono often felt conflicted about his status and his wealth, as evidenced by "Gone," a song that revealed these feelings in lyrics about being "spoiled rotten, and paid too much." He'd happily continue on with his craft at a much lower wage—he even suggested he'd "do it for free."

It's obviously a subject that he and another famous frontman, INXS' Michael Hutchence, talked openly about before the U2 singer's good friend took his own life. Following Hutchence's suicide, Bono would often dedicate the song to the Australian rocker's memory.

At the same time, "Gone"—underpinned by Adam's funk bass line—is a celebration of U2's accomplishments and a message to naysayers and envious shoe-gazers that life is good at the top. On the group's 2001 *Elevation* Tour, Bono, according to *U2—Live: A Concert Documentary*, introduced it to a Pittsburgh audience as "a song about self-mutilation, torture, and mortality, all kinds of confused things that happen to people in rock bands."

Released in September 1997 as the fourth single from *Pop*, "Please" was written about the troubles in Northern Ireland. In an unexpected move, the band put Northern Irish politicians Gerry Adams, David Trimble, Ian Paisley, and John Hume (clockwise from top left) on its cover.   *eil.com*

"Last Night on Earth" was the third single from *Pop*. Released as a four-track CD in July 1997, it included U2's Pop Mart Mix of M's 1979 one-hit wonder "Pop Muzik," the Soul Assassins' reworking of 1993's "Numb," and a unique take on the Beatles' "Happiness Is a Warm Gun."   *Author's collection*

8. "Miami": In the spring of 1996, U2 left Dublin with the hopes of reigniting a spark of creativity for its next studio album, which was falling behind schedule. But its trip to South Florida resulted in little more than a diversion, as the "trip rock" styled "Miami" affirmed.

Time was spent in South Beach Studios when the band wasn't sipping Mojitos and smoking cigars, the latter for which it developed an increasing appreciation. The sunshine and the socializing that took place rendered a tune that was a sonic travelogue, or what The Edge would later call "creative tourism."

And even if new material didn't come flooding out of them, the trip was a much needed distraction. "Generally we had a good time. We came, we saw, we conquered," said Bono of the trip on U2.com. "It's in the lyric. It was all there and our eyes were wide open—some of the time!"

9. "The Playboy Mansion": A symbol of the materialism and vanity that America had increasingly become, "The Playboy Mansion" is a sonic observation about the hedonistic party palace that Hugh Hefner called home. Experienced firsthand by the group's members, it's a place where plastic surgery and cocaine can be found inside its gates.

"People in America think if you don't have cash it's hard to believe in yourself," Bono told *Hot Press* of the only U2 song that mentions Michael Jackson by name. When it was first developed, its working title was "Hymn to Mr. Universe."

"It's almost like prosperity as a religion," Bono added. "'The Playboy Mansion' is a gospel song for American white trash. It's about how people demean the idea of heaven by seeing it as a Rolex watch, or a picture in *Hello* magazine, a day out at the Playboy Mansion."

10. "If You Wear That Velvet Dress": A somber, atmospheric track, "If You Wear That Velvet Dress" has an ambient feel, bolstered by the keyboards of Marius De Vries, previously known for his work with David Bowie and Annie Lennox. The track is unique from a percussive standpoint as it finds Larry Mullen, Jr. using brushes and playing in a softer style than is typical of him.

11. "Please": Inspired by the continued troubles in Northern Ireland, "Please" may not have the power of 1983's "Sunday Bloody Sunday," but its message is certainly direct. It begs the powers that be—presumably the four Northern Irish politicians on the single's cover—to "get up off their knees." Gerry Adams, David Trimble, Ian Paisley, and John Hume are urged by Bono to move forward with the peace process.

Released in Ireland on October 20, 1997, as a single, "Please" was *Pop*'s fourth extract. It charted in Ireland, making #6, but failed to have a significant impact in other parts of the world.

Larry Mullen revisits the military drumming he once regularly practiced for the track, which otherwise embraces strings and what producer Flood called "weird synthetic sounds." The album version has a less pronounced guitar than what can be heard on the single release.

12. "Wake Up Dead Man": The drab outlook of "Wake Up Dead Man" portrays a world on the verge of ruin. Bono's pained intonation, *"Jesus, Jesus help me/I'm alone in this world and a fucked-up world it is too,"* can't help but lend to the song's yearning for trust and optimism in a hopeless world.

Proof that even a singer in the world's most successful band can suffer from depression, "Dead Man" is a reference to God. Although the song had its start around the time of *Achtung Baby* and had morphed into an epic, gothic rock track during the *Zooropa* era, by the time it made it to its final form, it was a haunting shell of its former self.

"People want to believe but they're angry," Bono told *Hot Press* in 1997 at the time of the album's release. "If God is not dead, there's some questions we want to ask him."

Pop Flops

Released on March 3, 1997, the critical response to *Pop* was mixed. U2's core rock audience also continued to be baffled by some of its creative moves.

In the *Boston Globe*, Jim Sullivan called it "a moving record, but not a thrilling record. While not quite up to *Zooropa* or *The Joshua Tree*, it is by no means the misguided stretch of *Rattle and Hum*." The *New York Times*' Neil Strauss took it a step further: "From the band's first album *Boy* to 1987's *The Joshua Tree*, U2 sounded inspired. Now it just sounds expensive . . . U2 and techno don't mix any better than U2 and irony do."

Although *Pop* had impressive debuts, reaching #1 in dozens of countries, the disc quickly fell off of many surveys within weeks. Within three weeks, the album had fallen out of the U.S. Top Ten. In the U.K., the Spice Girls' *Spice* album bumped it out of the top spot after just one week.

The kitsch of the "Discothèque" video didn't launch the record as expected, so the band went for a more traditional approach for "Staring at the Sun," a song with a more familiar, guitar-based sound. But when the straight performance number failed to blow up after its MTV premiere, manager Paul McGuinness was quick to blame the video for the single's failure.

"We made a crap video," he explained to McCormick, but also admitted there could be more to it. "We all believed that 'Staring at the Sun' was a gold hit and all we had to do was release it and it would go to number one everywhere, and it didn't. We were so wrong. You know you can't really argue with the public."

U2 released five songs as singles from *Pop* in an effort to try and sustain the record; but when all was said and done, it was U2's biggest failure since *October*. Although it was certified for a million U.S. sales by the RIAA on May 5, 1997, sales since have been negligible, making it the lowest-selling record in the band's catalog.

Five Facts About *Pop*

1. Nellee Hooper was not given a production credit on the album because he left the project midway—in June 1996—to work on the film score for the Leonardo DiCaprio movie *Romeo + Juliet*. Hooper, who had worked with the likes of Bjork, Gwen Stefani, Sneaker Pimps, Garbage, Soul II Soul, and

Massive Attack, was not acknowledged because the shape of the album had drastically changed following his departure from *Pop*.

2. The Malaysian edition of *Pop* was censored due to the use of the word "fucked" in the song "Wake Up Dead Man." Profanity in U2 music is rare, although the word "shithouse" surfaced on "Silver and Gold" from *Rattle and Hum*.

3. The Edge and Howie B flew to New York City to master the record in late November 1996. Making changes to "The Playboy Mansion" and "Discothèque" up until the last minute, the guitarist later called the atmosphere "absolute madness."

4. Speaking to the press after the album's release, Larry Mullen explained that had the band had two or three more months to work on it, *Pop* would have turned out much differently. He expressed an interest in revising some of the songs. Singles from the album were in fact re-worked and re-recorded and those versions can be heard on the 2002 compilation, *The Best of U2:*

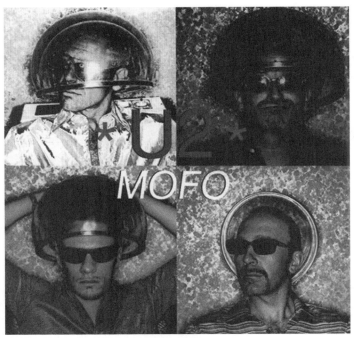

U2 goes to the hair salon for the cover of "Mofo," a song written about Bono's mother. Released in December 1997, it was the final single extracted from *Pop. eil.com*

1990–2000. The Edge concurred with Mullen's sentiment to a degree and suggested *Pop* was conciliatory in its final form, based on the difficulties he was having mixing the album upon its completion.

5. Paul McGuinness felt that the band had plenty of time to get the record done, but by having "too many cooks," *Pop* suffered. McGuinness felt that the use of technology was misguided, and there were too many hands in the production process.

36

Cigars and Big Hair

U2 Enjoys Its Fame and Wealth

Although the members of U2 were uncomfortable with their celebrity at first, the band has long since grown to appreciate it. "You get a little bit bent out of shape in terms of what's important," Adam Clayton told the *Observer* in August 2009. "Fame is like the dessert that comes with your achievements—it's not an achievement in itself, but sometimes it can overpower the work. . . . It opens doors and allows you to meet people, and you're in control. When fame first happened I didn't feel in control, and it closed doors to me."

Party On, Adam

Of the four men in U2, Adam Clayton was the first to embrace the partying aspect. While he was hardly in the realm of notorious imbibers like the Rolling Stones' Keith Richards and Ron Wood, Clayton was taking advantage of his rock star opportunities.

While his bandmates only drank on occasion, Adam was happy to hang out with members of the road crew, who were experienced in excess. One night, as their tour bus rolled through England on Adam's twenty-third birthday during the *War* Tour, the driver woke Bono from his sleep, screaming. According to the singer, Adam stood naked by the door, trying to step off the bus as it barreled down the highway. The bassist, as Bono explained it in *U2 by U2*, was "off his trolley."

Success in America

When U2's U.S. leg of the *War* Tour wrapped on June 29, 1983, at Pier 84, an outdoor venue on the Hudson River in New York, the band discovered it had—for the first time—turned a profit as a touring act. The group returned to Ireland with $2 million in gross receipts.

U2: The Homeowners

On the strength of *War* and *Live—Under a Blood Red Sky*, the members of U2 were now in the position to purchase homes. They were modest residences. Adam's home in Rathgar—where he lived with his then-girlfriend Sheila Roche (who worked for several years at Principle Management with Paul McGuinness) was little. Edge's place in Monkstown—where he and Aislinn began to raise a family—was only slightly larger. And Bono's house was downright unique.

If homeownership usually signified that young men were growing up, Bono's home was more like a cool fort than a house. It was actually a tower, designed by Martello and located in Bray, some fifteen miles south of Dublin. It was one in a series of seventy-four towers erected by the British around the coast of Ireland during the Napoleonic wars. The round structure—which resembled a lighthouse—was forty feet high and eight feet thick.

As for Larry, he was still being cautious, and didn't end up buying his place on the north side of Dublin until his father wound up remarrying. Unlike the others, who have since moved on, Mullen—definitely a creature of habit—has called it home ever since.

Junior's Tax Bill

Larry Mullen appended Junior to his name after his dad, Laurence, mistakenly received a tax bill from the Irish government for six hundred quid in 1984. The revenue office claimed the bill for three months of income belonged to the drummer's dad, and after his old man had a tough time sorting it out, Larry agreed to legally distinguish his moniker.

New Deal

With yearend accolades coming from Ireland's *Hot Press*, the U.K.'s *NME*, and beyond, coupled with the March 1984 honor from *Rolling Stone* writers, who name U2 as "Band of the Year" for 1983, Paul McGuinness approached Chris Blackwell to renegotiate a new Island deal.

Although the band's original contract, inked four years earlier, called for two more studio discs under the original terms of $50,000 with its respective low royalty rate, McGuinness had remarkable leverage. Coupled with the fact that other labels were already circling the band, he asked for Blackwell to return the band's copyrights.

Blackwell wisely agreed to new terms, which provided U2 with $2 million per album for the next four albums. He also doubled the band's royalty rate, agreed to pay for three music videos per disc at $75,000 per clip, and allowed the group the freedom to choose who would produce their albums.

When probed about the deal, Bono told the *Irish Independent*, "I don't want to say that money is not important to me, because it is disgusting for me to say that at a time when a lot of people don't have money. So I'm thankful that I don't have to worry about my next meal. [But] it is a threat to the band, because I don't want anything to take away from our focus."

Mother Records

Started by U2 in 1984 as a means of helping to promote bands it knew and liked, Mother Records' first-ever release was "Coming Thru" by Dublin outfit In Tua Nua. The band's members counted Vinnie Kilduff, who had contributed Uileann pipes on "Tomorrow." Steve Wickham, who had played electric violin on the *War* tracks "Sunday Bloody Sunday" and "Drowning Man," was also in the group.

Supporting other Irish acts like Cactus World News, who later signed with MCA, and the Hothouse Flowers, who inked with London/Polygram, Mother gave the bands from U2's own backyard a big boost in the mid-to-late 1980s.

By 1990, Mother had graduated from singles to albums in time to support the efforts of Engine Alley and the critically acclaimed Golden Horde. The former saw its debut disc, *A Sonic Holiday*, produced by Steve Lillywhite for release in 1992. Meanwhile the latter went on to tie U2's *Achtung Baby* with its eponymous release as the top album of 1991, according to *Hot Press*.

Other acts signed to Mother Records in the 1990s included Longpigs—who released *The Sun Is Often Out* in 1996—and eccentric chanteuse Bjork, who partnered with the label for four solo efforts including *Debut*, *Post*, *Telegram*, and *Homogenic*. The label ceased to exist in 2000.

Quality-of-Life Improvements

When the European leg of U2's tour got off the ground in the fourth quarter of 1984, the band's status as arena performers meant that it was starting to live a better quality of life on the road. Although it wasn't a drastic shift into wealth, the band was successful and its manager Paul McGuinness was all too happy to take the group to the best restaurants in the world.

If food and wine were becoming a significant part of the road, so were finer hotels. No longer would Larry need to sleep in a sleeping bag atop a mattress for fear of bed bugs, because U2 were being booked into the grandest facilities of accommodation in the world.

Groupie Policy

If the band was enjoying its just desserts, U2's "groupie policy" remained unaltered. Success and a shift into bigger venues also meant the band needed an expanding crew of roadies and technicians.

Larry Mullen kept a watchful eye on the conduct of the crew, and the rule was widely known. If a pretty young woman was backstage, you kept your hands to yourself.

Illegal drugs and heavy alcohol use were also taboo. In return, the band fostered a feeling of mutual respect and camaraderie, proudly interacting with those in its employ.

The Passengers

Coinciding with its *Rolling Stone* cover, U2 leased a passenger plane in March 1985 to make the final two months of the U.S. tour easier on the band. Although it was an aging plane, known as a Vickers Viscount, it was still quite a thrill for the band, who were happy to celebrate their ascent in the world of rock and roll.

Vegas, Baby

With a night off on April 6, 1987, in between shows in Tucson and Houston, U2's members were given the Las Vegas celebrity treatment when they flew into the city to watch the Sugar Ray Leonard–versus–Marvin Hagler fight at Caesar's Palace. After the event, they headed to the Golden Nugget for a performance by the legendary Frank Sinatra.

Sinatra proudly announced that U2 were in attendance for his show; and when the foursome stood up at the Hoboken, New Jersey native's insistence, he took the opportunity to poke fun at how the group was dressed. Afterward, Sinatra invited them to his dressing room where they hung out and talked about music.

After a run of shows in Texas and New Mexico, the band returned to Las Vegas for a performance at the Thomas and Mack Arena. Following the show, U2 filmed its music video for "I Still Haven't Found What I'm Looking For" under the bright lights of Las Vegas after deciding the song would be the second single from *The Joshua Tree*—and not "Red Hill Mining Town," as previously planned.

"I Shall Be Released"

Bob Dylan joined U2 for renditions of "I Shall Be Released" and "Knockin' On Heaven's Door" on April 20, 1987, in the middle of a five night stand at the Los Angeles Sports Arena. Dylan was in rare form and the crowd's response didn't just surprise the rock legend but gave him a much needed lift of esteem.

Back at U2's hotel, the Sunset Marquis, thousands of fans had flooded the area hoping to see the band, marking the first time the group experienced such a frenzy. Pulling Bono to the side, Dylan told him to be thankful that he had his bandmates to share in the pandemonium. Just two decades earlier, Bob had gone through it alone.

Tequila

With the massive success and fame U2 had achieved in the first half of 1987, the band found itself giving into its urges. The group began drinking often on the tour to support the *Joshua Tree* tour, partaking in margaritas and tequila on a routine basis.

The rest of the band was catching up to the partying ways that Adam Clayton had embraced for years, or what Bono would describe on U2.com as "a period of thawing out for the more uptight side of the band." It was U2's personal Glasnost.

The contrast between the roaring crowds and elation of a U2 gig and the silence of the other parts of the day had become more noticeable. For Bono, that void that existed during the downtime left him feeling hollow. Because of these feelings, he once admitted to understanding why Keith Richards might have become a junkie. Not that he condoned it.

Stadio Flaminio

On May 27, 1987, U2 began its European Stadium Tour in Rome with openers Lone Justice, Big Audio Dynamite, and the Pretenders on the bill as support. The band was so loud that hundreds of locals reportedly fled their homes and businesses fearing an earthquake had occurred.

Luminaries like Little Steven and the Rolling Stones' Ron Wood— who later interviewed the band for Italian television—were at the show. Brian Eno later told Bono of how he was brought to tears watching 35,000

Adam Clayton rocking the crowd during U2's 2005 *Vertigo* World Tour.

Photo by Mike Kurman

attendees—many who probably didn't speak English—sing along on the "Ha la la la de day" part of "Running to Stand Still."

Prison

In February 1987, before the ascent of *The Joshua Tree*, Bono had spoken to a *Rolling Stone* journalist about his discomfort in the role of a pop star for a May cover story. He suggested that he was "the wrong guy" with "the hands of a bricklayer."

By October, he spoke of the loneliness that fame brought. No longer could he go out into the street after shows and interact with fans, socialize with them or invite them back to his hotel room to hang out.

Things had changed. "I've got people who want to kill me, people who want to make love with me, so they can sell their story to the newspapers, people who want to hate you or love you or take a bit of you," he told the magazine. "So you end up going back to the hotel and back to your room, and even if it's a suite in the finest hotel, after being onstage in front of 10,000 or 100,000 people, it's almost a prison cell."

Money

U2's frontman had mixed feelings about his ever-growing wealth, and if 1987 was the group's best financial year yet, having money was still a challenge for the twenty-seven-year-old rock star. Bono liked having hits, he liked having a jet available to him so that the band could return to Dublin in the midst of its tours, but he also resented being a famous millionaire.

In fact, for a time he was in denial. The singer didn't want to see what he had earned. "All money's done is remove me from my friends and family, which are my lifeblood," Bono said in October 1987. And it wasn't only the notion that he needn't worry about his next meal or the cost of buying a round of drinks, it was the way in which people reacted to him.

"You've changed," they would tell him. Maybe he had changed but the way others were responding to him was equally different.

Meanwhile, Edge was also trying to forget about the financial end of things as well. Let someone else manage it, he thought. By early 1988, he had admitted he was fearful that with money he would become lazy, that he might get fat.

Money gave U2 the freedom to travel and record music whenever it felt compelled. It allowed the foursome to do things on a whim, but at times, it seemed to pose a threat of becoming the downfall of the band.

The Hamptons

As opposed to staying in hotels, U2 had decided to rent homes on the Hamptons on Long Island in New York during the East Coast run of dates that fall. The band would fly back after its performances in cities like Boston, Washington, and Philadelphia.

It discovered that the summer resort was deserted after Labor Day. There was little to do to keep from being bored and miserable, with the weather changing. It may have seemed like a good idea at the time to fly in and out of Long Island, but Edge later called the move a "miscalculation."

A Household Name

After a tremendous year, U2 was on its way to becoming the biggest band in the world. But the mere suggestion of that frightened The Edge, as he revealed in a March 1988 cover story with *Rolling Stone*, the group's third in a year.

"We're now a household name, like Skippy peanut butter or Bailey's Irish Cream, and I suppose that makes us public property in a way that we weren't before. And that's a bit weird, because we're getting so much mass-media attention."

The guitarist spoke of the U2 myth that had surfaced. Bono's personality had become caricatured, and he worried if that might impact his ability to continue to evolve creatively.

Hollyweird

Aside from nights spent living hedonistically during its 1988 L.A. stay, U2 had started to embrace its celebrity status. Adam partied at the Playboy Mansion as the guest of Vicky Iovine, Jimmy's wife, meeting bunnies and ex-bunnies while bumping into Motown brainchild Berry Gordy and aging actor Tony Curtis.

One time, Bono was driving a restored 1963 Chevy when police detained him. The singer had no ID. No driver's license. He did have a photo of himself with Bob Dylan which he showed the officers conducting the traffic stop. Although they didn't recognize U2's frontman, the sight of him with the legendary Dylan was enough for them to send the man born Hewson on his way.

Living the Rock-Star Life

If Bono and Edge were slow to take advantage of their rock star status, during the touring initiatives in support of *Achtung Baby* and *Zooropa*, and afterward, they fully embraced it. In the company of super models like Kate Moss, Helena Christensen, and Christy Turlington, among others, they partied at Bono's villa in the South of France.

For Bono, who remained loyal to his wife, it helped that Ali was friends with the models, and although they contend things were kept controlled with his and The Edge's children around, they were celebrating what they had achieved.

Bono and Edge may been living exhilarating and frequently hedonistic lives, but it allowed them both to rediscover music and become inspired by friends like Michael Hutchence and their model pals. Partying, swimming in the Mediterranean Sea, dancing, and cutting loose, Bono, speaking to McCormick, called it, "Frivolity, exactly when we needed some."

Famous Friends

In July 1999, while vacationing at his home the south of France, Bono wound up celebrating with rock's elite. Mick Jagger invited the U2 frontman to party with him on his fifty-sixth birthday. Along with superstars like Elton John and Jagger's Rolling Stones bandmate Ron Wood, Bono participated in a once in a lifetime jam session at Jagger's home, also in the south of France.

Top Hat

Bono flew to Modena on May 25, 2003, to join Luciano Pavarotti for a version of "One" which they would perform with a full orchestra two nights later. While in Italy, Bono realized he left his beloved hat back in London, so he spent an estimated £1,000 to have it flown to him before the performance.

Yacht Party

When Bono wasn't trying to save the world in the post-millenium, he was partying with celebrities like Jay-Z on yachts, as he did in late May 2006 while in Monaco for the Grand Prix Formula One race. At the request of the ship's owner, Renault racing head Flavio Briatore, Bono crooned a couple of tunes before heading on to a fundraising event for Haiti, where he and friend Wyclef Jean performed a version of Bob Marley's "Redemption Song."

37

They Said Be Careful Where You Aim

U2's Controversies

St. Patrick's Day

On a break from its spring 1982 commitment opening for the J. Geils Band, U2 returned to New York for a pair of gigs at the Ritz on March 17 and 18. While in town, plans were hatched by Paul McGuinness to put Ireland's biggest rock band in the city's annual St. Patrick's Day parade, playing a live show on a large float.

But the promotional gimmick went awry when parade organizers announced that Irish hunger striker Bobby Sands would be named Grand Marshall. U2—which feared its appearance could be interpreted as a show of IRA support—pulled out of the event.

Instead, U2 engaged in a photo shoot with noted photographer Lynn Goldsmith, walking with umbrellas along the rain-soaked parade route. When organizers found out about the activity, they threatened to have the band arrested.

Adam's Drunk-Driving Bust

On the evening of March 2, 1984, Adam Clayton was pulled over and arrested in Dublin. Charged with "dangerous driving and driving with excess alcohol after failing to stop at a police checkpoint," he spent a night detained.

Having ignored the checkpoint, a policeman on a motorcycle trailed him with a siren wailing until the bassist stopped his car. When approached, Adam reportedly told the officer that he was a "celebrity." He also questioned how he was supposed to know it was a police checkpoint.

On January 11 of the next year, he pled guilty to the charges, was fined £225, and had his driver's license revoked for two years.

Talking about the matter to *Hot Press* years afterward, Clayton admitted, "I was drunk. But it was pretty embarrassing to see it spread all over the papers."

I'm Your Boy

In the late 1980s, Culture Club's cross-dressing frontman Boy George kept himself in the newspapers during his waning career by telling reporters of his attraction to U2's handsome kitman Larry.

At the time, the headlines read: I FANCY THE DRUMMER IN U2!" Larry was completely mortified. But in the years since, Larry's perspective had changed. He now regards such advances as flattering.

Eamon Dunphy's *The Unforgettable Fire*

Subtitled *The Definitive Biography of U2*, the book commissioned by the band was released in October 1987 in advance of the Christmas season. But the band was unhappy with the end result, cited many inaccuracies, and ultimately took to the music press to express its frustrations after it was unsuccessful in its efforts to negotiate to have the text changed.

Dunphy, traditionally a sportswriter, made the mistake of calling U.K. punk band the Buzzcocks a local band. According to The Edge in an interview with the *NME* in October 1988, "The book was full of full of half-truths embroidered into phantasmagorical conclusions bearing no relationship to the truth. A certain amount of poetic license I can live with. But when somebody is putting two and two together and getting 198, that's when I get to thinking this guy is trying to do something other than portray the facts."

At one point Dunphy reacted to the band's criticism of his book, which received pretty strong reviews. He reportedly called Bono a "pompous git."

"Exit"

In 1989, a young television actress named Rebecca Schaeffer was murdered by a man who claimed that he was inspired to do so after listening to *The Joshua Tree* song "Exit." The man—Robert John Bardo—claimed that the song, which explores the thoughts of a violent man driven to kill, motivated his actions.

A rare ad that ran in New York's *Village Voice* promoting U2's St. Patrick's Day headlining shows at the Ritz on March 17 and 18, 1982.   *Courtesy of Angelo Deodato*

Responding to such suggestions, Bono said it sounded like a witty lawyer trying to build a unique case. The reality was that Bardo had stalked the actress from the *My Sister Sam* sitcom for three years before he murdered her.

Busted

On August 6, 1989, Adam Clayton was arrested in the parking lot of the Blue Light Inn in Glencullen on charges of marijuana possession and intent to apply the drug to another person. Police found him with nineteen grams of the drug. The offense came just seven weeks after the bassist's June 16 arrest in the Rathmines section of Dublin on suspicion of drunken driving.

The U.K. newspapers had a field day at Clayton's expense over the bust, running sensational headlines like: U2 MAN ON DRUGS CHARGES! When he went to court on September 1, with manager Paul McGuinness and Larry Mullen, Jr. by his side, the judge "invited" Clayton to pay £25,000 to the Women's Aid Refuge Centre in exchange for keeping his record clean.

With a tour of Australia looming at the end of the month, Adam was all too happy to keep from jeopardizing his traveling status. The entire band took a sigh of relief when this crisis was averted. But the judge offered this stern condemnation, according to the *Irish Independent:* "Taking into account the particular influence people like Mr. Clayton have on small children, it's a dreadful example to them to find one of their heroes caught in this situation."

According to Adam, he was hanging out with some friends—including members of Hothouse Flowers—in the lot of the pub that was located in the mountains and offered a great view of Dublin. A joint was being passed around, when undercover drugs officers came upon the group. After searching his car, they found his weed.

"The worst thing that ever happened to me was being busted," he revealed in the *Observer.* "It wasn't that I was treated particularly badly, it was just so stupid, so pathetic, to be busted for cannabis. It was a big newspaper story, and it becomes a whole talking point with your parents and your parents' friends and your friends' children, and you just don't want that debate opened up."

Carter Alan's U2: Outside Is America

Carter Alan may be U2's oldest U.S.-based ally. But when the Boston radio personality turned his relationship with U2 into a book deal, it was considered an act of treason by Larry Mullen.

Carter never presented himself as a journalist to the band, and while Bono, Edge, and Adam were hardly bothered by the act, Larry contended it was a betrayal of trust. Although it was written with complete admiration, Carter was specifically asked by Paul McGuinness not to write the book that was published in 1992 by Faber & Faber.

Despite the infraction, when it came time to be interviewed by Westwood One to promote the band in 1992, Bono and Edge requested that Carter be the man asking the questions. Still, Larry—who rarely does interviews—continued to feel burned.

"I think he took a chance and made a mistake," Mullen told Bill Flanagan. "There's no doubt that he knew the band was unhappy with the situation, but he thought he could do a really great book and we would be happy with it. I don't blame him for thinking that, but I blame him for blowing the friendship with U2."

Adam's Bender

In August 1992, after Adam Clayton and his girlfriend Naomi Campbell had an argument, the bassist went on a wild bender in London's Regent Hotel. When the story broke two months later in the British tabloids, U2's handlers did not deny the story—which claimed Adam got loaded and called out for a series of pricy call girls which he paid for on his credit card.

U2 spokeswoman Regine Moylett said in a statement, "Adam was in a fine mess at the time with Naomi. He went completely off the rails."

When the newspapers tracked down one of the prostitutes, she explained "We shared drugs, then had sex." Despite that, Adam and Naomi were able to fix the relationship for the time being and eventually became engaged.

Defending his bandmate months later, Bono told the *NME* in 1993, "Adam is not a sleazy guy. But when Adam bottoms out he goes way down. And that's what happened. He hurts no one but himself."

Tijuana Trouble

In San Diego in November 1992, Larry, Paul McGuinness, and Bono led assorted members of the U2 camp over the border into Tijuana, Mexico. Drinking beer in public, coupled with Larry's attempt at public urination, didn't delight local police, who also took exception to the drummer's Swiss Army Knife.

But these Mexican cops were on the take, and when McGuinness offered up prime seats for their show over the border the next night, they graciously accepted and agreed to let them go.

Christy Turlington

Bono and Christy Turlington made a tabloid splash in 1992, when pictures of the singer and the supermodel were seen kissing and holding hands. But Bono insisted they were only friends, having first met while shooting a cover together for British *Vogue* months earlier.

The paparazzi cleverly cropped out Ali and Bono's children, who had invited their model friend—who they met through Adam Clayton's relationship with Naomi Campbell—to join them on holiday.

Although Bono had fun flirting with Christy, he said would never act on the temptation. Besides, once the beautiful women had befriended his wife, Ali, they lost most of their interest in the singer.

It actually turned out Bono was more like a father figure to Turlington than anything else. He ultimately gave her away at her June 2003 wedding to actor Ed Burns in San Francisco.

Adam's Descent

While on the final dates of the ZooTV Tour in Sydney in November 1993, Adam Clayton became the first member of the band to ever miss a show. Adam's bass technician Stuart Morgan filled in for him that night, when the bassist was unable to perform as the result of a drunken binge brought on after his engagement to supermodel Naomi Campbell was called off.

Responding just days later, Adam—who had stopped drinking previously but relapsed—knew he had to beat alcohol to remain a useful member of U2. Inside the group, the situation was not taken lightly.

"I had to realize that every fuckup of mine, every problem over the last ten years that hasn't been quite so serious as that night, has been related to alcohol abuse," he confessed to Flanagan. "So I'm kind of glad I finally had to confront it."

Thinking about the his bandmate's propensity for partying, Bono once suggested that if it took Adam ten hard years, it probably took him another five to get past his addiction.

Speaking to the *Guardian* in 2009, Adam explained why he finally got sober in 1997: "I'd had enough of drinking, drugging, and nightclubs. It was a difficult decision to change my life, and it took a while to reprogram, but I've no regrets at all. I've enjoyed every bit of my life. I've had the best of it both ways."

F-Bombs Fly

In 1994, Bono walked onstage at the Grammy Awards to accept U2's Best Alternative Album award for *Zooropa*.

"I think I'd like to give a message to the young people of America. And that is: We shall continue to abuse our position and fuck up the mainstream," he said on national television. Understandably, TV censors freaked out.

Later, the singer wasn't quite sure what the big deal was about. He said "fuck" every day; and in his opinion, it was a harmless slip of the tongue. One that was undoubtedly helped by an afternoon sipping whiskey with Frank Sinatra in the legend's Grammy dressing room.

When it came time for Bono to return to the stage to pay homage to Sinatra, who was getting the Lifetime Achievement honor, the show's producers were on the edge of their seats in fear of another verbal infraction.

But Bono played it cool as he spoke. "Rock and roll people love Frank Sinatra because Frank's got what we want: swagger and attitude; he's big on attitude," the *Free Republic* reported him saying. "Serious attitude. Bad attitude. Frank's the Chairman of the Bad. Rock and Roll plays at being tough but this guy, well, he's the Boss. The Boss of Bosses. The Man. The Big Bang of Pop. I'm not gonna mess with him, are you?"

As the censors took their hands off of their seven-second delays and breathed a sigh of relief, Sinatra was clearly thrilled, although the telecast's producers cut off the Lifetime Achievement winner midway through his speech. Later, Sinatra—according to Grammy.com—reportedly told Bono his introduction was "maybe the best I've ever had."

Jamaica Mistake-a

On January 16, 1996, Bono and his family wound up on the receiving end of police gunfire when his plane landed in Negril, Jamaica. Planning to meet up with Adam Clayton on the island, somehow local police were of the belief that a plane loaded with drugs would be landing in the same area around the same time.

When the gunfire finally stopped, the Hewsons, Chris Blackwell, and Jimmy Buffett were offered an apology by local police, who had fired at the wrong plane.

Oasis Kiss

In March 1996, a photo of Bono and Liam Gallagher of Oasis sharing an open-mouthed kiss caused a stir. Taken backstage at the Point Depot in

Dublin, fans of both bands quickly derived that it was an alcohol-fueled joke, but not before the media got a lot of mileage out of it.

Bono confirmed this to *Rolling Stone* in 1999, saying, "Actually, what happened was he had a guitar pick in his mouth, and he dared me to take it off him while the paparazzi were standing around. I couldn't resist."

Adam's Stalker

In March 1996, police near Adam's home to the south of Dublin arrested a crazed Canadian U2 fan who had been stalking him with repeated phone calls and letters. The man was arrested while lurking on Adam's property, and he was escorted to the airport for a forced trip back to North America.

Eighteen months later, before U2's October 27, 1997, show at the Skydome in Toronto, police arrested the city man, who had first started stalking Adam three years earlier. The crazed fan had been calling Adam as often as two hundred times in one day.

Me Rattler

In October 1996, Bono got in hot water while attempting to help out with a fundraiser for Romanian orphans held by the Irish National Parents Council. Asked to donate "his favorite childhood toy," the singer drew a picture of his penis, which he called "Me Rattler." The Council called his artistic contribution "tasteless."

"Last Night" in Kansas

On May 19, 1997, while in town for a stop on its PopMart Tour, U2's video shoot for "Last Night on Earth" angered Kansas City, Missouri locals when busy highways in the area were shut down to accommodate the band and its video crew. To make matters worse, the news of the road closures came with less than a day's warning, prompting officials to get dozens of complaints, according to a local report.

"I'd never heard of U2, though I now know they're one of the most popular bands on the planet," Mayor Emanuel Cleaver told the *Kansas City Star*. The following day, the video—which was designed to spoof 1950s science-fiction movies and marked one of the last appearances of eighty-three-year-old beatnik poet William S. Burroughs before his death—forced the closure of several downtown streets.

"I can't believe the stupidity of it," a representative of the AAA Auto Club of Missouri told the *Associated Press*. "They're going to close down an interstate highway that serves downtown Kansas City for a . . . music video?"

Terrorist Threats

On August 7, 1997, U2 announced plans to play at Belfast's Botanic Gardens later in the month. Skipping a week's vacation they had scheduled, the group planned to play its first performance in the city in about a decade.

As soon as it received word, the extremist Loyalist Volunteer Force released an announcement suggesting it intended to disrupt the August 26 event. Although no specifics were given, Northern Irish police took the threat very seriously.

"We are taking no chances," the police explained in the *Irish Times*. "Intelligence sources report that this is exactly the sort of [threat for which we need to] pull out all the stops." U2 and opening act Ash, who were from Northern Ireland, performed the show without incident.

"Macarena"

During a September 1997 performance at Barcelona's Olympic Stadium, U2's nightly karaoke exercise went horribly wrong when Edge sang a rendition of "Macarena," a song that U2 later learned was universally loathed in this part of Spain.

The crowd's angry booing prompted the guitarist to stop the song before he could finish it. Asked afterward, Paul McGuinness admitted the song selection was one of the biggest mistakes of the entire PopMart trek.

Pot Bust

Howie B.—the DJ and producer who was instrumental in the creation of *Pop*—got popped for drug possession on October 29, 1997, while traveling from Toronto to Minneapolis. Customs officials found a small amount of marijuana in his possession, which resulted in the cancellation of his work visa. As a result he was kicked off of the tour.

Mexico City

U2's first-ever show in Mexico City at the Foro Sol Autodromo on December 2, 1997, was stained by an offstage incident that left a member of the band's security detail seriously injured. It began when the three sons of Mexico's

President Ernesto Zedillo arrived backstage at U2's concert uninvited and with their bodyguards in tow.

Entering the band's restricted area in a black car, Zedillo's offspring were approached by Jerry Meltzer, who tried to block them from entry. One of their bodyguards pistol-whipped U2's man, and he fell to the ground unconscious and bleeding heavily.

When the band's security chief, Jerry Mele, stepped in thinking Meltzer had been shot, a second car affiliated with the Zedillo sons hit him. Both were hospitalized, and Meltzer incurred five stitches and was sent home to recover. Mele was not so lucky—he suffered spinal injuries that forced him into retirement.

The day after the incident, U2 was brought to President Zedillo's home, where the band was asked not to publicize the incident. U2 instead demanded a public apology, but its request was denied. The way Zedillo's children explained it to their father, they were roughed up by U2's guards. U2 informed Zedillo that his sons lied to him to cover up their atrocious behavior.

Tabloid Trash

In September 1998, U.K. tabloid the *Daily Star* published photos of Bono's bare ass. Bono had been changing his clothes on an Italian beach during a vacation with his wife Ali at the time the paparazzi snapped his bottom. The couple sued the paper for invasion of privacy.

Cancer Scare

In the autumn of 1998, Bono's on-again, off-again throat issues became scary when doctors were unable to control the swelling of his vocal cords. When one doctor suggested it could be cancer, Bono pondered his own transience. He was later relieved to learn it was not a fatal diagnosis after all, and that he would be able to continue his singing career.

NRA

During the first leg of U2's 2001 *Elevation* Tour, a video leading into performances of "Bullet the Blue Sky" was shown overhead. Depicting National Rifle Association head Charlton Heston defending the American right to bear arms, the band took this clip and appended another to it. It's a divisive but thought-provoking home video of a little girl picking up a pistol that she finds while playing in her house.

Not Splitting

In March 2002, U2 canceled plans for a European summer tour that caused media conjecture that the band had broken up. Manager Paul McGuinness was forced to shed formal light on the situation: "U2 would like to clarify that contrary to certain speculation in the press, they will be neither touring Europe this summer, nor splitting up. Instead, they are spending time in the studio working on new material for a possible release later this year."

More F-Bombs

In January 2003, U2 was awarded a Golden Globe for Best Original Song for "The Hands That Built America," which appeared on the soundtrack to the film *Gangs of New York*. Bono, who caused a controversy in 1994 for obscenities at the Grammy Awards, was heard saying "fucking brilliant!" as he and Edge accepted the honor.

It rekindled the debate over obscenity on television in the U.S., where over-the-air broadcasts are governed by the Federal Communications Commission. Late in the year, however, the FCC decided that his use of the word "fuck" did not violate indecency laws because he didn't describe a sex act.

Overruling its own previous decision in March 2004, however, the FCC announced that Bono's use of the F-word during the live NBC Golden Globes telecast was indecent and profane. However, the FCC didn't fine him.

Death Threats

British Royal Mail officials confirmed to the media in June 2003 that they were investigating death threats against Bono that began in 2001. An officer revealed that they had seized two dozen letters originating in London threatening the frontman. The Royal Mail believed that others it may not have intercepted could have reached U2's Dublin compound.

No Thanks

In early 2004, Bono approached the NFL with an offer to perform an unreleased duet that he had recorded with singer/actress Jennifer Lopez during that year's Super Bowl halftime performance. Called "American Prayer," the organizers declined the proposal, telling U2's politically connected singer that the AIDS anthem was an ill fit for the show, which was designed for entertainment, not to promote causes.

Another Cancer Scare

In 2000, Bono revealed to a *Rolling Stone* reporter that he had a huge health scare but wouldn't discuss it. Five years later, Bono confessed that at one point prior to the sessions for *All That You Can't Leave Behind* he thought he had throat cancer.

It was a problem he noticed after the ZooTV Tour started that he had kept a secret from the band. U2's singer noticed a decline in power, and he admitted that he struggled on tour and in the studio sessions for *Pop* and its subsequent world trek. It was an emotional time for Bono, who feared he might die at a young age and leave his wife and children behind.

Lola Cashman

A stylist who worked for U2 in the 1980s, Lola Cashman was taken to court by the U2 organization on June 28, 2005, when the band sought to get back items it valued at £3,500. Bono, Larry, and Paul McGuinness appeared in court to allege that she stole pants, earrings, a Stetson hat, and other materials that Cashman insisted were gifts.

When the woman tried to sell these possessions, auction outfits contacted the group's offices to try and authenticate them, which was how she was brought to court. Bono reportedly cracked wise when under oath, and court employees asked for autographs.

Kanye West

Hip-hop star Kanye West didn't go over well as U2's opening act on December 14, 2005, in St. Louis. Months prior, on September 2, West had made controversial remarks during an NBC fundraiser for victims of Hurricane Katrina, saying, "I hate the way they portray us in the media. You see a black family, it says, 'They're looting.' You see a white family, it says, 'They're looking for food.' And, you know, it's been five days [waiting for federal help] because most of the people are black."

Kanye hadn't endeared himself to U2's heartland crowd, even though Bono tried his best, personally introducing the conflict-ridden rapper to the crowd before West picked up his microphone. Later, during the headlining set, Bono thanked West for opening the gig. U2's own fans booed him for the mere mention of Kanye's name.

Bono to Geldof: Fuck Off

In February 2006, Bono's videotaped appearance at the *NME* Awards, in which he introduced Bob Geldof—the winner of the Hero of the Year award for his work on Live 8—was addled with obscenity, as the singer said "fuck" fourteen times, according to the publication.

"Bob Geldof has told me to fuck off perhaps hundreds, maybe thousands of times," Bono snorted to the audience. "Thank you very much for this award and to my friend who is picking it up in all our honor—fuck off."

Finger-Food Fuck Off

When Bono and Ali appeared at a Hudson Hotel event in New York in September 2006 for the launch of their new EDUN-ONE Campaign shirt, things quickly went sour. The party, designed to publicize the forty-dollar African-made shirts from which ten dollars of each one sold went directly to fight AIDS, didn't go as planned. During a performance by Ireland's own Damien Rice, Bono lost his cool.

Upset about the loud voices that were impacting his ability to hear Rice perform, the U2 singer gave the VIPs of fashion and music at the event a piece of his mind. Taking a microphone, he told those in the Hudson ballroom to "take your fucking finger food and fuck off."

Stroke Me

Bono and his neighbor, Billy Squier—best known for the 1981 album *In the Dark*—were in the middle of a dispute, according to a May 2007 report in the *New York Times*. Both live in Manhattan's San Remo building, but Bono—who only stays in his penthouse duplex part time—was griping about smoke from Squier's chimney below making its way up into his home.

Other past and current residents of the building on Central Park West include Tiger Woods, Steven Spielberg, Steve Jobs, Demi Moore, Glen Close, and Dustin Hoffman.

Paparazzi Nazis

After attending a party in a St. Tropez nightclub the night before, Bono and actress Penelope Cruz were photographed together holding hands on the beach on July 26, 2007. The pictures made their way to the newspapers, which speculated that the celebrities were involved. But the cropped picture left out the fact that Bono and his children were nearby. There was no romance; the movie star was visiting the Hewson family on holiday.

Cruz felt compelled to explain to *Vogue* in November 2007 what happened anyway. "We were walking along holding hands because we're very good friends, and do you know want the paparazzi did to us? They took photos and cropped out Bono's wife and children. So they made up a story about us being together."

Kidnapping Plot

In October 2007 it was revealed that Bono's daughter, Jordan Hewson, was the target of an abduction plot in 1994. According to a book written by Frances Cahill, the daughter of gangster Martin "The General" Cahill, five Irish criminals had planned to demand $8 million in exchange for the singer's daughter, then only four years old. Cahill's father supposedly had a change of heart and called off the kidnapping after spending six months monitoring Bono's Dublin home.

Shut Up, Paul

In June 2008, after Paul McGuinness suggested that Radiohead's 2007 pay-what-you-like download release of *In Rainbows* had backfired, Bono announced his disagreement with U2's long running manager. Bono called the Thom Yorke–fronted band "courageous and imaginative in trying to figure out some new relationship with their audience," in an open letter to the music weekly *NME*.

Calling Radiohead a "sacred talent," Bono added, "such imagination and courage are in short supply right now," and explained that U2 "feel blessed to be around at the same time."

Oasis Bump U2 from Abbey Road

When Oasis guitarist Noel Gallagher wanted to get down to work on what would become the band's swansong album, *Dig Out Your Soul*, in December 2007, he hit a snag. London's legendary Abbey Road Studio was already booked by U2 for sessions with producer Rick Rubin.

Gallagher told *Mojo* the following year that he did what any self-respecting rock star millionaire would do. He paid off the owners of the facility made famous by the Beatles. "I was like, 'U2? U2 have to have a fucking six-hour meeting [to decide] whether to get tea or coffee in the rehearsal room! They are not coming in here any time in the next five years.'"

With a bag of cash in hand, Gallagher said, "The guy from Abbey Road was like, 'I've got it block-booked for the exact time you want it.'"

Begging for Bono's Retirement

Organizers launched an online petition in August 2008 hoping to get Bono to retire in order to "stop [his] leading misguided counterproductive philanthropy efforts."

Aaron With, the brains behind the lobby, cited the U2 frontman's inadequacy as a force for social change as the reason for the protest. Of course, With's own activities were kind of suspicious. He asked for donations that he assured would go to charity when Bono finally gives up on his anti-poverty efforts.

Drummer Condemns Singer's Political Relationships

By January 2009, U2's drummer Larry Mullen, Jr. was publicly criticizing Bono over his bandmate's relationship with politicians. Mullen told *Q* magazine that he was specifically distressed by the singer's relationship with former British Prime Minister Tony Blair.

"My biggest problem really is sometimes the company that he keeps," Mullen said. "And I struggle with that. Particularly the political people, less the financial people. Particularly Tony Blair—I mean, I think Tony Blair's a war criminal. And I think he should be tried as a war criminal. And then I see Bono and him as pals, and I'm going, 'I don't like that.'"

Mullen went on to say that he understood why people might find it distasteful but also knew his remarks would hardly come as a surprise to his longtime friend and colleague. "Bono [is] prepared to use his weight as a celebrity, at great cost to himself and his family, to help other people," Mullen added. "I don't think there's much of an upside for him and I don't think he chooses where he goes and who he meets. But as an outsider, looking in, I cringe."

Wal-Mart Leaks *No Line*

U2 fans that frequented Wal-Mart's website in February 2009 got an early taste of the group's new studio album, *No Line on the Horizon*. It seemed the big box store made an epic blunder when it prematurely posted twenty-two-second samples of all of the disc's tunes over the second weekend of the month.

No formal apologies or explanations were given by the company, but the song clips had been removed by the following Monday. Of course, eager fans had already gotten their boots on, posting snippets of the material across music blogs and bit torrent sites.

U2 Fears Its Competition

In support of its *No Line on the Horizon* album, Bono and Edge had admitted that they were afraid of losing their foothold to younger acts like Coldplay, the Killers and Kings of Leon. Speaking to BBC.com in late February 2009, Bono said he was equally frightened and inspired by said up and comers.

"In our heads that's who we're up against," Bono said. "You've got to keep an eye on the youth. Coldplay are such an extraordinary band with such song writing talents. [Chris Martin] is one of the most important melodists since Noel Gallagher, since Ray Davies, since Paul McCartney. I love the fact that the Killers want to get their songs on the radio, too."

Meanwhile, Edge used the feature as an opportunity to praise U2's *Vertigo* Tour openers Kings of Leon, for "taking a southern American idiom and moving it into the twenty-first century. I think they're a band to watch for the future."

David Byrne Knocks U2

David Byrne gave U2 some of its earliest breaks, when the band opened for Talking Heads in 1979 and 1980. But by the time U2's massive 360° Tour had started in the summer of 2009, Byrne criticized the group's "extravagant and expensive" endeavor and it's enormous carbon footprint.

"$40 million to build the stage and, having done the math, we estimate two hundred semi trucks crisscrossing Europe for the duration," Byrne wrote on his blog. "It could be professional envy speaking here, but it sure looks like, well, overkill, and just a wee bit out of balance given all the starving people in Africa and all."

The latter was aimed squarely at Bono's humanitarian efforts, but at least Byrne was honest about his jealousy. "Maybe it's the fact that we were booted off our Letterman spot so U2 could keep their exclusive week-long run that's making me less than charitable? Take your pick—but thanks, guys!"

Edge Responds to Byrne

Although U2's guitarist doesn't mention David Byrne by name, days after the former Talking Head disrespected the band over its carbon footprint, Edge spoke about the matter to BBC6 Music.

"We're spending the money on our fans," Edge told BBC.com. "I don't think there's a better thing you could spend it on. I think anybody that's touring is going to have a carbon footprint. I think it's probably unfair to single out rock and roll. There's many other things that are in the same category but as it happens we have a program to offset whatever carbon footprint we have."

U2 Fined $53,000 for Noise Pollution

While some have argued that 1997's *Pop* was U2's version of noise pollution, the city of Dublin said that the band has officially committed the act when its hometown heroes breached noise levels during their July 2009 Croke Park concerts.

Concert promoters MCD were fined 36,000 euros (approximately $53,000) for Bono and the boys' offense, according to Ireland's *Evening Herald.* Dublin City Council levied the penalties against the firm for allowing U2 to exceed allowed noise limits on a number of occasions during the shows.

U2 was responsible for twelve breaches over three nights of concerts, racking up 3,000 euros for each violation. But considering the $20 million in profits the band and promoters made during the three stadium performances, another local newspaper—the *Irish Independent*—called the fine "paltry."

U2's Berlin Barrier

Fans expecting to watch U2's free mini concert in Berlin in October 2009 were annoyed to discover that a twelve-foot metal barrier had been erected to block the view for those without tickets. Considering the concert—which included a guest appearance by Jay-Z—was planned to mark the twenty years since the fall of the Berlin Wall, the irony was hardly lost on both Berliners and travelers.

A white tarp draped over the newly installed fence blocked fans from seeing the stage, which was placed adjacent to Berlin's legendary Brandenburg Gate, from the street. MTV—the network that organized the gig with a local promoter, the city and Berlin police—said the temporary fence was placed "around the site to ensure the safety and security of the attendees at the event as well as residents and businesses in the area." The 10,000 free tickets made available online to fans were gone within three hours of release.

Bono Admits He's Overpaid

In December 2009, U2's singer admitted he has no financial worries. "I've been blessed and I've been over-rewarded for what I do, and I'm trying to give my time and my resources but you know, I'm a rich rock star, so shoot me," Bono told London's *Daily Mail*.

Despite his good fortune, Bono was happy to encourage his less-privileged fans to pony up for his next charity endeavor, a (RED) project with Nike called Lace Up Save Lives. "I think it's okay to criticize me as long as the ones who are doing so are doing their bit," he explained. "You can still contribute even if you are not as fortunate as I am."

Adam Gets Ripped Off

In December 2009, Adam Clayton received a court order to temporary freeze the assets of his former assistant, Carol Hawkins, after discovering that she stole roughly $2.5 million from him. The month before, Clayton fired Hawkins after she admitted to misappropriating the bassist's money, using his credit and debit cards for her own purposes.

Reports at the time suggested that Hawkins used Clayton's money to finance vacations and a New York City apartment.

Broken Grammy

It was a beautiful day for trophy maker Stuart Allcock when he got a call from his favorite band looking for help in early 2010. One of the two Grammy Awards that U2 were awarded for *The Joshua Tree* had been dropped and wound up in three pieces.

Allcock—a big fan who caught his first U2 show during that album's campaign back in 1987 and ran Alpha Trophies—told the *Daily Telegraph* that although working on the iron statue was stressful and "complex," he was stoked that U2's management had asked him to fix the coveted prize. The gramophone had to be welded back on and other parts had to be glued together and re-sprayed.

As for the call from the band's camp, at first Allcock, of Taunton in Somerset, U.K., thought his friends were pulling a gag. "I thought it might be a joke and said, 'Is this Bono?'" he said, adding, "If it wasn't a U2 Grammy, I wouldn't pay a fiver. But it's priceless."

In 1988, U2 was awarded Grammy honors for "Album of the Year" and "Best Rock Performance by a Duo or Group with Vocal."

Malibu, Man

In March 2010, The Edge was fighting a campaign by his California neighbors to prevent him building a five-home development on the 156 acres of land that he purchased in Malibu for $9.6 million. Although Edge was careful to explain that the houses he was looking to construct would not intrude on the landscape of the ocean town's exclusive Sierra Canyon district, the area's temporary mayor, Jefferson Wagner was adamant that the development project was out of character for this part of California.

"This is not what Malibu is about," Wagner balked to the *O.C. Register*. "These kinds of places are ego run riot."

U2's guitarist was still hopeful that when he his case went before the Californian Coastal Commission later in the year, he had a shot at gaining approval for the development.

38

I Got No Home in This World

The Million Dollar Hotel

Directed by Wim Wenders and starring Mel Gibson and Milla Jovovich, *The Million Dollar Hotel* is a motion-picture drama based on a story by Bono and Nicholas Klein. Although formally released in March 2000, Bono had been working on the idea for the film since 1987, when he came up with the notion during a photo shoot on top of the actual Los Angeles building of the same name.

With a relatively small budget of $8 million, the film follows the lives of a number of different people who have taken up residency in a Los Angeles hotel. When the son of a senator, played by Tim Roth, commits suicide, his father commissions an FBI agent played by Gibson to investigate his passing.

Featuring music by U2 and other artists, the film performed poorly when it opened, pulling in just under $30,000 in U.S. box-office receipts. Reviews were largely negative; and although it earned a Silver Berlin Bear at the Berlin International Film Festival in 2000, some of its international success was hampered by Gibson, its star and the film's distributor.

On a press junket to his native Australia in October 2000, Gibson told journalists at a Sydney press conference, "I thought it was as boring as a dog's ass." Later, Gibson did damage control, explaining that the remark was at the end of a long day of interviews where a journalist was heavily criticizing the movie.

"Later, I thought, 'God, why did I say that? I'm an idiot! I produced this film. I'm distributing it!'" Gibson told the *Miami Herald*. "It was pretty thoughtless of me, because a lot of people worked very hard on that film, and the fact is there are moments of genius in it. The soundtrack is by U2, and it's phenomenal. So I really regret saying that. I have written a lot of apology letters about it."

The Million Dollar Hotel **Soundtrack**

After bringing the script to longtime friend, collaborator, and director Wim Wenders, *The Million Dollar Hotel* was filmed in 1999. Early the same year, before throwing his attention fully into U2's next proper studio album, Bono served as the executive producer of the movie's soundtrack, performing on many of the tracks on the disc, with and without U2.

Led by the first U2 release of the millennium, "The Ground Beneath Her Feet" was performed by U2 and produced by Daniel Lanois, who also performed pedal steel on the track, and Brian Eno. Boasting original music by the band and lyrics by Salman Rushdie from his book of the same name, the track was distributed to U.S. radio for airplay on February 8, 2000, but it was widely overlooked because U2's record label Island/Interscope was concerned about heavily promoting a non-album track so close to its long-awaited new studio effort.

U2 had considered the song for its upcoming studio album, due later that year, but the group had decided it was better as an anchor for Bono's film project. In Europe, the tune was appended to *All That You Can't Leave Behind* as a bonus track. A video was also created for the song; however, it

All That You Can't Leave Behind is U2's tenth studio album. The second track on the record, "Stuck in a Moment You Can't Get Out Of," exemplifies a type of song U2 learned to perfect over the decades—a mid-tempo, melodic anthem with a universal lyric.
Author's collection

received little airplay. Speaking about the song upon completion, Rushdie told U2.com, it had "some of the most beautiful melodies [Bono] had ever come up with."

Two other U2 inclusions, "Stateless"—another new song also produced by Lanois and Eno—and the *Zooropa* track "The Last Time," rounded out the soundtrack, but Bono's appearances were plentiful as he performed as Bono and the MDH Band with Lanois and Eno on credible vocal tracks like "Never Let Me Go" and "Dancin' Shoes." Bono and Lanois were also credited on the memorable track "Falling at Your Feet," which was one of several songs that credited producer Hal Willner.

Elsewhere, Milla Jovovich performed a cover of Lou Reed's classic "Satellite of Love" with the MDH Band. And Larry Mullen and Adam Clayton performed on the soundtrack's altered take on the Sex Pistols' "Anarchy in the U.K." Performed by Tito Larriva—formerly of L.A. punk band the Plugz and rock outfit Cruzados—with the MDH Band, the tune is re-titled "Anarchy in the U.S.A." and sung in Spanish.

39

See the World in Green and Blue

U2 on Home Video

Live at Red Rocks: Under a Blood Red Sky

The companion concert film to U2's live 1983 mini-LP, *Live at Red Rocks: Under a Blood Red Sky*, was released on VHS after first being broadcast on Showtime and MTV in the U.S. The album—which dropped on November 21—counts the first North American appearance of "Party Girl." The track first appeared as a B-side in early 1982, on LP.

The band's performance of "Sunday Bloody Sunday" from the film was listed in *Rolling Stone*'s "50 Moments That Changed the History of Rock and Roll." Twenty-five years after its November 1983 VHS release, the clip was remastered for release on DVD in September 2008.

The Unforgettable Fire Collection

This VHS release from 1985 originally included the four music videos shot for *The Unforgettable Fire*—"Bad," "Pride (In the Name of Love)," "A Sort of Homecoming," and the title track, plus a thirty-minute documentary of the band making the album. The documentary was re-used as a bonus feature on *U2 Go Home: Live from Slane Castle* [see later entry].

Achtung Baby: The Videos, the Cameos, and a Whole Lot of Interference from ZooTV

Released in May 1992, this hour-long VHS included the three music videos shot for "One," plus clips of "The Fly," "Mysterious Ways," and "Until the End of the World." The interference referenced in the title was documentary footage and shots from the band's ongoing tour.

Zoo TV: Live from Sydney

Shot on the last leg of ZooTV—known to the band as the Zoomerang trek—this video shot in Sydney Football Stadium on November 27, 1993, and released the following May on VHS and laserdisc earned the band a Grammy. It was reissued on DVD in September 2006.

Adam Clayton missed the show the night prior, the band's dress rehearsal for the shoot, with his bass tech Stuart Morgan filling in. Clayton was terribly hung over, but he recovered in time to play before the cameras.

PopMart: Live from Mexico City

Shot in December 1997 at Foro Sol in Mexico City, this two-hour twenty-five song VHS was released in November 1998 and earned U2 a Grammy nomination. It was released on DVD in 2007, with bonus material, including performances shot in Rotterdam and Edmonton, two music videos—including a version "Staring at the Sun" directed by Edge's future wife Morleigh Steinberg—and four documentaries: *Lemon for Sale, The Road to Sarajevo, A Tour of the Tour, and Last Night on Earth—One Day in Kansas.*

Elevation 2001: Live from Boston

Shot by Hamish Hamilton during U2's three Boston June 2001 gigs at the Fleet Center, this DVD chronicles U2's return to arenas for more intimate performances. Counting nineteen performances from the *Elevation* trek, bonus material includes concert footage of the band in locales like Dublin and Miami.

U2 Go Home: Live from Slane Castle

Also directed by Hamish Hamilton, *U2 Go Home* is an exceptional concert film shot live on September 1, 2001, at the band's Slane Castle homecoming. Released on DVD in November 2003, it chronicles the band at the height of its *Elevation* Tour powers. It's an emotional performance, undoubtedly driven by the fact that Bono had lost his dad to cancer just days prior to the gig.

Vertigo 2005: Live from Chicago

Recorded live in May 2005 and released in November of that year, *Vertigo 2005: Live from Chicago* was lensed by Hamish Hamilton, a veteran of other

Bono gives his cameraman a break and shoots footage of U2's excited fans before the band's November 14, 2005, show at Miami's American Airlines Arena.
Photo by Mike Kurman

U2 concert DVDs. Credibly, this is a warts-and-all clip, with errors left in—specifically a moment when Bono clears his throat during "Elevation." The DVD is a fine example of U2 mixing early classics like "An Cat Dubh/Into the Heart" and "Running to Stand Still" with late-model winners like "City of Blinding Lights" and "Yahweh."

Live from Paris

Live from Paris is both a DVD and a digital live album recorded at U2's July 4, 1987, concert at the Hippodrome de Vincennes in Paris. Included as a bonus DVD with the box-set version of the expanded and remastered November 2007 reissue of *The Joshua Tree*, the audio of the show was subsequently made available via iTunes on July 21, 2008. A strong representation of U2's concert experience at the time, eighteen of the gig's twenty-one tunes made the cut. Those left off were covers—Ben E. King's "Stand By Me," Eddie Cochran's "C'mon Everybody," and the Beatles' "Help!"—presumably due to clearance issues.

40

The Heart Is Abloom

All That You Can't Leave Behind

By January 1999, the members of U2—spearheaded by drummer Larry Mullen—began to dismiss the heavy experimentation of its previous two albums and decided to revert back to the idea of "four people working in a room." Spending much of the year working on song ideas for its next record, Bono suffered a major setback in late 1999 when his laptop was stolen in Dublin.

After the U2 camp took to the local media to report the missing computer, a Dublin man who had bought the laptop secondhand for £300 came forward and turned it in after reading about it in the *Star*. An appreciative Bono replaced it with a brand new laptop, and told the paper, "Everything I've written since August was on this and I hadn't backed up any of it—so I would really have been a goner. This is like my portable brain—unfortunately I've got a smaller one so this stores all my information. Now the album is back on track. Thanks so much."

With that close call averted, Bono dropped in on Dave Fanning's RTE television show *Saturday Night Live* to give a progress report while plugging the soundtrack and movie for the *Million Dollar Hotel*. "U2 is ready to make the best record of our lives," he boasted. "Oasis? Radiohead? They are good. They're the boys. But we're the men."

Elsewhere, Edge promised a simple approach akin to U2's earlier records with guitar, bass, and drums taking the priority this time out. A reaction to the lackluster commercial response *Pop* received, the alternative rock and electronic dance approaches of the band's past two albums were gone. Reuniting with their proven rock producers Brian Eno and Daniel Lanois, the band allowed itself the necessary time to craft the giant rock album it needed, allowing room for Bono's involvement with the aforementioned soundtrack and his Jubilee 2000 social efforts.

Writing and recording its own Hanover Quay Studios, plus Windmill Lane, Westland Studios, and Totally Wired Studios, the first song to take shape was "Kite." But the album gained serious momentum when The Edge turned heads by using a tone that he hadn't used since 1983, on the song that wound up being known as "Beautiful Day."

Upon the album's completion in July 2000, U2 announced it would be called *All That You Can't Leave Behind*, taking its title from one of the lyrics of the disc's most poignant numbers, "Walk On." Although the album wasn't released for nearly two months, the lead single, "Beautiful Day," started getting major airplay on rock and Top Forty radio upon its August 31 broadcast release. A formal single followed in three weeks' time.

1. "Beautiful Day": This uplifting and upbeat number meshed Edge's classic Gibson Explorer with a mesmerizing melody to create one of the finest U2 songs in years. It was written by Bono at his Eze Beach villa in France, and based lyrically on the story of a man who has lost most of his material possessions but is somehow capable—according to the singer—of "finding joy in what he still has."

With its ringing guitar notes, its little surprise that "Beautiful Day" became a chart topper in the U.K., Ireland, Canada, and Australia. Although it wasn't formally released as a single in the U.S., heavy airplay and a tremendous popularity in an array of radio formats propelled it to #21 on the *Billboard* survey.

In an interview with the Sundance Channel program *Iconoclasts*, Michael Stipe spoke of his appreciation of the tune. "I love that song. I wish I'd written it, and they know I wish I'd written it," R.E.M.'s singer said. "It makes me dance. It makes me angry that I didn't write it."

2. "Stuck in a Moment You Can't Get Out Of": Penned by Bono after the suicide of INXS frontman Michael Hutchence, one of his dear friends, "Stuck in a Moment You Can't Get Out Of" sounds gospel-like and is written from the heart.

"I feel the biggest respect I could pay to him was not to write some stupid soppy fucking song, so I wrote a really tough, nasty little number, slapping him around the head," Bono said to U2.com of the tune, which is the frank discussion he only wishes he could have had with Hutchence.

It won the Grammy Award for Best Pop Performance by a Duo or Group with Vocal in 2002. Few could argue with the power of the album's second single, which reached U.K. #2 but only made U.S. #52, again based on radio play. U2's label was looking to drive U.S. CD sales and opted against releasing any proper Stateside singles.

3. "Elevation": An infectious guitar rock song with a thumping beat and a memorable lyric, U2's third single from *All That You Can't Leave Behind* was a hit in both the U.K. and the U.S. Although its message seems cryptic, lines like *"Love, lift me up from out of these blues/Won't you tell me something true, I believe in you"* seem to assert Bono's faith in God.

Propelled by its exposure in the movie *Lara Croft: Tomb Raider* and its increasing popularity at football games in the United States, "Elevation" continued to thrive in the public's conscience. In U2's 2002 Grammy sweep, the song earned the band the gong for Best Rock Performance by a Duo or Group with Vocal. The track's title later lent itself to Elevation Partners, the $1.9 billion private equity firm Bono co-founded.

4. "Walk On": The inspirational fourth single from U2's tenth studio album was written about Aung San Suu Kyi—an Oxford scholar who left her husband and child behind in England in the late 1980s to push for human rights in her native Burma. Putting her fears aside, Suu Kyi founded the National League for Democracy. Although she was placed under house arrest in 1989, where she was prevented from seeing visitors or communicating with others, she was released the following year when democratic elections were held and a four-fifths majority voted for her National League for Democracy.

Although the Burmese military didn't respond well to the uprising, keeping her under house arrest until 1995, she was awarded the Nobel Peace Prize in 1991. The song itself—which was dedicated to the activist—and its parent album have been outlawed in Burma, and any person caught in possession of the single or the album could reportedly face a prison sentence.

The musical structure of the song came from two different U2 demos that weren't going anywhere, according to bassist Adam Clayton, until the band combined them. The result was another Grammy honor for U2 in 2002, when "Walk On" was named Record of the Year.

5. "Kite": This song originated from a kite-flying expedition Bono took with his daughters Jordan and Eve to Killiney Hill on the Dublin Bay in late 1998. The singer later revealed he was compelled to write the tune about coming to terms with the fact that his children were growing up and they would get to the age where they—as he explained—"no longer need him."

Edge, however, believed that the song was written for Bono's father, whose health had been waning at the time the album was being made. When the singer asked the guitarist to help him with the verses, Edge told *Hot Press* in 2000, "It was one of those weird scenes. I was throwing in lines and he didn't like them at the time, but we went through this circular process [where] they went back in."

6. "In a Little While": Referring to a "lovestruck hangover" the tune is similar terrain topically to the *Achtung Baby* track "Tryin' to Throw Your Arms Around the World."

Written for Ali as an apology for his drunken behavior, Bono later learned that the track—which he has since described in live performances as a gospel song—was one of Joey Ramone's favorite songs to listen to in his final days before he succumbed to cancer.

7. "Wild Honey": This warm acoustic song found U2 operating in its purest state. "It was never monkeyed with," producer Daniel Lanois remembered. If it at first seems out of place it's actually the ideal, infectious song of devotion needed to keep the album on track.

For The Edge, who once suggested that the song was a bit of a toss-away pop ditty in the vein of the Beatles' "Ob-La-Di, Ob-La-Da," keeping the tune on the album might have been a mistake. But Brian Eno was infatuated with it and pushed for it to stay.

As for its pop direction, it was one of those songs that Bono described as a pallet cleanser that made the listener want to get out of bed, rather than hide under it.

8. "Peace on Earth": Written about the IRA bombing in Omagh, County Tyrone on August 15, 1998, this moving and politically charged song was Bono's instant reaction. Written the same day the Omagh bomb went off, a stunned Bono used his rage and disbelief to fuel the lyrics. The song was a direct reflection of the shock he—and many throughout Ireland—felt when the RTE read the names of all the people who had just died on the six o'clock news.

The song, which listed the first names of some of those killed (Sean, Julia, Gareth, Anne, and Breda) had a lasting impact on the band and its many countrymen, and tested Bono's faith as evidenced by lines like *"Jesus can you take the time/to throw a drowning man a line?"*

In the wake of the terrorist attacks on the United States on September 11, 2001, the song had a chilling effect on Americans, as its theme of loss was universal. It—along with "Walk On"—became poignant moments in the band's post 9/11 leg of the *Elevation* Tour. The band paired these meaningful songs during its appearance on the telethon *America: A Tribute to Heroes*, which aired globally in October 2001.

9. "When I Look at the World": "I still think that the world is a really unfair and often wicked place," Bono told Niall Stokes, when asked about this song, which was written from the point of view of someone "who is having a crisis of faith."

U2's singer has also suggested he was inspired to pen the song about his wife Ali Hewson's dedication to the victims of the Chernobyl nuclear disaster.

As for the track itself, it came together so quickly in the studio that The Edge was unable to remember how to play it, which was why it was overlooked as a possibility for the band's live set.

10. "New York": As tense as the pace of the city that bears its name, "New York" first started out with verses about famous residents like Lou Reed and Frank Sinatra, but Bono eventually went with his own observations of the Big Apple, where he had just bought a place on Central Park West.

If it felt like the center of the earth to Bono, the city and the song also offered the singer clarity after the 9/11/01 terrorist attacks as to why Osama Bin Laden singled it out. A staple of the *Elevation* Tour that has since been retired, it's a powerful anthem built atop Larry Mullen's drumbeat with the studio prowess of Eno and Lanois. *"Hot as a handbag and a can of mace"* indeed.

11. "Grace": A beautiful lilting album closer up there with the likes of "MLK," "Grace" was a song that came together sometime during the creative process for *All That You Can't Leave Behind*. When a suitable melody didn't come along in reasonable time, Brian Eno tucked it away.

At the end of the record, U2 was looking for something memorable and meaningful to close out its disc. The band revisited the musical piece and Bono was inspired to write his lyrical appreciation of womankind. Not only a woman's name, but—as Bono sings on the heartening album closer—*"a thought that changed the world."*

Release and Reception

Topping the charts in twenty-eight countries after its October 30, 2000, release, *All That You Can't Leave Behind* debuted at #3 in the U.S. Eighteen days in advance of its proper release, the full album found its way onto illegal file sharing applications such as Napster.

But Paul McGuinness was more bothered by the fact that his band was in competition with another Universal Music title when Jay-Z's *Roc La Familia 2000* debuted at the top spot. It was bad enough that U2 didn't go

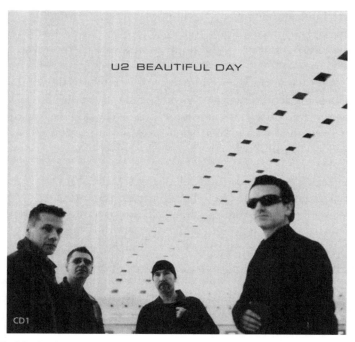

The U.K. CD single sleeve for "Beautiful Day," which was never properly released in the U.S. in an effort to bolster album sales, was backed by two solid B-sides: "Summer Rain" and "Always." The song topped the charts in the U.K. and Canada.

U2Wanderer.org

to number one, but the fact that the group was kept from the top perch by another artist from the same company really pissed him off.

But praise for the album and its enduring success—it went on to sell more than eighteen million copies worldwide—far outweighed any chart position. *Rolling Stone*'s James Hunter called it U2's "third masterpiece" after *The Joshua Tree* and *Achtung Baby*, while *Entertainment Weekly* gave it an A-rating, and said "it's as if they decided it was time to write and record an album of very good, extremely substantial traditional rock songs with an underlying spiritual bent."

Meanwhile *Spin* called it "the happy aftermath of a mid-life crisis" and the *Village Voice* wrote "Practically every song a potential hit single. . . . Soulful, exuberant, at peace with its own clichés, this is one U2 record that will never be called anti-anything."

With *All That You Can't Leave Behind*, U2 finally acknowledged the rich history it had been dodging creatively for the previous decade. "It wasn't just rushing headlong forward, jettisoning the past as we went," The Edge told McCormick.

41

It's You When I Look in the Mirror

Bono on Bob Hewson

When Bono lost his father, Bob Hewson, in August 2001 to Parkinson's Disease, the U2 singer paid tribute to his dad with a new song, "Sometimes You Can't Make It On Your Own." It eventually wound up on the band's next studio album, 2004's *How to Dismantle an Atomic Bomb*, and earned the group a 2006 Grammy for Song of the Year.

At Mr. Hewson's funeral, at a Catholic Church in Howth, Bono thanked his dad for giving him his voice and heard him recall his childhood, telling hundreds of mourners, according to Reuters, "Our house was filled with music. It was the kids who had to ask the father to turn it down."

It wasn't the first time and it wouldn't be the last time Bono got laughs talking publicly about his dad. Here are ten classic revelations about the retired post office worker.

1. According to his youngest son, Bob Hewson acted somewhat jaded. He acted as if the world couldn't impress him. So Bono took the opposite point of view, making them enemies on most topics. Mr. Hewson was deeply bothered by the fact that his son had rejected his wit, after all he needed someone to bounce his sarcasm off of.

2. Despite the many conflicts between them in his teens, Bono continued to live with his father—who began to mellow out—after he finished school. He had just one year to goof off free of charge and explore a career with his silly rock and roll band. Luckily for Bono, U2's fortunes started looking brighter just as his time ran out.

3. After the death of his mother, Iris, things got very ugly at 10 Cedarwood. At one point, Bono remembered his father tried to punch him. He ducked and Bob missed. He wanted to hit back, but he resisted the urge

4. Bob was a tough man emotionally. After his wife's death he worked diligently to keep the house together. Three men living in a house without a woman was not an ideal arrangement, but Bono's dad implemented rules and he and Norman had to follow them, or there would be consequences.

5. After Bono became wealthy, his father cackled at the irony of a kid who never cared much about money who now had more than he could ever spend. Bono kind of disappointed Bob, however, when he began to make some smart investments instead of pissing it up a rope as he had imagined his son might do.

6. Bob Hewson loved children, especially his grandkids. In fact, every time Ali became pregnant with another child, Bob imagined God was helping him have his revenge.

7. Bono once introduced his dad to one of the world's most beautiful women, Julia Roberts. Full of piss and vinegar, Bob—according to *Bono in Conversation*—snapped back to his son, "Pretty Woman? My arse."

8. The singer says his father's advice to him, without ever speaking it, was to avoid dreaming. Dreamers would be met with disenchantment and frustration. Such was why he chose a simple Post Office existence. No wonder his kid turned out to be such a megalomaniac.

9. Although he was raised Roman Catholic, Bob Hewson soured on the church after all the scandals and hypocrisy. Although he lost his own faith, Bono's dad was extremely proud of his spiritual essence. As for U2, even over the music, he was most impressed with the group's faith.

10. When his father had Parkinson's disease and was dying, Bono would come to visit him in the hospital. But even then all his dad could do was whisper. Occasionally Bono would read his father Shakespeare but if he tried to read from the Bible, his dad would tell him to "Fuck off." According to *Bono in Conversation*, his father's final words were in fact "Fuck off!" He was in the hospital room with the nurse at the very end when Bob whispered these very last words to them, "Would you ever fuck off and get me out of here?" he said. "I wanna go home. This place is a prison cell."

42

I Won't Heed the Battle Call

Can Bono (and the Rest of U2) Save the World?

ong before he had meetings with the leaders of the free world, U2's frontman was a free thinking humanitarian. Sometimes with and sometimes without the full support of his bandmates, Bono used his position in front of thousands and his ultimate sway with record and concert ticket buyers the world over to try and right the wrongs.

It's hard to believe that the man born Paul Hewson in Ballymun set out to save the world, but as U2's profile rose, he certainly made his feelings known. Although the singer's political awakening probably didn't come until his service work in Ethiopia in September of 1985, as the band's mouthpiece he started probing thought among fans and pissing off politicians in the early 1980s.

Denouncing the IRA

In the early 1980s, Bono began condemning the Irish Republican Army from the stage in Ireland. On its first tours of the United States, U2 worked hard to prevent Irish-Americans, who were a large part of their fan base, from sending money to the cause. Through awareness, it drove the point home that the money would end up funding the placement of bombs in British supermarkets and pubs that would result in the murders of innocent women and children.

The Provisional Army did not respond kindly to these efforts, and the band was on the receiving end of threats, some more idle than others. Gerry Adams, who has been the president of Sinn Fein—the largest political party in Northern Ireland—since 1983, once called Bono "a little shit" in a major interview.

Although they later made peace, in one specific incident, U2's car was surrounded by IRA supporters who called them traitors and scared the group quite effectively. But U2 wouldn't be silenced. In another brouhaha, there was a threat of kidnapping, which resulted in the police requesting the fingerprints and toeprints of Bono, Larry, Adam, and Edge.

Bono Backs Fitzgerald

As U2 was wrapping up work on *War* in late 1982, a general election in Ireland was making headlines. Bono spoke out in support of Garret Fitzgerald, the liberal democratic candidate representing the Fine Gael, or United Ireland Party.

Months before, Bono and Fitzgerald had met in London waiting for a plane ride to Dublin. Fine Gael's publicist took advantage of the relationship that was forged. In an effort to pull in the populist vote, Fitzgerald and his wife visited Windmill Lane for a photo opportunity.

In advance of the election for Taoiseach, the picture ran on the front page of Ireland's newspapers. The following week, Fitzgerald won.

In 1984, Fitzgerald asked Bono to serve on a government committee on unemployment. He accepted, but eventually found himself disenchanted by the experience, and didn't care for the language spoken by the team, which the singer called "committee-speak."

Ethiopia

In September 1985, with U2 on the first notable break of its career, Bono and his wife Ali decided to travel to Africa to perform relief work. Having met Bob Quinn, a filmmaker and TV producer based in Connemara, Ireland—who believed the origins of Irish music and art could be traced back to Africa—the couple were given a list of contacts in Ethiopia.

First stopping in Cairo, Egypt, the Hewsons toured a "city of the dead"—a population of millions who were forced to live in the cities enormous cemeteries because of an ongoing housing disaster—before they flew on to their main destination. In Ethiopia, the U2 frontman teamed with World Vision—a passionate organization whose people Bono credited with changing his life.

The Hewsons were sent by Steve Reynolds to a feeding center in Ajibar, Ethiopia. After assessing the couple, Reynolds thought they wouldn't last a week, but they actually stayed for a month and assisted the World Vision staff in developing music and drama programs for the children in the facility.

During his stay, the children referred to Bono as the "Girl with the Beard" because of his long hair and newly grown facial hair.

Perhaps the most jarring experience occurred when an Ethiopian man brought his son to see the singer and asked him if he would take his boy. The father was afraid that if the child stayed he would die.

Talking about his work in the desert Ajibar the following year, Bono claimed he got more than he gave in Ethiopia. He found his interactions with the people there, who lived in abject poverty, quite inspirational. There was a wealth in character that was absent in the Western World. Returning to Dublin and, soon after, New York, Bono couldn't help but feel disgusted by the wastefulness and spoiled outlook of those in the U.S. and the U.K. The time spent in the desert significantly affected U2's next studio album.

Amnesty International

Few could argue that U2's appearances at Live Aid in 1985 and its run with Amnesty International's "Conspiracy of Hope" Tours helped establish U2 in the big leagues of rock. And if getting behind human rights today seems like a no-brainer, at the time the group was one of the few to put its money where its mouth was with benefits and service work.

At point, however, U2 had to be careful not to devalue what it had already done. But continuing to support Amnesty International by putting up booths at its shows for years to come to drive up enrollment was one thing it would not abandon.

The ambition of the organization seemed so basic and so essential. The fundamental belief in human rights was indispensable to both the band and its like-minded fan base.

Central America

In 1986, Bono and his wife, Ali, went to Central America, where they worked in the hills of El Salvador, one hundred miles from the main city of Salvador. In an area controlled by rebels, the U2 singer was bringing financial help to a small, co-operative farm. During the visit, the singer was stunned by the sight of teenage girls carrying rifles.

In transit from the airport, the Hewsons witnessed a body being thrown out of a van on the road. With "military sponsored by the Land of the Free, terrorizing peasant farmers" as the frontman described it in *Bono in Conversation*, he admitted years later that he really didn't need to put himself and his young wife in that sort of danger.

A more suitable vacation for a rock star was always waiting at the Chateau Marmont in Los Angeles. But the trip did result in "Bullet the Blue Sky," easily the most ferocious track on *The Joshua Tree.*

Another track, "Mothers of the Disappeared," didn't only become a comment on his experience, it is now notorious throughout Central and South America. To this day, the song is played as an act of defiance by women in places like Chile who have had their children abducted and killed by the secret police.

The Gulf War (1991)

U2 were in the studio working on *Achtung Baby* when the Persian Gulf War began in Baghdad on January 17, 1991. Watching CNN's live coverage of the bombing, the group marveled at how easily they could turn it off and on. It gave them an idea for their next tour.

If the footage seemed to Bono and Edge like a video game being played by someone else on their televisions, they weren't alone. U.S. pilots weren't even sure it it was real when they were heard telling news reporters that their bombing mission was "so realistic."

Of course, Bono condemned what he called "war in the comfort of your own home" when a BBC reporter reenacted the path of Cruise missiles. It very nearly resulted in *Achtung Baby* being christened *Cruise Down Main Street.*

We Will Rock You

One of U2's most memorable moments from the first leg of the ZooTV Tour was a film of existing President George Bush, looped and edited so that it appeared as if Bush were chanting the lyrics to Queen's 1977 stadium anthem "We Will Rock You" while pounding the Presidential dais. The year 1992 was an election year in the U.S., and although Bush was considered unconquerable after the success of the Gulf War, U2 did its part to poke fun at Bush and suggested that there might be a weakness. The Texas-reared President opened U2's concerts.

Sellafield

In June 1992, U2 began planning a trip to the Sellafield nuclear plant as a means to protest the plan for a second nuclear facility on the grounds of the existing site, on the coast of the Irish Sea in Cumbria, England. Before the band descended on the site on June 20, it headlined its own "Stop Sellafield" show with support acts Kraftwerk, Public Enemy, and Big Audio Dynamite

II. During the audio-visual barrage of "The Fly," the words "Leukemia". . . "Child". . . "Plutonium". . . "Stop". . . "Sellafield". . . "Now". . . flashed on the tour's $5 million "Vidiwall."

After the gig, a small boat took U2 to the Greenpeace "Solo" ship, which was headed toward the nuclear plant. The band took to the water because original plans for a demonstration concert on the Sellafield Grounds were blocked days earlier by a British High Court at the request of its operator, British Nuclear Fuels (a.k.a. BNFL).

Although Greenpeace and U2 were forced to publicly declare that there would be no protest, they conspired to secretly approach the facility by water. From the Greenpeace ship, rubber dinghies carried about five dozen demonstrators that went onshore at 7:00 the following morning. The press was notified of their actions, in which they help created a three-kilometer-long line of seven hundred placards that said REACT—STOP SELLAFIELD.

In white radiation suits, U2 railed against both the Irish and British government's inaction against BNFL during an impromptu press conference held on the beach. The group brought with them barrels of contaminated mud from coastlines across the Irish Sea. As Bono said in the *Glasgow Herald*, "They can call us mad Paddies if they want to, but we can't put a lot of faith in politicians."

Following the lead of his wife, Ali Hewson, U2's singer was becoming increasingly involved in Adi Roche's Irish Campaign for Nuclear Disarmament, which also supported the Chernobyl Children's Project. The band's efforts for Greenpeace were a big step up from the financial donations that U2 had made to the group in the past.

"We've never actually been involved in an action," Larry Mullen told reporters, including *the Associated Press*, at Sellafield. "When this came up, it was an opportunity."

Bosnia

By July 1993, as the ZooTV Tour reached Bologna, Bono's activist conscience triumphed over his playful characters "The Fly" and "MacPhisto," if only for a moment. Calling Sarajevo through a live satellite link as a means of pointing out how close they lived to the massacres resulting from the ongoing Bosnian War, Bono told the crowd, "We're only about five hundred kilometers here from a city very different to this city."

Meanwhile, U2—who were funding a caravan of supplies into Bosnia—took to the media to publicize the need to take risks in getting supplies past Serbian guns. Adam held a press conference attended by the BBC and

Reuters that noted: "It is unacceptable in the world that we live in that these things can still be allowed to go on without being challenged!"

The Bosnia segment expanded in subsequent shows to include a satellite link to Sarajevo featuring interviews with artists and writers from war-torn Bosnia. After first being invited by Bill Carter, Bosnian TV's (Radio-Televizija Bosne I Hercegovina) foreign associate to Sarajevo, U2 was uninvited. The band's presence was considered too dangerous, although its financial assistance and awareness-raising was appreciated.

During one show in Marseille in July, Bono called Carter for a status report on Bosnia, who told the stadium by telephone that they had no water, food, or electricity. "Old people are starting to die because there's no food," he told the crowd, according to *U2 Live: A Concert Documentary*. But the nightly introduction to "One" was starting to wear on U2's rhythm section. The onscreen testimonials of Bosnian women who had been raped were excruciating. It was a rock show, after all.

Bono was committed to publicizing the horrors of life and the violence and death that surrounded those in Sarajevo, even if it was killing his audience's good time. By the time the tour made it to the United Kingdom six weeks later, the British music press suggested the segment was equally uncomfortable and manipulative. The band decided to cut it from the live show, but not before Bono sent an axe to *NME* scribe Stephen Dalton for doing a hatchet job on the idea.

"The Bosnian linkup was beyond bad taste. It was insulting," Dalton wrote. "Faced with the horrific description of the situation in Sarajevo, Bono was reduced to a stumbling incoherence that was probably the result of genuine concern, but came across as bog-standard celeb banality. What does the band who have virtually everything buy with their millions? The one thing they've never had—credibility. Shame it's not for sale."

Bono and his wife, Ali, finally traveled to Sarajevo on December 30, 1995, spending the New Year in a city that had been devastated by ethnic war. The media followed them everywhere, from a meeting with city officials to a Sarajevo nightclub. During a press conference, he talked about "Miss Sarajevo," the recent chart hit from Passengers, and his telephone reports from Bill Carter from the ground in Bosnia during the summer of 1993.

What a Mistake

On November 23, 1995, at the MTV European Music Awards, French President Jacques Chirac became the target of an angry outburst from Bono. "What a city, what a crowd, what a bomb, what a mistake . . . what a wanker you have for president," Bono ranted according to an *Independent* report, referring to French nuclear testing in the South Pacific.

D-I-V-O-R-C-E

Also in November 1995, the Emerald Isle had its closest referendum in history when 50.3% of the Irish electorate voted in favor of divorce. Bono—who was still happily married—declared his support for Taoiseach John Bruton in the campaign for a Yes vote. He participated in a pro-divorce rally on the Sunday before the votes were cast.

Chile Reception

In February 1998, U2 performed in Santiago, Chile before a full soccer stadium in a performance that was also broadcast on national television. During the group's emotional performance of "Mothers of the Disappeared," Bono brought out the mothers and relatives of those who had "disappeared" and ordered the country's president, Augusto Pinochet, to tell the victim's families where their children were buried.

"Where are the bones of these mothers' sons?" Bono asked. With that pointed inquiry, all of the police and security left the stadium. The situation turned frightening when half the crowd began booing. They might have loved U2's music, but they were not in alignment with Bono's stance. As the singer would acknowledge to *Rolling Stone*, "There was a 'gringo, go home, you don't understand this' aspect."

The Good Friday Peace Agreement

Bono was instrumental in putting an end to the troubles in Northern Ireland. He has publicly proclaimed April 10, 1998, to be one of the proudest moments in his life. It was on this date that he brought together the two opposing leaders in the long-standing conflict, John Hume and David Trimble, to shake hands onstage during a U2 gig in Belfast to support the initiative.

This major feat was the next logical step after the Provisional Irish Republican Army's ceasefire initiative, which started in 1994 but took four years of talks to achieve. Many believed—including the singer himself—that U2's concert and the photo opportunity with opposing sides prompted the leaders to ratifying the peace agreement.

Drop the Debt

In 1997, U2's frontman was asked to join a campaign—Jubilee 2000—to use
the occasion of the millennium to eliminate the debt burdens of the poor-
est countries in the world. Politicians had hoped for something symbolic
to mark the effort, a milestone to help these nations wrought by extreme
poverty. Bono considered it the obliteration of economic slavery.

Calling these loans "obscene," Bono was appalled that countries like
Tanzania and Zambia were spending twice as much to service decades-old
Cold War loans than they were on the education and medical needs of their
own citizens. Western governments provided these loans to non-Communist
African nations in the 1960s and 1970s. Unfortunately, in some cases—such
as when Mobutu, the Dictator of Zaire took the bulk of his loan and stuffed
it in a Swiss bank account—the money landed in corrupt hands.

Less about charity than about justice, the singer was integral in the cancellation of $100,000,000,000 of these debts. In order to do so, Bono went
straight to the decision makers, first contacting Eunice Kennedy Shriver, who
put him in touch with her son Bobby. With the support of Shriver's brother
in law, Arnold Schwarzenegger, they connected with Ohio Congressman
John Kasich. DATA's forerunner Jubilee 2000 eventually got the support of
then-President Clinton.

The outcome resulted in three times as many children going to school
in countries such as Uganda. In other developing countries, hospitals were
erected.

"New Day" and Net Aid

Collaborating with the Fugees' Wyclef Jean, Bono recorded the charity song
"New Day" at Wyclef Jean's basement studio in New Jersey in the summer
of 1999. The tune—released on September 14 and aimed to benefit Kosovo
and the Wyclef Jean Foundation—served as the theme for the Net Aid charity concert slated for Giants Stadium on October 9, with other performances
scheduled in London and Geneva.

Bono helped launch the Net Aid effort in front of the United Nations
building in Manhattan on September 9, announcing the www.netaid.org
website to "fight extreme poverty" and performing "New Day" with Wyclef
outside of the world-famous Manhattan landmark.

Despite the help of many artists, and a collaboration on "One" with
Quincy Jones, the New Jersey concert was sparsely attended. According to
the *New York Post* the next day, "nearly three quarters of the stadium was
empty." Insufficient publicity coupled with what some call "compassion

fatigue" had kept the event from being the success that these compassionate artists had hoped.

DATA

In the post-millennium, Bono has become almost as famous for his political and humanitarian issues as he is for his work with U2. In 2002, for instance, after the singer became active as a world ambassador for the DATA (Debt, AIDS, Trade, Africa) Organization, he was placed on the cover of *Time* for his efforts with the group that he co-founded with Bobby Shriver.

Frustrated by the notion that AIDS was taking the lives of 6,500 Africans a day from a treatable and preventable disease, Bono and DATA (which also stands for Democracy, Accountability, and Transparency for Africa) sought to raise awareness of the fact that Americans and Europeans don't put the same value on African lives. The ultimate goal of DATA was and is to get antiretroviral drugs to Africa to save lives.

A Bold Brave Man

On June 13, 2001, during his efforts to get financial help for Debt Relief and AIDS in Africa, Bono was invited to a lunch hosted in Washington by North Carolina Republican Senator Jesse Helms, a man not known for his open mindedness through the years. Bono publicly proclaimed Helms a "bold brave man" for inviting him to lunch, and said he was impressed that the Senator had changed his way of thinking about AIDS relief.

Bono had genuine gratitude and praise of Helms, who admirably asked forgiveness for his misunderstanding and insensitivity to HIV/AIDS. In doing so, Helms prompted his stern Republican peers to rethink how they thought about the disease.

The night after the luncheon, Bono invited Helms backstage at the MCI Center in Washington. Helms was fascinated by the U2 concert experience, calling it "the noisiest thing I ever heard."

"It was filled to the gills," Helms told reporters. "People were moving back and forth like corn in the breeze," Helms said. "They had that crowd going wild. When Bono shook his hips, that crowd shook their hips."

9/11

Following the terrorist attacks on the World Trade Center on September 11, 2001, many of the concerts and tours routed through the New York area were canceled out of respect for the lives lost and the general mourning that was occurring. U2 was one of the first acts to play Madison Square Garden, and when they took the stage on October 24, the appearance was affecting, heartfelt, and uplifting.

Using giant screens, the band projected the names of those that lost their lives. Although the entire audience wept in unison at the grief they felt individually and universally, U2 reminded fans in New York that they were all connected to the tragedy.

Bono would call the show one of the most extraordinary moments of his life. The band would later repeat this presentation for all the world to see when it performed during the halftime show of the 2002 Super Bowl.

At the time of the tragedy, Bono was walking in Venice with his young son Elijah and his nanny when he heard the news of the terrorist attacks on New York and Washington. Bono went to an American hotel, where he saw what had occurred on television, standing amid the stunned guests who similarly couldn't believe their eyes.

Millennium Challenge

Ever wonder how Bono wiggled his way into a photo opportunity with President George W. Bush? The infamous picture, where U2's frontman throws up the peace sign took place after the Republican President committed to help with Millennium Change, the name of an initiative designed to help with $10 billion in foreign assistance over three years.

According to Bono, Bush was amused enough by the peace sign to whisper to him under his breath: "There goes a front page somewhere: Irish rock star with the Toxic Texan."

Bono admitted to Assayas that he really liked Bush as a man. "I couldn't come from a more different place, politically, socially, geographically," he explained. "I had to make a leap of faith to sit there. He didn't have to have me there at all. But, you know, you don't have to be harmonious on everything—just one thing—to get along with someone."

Although Bush had ultimately promised $5 billion a year for three years to Millennium Change, three years after that pledge, the assistance was far less: $1.75 billion a year. But rather than be critical, Bono was appreciative in the media, admitting that part of a very large loaf was way better than what he started with.

Bono: The Political Insider

Interacting with politicians, many with whom he had opposing views, Bono acknowledged he had changed his idea of what made a person good and bad as his political connections ballooned. His view of the world was changing. And he wanted to be more than just the problem—he wanted to be part of the solution.

Bono would argue that he didn't really have any political sway; it was U2's fan base that had the power. It was this constituency that got him in the door with the world's leaders.

Even if it meant getting a newspaper thrown at him by a senator after a meeting with Bush in which he criticized the slow reaction to the Millennium Challenge. According to the singer, the unnamed politician was angered with him for disrespecting the President of the United States.

Can Bono Save the World?

In February 2002, Bono was placed on the cover of *Time* with a headline that read CAN BONO SAVE THE WORLD? Inside, the magazine featured two articles that discussed his recent efforts to get AIDS relief to Africa and encouraged Industrial nations to forgive the debts of the Third World. It was Bono's first time on the cover of the magazine since he appeared with U2 fifteen years earlier.

In April 2004, Bono again made the cover of the magazine when *Time* listed him as one of the 100 Most Influential People in the World. Bono ranked among the "Heroes and Icons" on the list, and appeared next to the likes of Nelson Mandela.

Operation Christmas Child

Bono and Senator Bill Frist joined the Reverend Franklin Graham and others at Kennedy Airport in December 2002 to airlift 83,000 Christmas gifts to HIV-positive children in Africa and participate in a press conference to raise awareness of the extreme poverty that still exists in Third World countries. A cargo plane, part of evangelist Billy Braham's effort Operation Christmas Child, transported the gifts that were financed through charitable donations.

Pain in the Neck

By July 2003, Bono's debt-relief efforts were being heavily scrutinized. In the *Sunday Times*, Liam Fay protested the singer's mission by writing, "There is something undeniably grotesque about a campaigner against world poverty, with an estimated personal fortune of more than 100,000,000 euros, who contributes so little to the welfare state of the country in which he lives, much less anywhere else. With typical self-aggrandizing bluster, Bono characterizes himself as a stone in the shoe of the developed West, the squeaky wheel that won't be silenced. What he has yet to realize is that, beyond the confines of his newfound establishment fan club, he's increasingly seen, rather more prosaically, as a pain in the neck."

ONE and Product (RED)

In 2004, Bono co-founded ONE, a campaign to make poverty preventable and history through advocacy and campaigning. By 2008, DATA had merged with ONE, assuming the name of the latter while successfully lobbying U.S. Presidents and Congressional leaders, plus the heads of many other G8 nations.

2006 also saw the launch of Product (RED), a joint effort of Bono and Bobby Shriver to help raise money from businesses to provide AIDS drugs for Africans that were unable to afford them. Brands embracing Product (RED) included Apple, Dell, American Express, Converse, the Gap, and many others.

Motorcycle Safety

Larry Mullen, Jr. easily the biggest motorcycle enthusiast in U2, signed on in the spring of 2004 for a campaign promoting motorcycle safety in Ireland by supporting a new booklet called *This Is Your Bike*. A collaborative effort of the National Safety Council and the Irish Safety Council, Larry participated in an interview on RTE radio about the initiative, revealing that the previous summer he had barely averted a tragedy when he accidentally ran a red light after a long night in the studio.

Mullen also explained during the promotion that he was never formally trained in motorcycle operation, but acknowledged the need for driving-school lessons. "I went into town, bought a bike, and just got on it," he said. "When I think back now, I wonder how I could have been so stupid. People just don't have the basic training."

The War in Iraq

If U2's position on the War in Iraq was largely suspected, the band's positions weren't widely known despite being artistically active during the era with the albums and tours for *All That You Can't Leave Behind* and *How to Dismantle an Atomic Bomb*. According to Bono, not campaigning against it—and the world leaders behind it like Tony Blair and George W. Bush—was a compromise he made when he began to work on DATA, the Millennium Challenge, and ONE.

According to the singer, he chose silence when he began working for the 180,000 people in Africa who owe their lives to the American money that paid for their lifesaving drugs. But Bono acknowledged that not shooting his mouth off on the subject was tough at times. As a rock and roll blowhard, that commitment couldn't help but leave him frustrated.

Backlash from Bono's Humanitarian Work

Bono's bandmates at times worried about how his crusades might impact their fan base. At first, U2's other members feared Bono's causes might turn off the millions around the world they worked so hard to win over.

But Bono came to believe that his audience felt empowered to follow suit when he raised his voice about right versus wrong. However, the bottom line was that U2 was a rock band above all else. After the release of *How to Dismantle an Atomic Bomb* he insisted that if U2 developed "fat arses" or made a "crap album" they would toss in the towel.

For all of the singer's efforts with AIDS and world debt, he had the ability to poke fun at himself, affirming that if he took his positioning seriously, he didn't take himself that way. Upon being named "The Most Powerful Man in Rock" by *Q* magazine, Bono cracked wise: "If there's one thing worse than a rock star, it's a rock star with a conscience."

Despite such self-deprecation, Bono revealed in December 2005 while speaking on BBC's *Today* program that his humanitarian work had at times strained relationships in U2. "There was one point when I thought, 'I'm going to be thrown out of the band for this stuff,'" he acknowledged.

Live 8

With the 2005 G8 Summit slated for Scotland that summer, Bono began to suggest to Bob Geldof in February of that year that a new Live Aid–styled concert would be an ideal way to get the globe behind the idea. Geldof told Bono to forget it even when the singer suggested that U2 and Paul McCartney could launch the show with a rendition of "Sgt. Pepper's Lonely Hearts Club Band."

By April, Bono had confirmations from McCartney and Coldplay's Chris Martin. Through Bono's persistence, Geldof ultimately relented by May, and together they continued to seek out other acts for the main gig, which was tentatively slated for July 2 at London's Hyde Park on the Saturday prior to the G8 Summit. Other shows were also planned for Philadelphia, Paris, Rome, Berlin, Barrie, Tokyo, Johannesburg, and Moscow.

On May 26, before the group's show at the Fleet Center, Adam Clayton confirmed to the *Boston Globe* that U2 would in fact perform at the July 2 event. When the time arrived, the band opened the show in London and then flew to the Vienna stop of its *Vertigo* trek later in the day.

A day before Live 8, on July 1, U2 and Macca ran through "Sgt. Pepper's," but the next day there was a bit of a wardrobe crisis. McCartney and Bono were both wearing the same designer jacket backstage before the show began, an argument the one-time Beatle evidently won. When they came out onto the stage at Hyde Park, Bono was in a different coat.

For the Beatles tune, a four-piece horn section accompanied them. Afterward, U2 moved forward with "Beautiful Day," "Vertigo," and "One" as Bono asked the G8 leaders to "make poverty history."

Katrina

As U2 prepared for the third leg of its *Vertigo* Tour to get underway in early September 2005, the band took time out to tape a performance designed to aid New Orleans, which had been devastated by Hurricane Katrina.

First the group teamed up with Mary J. Blige for a genre-defying but somber rendition of "One," which was shown during the "Shelter from the Storm" telethon. The program aired on every U.S. broadcast network and countless other channels shown around the world.

"To know that it's mainland U.S.A. is jaw-dropping and bewildering," Edge told the *Toronto Sun*. "Because you couldn't ever have imagined that a natural disaster could have presented so many problems for such a powerful country. I think that's the thing that's hit everybody."

The Statesman

On September 18, 2005, Bono appeared on the cover of the *New York Times Sunday Magazine* in a feature written by author James Traub. Titled "the Statesman," Traub describes his time spent with the singer over the past year.

"He's a kind of one-man state who fills his treasury with the global currency of fame," Traub writes. "He is also, of course, an emanation of the celebrity culture. But it is Bono's willingness to invest his fame. And to do so with a steady sense of purpose and a tolerance for detail, that has made him the most politically effective figure in the recent history of popular culture."

After first joining up to perform on a duet of "One" on the Hurricane Katrina tele-thon "Shelter from the Storm" weeks earlier, Mary J. Blige again duets with U2 on its famous song during the band's second in a five-night stand at New York's Madison Square Garden on October 8, 2005.   *Photo by Mike Kurman*

Music Rising Auction

In April 2007, U2 artifacts were donated at Music Rising's "Icons of Music" fundraiser. The event, co-sponsored by The Edge, helped raise $2.4 million toward replacing instruments damaged during Hurricane Katrina. The guitarist's Gibson Les Paul sold for $240,000.

Rounding out the auction, Bono's autographed Gretsch earned $180,000, a bass belonging to Adam went for $22,000, and a tom-tom drum belonging to Larry sold for $19,000.

Man of Peace

In December 2008, Bono was given Nobel's "Man of Peace" award for his humanitarian efforts. In a Paris ceremony, U2's singer was praised for his crusades to conquer African debt, poverty, and disease.

"This is a very big award for me, because let's be honest this is as close as I am going to get—as close as a rock star is ever going to get to the Nobel Peace Prize," Bono told attendees.

"I am an over-awarded, over-reward⟨   ⟩star," Bono continued. "You are the people who do the real work,⟨   ⟩l to the audience, which included Nobel Peace Prize winners F. W. ⟨   ⟩: of South Africa, Lech Walesa of Poland, and Northern Ireland's J⟨   ⟩ne. "So I am very, very pleased to be in such esteemed company."

We Are One

U2 proudly performed at the "We Are One" concert at Washington's Lincoln Memorial on January 18, 2009, as part of a celebration of Barack Obama's inauguration. At President-Elect Obama's request, U2 delivered his favorite song by the band, "City of Blinding Lights." In addition to that number—which was played on most of his campaign stops on his road to White House victory—the band performed its Martin Luther King, Jr. tribute "Pride (In the Name of Love)."

Speaking directly to Obama, who was in attendance, Bono—according to a *Reuters* report—told the 400,000 people who witnessed the show, "What a thrill for four Irish boys from the Northside of Dublin to honor you, sir, the next President of the United States, Barack Obama, for choosing this song to be part of the soundtrack of your campaign, and more besides."

Bono altered the line "Neon hearts, Day-Glo eyes/A city lit by fireflies" and instead sang, "America, let your road rise/Under Lincoln's unblinking eyes." Later in the performance, Bono also acknowledged Vice President-Elect Joseph Biden. It was a colossal moment of change that many Americans won't soon forget.

43

I'm Hanging Out to Dry with My Old Clothes

Side Projects, Collaborations, Compilation Tracks, Soundtracks, Benefits, Books, Movie Roles, and More

"Snake Charmer"

Released in October 1983, this EP with Jah Wobble and Holger Czukay featured slide guitar by The Edge on the title track, plus lead guitar on the number, "Hold Onto Your Dreams." Edge teamed with Wobble, once the bassist in Public Image Ltd., on this one-off project.

The Royal Dublin Ballet

By mid-1983, U2 had announced its intentions of writing the music score for a production by the Royal Dublin Ballet. The plan was for the project to be piano-based and balanced by what Bono called "metronomic-type work."

With Bono and Edge supposedly getting the creative ball rolling, they hoped to engage Larry and Adam upon the group's return to Dublin that summer. The project was evidently abandoned, as it never came to fruition.

Behind the Trap Door

Released in November 1984, T Bone Burnett's *Behind the Trap Door* EP included a track co-written with Bono called "Having a Wonderful Time, Wish You Were Her." Aside from Bono, the project featured collaborations with Richard Thompson and folksinger Bob Neuwirth.

The song was a product of their first-ever meeting at London's Portobello Hotel that year. The performer/producer and the U2 singer would become friends and collaborators who would work together again in the future.

Band Aid

While on tour in Germany, Bono was tracked down by Boomtown Rats singer Bob Geldof on November 21, 1984. Geldof—who was putting together an all-star charity recording with Ultravox frontman Midge Ure to raise money for Ethiopian famine victims—asked U2's singer to come to London on the twenty-fifth to lend his voice to a song that featured U.K. pop stars of the day like Culture Club's Boy George, Simon Le Bon's Duran Duran, and George Michael of Wham!

U2's singer was caught off guard by Geldof's call, but Bob was persuasive. When he hung up the phone after a lengthy discussion about the African plight, Bono wondered how he might convince the rest of the band to agree to participate.

Ultimately, he didn't. The band had a week off before it was due to fly to the U.S. for a short run of dates and Edge had family matters to tend to at home. Larry was also otherwise committed. But Adam went with Bono to Basing Street Studios to lend support and chaperone the singer for his participation in the song, titled "Do They Know It's Christmas?"

U2's singer was hesitant to sing the line, "*Tonight, thank God, it's them instead of you,*" but Geldof guilted him into it. Discussing it in *U2 by U2*, Bono recalled Bob's assertive and persuasive approach. "He said, 'This is not about what you want, okay? This is about what these people need.'"

The song, bolstered by Bono's powerful, emphatic delivery, debuted at #1 in the U.K. and twelve other countries. Raising £8 million for Ethiopian famine relief, "Do They Know It's Christmas?" went on to become the best-selling U.K. #1 single of all time, until Elton John's "Candle in the Wind 1997" eventually supplanted it.

Sun City

A day after returning to Dublin from Africa in October 1985, Bono flew to New York City where he participated in an all-star charity effort known as Artists United Against Apartheid. Helmed by one-time E Street Band guitarist Little Steven, the recording session and video again put the U2 singer in the company of Bruce Springsteen and Peter Wolf—who Bono hadn't seen since the 1982 J. Geils tour. During the creation of the song "Sun City," Bono also met one of his childhood heroes, Lou Reed, for the first time.

The track itself protested apartheid in South Africa and also counted Bob Dylan, Midnight Oil's Peter Garrett, Peter Gabriel, Hall and Oates, and Run-DMC, among others. Its parent album was released on December 7, 1985, and although it wasn't a smashing commercial success, the project went on to earn over $1,000,000 for anti-apartheid education and other projects. It was also acclaimed. In late 1985, the *Village Voice* ranked it as the #5 album of the year in its "Pazz & Jop" Critics Poll.

"In a Lifetime"

After lending his voice to the Clannad song "In a Lifetime" Bono has been asked to appear in a video for the song which the revered Irish folk band has decided to release as a single. On December 11, 1985, Bono and Adam Clayton traveled to the northwest corner of their homeland so that the singer could join the video shoot.

Part of the video was shot at the Poison Glen, where British soldiers supposedly died after drinking poison water. The clip—directed by longtime U2 ally Meiert Avis—was based around a concept Bono and The Edge had developed. Following its release in early 1986, the song peaked at #20 in the U.K. survey.

"Heroine"

Recorded for the 1986 movie *Captive*, which The Edge also scored, "Heroine" marked a collaboration with up and coming singer Sinead O'Connor, who had been with In Tua Nua at the time. This was O'Connor's first-ever recorded release. Featuring Larry Mullen on drums, the track was remixed by Steve Lillywhite and can be heard on O'Connor's compilation album, *So Far . . . The Best Of.*

Robbie Robertson

Produced by Daniel Lanois, the self-titled 1987 album by Robbie Robertson, a former member of The Band, featured backing by U2 on two tracks. "Sweet Fire of Love" was practically a duet between Robertson and Bono, and "Testimony" also featured the singer in the background. The music on these tracks, which was recorded in August 1986—the same time U2 was working on its fifth studio album—sounded remarkably similar to the band's approach on *The Joshua Tree*. Elsewhere, the disc featured assistance from Peter Gabriel, members of the BoDeans, Maria McKee, and Robertson's former Band-mates Rick Danko and Garth Hudson.

"Royal Station 4/16"

Released on Melissa Etheridge's 1989 sophomore album *Brave and Crazy*, the song "Royal Station 4/16" featured guest harmonica work by Bono. At the time he stopped by the studio to help her out, Etheridge and U2 were label mates. According to legend, the U2 frontman was with Chris Blackwell the night he decided to sign the Kansas-bred lesbian rock singer.

Acadie

Released on September 20, 1989, the debut solo album of U2 producer Daniel Lanois featured Adam Clayton and Larry Mullen performing on the tracks "Jolie Louse" and "Still Water." Brian Eno also appears on the latter.

A Clockwork Orange

In the spring of 1989, Bono and Edge were approached by Ron Daniels, the director of the Royal Shakespeare Company, to ask if they would like to compose music for an upcoming production of *A Clockwork Orange*.

In August, the vocalist and guitarist went to London to watch the RSC's production of *Macbeth* and were very impressed. They agreed to write the music for the production of *A Clockwork Orange*, which was due in 1990.

On February 6 of the next year, *A Clockwork Orange 2004* opened at the Barbican Arts Centre in London. But the score written by Bono and Edge—which Ron Daniels commissioned—didn't sit well with Daniels's collaborator, Anthony Burgess. Burgess hated the music and called the score "neo-wallpaper." Bono in turn said Burgess was "a cranky old sod."

A complete shift from the musical approaches of U2's last two albums, Edge had been drawing on industrial material like Einstürzende Neubauten, Ministry, the Young Gods, and KMFDM for inspiration. When U2's next studio album surfaced eighteen months later, the approaches heard in these industrial and electronic subgenres would have a significant influence on the band's direction.

The Neville Brothers

In March 1990, Bono, Ali, and baby Jordan rented a van and took a road trip across America. The month-long trip was anchored by a two-week stay in New Orleans, where Bono teamed up with the Neville Brothers and wrote two songs, "Jah Love" and "Kingdom Come" for the group's upcoming album,

Brother's Keeper. The former made the album's final track listing and was released on August 7 of the same year.

Red Hot + Blue: A Tribute to Cole Porter

In June 1990, the members of U2 came together in Edge's basement studio to record a cover of Cole Porter's "Night and Day," which was used on an AIDS fundraising compilation album, *Red Hot + Blue*, released in the fourth quarter of the year.

In support of the project, a promotional single was released in December 1990, although the song didn't get much attention at radio. But the album—which was one of the first album benefits for the disease—was a remarkable success, selling over one million copies.

The Call

The Call were among the most underappreciated American bands of the 1980s. Fronted by Michael Been, the band had its share of minor hits like 1982's "When the Walls Came Down" and 1986's "Everywhere I Go"—which featured backing vocals by both Peter Gabriel and Simple Minds' Jim Kerr—and 1989's "Let the Day Begin."

In an effort to try to keep the momentum going and show his allegiance to a great band, Bono lent backing vocals to the Santa Cruz, California–bred band's 1990 album *Red Moon*, singing on "What's Happened to You."

"Put 'Em Under Pressure"

In April 1990, Larry Mullen, Jr. wrote and performed drums on this single, which became the official anthem of Ireland's 1990 World Cup soccer team. Released on Son Records, an imprint of U2's Mother Records, the song topped the Irish singles chart.

Up and coming London DJ Howie B assisted the U2 drummer with the track's completion.

"New York, New York"

Released on the Australian Roo Art label, Ecco Homo was a Melbourne band produced by Michael Hutchence and his Max Q conspirator Ollie Olsen. During U2's 1989 Lovetown Tour, Hutchence got The Edge and Bono to contribute to the track. A video for the song was released down under in 1990 and featured a cameo by Bono.

"Can't Help Falling in Love"

Culled from the soundtrack to the movie *Honeymoon in Vegas*, it featured Elvis Presley classics covered by established stars. Released in 1992, Bono's solo rendition—which was supposedly recorded during Sun studio sessions for *Rattle and Hum*—was eventually incorporated into the ZooTV shows, with him singing it nightly to end the concert, as evidenced by the *Zoo TV: Live from Sydney* video. It was also a B-side on the single "Who's Gonna Ride Your Wild Horses."

Slide on This

Edge played guitar on Ron Wood's solo disc, *Slide on This*, which was released in September 1992. Edge can be heard on the tunes "Show Me," "Somebody Else Might," and "Ain't Rock & Roll."

Automatic Baby

In late January 1993, Adam Clayton and Larry Mullen were in Washington for Bill Clinton's swearing-in ceremony as president. At a party, they met up with Michael Stipe and Mike Mills of R.E.M., half of another popular band who helped Clinton with voter registration during its 1992 tour.

Stipe—who would sing with 10,000 Maniacs at MTV's televised inaugural ball—informed them that he and Mills were thinking of doing an acoustic version of "One." Of course, he wanted to know if U2's rhythm section would like to join them.

After hemming and hawing, Stipe talked them into it, with Larry playing congas instead of a full drum set. After a quick afternoon rehearsal, they named themselves Automatic Baby by taking the first word in the title of R.E.M.'s latest album, *Automatic for the People*, and the last in U2's latest.

News of the collaboration caused excitement, prompting MTV boss Tom Freston to shift things around so that the supergroup could close the show. But Don Henley, an aging superstar, who was playing a full set, balked at the demand and threw a tantrum. As a result, Mullen, Clayton, Stipe, and Mills didn't close the show—but their gorgeous performance of the anthem was long remembered as the highlight.

"I've Got You Under My Skin"

In 1993, Bono's duet with Frank Sinatra, which was recorded in different studios, was selected as the lead single from the Hoboken, New Jersey, native's

Duets album. The long-player debuted at #2 on the U.S. charts behind Pearl Jam's second effort, *Vs.* The song was praised for being an intergenerational effort that brought Sinatra fans that might otherwise not have appreciated his music.

Still, the part of the song where Bono intones, *"Don't you know, Blue Eyes, you never can win"* sounded a bit contrived. While it didn't stop it from being a massive global favorite, the *NME* trashed the exercise, writing, "A crappier and more, well, insulting record would be hard to imagine . . . Bono's mumbling take on 'I've Got You Under My Skin' confirms his covetable status as World's Most Pretentious Human Being."

In the Name of the Father

In the fall of 1993, Bono spent a good amount time with Gavin Friday at Dublin's STS Studio where they worked together on the *In the Name of the Father* soundtrack. Sinead O'Connor, who had since patched up her war with U2, joined the session to record her vocals for "You Made Me the Thief of Your Heart," which became the project's single and signature track.

The following January, the song was nominated for a Golden Globe alongside U2's own "Stay (Faraway, So Close!)" from the Wim Wenders film of the same name. They both lost, however, to Bruce Springsteen's powerful "Streets of Philadelphia."

Flyer

In April 1994, with Adam and Larry both living in New York City and enjoying time off from U2, they recorded four tracks with Nanci Griffith for her upcoming *Flyer* album.

Released in September of that year, and also including performances by Peter Buck of R.E.M., Mark Knopfler, the Chieftains, the Indigo Girls, Emmylou Harris, and Adam Duritz of Counting Crows, it was nominated for a Grammy in the Best Contemporary Folk Album category at the 1995 awards ceremony.

Born Again Savage

In May 1994, Adam Clayton guested on sessions for Little Steven's next studio album, *Born Again Savage.* U2's bassist played on every track.

Sadly, because of contractual matters, the raw, edgy follow up to 1989's *Revolution* was not released until 1999.

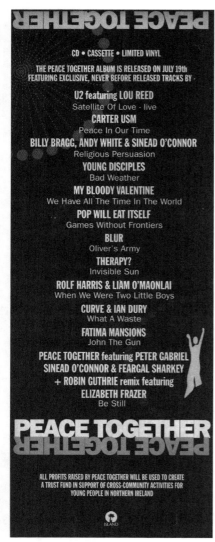

This ad, which ran in the short-lived U.K. music publication *Lime Lizard* in July 1993, was created to promote the *Peace Together* all-star compilation. Featuring U2 and Lou Reed's live collaboration of "Satellite of Love" as its lead-off track, the project aimed to raise funds for cross-community activities for the youth of Northern Ireland.

Author's collection

"Hallelujah"

In May 1994, Bono recorded a mostly spoken-word rendition of Leonard Cohen's "Hallelujah" at Dublin's STS Studios. DJ Howie B tweaked the track at the request of the band, marking the beginning of a fruitful relationship with the U2 organization.

The song eventually surfaced on the March 1995 tribute album, *Tower of Song*, released by A&M Records. The compilation also boasted the likes of Don Henley, Sting, Tori Amos, Elton John, Peter Gabriel, Billy Joel, and Depeche Mode's Martin Gore covering Cohen's songs.

"Hold Me, Thrill Me, Kiss Me, Kill Me"

Following a year and a half out of the public eye, U2 returned to its *Zooropa* leftovers in order to craft a track to be included on the 1995 *Batman Forever* soundtrack. The net result, "Hold Me, Thrill Me, Kiss Me, Kill Me" was written by Bono about "being in a band" and "being a star."

Although the song did well in the U.K. upon its June release in that year, hitting #2, it stalled at #16 in the U.S. It fared better on the American Rock and Modern Rock airplay charts, however, reaching #1 on both surveys.

The song's animated video was the work of Kevin Godley and Maurice Linnane who hurriedly crafted the clip, which featured drawn renderings of Bono's ZooTV aliases "The Fly" and "MacPhisto." Interspersed with footage from the film, the band—replete with its guitars as flamethrowers—was shown chasing the Batwing in a yellow supercar.

On a related note, the filmmakers reportedly offered U2's frontman $5 million to play the role of MacPhisto as a villain in the film. He declined.

Shag Tobacco

Gavin Friday's 1995 album included backing vocals by Bono and Edge on the song "Little Black Dress." Released in the U.S. in January 1996, the disc also counted "Mr. Pussy"—an ode to the Dublin café he co-owned with Bono—and a unique cover of T. Rex's classic, "The Slider."

Wrecking Ball

Produced by Daniel Lanois, Emmylou Harris's 1995 album *Wrecking Ball* featured Larry Mullen, Jr. drumming on nine of twelve tunes and playing among dignitaries like Steve Earle, Lucinda Williams, and Neil Young, who wrote this acclaimed project's title track. Released in September, it was recorded in Lanois' New Orleans studio.

"Save the Children"

Released in October 1995, the Marvin Gaye tribute album *Inner City Blues* featured a solo cut by Bono delivering his rendering of "Save the Children." Elsewhere, Madonna and Massive Attack; Stevie Wonder; and Neneh Cherry contribute tracks.

"GoldenEye"

Performed by Tina Turner as the theme to the James Bond film of the same name released in November 1995, it was written by Bono and The Edge. Because the producers of the film did not collaborate with U2's principals, alternate takes of the song did not appear throughout the film, which was the case with most other Bond films.

GoldenEye was the first film starring Pierce Brosnan in the Bond role.

"Let the Good Times Roll"

Bono can be heard singing alongside Ray Charles and Stevie Wonder on Quincy Jones's 1995 album *Q's Juke Joint*. Released in November, the disc's liner notes explained how U2's singer and Jones befriended one another. They met in 1987 while Bono was in L.A. on *The Joshua Tree* Tour.

The following year, during the *Rattle and Hum* efforts in that city, Bono, Larry, and Adam leased the house next door to Jones, and their friendship grew.

"We've been friends ever since," Quincy explained in that album's liner notes. "He is smart, perceptive, curious, warm, real, and strongly connected to music's roots. His introduction of Sinatra at the Grammy Awards was so on the money that I asked him to send me a copy of it. He is the perfect fit for the middle of this. The addition of Bono simply felt natural, the way things should be."

Passengers

In November 1995, U2 released *Passengers: Original Soundtracks, Volume One* in collaboration with Brian Eno. Much to U2's objections, Island Records told the band and its producer/collaborator that it was unwilling to release it as a U2 and Brian Eno title for fear that fans of the band would be put off by the collaboration.

The experimental *Zooropa* had not been the blockbuster of its predecessors and the label didn't want the band to lose any more of its commercial footing. The "Passengers" moniker was suggested and approved.

A mix of instrumentals, only two of the songs were immediately identifiable as U2 efforts. It's a record which Larry Mullen famously dislikes. Deeming it self-indulgent, critics agreed with the drummer about the group's droning effort. The *Washington Post* called it "seldom anything more than high-tech slug music."

With that said, "Miss Sarajevo" still made #6 in England. The band donated its proceeds to War Child, an organization designed to aid children in war-torn areas.

"Drinkin' in the Day"

Bono co-wrote the track "Drinkin' in the Day" for Ronnie Drew's album *Dirty Rotten Shame*. The solo album by the Dubliners member was released in December 1995.

"Tomorrow ('96 Version)"

Released on the May 1996 compilation Common Ground, "Tomorrow ('96 Version") was an updated take on the *October* track that Bono and Adam worked on with Donal Lunny and Sharon Shannon. It features traditional

Irish instrumentation by modern musicians from the Emerald Isle and was designed to showcase emerging talent performing traditional Irish music. Bono added a new verse to this rendition.

"Mission: Impossible"

In May 1996, the *Mission: Impossible* soundtrack—which featured the theme by Larry Mullen, Jr. and Adam Clayton—was released. The successful side venture was tracked while on hiatus from U2 in 1995 when both bandmates had taken temporary residence in New York City the previous fall.

Released as a single in June, it went Top Ten in the U.K. and U.S. The following January, the high-energy rendition of the classic espionage theme was nominated for a Grammy Award in the Pop Instrumental Performance for an Orchestra, Group, or Soloist category.

"'Mission: Impossible' is such a great tune that we thought we'd try to do an updated version, and I think it fit more as something that would work in clubs rather than something that would promote the movie," Adam told *Propaganda* in July 1996, soon after its completion.

"Give Me Back My Job"

Recorded with Carl Perkins, Johnny Cash, Willie Nelson, and Tom Petty, Bono sang backing vocals on the song "Give Me Back My Job" from Carl Perkins's 1996 album *Go Cat Go*. It turned out to be the final album by the rockabilly legend.

"I'm Not Your Baby"

During the eight days U2 rehearsed for the PopMart Tour at Sam Boyd Stadium in Las Vegas, the band wrote three new songs. One, called "I'm Not Your Baby," wound up becoming a duet between Bono and Sinead O'Connor that was slated for the soundtrack to the Wim Wenders film *The End of Violence*.

Bono finished the lyrics during this Vegas stay, and tracked his vocals. Sinead added hers later.

"Dreaming with Tears in My Eyes"

On August 19, 1997, Bono contributed to the tribute album *The Songs of Jimmie Rodgers*. The song "Dreaming with Tears in My Eyes" featured drums by Larry Mullen and was part of a compilation overseen by Bob Dylan to draw attention to Rodgers's work. The album also featured Alison Krauss, Willie Nelson, Van Morrison, John Mellencamp, and Dylan, among others.

"Perfect Day"

Originally written by Lou Reed for his landmark album *Transformer*, "Perfect Day" was reworked as a tribute to live music and the BBC's support of it. Featuring Reed, Bono, David Bowie, Suzanne Vega, Elton John, Lou Reed, Emmylou Harris, Tammy Wynette, Shane McGowan, Dr. John, Robert Cray, the Lemonheads' Evan Dando, Suede's Brett Anderson, and Laurie Anderson, the song and video was originally issued in November 1997. Bono, who was unable to be in London during the tracking of the song because of his PopMart Tour activities, recorded his parts in New York.

"Sweet Jane"

On January 12, 1999, Lone Justice released its cover of the Velvet Underground's "Sweet Jane" on the album *This World Is Not My Home*. Featuring Bono on vocals with frontwoman Maria McKee, this version was recorded live when the country-rock band opened for U2 in 1987.

Entropy

Released on April 15, 1999, the Phil Joanou–directed film *Entropy* debuted at the Los Angeles Film Festival and featured Bono and Larry Mullen with speaking parts. It is a semiautobiographical film that traces a film director who is assigned to shoot a U2 music video while his personal life is in crisis.

Featuring footage from U2's performance in Cape Town, South Africa in March 1998, U2 happily agreed to let Joanou have the rights to five songs for a licensing fee of just $1,000, which was unheard of for a band of U2's stature. The group could have insisted upon a payment of about $250,000. Despite the help of his famous Irish friends, Joanou's *Entropy* was never in wide release. It went straight to video in February 2000.

Sightings of Bono

Written by Paul McGuinness's wife Kathy, this short film—which was released in September 2000—starred U2's singer as himself. *Sightings of Bono* tells the story of a Dublin girl who sees the rock star everywhere and finally meets him in the store where she works.

"Air Suspension"

This track by Mocean Worker features guest vocals from Bono. His singing parts on "Air Suspension" had originally been planned for another song that was to be included on *The Million Dollar Hotel* soundtrack. When that fell through, Adam Dorn—the man behind Mocean Worker—got the U2 singer's permission to release the vocals on *Aural & Hearty*, which was released on September 26.

"Children of the Revolution"

Recorded by Bono with Gavin Friday and Maurice Seezer, this bastardized cover of the T. Rex classic "Children of the Revolution" was released as part of the *Moulin Rouge* Soundtrack on May 8, 2001. Elsewhere on the album, alt-pop chameleon Beck did a cover of David Bowie's "Diamond Dogs."

"Joy"

In the summer of 2001, Bono helped his friend Mick Jagger out by lending his voice to a track called "Joy" from the Rolling Stones' frontman's latest solo album *Goddess in the Doorway*. He appeared alongside the Who's guitarist Pete Townshend, recording in Mick's personal studio in the South of France.

Upon its release on November 19, 2001, Jagger told *Rolling Stone*, "As for Bono, when you've done so many records for so many years, you have to give young people a go. It worked really well—I'd already

This artwork commemorates an event to celebrate the release of the hardbound illustrated book and CD of "Peter and the Wolf," which was narrated by Bono's longtime friend Gavin Friday. The illustrations in the book were the work of the U2 frontman and his daughters Eve and Jordan. The project benefited the Irish Hospice Foundation.

Author's collections

done the vocal and then I took it to him. He took it and did a lot of stream of consciousness at the end."

Live in Dublin

Recorded at Ardmore Studios in County Wicklow on January 25, 2002, in an intimate setting, Bono performed two songs with the Corrs for their album *Live in Dublin*, released that March 2002. Together he sang duets with Andrea Corr, reworking the recent Ryan Adams song "When the Stars Go Blue" and the classic Lee Hazelwood/Nancy Sinatra tune "Summer Wine."

"That's Life"

Recorded for the soundtrack to *The Good Thief*, Bono's rendering of this Frank Sinatra classic was released in March 2003. It is believed Bono's vocals were tracked at Windmill Lane Studios.

"Falling at Your Feet"

Written and recorded for *Million Dollar Hotel* soundtrack, 2003's *Shine* found Daniel Lanois re-working this track with an assist from Bono for his first studio album in ten years. The longtime U2 producer revised "Falling at Your Feet," removing most of Bono's vocals and all of the original instrumentation—including Larry Mullen's drums. Bono still received a vocal credit, but the song has been claimed by the group's Canadian-born accomplice.

"Class Reunion"

The Edge was invited to collaborate with Wyclef Jean on his 2003 project, *The Preacher's Son*, after the guitarist arrived and performed at one of the Haiti native's Dublin gigs. An instrumental at the time Edge tracked his guitar part, R&B singer Monica was later brought in to finish off the tune.

Peter and the Wolf

Bono launched an art exhibition in the fall of 2003 that featured material he had drawn and painted with his daughters Jordan and Eve for an updated take on the classic children's book *Peter and the Wolf*. In addition to the Hewson family's art contributions, a CD accompanied the project with music and voices by Gavin Friday and his musical collaborator Maurice "the Man" Seezer.

Bono earmarked proceeds from the project to go to the Irish Hospice Foundation, which assisted his father Bob Hewson up until his death. The following month, the artwork was shipped for display in London and an ultimate auction at Christie's in New York. Sixteen paintings raised $368,000 at auction.

"American Prayer"

Released on April 3, 2004, as part of the album, *46664 Part I: African Prayer*—which also featured tracks by Beyonce, Bob Geldof, Queen with David A. Stewart, Paul Oakenfold, Baaba Maal, Peter Gabriel, and Youssou N'Dour, "American Prayer" was written by Bono and Stewart and was performed by them with The Edge and Beyonce.

Originally designed as a song that would be written with Joe Strummer of the Clash and titled after Nelson Mandela's Prison Number "46664," Bono had hoped to bring attention to the AIDS crisis in Africa. When Strummer died unexpectedly in December 2002, Bono moved forward with "American Prayer."

"Two Shots of Happy, One Shot of Sad"

Written by Bono for Frank Sinatra, who was unable to record it before he passed away, the song was later tracked for the flipside of U2's 1998 single "If God Will Send His Angels." Larry Mullen and Adam Clayton perform on Nancy Sinatra's rendition, which was produced by Sinatra's granddaughter A. J. Azzarto and her then-husband Matt. It was released in the fall of 2004.

"Do They Know It's Christmas?"

Released on the twentieth anniversary of the original in November 2004, Band Aid 20's "Do They Know It's Christmas?" also features a line from Bono and was produced by Radiohead veteran Nigel Godrich. Coldplay's Chris Martin, Joss Stone, Keane's Tom Chaplin, Robbie Williams, Dido, and the Darkness' Justin Hawkins were among the British stars who appeared on this single which benefitted the "Make Poverty History" campaign.

U2 Jukebox

Compiled for *Mojo* magazine's June 2005 issue, this fifteen-track disc was compiled exclusively by Bono. Whittling a total of thirty songs down to the final list, the album counts current favorites and influential material alike. The songs as follows are: "Wake Up" by the Arcade Fire, "Float On" by Modest Mouse, "Grey Will Fade" by Charlotte Hatherly, "Obstacle 1" by Interpol, "Pagan Lovesong" by the Virgin Prunes, "Dream Baby Dream" by Suicide, "30 Seconds Over Tokyo" by Pere Ubu, "Hounds of Love" by the Futuresmiths, "Cattle and Cane" by the Go-Betweens, "A Forest" by the Cure, "The Cutter" by Echo & the Bunnymen, "Christine" by Siouxsie & the Banshees, and "Glad to See You Go" by the Ramones.

"Don't Give Up (Africa)"

Bono's duet with Alicia Keys, "Don't Give Up (Africa)," was released in December 2005. The charity single was a cover of the 1986 Peter Gabriel/Kate Bush collaboration "Don't Give Up," which originally appeared on the album *So*. It was recorded a month earlier for Keys's New York–based Black Ball fundraiser.

"Tower of Song"

Recorded in the Slipper Room in New York City in May 2005, U2's collaboration with Leonard Cohen surfaced the following year on the soundtrack to the movie *Leonard Cohen: I'm Your Man*. Tracked in a burlesque club, Bono performs just one verse before Cohen takes over, with Edge, Larry, and Adam gleefully backing them.

Rogue's Gallery: Pirate Ballads, Sea Songs & Chanteys

Following his role in *The Pirates of the Caribbean*, actor Johnny Depp worked with Gore Verbinski to put together this collection of songs, released in 2006. Produced by Hal Willner (*Million Dollar Hotel*), it features musical contributions from the likes of Richard Thompson, Nick Cave, Bryan Ferry, Sting, Lou Reed, and Bono.

The song penned and performed by U2's singer—according to the liner notes—is "a haunting ballad of the nineteenth-century whaling ships. As well as being musical, sailors often displayed great poetic ability, as in the lyrics of this powerful song."

Maurice Seezer and Gavin Friday appear on the project, as do former Virgin Prune and Lypton Village members Guggi and Day-Vid who join Friday as "Three Pruned Men."

U2 by U2

In March 2004, U2 sold the rights to an upcoming book tentatively titled *In the Name of Love: U2* to Harper Entertainment in the U.K. for a reported $3 million. When the book surfaced in the fall of 2006, it was in a coffee-table style, replete with great, rare photos and extensive and insightful comments from the band. Its official title is *U2 by U2,* and it first retailed for $39.95.

While fans loved it, critics took aim at the band's project. The *Irish Book Review* said, "What comes across most strongly is a degree of self-obsession that becomes tedious and dismaying." Ouch.

"Love's in Need of Love Today"

Bono and Stevie Wonder came together in 2007 to record a version of the latter's classic, "Love's in Need of Love Today." A memorable track on the soundtrack to the film, *Darfur Now,* the album was released on November 27 of that year.

"I Am the Walrus"

Bono performed the Beatles' classic "I Am the Walrus" on November 20, 2005, on the set of the movie, *Across the Universe.* The Julie Taymor–directed film in which he appeared was shot in New York.

The singer starred as a mustachioed hippie in the role of "Dr. Robert," a character based on Jack Kerouac's muse Neal Cassady. "We studied film of him and the way he worked, and it's almost like he wanted to be a rock star," Bono said in a statement about Cassady.

"He has all these jerky moves, a lot of self-confidence, always plays to the women in the room," the singer added. "For my first acting role, I thought this would be interesting and a little bit special."

When the soundtrack to the project was released in tandem with the film in September 2007, Bono had rendered two Fab Four classics with up-and-coming rock band the Secret Machines. In addition to "Walrus," U2's frontman turned out a version of "Lucy in the Sky with Diamonds."

Ten Feet High

Andrea Corr's 2007 solo album was executive produced by Bono and Gavin Friday. Although neither were credited on the record, Andrea did thank both, along with producer Nellee Hooper for "breathing life into my songs," in the liner notes. The disc also boasts a unique cover of the Squeeze classic "Take Me I'm Yours" and the single "Shame on You."

"The Ballad of Ronnie Drew"

Written by Robert Hunter—longtime lyricist for the Grateful Dead—with Bono, The Edge, and Simon Carmody, this all-star song was released as a digital download in Ireland only on February 22, 2008. It was recorded the month prior at Windmill Lane Studios.

Originally written with the hope that Drew—an Irish music legend as part of the Dubliners—would sing a part of the tune, his waning health prevented his involvement, but a who's-who of modern Irish music—including Christy Moore, the Pogues' Shane McGowan, Sinead O'Connor, and the Frames' Glen Hansard, all the members of U2, the Dubliners, and Kila, the song's profits benefitted the Irish Cancer Society.

Drew died on August 16, 2008.

"Sugar Daddy"

When it came time for Tom Jones to release his first new studio album in fifteen years, he called on Bono and Edge to write him a new tune. The end result, "Sugar Daddy," also featured a performance by U2's guitarist.

Although Jones said he immediately loved the song, he revealed his concerns about the title for reassurance. "I said, 'Is that what you think of me?'" Jones told *Spinner* in 2009. "Bono said, 'I just like the sound of sugar daddy.'"

The New York Times

In his first-ever *New York Times* Op-Ed piece in 2009, guest columnist Bono tackled an unexpected subject—the late, great Frank Sinatra.

In a piece titled "Notes from the Chairman," Bono wrote of how he first met and befriended Sinatra when recording "I've Got You Under My Skin" for his 1993 *Duets* album. In appreciation, Sinatra—who also dabbled in painting—gave Bono one of his canvases, titled "Jazz."

"We had spent some time in his house in Palm Springs which was a thrill—looking out onto the desert and hills, no gingham for miles," Bono wrote. "Plenty of miles, though, Miles Davis. And plenty of talk of jazz. That's when he showed me the painting. I was thinking the circles were like the diameter of a horn, the bell of a trumpet, so I said so."

Bono also wrote that Sinatra offered up some "little pithy replies," including: "I don't usually hang with men who wear earrings"; "Miles Davis never wasted a note, kid—or a word on a fool" and "Jazz is about the moment you're in. Being modern's not about the future, it's about the present."

In a subsequent editorial published in January 2010, Bono addressed subjects like illegal file-sharing of music and the state of medicine.

It Might Get Loud

Directed by Davis Guggenheim, this 2009 film chronicles three guitarists—the young fire-starter known as Jack White, the legend they call Jimmy Page and the technician from U2 dubbed The Edge.

Chronicling the power that these notorious guitarists, from three of rock's four generations, exhibit in pursuit of their art, the part of the movie tracing The Edge follows him to the band's origin at Dublin's Mount Temple School, shows the young U2 playing "Street Mission" on RTE in 1978, and finally catches up with the musician as he talks about his guitars.

"Stranded (Haiti Mon Amour)"

In response to the devastating earthquake in Haiti in January 2010, a television benefit was held eleven days after the crisis called *Hope for Haiti Now—A Global Benefit for Earthquake Relief.* Organized by actor George Clooney, it starred Bruce Springsteen, Sting, Coldplay, Haiti native Wyclef Jean, and Neil Young, who each donated their performances for digital download.

Bono and The Edge also performed on the program and the subsequent album with Jay-Z and Rihanna appearing on the track "Stranded (Haiti Mon Amour)" which was made available on the benefit album in both a live and studio versions.

Spider-Man: Turn Off the Dark

By 2010, the Broadway musical version of *Spider-Man*, featuring words and music by U2's Bono and The Edge, had seen a number of delays. The $50 million production had been slated for the stage in 2009, but financial woes caused its funding to vanish. Plans for February 2010 previews were also scratched, with ticket holders being given refunds.

"We were open to the idea of musical theatre, but *Spider-Man?* That's a different thing again because that's comic books and there's a whole relationship between comic books and rock that goes back years," Bono said of the idea in a Marvel.com interview in the summer of 2009, before the production ran into trouble. "To mess with all these different aspects of pop culture and put them in a blender and see what could come out the other end."

The Edge added that the story of Peter Parker was one he identified with. "It's a bit like every rock and roll star's story in a weird way," he said. "Every rock and roll star started out as the geek who was bullied in school and eventually their form of revenge was to write songs."

The front and back sleeves for the *Mojo* magazine compilation U2 put together in July 2005 during its *Vertigo* tour. A mix of the band's favorites from the past by the likes of the Ramones, the Cure, and Echo & the Bunnymen, plus up-and-comers of the time like the Arcade Fire and Interpol, it's an exhilarating compilation.   *U2Wanderer.org*

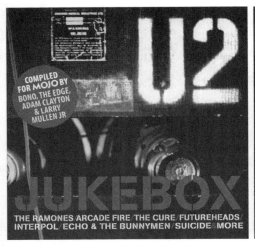

44

It Could Be Yours Tonight

Gettin' Paid

Cashing In

In September 1998, London's *Financial Times* reported that U2 intended to sign an additional $50 million record deal with PolyGram for the release of three *Best of* discs.

First up was *U2: The Best of 1980–1990*, a compilation that includes one limited edition bonus disc of B-sides. The band intended to re-work its 1987 B-side "Sweetest Thing"—Bono's ode to Ali—as the project's single.

iTunes

Apple Computer launched the iTunes Music Store with U2's help on April 28, 2003, with Bono joining the announcement, explaining that an exclusive U2 EP would be made available. An acoustic version of "Stuck in a Moment," plus two tracks recorded live in Boston, marked the first of several business arrangements with Apple during the next five years.

Elevation Partners

Elevation Partners, according to a June 2004 *Wall Street Journal* report, was a Silicon Valley venture capital fund that Bono had joined forces with. Bono, serving as managing director, guided the firm in its investments and acquisitions of media and entertainment businesses.

In a statement, Bono announced, "I want U2 to be a part of the future, and a part in shaping the future. This opportunity with Elevation Partners is, for me, a chance to involve myself in the business that runs my life. I don't want to be a casualty."

In 2006, the singer was criticized for his role in the fund after it bought a stake in *Forbes* magazine, which was owned and steered by American conservative Steve Forbes.

Then in March 2010, Bono was named "the worst investor in America" after a number of trade papers called Elevation Partners "arguably the worst-run institutional fund of any size in the United States." Part of that criticism came from Elevation's investment in Palm, whose Android-based Pre Smartphone had come up short in its bid to compete with Apple's iPhone.

The Big Apple

On October 26, 2004, U2 teamed up with Apple to release a special limited-edition black iPod; the machine also came with a fifty-dollar voucher to enable users to download the band's entire back catalog. Screams of "sell-out!" rang out across the world.

In a statement Bono said, "We want our audience to have a more intimate online relationship with the band, and Apple can help us do that. With iPod and iTunes, Apple has created a crossroads of art, commerce, and technology which feels good for both musicians and fans." In a cross promotion, U2 lent its song "Vertigo" to an iPod television campaign.

Responding to fan allegations that the endorsement was a sell-out, Edge balked in a 2004 *Rolling Stone* piece. "Our position on sponsorship hasn't changed," he insisted. "It's always been that we do not sell our reputation or our work to anybody. But this is a different thing: this is a technology partnership. We're selling U2-branded iPods—the U2 iPod."

It was the band's position that it was merely selling its music on iTunes and getting its entitled share of revenues for its products—which included the digital box set *The Complete U2*. As for the iTunes ad, Edge argued that it was merely using the new music-distribution system to promote its music.

U2 Corp.

In May 2005, the *Chicago Tribune*'s Greg Kot knocked U2 by writing "this once-vital band is turning into the Rolling Stones, more of a corporation focused on perpetuating itself than a creative force."

Bono was not pleased. "Some of what is going around as a result of your article is not just unhelpful to our group and our relationship to our audience," the singer responded to the paper, "but just really problematic for what in the broad sense you might call rock music. The things you think are wrong with it, and the things that I think are wrong with rock music, are polar opposites."

Royalties

Reports surfaced in August 2006 that U2 had shifted control of its publishing royalties to the Netherlands, where they were under the control of Dutchman Jan Favie, who also handled the same responsibility for the Rolling Stones. The band made the move in early June to sidestep a substantial tax increase about to take effect in Ireland. Under the new law, Irish artists' tax exemption was capped at €250,000.

Critics and the Irish parliament reacted to the report—which explained there was no tax on royalties in the Netherlands—by criticizing Bono, who had asked the government of Ireland to offer more assistance in Africa. A *Sunday Times* editorial said, "How can [Bono] be taken seriously on issues like the government's contribution to overseas aid, when he himself is reducing the pool of income from which that funding comes?"

In a *Hot Press* interview almost two months later, manager Paul McGuinness defended the band's decision. "The reality is that U2's business is ninety percent conducted around the world. Ninety percent of our tickets and ninety-eight of our records are sold outside of Ireland. It's where we live and where we work and where we employ a lot of people. But we pay taxes all over the world— of many different kinds. And like any other business, we are perfectly entitled to minimize the tax we pay."

Basquiat

A painting that hung in U2's recording studio in Dublin for almost twenty years was sold on July 1, 2008, at a Sotheby's Contemporary Art auction in London for more than £5

This ad not only announced U2's first album in nearly five years, it also plugged *No Line on the Horizon*'s individual lead singles, "Get on Your Boots" and "Magnificent."

million. U2 bought the painting, by Jean-Michel Basquiat, in 1989 after Clayton saw it in the Robert Miller Gallery, and it had remained in the band's joint collection since.

Known as "Untitled (Pecho/Oreja)," the six-foot-square acrylic, oil stick, and collage canvas—which was created in 1982 when the former graffiti artist was twenty-two years old—featured Basquiat's trademark primitive-mask motif. New York–based Basquiat died in 1988 of a suspected drug overdose, but his work continues to inspire artists.

Live Nation

U2 signed on with concert promoter Live Nation in March 2008 for a twelve-year, $25 million stock arrangement that the *Wall Street Journal* once called a "sweetheart deal." But after the economy tanked later in the year, the band moved to sell the 1.6 million shares—which Live Nation had guaranteed—when they fell to just $6.1 million in worth. U2's new business partner had to make up an estimated $19 million in losses to the band.

Biggest Earners

Although 2009's *No Line on the Horizon* was the group's worst-selling album yet, the band still made more money in the U.S. that year than any other act on the strength of its 360° Tour.

Touring receipts from the spectacular trek—which counts the largest concert stage ever built—along with album sales and royalties resulted in a staggering $109 million. Second behind the Dublin foursome was U2's old pal, Bruce Springsteen, who earned just over $57 million.

Blackberry

In a partnership with Research in Motion, the manufacturers of BlackBerry, the Windows-based PDA manufacturer, sponsored U2's 360° Tour. Signifying the end of U2's previous relationship with Apple, Bono spoke out about the potential to collaborate with Research in Motion on mobile music applications. "I'm very excited about this," he said in a statement. "Research in Motion is going to give us what Apple wouldn't: access to their labs and their people so we can do something really spectacular."

If the blatant sponsorship was overdue for U2, considering the corporate involvement of other major acts, it wasn't a surprise. It needed help with the mounting production costs behind its tour, and this allegiance made it manageable.

Commercials for Blackberry's "U2 Mobile App," began airing in early July 2009, helping to plug "I'll Go Crazy If I Don't Go Crazy Tonight." The application allowed the user to hear the new album, read news about the band, and see where they were in relation to the band during its concerts.

45

I Have No Compass, and I Have No Map

U2's Side Businesses

The Clarence Hotel

In November 1992, U2 and Point Depot owner Harry Crosbie partnered to purchase the notorious Clarence Hotel in Dublin for a reported £2 million. The band began renovating the building and put a nightclub on site.

The building was built in 1852, and was one of the more prestigious hotels in the city of Dublin.

The Kitchen

On Valentine's Day 1994, U2 opened the Kitchen, its nightclub housed in the basement of the Clarence Hotel. Although the band's major celebrity pals were largely absent from the opening, Cranberries frontwoman Dolores O'Riordan, Def Leppard's Joe Elliot, and rock pioneer Jerry Lee Lewis made the scene.

The Kitchen was touted as "a brave new era in Dublin nightlife." But on May 4, 2002, U2 closed the nightclub after eight years. Falling attendance and new licensing laws—which allowed pubs to now stay open later—were blamed on the decision. The media suggested the venue's turbulent relationship with the local Garda Siochana could also have been to blame. The unoccupied space would reportedly be used as an extension of the Clarence Hotel's Therapy Room.

Kitchen Records

In February 1998, U2 launched Kitchen Records. With Bono and his old friend Reggie Manuel (a.k.a. J. Swallow) working in A&R capacities, the label—named for its nightclub—focused on releases aimed at club DJs.

Café Nude

A company founded by Bono and his brother Norman designed to provide a healthy fast-food option, Café Nude was opened at 21 Suffolk Street in Dublin, the former site of Mr. Pussy's Café De Luxe, the cabaret café Bono had owned with Gavin Friday and filmmaker Jim Sheridan.

This long closed venue was briefly visible in U2's 1995 video "Hold Me, Thrill Me, Kiss Me, Kill Me." It was located next to another now defunct Norman Hewson enterprise, the Italian restaurant Tosca—which closed its doors in 2000.

Hanover Quay Studios

U2's Hanover Quay Recording Studio and building was renovated to completion in 1994 and has been the home to much of its studio work since 1995. Located in the Dublin docklands area, U2 fought to stop the forced demolition of its building when the Dublin Docklands Development Authority announced a redevelopment project in the early 2000s.

Calling for 1,200 new homes, an amphitheater, shops, and restaurants, and a purported 20,000 jobs, it meant Hanover Quay would be a goner. Shortly after U2 lost its June 2002 petition, the band and the DDDA agreed to replace their studio building, but by 2009 the building was one of just two original buildings remaining.

If and when the project breaks ground it will keep the band in the area of the city where it has worked, recorded, and invested over the past twenty-five years.

The U2 Tower

Six months after it lost its ruling, U2 announced in November 2002 that the Dublin Docklands Development Authority and U2 would build a new high-rise building, "the U2 Tower" in Dublin, that would include a new penthouse recording studio.

The new building was to be designed to replace U2's Hanover Quay studio, which the DDDA planned to tear down as part of a redevelopment project. But by October 2008, plans to break ground on the project—which would have been completed by 2011—were suspended indefinitely due to an economic downturn.

EDUN

A clothing line belonging to Bono and Ali and featuring fashions produced in Third World countries was launched in New York on March 11, 2005, when Saks Fifth Avenue began to retail the designs.

They called it "a marriage of social activism and aesthetic innovation." EDUN items started in Saks Fifth Avenue stores and moved to other retailers later in the year.

But by May 2006, a *New York Post* piece said that EDUN was failing. With poor sales, certain retailers dropped the line. "We've experienced bumps in the road," a representative of the company told the newspaper.

46

The Songs Are in Your Eyes

How to Dismantle an Atomic Bomb

F ollowing the multiplatinum success of 2000's *All That You Can't Leave Behind*, U2 continued working with its successful rock formula on the follow up, which was recorded between February 2003 and August 2004 and was ultimately released on November 22 of that year.

In early 2003, Bono described a new song, then called "Full Metal Jacket," as "the reason to make a new album" to *Rolling Stone*. But this "mother of all rock songs," as Edge called it to *Planet Sound*, morphed into a demo known as "Native Son" and finally emerged as "Vertigo." Other songs from these sessions that were attempted but never properly released—included the sprawling, six-plus-minute "Mercy" and titles like "Shark Soup," "Viva La Ramone," "Lead Me in the Way I Should Go," and "You Can't Give Away Your Heart." Another track, called "North Star," purportedly included guest vocals by Christian artist Michael W. Smith and was penned in homage to Johnny Cash.

Using an array of producers, beginning with Chris Thomas—the man behind the Pretenders' 1979 eponymous classic and the Sex Pistols' iconic 1977 set *Never Mind the Bollocks*—the group subsequently tapped its old friend Steve Lillywhite to oversee the project when efforts with the former went awry. Working in Air Studios in London in October 2003 with a fifty-piece orchestra, the session was disastrous. According to reports, Thomas called it the worst day he'd ever spent in a studio.

With Lillywhite on board and Jarrett "Jacknife" Lee assisting him, things began to progress in the New Year. One of the final songs the band recorded before the album's completion was a bonus track in certain international markets known as "Fast Cars" which contained a lyric that would give the album its title.

By summer, as with past U2 albums, *How to Dismantle an Atomic Bomb* endured its share of band-initiated drama after an incomplete version of the disc belonging to The Edge was stolen during a July 2004 photo shoot in France. For fear that these unfinished tracks might leak onto the internet, the band announced that should the songs hit the web it was prepared to release its proper version immediately.

The move wasn't necessary; however, much closer to the disc's scheduled drop date, some tracks from advance copies of the CD made it into the realm of illegal file sharing. In an effort to let fans try it before they could buy it, U2 streamed the album in its entirety via its official website a week prior to its proper release.

Upon its completion, Adam Clayton spoke of the disc's guitar-driven tunes to U2.com. "A lot of them are a kick-back to our very early days," the bassist revealed, "so it's like with each year we have gathered a little bit more and this is what we are now."

Elsewhere—in the album's bonus documentary *U2 and 3 Songs*—Bono described the record's lyrical direction, saying, "Although [it's] not a concept album in the traditional sense, most of the music on the record deals with the world at the crossroads of its existence. Love and war, peace and harmony, and approaching death are themes of the album."

1. "Vertigo": Originally known as "Native Son," with lyrics inspired by Leonard Peltier, an American activist and member of the American Indian Movement who some say was unfairly convicted for the 1975 murders of two FBI agents during a shootout on the Pine Ridge Indian Reservation, this song was soon enough lyrically altered. The impetus for the shift came when Bono realized that the idea of performing such a controversial tune in a live setting might be upsetting for him.

"Vertigo," as it became known, was a far less serious, rave-up of a song that first earned the attention of television viewers in September 2004 as part of an animated television commercial for the Apple iPod. It was part of a shared marketing initiative to promote U2's upcoming album, its own Special Edition iPod (which was laser-engraved with autographs), and the band's exclusive digital box set, *The Complete U2*.

A count off in Spanish of "¡Unos, dos, tres, catorce!"—which strangely translates as "some, two, three, fourteen!" and was blamed by Bono on his own alcohol consumption during the session—gives way to Edge's savage guitar line. Coupled with a superb "Hello, hello" line hollered by U2's frontman, some fans have suggested it harks back to the same utterance on 1980's "Stories for Boys." Although the songs have no other similarities, the band had the recipe for a brilliant single.

As for the actual lyrics to the song, its message of staying true to one's beliefs and faithfulness in the face of temptation is evidenced by lines,

"I can't stand the beat, I'm asking for the check / The girl with crimson nails has Jesus 'round her neck."

Released in advance of its parent album on November 8, the song—for which the band's 2005 tour was named—was an instant smash, reaching #1 in the U.K. and debuting at #1 on the Hot Digital Tracks survey (selling 200,000 downloads) in the U.S. It only reached #31 on the Hot 100, however, because *Billboard* didn't begin including digital downloads as part of its charting calculations until the beginning of 2005.

2. "Miracle Drug": The contemplative but uplifting second track on *How to Dismantle an Atomic Bomb* was written about the Irish writer Christopher Nolan, who had been a student a few years behind U2 at Mount Temple Comprehensive School. Deprived of oxygen for the first two hours after his birth, Nolan suffered from cerebral palsy, was wheelchair bound and unable to communicate for the first thirteen years of his life until they discovered a medication that gave him movement of one muscle in his neck.

"They attached this unicorn device to his forehead and he learned to type," Bono marveled to *Blender* in late 2004. "And out of him came all these poems that he'd been storing up in his head. Then he put out a collection called *Dam-Burst of Dreams*, which won a load of awards, and he went off to university and became a genius. All because of a mother's love and a medical breakthrough."

Through the song, which has been compared structurally to "With or Without You," U2 gives praise to the medical advancements made in our lifetime. "Miracle Drug" was just the second recorded instance of Larry Mullen, Jr. joining Bono and Edge on vocals. The first was 1993's "Numb."

3. "Sometimes You Can't Make It on Your Own": Written in memory of Bono's father, Bob Hewson, "Sometimes You Can't Make It on Your Own," was released as a single in the U.K. on February 7, 2005. Chronicling the relationship that they nurtured in his father's final months, the tune he initially called "Tough" is among Bono's finest vocal performances ever which might explain why it debuted at #1 on that singles survey.

"And it's you when I look in the mirror," Bono crooned on the number that he first sang at his father's 2001 funeral after Bob Hewson succumbed to cancer. If it was deeply personal, "Sometimes" was also the arguable high point of *How to Dismantle an Atomic Bomb,* and the singer knew it.

Bob Hewson was also the inspiration for the album, which Bono at first called *How to Dismantle an Atomic Bob.* "My voice is the best it's ever been on this record," he told *Hot Press* in 2004. "And I believe that it's my father's gift to me. He was a great tenor and when he died he passed that on to me."

4. "Love and Peace or Else": Dating back to the sessions for *All That You Can't Leave Behind*, U2's political missive for 2004 got its start with a distorted bass part producer Brian Eno imagined. Topically driven by the war in Iraq, the song—which often segued into "Sunday Bloody Sunday" during its *Vertigo* Tour performances—transformed Bono from rock star to preacher in order to proclaim, *"Lay down, Lay down your guns/All you daughters of Zion, All ye Abraham's sons."*

"It's worth reminding ourselves of those days after 9/11, and what they felt like," Bono told *Hot Press*, discussing it in 2004. "No one knew whether we were going to wake up and a quarter of London, maybe Kilburn, would be gone."

5. "City of Blinding Lights": As the third U.K. single, "City of Blinding Lights" reached #2 there on the strength of its musical muscle and powerful melodies. Although it didn't make a big impact commercially in the United States, the song was acclaimed and used regularly by Barack Obama during his 2008 presidential campaign. The U.S. President has since named it one of his favorite songs.

Formed from a song named "Scott Walker" that was inspired by the cult songwriter and first developed during the recording of *Pop*, U2 had returned to it in 2000, but it was left incomplete until work started on its eleventh studio set.

Rebuilding it musical part by musical part, Bono has said that the lyrics were in part inspired by a photo exhibition he attended by the group's photographer Anton Corbijn in the Netherlands. When Bono saw a picture of himself from December 1982 as he boarded a helicopter to film the "New Year's Day" video, Neil McCormick wondered what he might say to his younger self if time travel were possible. "I'd tell him to stop second-guessing himself," Bono answered.

Elsewhere, Bono has suggested that lines for the song reference his first-ever trip to London with his wife, Ali, and the experience of performing in Madison Square Garden just six weeks after the 9/11 attacks on New York.

"*'Oh you look so beautiful tonight.'* It is such a naïve and innocent line," he explained to U2.com. "That's what this song is about, remembering those times. . . . It's not necessarily a curse, it's that part of us is missing. It's about recapturing a sense of wonder, being in a city and reminding yourself that you don't have to lose your soul to gain the world."

6. "All Because of You": This hard-charging, punk-like single is also somewhat revelatory for Bono, who calls himself an "intellectual tortoise." When asked for an explanation, bassist Adam Clayton told *Hot Press*, "He is. He is a unique character. He is organized intellectually, but he wouldn't know where his car keys are."

A radio favorite on U.S. rock outlets, the song reached U.K. #4 as a single. When the group played it live on the *Vertigo* Tour, Bono introduced it as "a love song to the Who." A video for the song was shot in New York City in the fall of 2004 with the band playing atop a flatbed truck as it rode around the city with fans chasing it. Upon their arrival in Brooklyn, at Empire Fulton Ferry State Park, the band played an impromptu mini concert recorded for MTV, which fans learned about through local radio and the internet.

7. "A Man and a Woman": Described by U2's frontman to *Q* in November 2004 as a cross between Marvin Gaye and the Clash, the stylistic inspiration for the song came from Thin Lizzy's Phil Lynott. The lyrical brainwave, however, came from his companion of nearly thirty years.

This promotional red, grey, and white CD single was released to radio outlets throughout Europe during the week of September 24, 2004.   *U2Wanderer.org*

Written with Ali in mind, and for couples who have been together for a long time and were still spiritually connected, for Bono it was a way of asserting his fidelity and celebrating their union.

8. "Crumbs from Your Table": A musical accompaniment to his Drop the Debt initiative, Bono's lyrics (*"Where you live should not decide/Whether you live or whether you die"*) hone in on the fact that rich nations such as the United States provide very little relief to third-world nations.

"I went to speak to Christian fundamentalist groups in America to convince them to give money to fight AIDS in Africa," Bono griped to *Q* in November 2004. "It was like getting blood from a stone. I told them about a hospice in Uganda where so many people were dying they had to sleep three to a bed."

As for the song itself, the melody and music came together quite quickly while Bono and Edge were drinking. As for the lyrics, which U2's singer has called "one of the most vicious songs ever," Bono wrote them after he sobered up.

"It's full of spleen about the church and its refusal to hear God's voice on the AIDS emergency," he added of its biting albeit effective content.

9. "One Step Closer": This was reportedly written after Bono and Noel Gallagher shared a conversation about Bob Hewson's waning health and the fact that he had lost his faith in the later years of his life. "Do you think he believes in God?" U2's frontman wondered. "Well, he's one step closer to knowing," the Oasis guitarist responded matter-of-factly.

With origins dating back to 2000, the slow, somber song finds Bono marooned on an island. When asked if he ever thanked Gallagher for the song's title U2's frontman cracked to *Hot Press*, "He's on a pint of Guinness and a packet of crisps for coming up with the title."

10. "Original of the Species": Bono had his goddaughter, Edge's then-teenage daughter Hollie, in his thoughts when he first started working on "Original of the Species" for the band's album *All That You Can't Leave Behind*. The song became less specific as it progressed and was designed to reassure young people who were full of self-doubt.

By the time it was finished for *How to Dismantle an Atomic Bomb*, it was a sorely needed commentary on the concern young people have with how they look and what they weigh. It was a message to teenagers to accept who they were. Bolstered by Edge's piano work, the tune—which was also featured in commercials promoting Apple's iPods in 2005—received some radio play in the U.S., specifically on the adult-alternative format, where it charted at #6.

11. Yahweh: A swooning parting shot of a song built from a title that means "God" when the letters are individually translated to Hebrew letters, this song was originally recorded with Chris Thomas. "Yahweh is the name for the most high," Edge would explain to *Q*, "which Jewish people do not utter. It is written, not spoken. It's a sacred name for God and in this song it's a prayer."

Talking about the song, Bono said the fact that he sings it instead of speaking it justified his use of the moniker. "It just formed in my mouth, as a lot of U2 songs do," he said later. "There's the sound, and then trying to figure out what that sound is—and it was this word, 'Yahweh.'"

Reception and Reaction to *How to Dismantle an Atomic Bomb*

Upon its release on November 22, 2004, U2's eleventh studio album debuted at #1 in the United States, with first-week sales of 840,000—twice that of its predecessor, *All That You Can't Leave Behind*. Globally it topped the charts in thirty-four countries. It eventually sold nine million copies worldwide.

But despite its commercial reach, Bono confounded the media when he said of U2's latest achievement, "There are no weak songs. But as an album, the whole isn't greater than the sum of its parts, and it fucking annoys me."

Despite that odd decree, the album was praised around the world. *Rolling Stone* touted it as "grandiose music from grandiose men," and although it was released late in the year, it topped the year-end best-of rankings in esteemed publications like the *New York Times*, *Paste*, and *USA Today*. The latter called it "U2's best album, eclipsing *Achtung Baby* and *The Joshua Tree*. Meanwhile, *Q*, the *Village Voice*, and the *Los Angeles Times* placed it in their Top Ten lists for 2004 at #4, #8, and #2 respectively.

I Believe You Can Dance with Me

Rare, Unreleased, and Collectible Releases

Rare A's and B's

The following releases represent songs that made it onto officially sanctioned 45s, but for one reason or another did not see wide release. Some tracks have been reissued in other, more readily available formats; others have not.

"A Celebration"

At the outset of 1982, in advance of its U.S. touring commitments, U2 hit the studio to record an upcoming single, "A Celebration." The non-album release—which was backed by the acoustic number, "Trash, Trampoline and the Party Girl"—was another modest chart performer, stalling at #47 in the U.K. Top Fifty.

With its lyrics about believing in the "atomic bomb" and "the Third World War," Bono would joke to Timothy White in his 1991 book that "it was sort of Apocalypse Next Week." With a video for the clip shot in April 1982 again with Meiert Avis in Dublin's Kilmainham Jail, it didn't have the success on MTV of its predecessor, "Gloria."

Speaking of the clip in 1983, Larry said it had been shot on the site of the 1916 uprising. "We filmed it with the idea of breaking out," he said in an April 1983 fanzine interview with *White Lucy*. "It was very much a look at ourselves. Like when we were in school and everyone was telling us 'you're crap' and we couldn't get a record deal, it was the triumph of breaking through."

Released in 1982 for the German and Netherlands markets only, the sleeve of this rare single exhibits one of the earliest images of Bono holding a flag as a stage prop. The A-side, a live rendition of the band's first global hit, "I Will Follow," was recorded at Veronica's Countdown at Hattem in Holland on May 14, 1982.   *991.com*

Just the same, the song was quickly forgotten. A year after its release, Bono was telling reporters that the band had forgotten how to play it. But the reality was that the group was trying to bury it. The single was unavailable on CD for twenty-five years until it was appended to the 2008 expanded reissue of *October.*

"Pete the Chop"

No, it's not the U2 B-side "Whatever Happened to Pete the Chop?" This track is a different tune from the early days of U2 that the band kept as its secret weapon. A surefire single that they held in reserve in the event Island ever dropped them—something the company probably considered after the initially poor reception to *October*—they never had to use it.

"I Will Follow" Again

In May 1982, U2 was asked to perform "I Will Follow" for a Dutch television program. When the show aired on July 7, fans began to clamor for the song in the shops. Island Records rush released the version from the show in the Netherlands and Germany, where it peaks at #12.

Unreleased

What follows is a list of the U2 songs that have only surfaced via bootlegs or in another, similar unofficial capacity. Most of this material is indispensable for those seeking to be U2 completists.

"Be There"

Still in pursuit of a replacement for Steve Lillywhite, U2 cut a demo with another potential producer, Blondie's Jimmy Destri in March 1982. In this session, the band tracked a rarity called "Be There," which would eventually be released in bootleg form. During the studio experiment,

A one-off single released in the spring of 1982 that never surfaced on any actual album and was quickly disowned by the band until it resurfaced as a bonus track on the expanded CD reissue of *October*. The Japanese pressing above was released via Island/Polystar. It counts different artwork and a different B-side, choosing "Fire" over the non-LP track "Trash, Trampoline and the Party Girl," which backed the tune in European markets.   *Author's collection*

they also developed ideas that would eventually become "Endless Deep," a future B-side, and "The Unforgettable Fire."

"In Cold Blood"

This unreleased track was one of fourteen prepared for *Zooropa*, but late in the session four of the most guitar-based tracks were eliminated, leaving the final count at ten. "In Cold Blood," reportedly featured somber lyrics courtesy of Bono, but little else is known about the song.

"Break of Dawn"

A rarity recorded as a duet by Bono and Bruce Springsteen that had been slated for the bonus disc of rarities included on limited copies of the Boss's *The Essential Bruce Springsteen*, "Break of Dawn" never surfaced. Fans expecting the track when the project was released in October 2003 were indeed disappointed.

Reel to Reel

On March 26, 2004, rare U2 memorabilia was offered for auction on eBay, including a reel-to-reel copy of U2's first-ever recording session. Plans for a big payday, including an opening bid of $18,000, were squashed, however, when Paul McGuinness told the *Irish Times*, "I've seen it on the site and it's clearly genuine. Someone can buy the tape but they can't release anything from it without the band's permission."

McGuinness also suggested that permission to release the tracks, which he called "pretty rough," will not be granted, killing any possibility of a buyer. Other items in the collection reportedly included Bono's handwritten lyrics to "Shadows and Tall Trees" and typed lyric sheets for "Street Missions" and "The Fool," plus proof pictures from one of the group's early photo sessions.

Digital Rarities

From *The Complete U2*: This entirely digital box set was released by U2 on November 23, 2004, via iTunes. Boasting the complete U2 album catalog it featured 446 songs and a PDF that included album art, track listings and band comments. Among the previously released material, the set—which retailed for $149.99—possessed three exclusive albums and an EP of rarities and unreleased material, plus the groups hard-to-find early singles. As of late 2007, it was no longer available.

Early Demos

Recorded at Keystone Studios in Dublin in 1978, these three songs were produced by Horslips' Barry Devlin. Tracks included "Street Missions," "Shadows and Tall Trees," and "The Fool."

Live from Boston 1981

This digital live album was released exclusively as part of the band's iTunes digital box set *The Complete U2*. Recorded at the Paradise Rock Club on March 6, 1981, the thirteen track concert recording found the band recycling "The Ocean" and "11 O'Clock Tick Tock," its opening numbers that night to accommodate the unexpected encores that the audience requests.

Live from the Point Depot

Another digital live album, this was also released as part of the band's iTunes digital box set. Recorded on New Year's Eve 1989 at the Point Depot in Dublin, the show was initially broadcast internationally on the radio and was a popular bootleg until the band decided to release it as a bonus in this format. These tracks could not be purchased individually and were only available to those who purchased *The Complete U2*.

The concert highlights include "I Still Haven't Found What I'm Looking For" with an excerpt of the Bob Marley song "Exodus," a medley of "Running to Stand Still," and "Dirty Old Town" with a snippet of Bob Dylan's "The Times They Are a Changin'" and the assistance of the legendary B. B. King on "When Love Comes to Town" and "Love Rescue Me."

Unreleased & Rare

Also part of this massive but now-defunct digital box set, *Unreleased & Rare* was an eighteen-track compilation of largely unavailable material culled largely from the group's *All That You Can't Leave Behind* and *How to Dismantle an Atomic Bomb* eras, with three and six songs represented, respectively.

In many cases, U2's cast-offs are remarkable, including "Levitate," a song that didn't make the cut for *All That You Can't Leave Behind*. Other winners from that era include the hard-rocking "Love You Like Mad" and the strummed delight "Flower Child." The *How to Dismantle an Atomic Bomb* leftovers "Native Son"—the politically charged blueprint that became "Vertigo"—and "Xanax & Wine" are also stellar.

Other Digital Releases

U2 has seen a remarkable shift in music-storage formatting in their thirty-two-years-and-counting career. Vinyl, magnetic tape, and compact disc all predated the current method of choice: audio download. Here are some difficult-to-classify releases thereto:

Live from Under the Brooklyn Bridge

Four tracks released as an EP from a performance at Empire-Fulton Ferry State Park in Brooklyn, New York on November 22, 2004, this digital release—via iTunes—surfaced on December 9 of that year. Featuring performances of "All Because of You," "Sometimes You Can't Make It on Your Own," "I Will Follow," and "Vertigo," it is no longer available for purchase.

Exclusive

Released via iTunes on April 24, 2003, this digital EP featured an acoustic take of "Stuck in a Moment You Can't Get Out Of," which had been a B-side release in various formats outside of the U.S. and was included on 7. It appended two concert tracks—"I Will Follow" and "Beautiful Day"—from *Elevation 2001: U2 Live from Boston*.

Collectible Physical Releases

These are extended- or long-play recordings that the band has produced but might not be readily available in your local record store. Some contain gems and are worth the effort of tracking down.

Please: PopHeart Live EP

Never released in the United States in this format, this EP—released in 1997—boasts four live tracks from U2's PopMart Tour. The four live tracks were instead released on the "Please" single, itself a collectible.

Hasta La Vista, Baby!

Released with the August 2000 Issue of U2's *Propaganda* magazine, this fan-club-only release is a live recording from the group's PopMart concerts in Mexico City in December 1997. The track listing is as follows: "Pop Muzik," "Mofo," "I Will Follow," "Gone," "New Year's Day," "Staring at the Sun/ Bullet the Blue Sky," "Please," "Where the Streets Have No Name," "Lemon,"

"Discothèque," "With or Without You," "Hold Me, Thrill Me, Kiss Me, Kill Me," and "One."

Sunday Times U2 Exclusive (Promo)

Released in tandem with a June 3, 2001, cover story on U2, the magazine's free disc included five songs and two videos. Featured were album renditions of "Beautiful Day," and "The Ground Beneath Her Feet," a cover of the Ramones' "I Remember You" and their own "New York" plus "I Will Follow"—recorded live at Irving Plaza in New York in December 2000—and videos for "Beautiful Day" and Johnny Cash's "Don't Take Your Guns to Town."

7

This exclusive EP, which was only available through Target stores in the United States, was released on January 22, 2002. Counting the B-sides that were available recently on singles released in other territories, it includes "Summer Rain," "Always," "Big Girls Are Best," "Beautiful Day (Quincey & Sonance remix)," "Elevation (influx remix)," "Walk On (single version)," and "Stuck in a Moment You Can't Get Out Of (acoustic)."

U2.COMmunication

This live album was released exclusively to U2.com members in November 2005. Recorded at two different May 2005 Chicago performances and two subsequent shows in Milan in July of that year, the eight-track disc includes a moving rendition of "Miss Sarajevo" from the Italy shows that includes Bono tackling the aria originally recorded by Luciano Pavarotti. The track was dedicated to the victims of the July 2005 terrorist bombings in London.

This project also came with a CD-ROM of U2 wallpapers, screensavers, and a video clip of "Vertigo" live in Milan. The exclusive release was discontinued in November 2006.

Zoo TV Live

Captured in concert at the Sydney Football Stadium on November 27, 1993, *Zoo TV Live* was a double CD made available to subscribers of its official website in November 2006. Featuring the same live material that was included on the *Zoo TV: Live from Sydney* home video, it also appends a bonus rendition of "Tryin' to Throw Your Arms Around the World" recorded at the band's August 1992 Yankee Stadium show. The project also

In contrast to the Japanese sleeve, the U.K. pressing of "A Celebration" lacks a cover photo of the band.

U2Wanderer.org

included a double-sided poster with two images from the band's 1992–93 tour.

This release came with two limited-edition posters (on one double-sided pressing) from the ZooTV era, pictured above with the "cover art," of which there is little except for what's on the sleeve.

Medium, Rare & Remastered

When *The Complete U2* digital box set could no longer be had, U2 improved on *Unreleased & Rare*, altered its title and artwork and made it available exclusively to U2.com subscribers in 2009 as *Medium, Rare & Remastered*.

Tweaked with most of the original B-sides fans might have missed during the release of its post-millennium singles output, songs like "Summer Rain" and "Fast Cars" and early rarities like "Saturday Night," "Trash, Trampoline and the Party Girl," and "Angels Tied to the Ground" add additional value.

If those peak bonus numbers from U2's remastered and expanded versions of *Boy*, *October*, and *War* weren't enough, *MR&R* included a pair of lost tracks from *The Joshua Tree*! With extra material this strong, one can't help but wonder why this compilation hasn't been released earlier.

Artificial Horizon

Similar to *Melon: Remixes for Propaganda*, U2's second remix project *Artificial Horizon* was made available to U2's subscribing members on CD in March 2010. A compilation album of thirteen tracks from U2, it was reworked by the likes of Trent Reznor, Hot Chip, Snow Patrol, and Jacknife Lee. The material was also subsequently released to the general public as three purple vinyl LPs which were first available as a pre-order through the band's official website for a May 2010 delivery.

U2.COMmunication was a live album recorded exclusively for members of the band's official website. Released in November 2005, it included material recorded earlier that same year during shows in Chicago and Milan.   *eil.com*

48

Papa Sing My Sing My Song

Tunes U2 Has Written for Others

"Purple Heart"

Written by Bono and T Bone Burnett for the latter's 1988 Columbia album *The Talking Animals*, Bono also sang backing vocals and produced the song "Purple Heart." It also featured help from session veterans such as Tony Levin, the late T-Bone Wolk, and Mitchell Froom.

"She's a Mystery to Me"

Written for Roy Orbison by Bono and Edge, the impetus for this brilliant song began when the latter's former wife Aislinn gave the singer a copy of the soundtrack to *Blue Velvet*, the David Lynch film, when U2 was in London for a gig.

With the disc on repeat, Bono fell asleep. When he woke up he had a melody and words in his head. When he realized his song was different from any of the tracks on the soundtrack, he wrote it down and brought it to soundcheck.

Bono claims that he was telling the band how he thought the song would be perfect for Roy Orbison before the show. Later, he was completely surprised when Orbison—who happened to be in London—dropped by the band's backstage area.

"I had no idea he was coming over, and neither had the band," Bono remembered. "They all looked at me like I had two heads. Somehow God had agreed with me about Roy Orbison."

Later, Bono finished the song with Roy, which appeared on his final studio album and became its first single. Released posthumously in 1989, the disc's title, *Mystery Girl*, was also derived from Bono's lyrics.

"Conversation on a Barstool"

This was a song Bono wrote for Marianne Faithfull with the understanding that she would record the song for her 1990 album *Blazing Away*. But "Conversation on a Barstool" was left off of the album, and Faithfull's version didn't surface until her 1998 set, *A Perfect Stranger*.

"Slow Dancing"

Originally written in 1992, "Slow Dancing" is a country-tinged song that Bono had in mind for Willie Nelson. A beautiful number about yearning and untrustworthiness, Nelson was slow to commit to it at first. It eventually surfaced in 1998 with the country legend singing lead vocals on the track, and wound up on the flip side of "If God Will Send His Angels."

"Time Enough for Tears"

Released in November 2003 on the *In America* soundtrack, "Time Enough for Tears" was penned by Bono for Andrea Corr with Gavin Friday and Maurice Seezer. Friday and Seezer produced the track, which ran over the credits of Jim Sheridan's film. Recorded in late 2002 with Corr putting down her part in just one take, the movie and its subsequent soundtrack surfaced a year later. The song was nominated for a 2004 Golden Globe Award.

49

Joyful Noise

U2's Hits Compilations

The Best of 1980–1990

U2's first greatest-hits effort, released in November 1998, *The Best of 1980–1990* contains most of the group's singles, a couple fan favorites, and one new recording—a reworking of the 1987 B-side "Sweetest Thing." For fans, however, the real lure was a limited edition version with a bonus disc of essential B-sides.

This reworking of U2's 1987 B-side became the pop hit it needed in 1998, helping to propel the band into the Top Ten in the U.S., the U.K., and Canada, among other markets. It was the anchor track of the band's *Best of 1980–1990* campaign that fall. The sleeve features—you guessed it—Peter Rowan photographed in a gas mask circa 1983.

U2Wanderer.org

Also featuring Guggi's brother Peter Rowen on the cover in a previously unreleased *War*-era photo in which he sports a combat helmet, the project—bolstered by its aforementioned hit single—was the commercial success U2 needed after the mixed reaction to *Pop*.

A subsequently released home video DVD with the same title, boasting all of the band's best-known formally issued music videos from this era, was also made available in April 1999.

The Best of 1990–2000

Offered in November 2002, the second greatest-hits compilation from U2 spanned the band's second decade and included two new songs, the project's single "Electrical Storm" and "The Hands That Built America" which also appeared on the soundtrack to Martin Scorsese's *Gangs of New York* in a slightly altered form.

The project also marks the first U2-branded release of the *Batman Forever* tune "Hold Me, Thrill Me, Kiss Me, Kill Me" and "Miss Sarajevo."

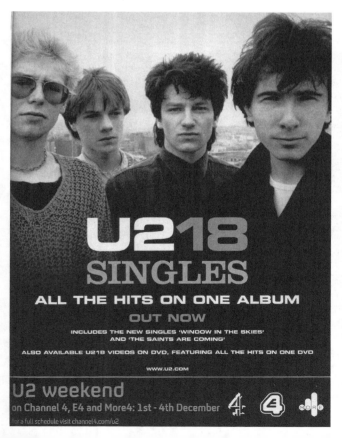

Released in conjunction with *U2 by U2*, the band's official coffee table book and biography, *U218* counts the bulk of the group's best-known songs. This ad promoted the hits compilation in the U.K.

Cathleen Penyak

U2 also took the opportunity to rework several experimental *Pop* tracks like "Discothèque," "Staring at the Sun," and "Gone" into approaches more in keeping with its established guitar sound.

Like its 1980–1990 predecessor, the project also featured a bonus B-sides disc, which included such must-haves as the band's take on the Beatles' "Happiness Is a Warm Gun" and its co-writing collaboration with Christy Moore, "North and South of the River." Fans of the group's dance mixes really hit the mother lode, however, with a total of nine reworked mixes.

A home video DVD of U2's music videos from this era, replete with commentary from the clips' respective directors, was released separately but in tandem with the audio CDs.

U218 Singles

Some have argued that *U218 Singles*, another greatest hits compilation boasting artwork identical to the band's *U2 by U2* coffee-table book—was a

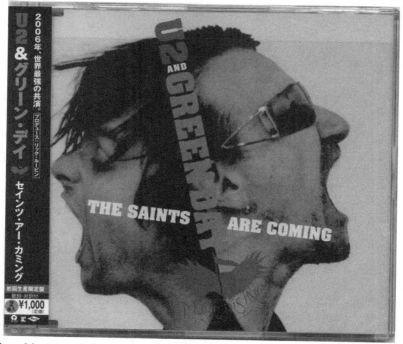

Produced by Rick Rubin, this is the Japanese CD single pressing of the 2006 U2/Green Day collaboration "The Saints Are Coming," which was originally performed by Scottish punk band the Skids and appeared on *U218*. Proceeds from the single went to Music Rising, an organization co-founded by The Edge that was designed to restore a musical presence to New Orleans after the wreckage caused by Hurricane Katrina.

U2Wanderer.org

cash grab. With sixteen of the band's best-known tunes and a pair of new songs, the album was a strong commercial performer, reportedly becoming the seventh best-selling disc in the world for 2006.

Two new singles emerged from the set, including its Rick Rubin–produced collaboration with Green Day on the Skids' "The Saints Are Coming," plus a new original song "Window to the Skies."

Fans who bought the deluxe edition of *U218* were treated to a bonus DVD called *Vertigo 05: Live from Milan*. It included ten of the twenty-five songs performed during the group's 2005 Milan, Italy show. The digital version of the deluxe edition sold via iTunes also made nine of the ten songs here available as bonus audio tracks.

50

Three Chords and the Truth

U2 and the Rock and Roll Hall of Fame

The Who

On January 17, 1990, all of U2's members were on hand as Bono inducted one of their all-time favorite bands, the Who, into the Rock and Roll Hall of Fame at the annual ceremony in New York City. In his remarks, Bono poked fun at Townshend's big nose, suggesting that it's the key to a great rock and roll band.

This may very well be the last time Bono appeared in public wearing his brimmed hat and vest in public. The next time he emerged, he had an extremely different public image.

The Yardbirds

U2 guitarist The Edge took an early morning flight to New York on January 15, 1992, so that he could induct 1960s blues-rock favorites the Yardbirds into the Rock and Roll Hall of Fame. He wrote his speech honoring the band, which produced three of the best guitarists of all time—Eric Clapton, Jeff Beck, and Jimmy Page—while sitting in first class.

At the end of the ceremony, Edge joined in the traditional jam session, performing alongside Neil Young, Johnny Cash, Keith Richards, Jeff Beck, Jimmy Page, Steve Cropper of Booker T and the MG's, Robbie Robertson, Carlos Santana, and Creedence Clearwater Revival founder John Fogerty.

Bob Marley

In January 1994, Bono inducted Bob Marley—the man whose album sales first gave Island Records its financial power—into the Rock and Roll Hall of Fame.

According to Edge, the Clash—pictured above in 1980—were inspirational in writing "Sunday Bloody Sunday" among other songs. The U2 guitarist helped to induct the band into the Rock and Roll Hall of Fame in early 2003, just over a month after the passing of the band's outspoken singer/guitarist Joe Strummer.   *Photofest*

"I know claiming Bob Marley is Irish might be a little difficult here tonight," he told the crowd, "but bear with me. Jamaica and Ireland have a lot in common. Naomi Campbell, Chris Blackwell, Guinness, a fondness for little green leaves—the weed, religion, the philosophy of procrastination—don't put off 'til tomorrow what you can put off till the day after. Unless, of course, it's freedom."

ZooTV Exhibit

On September 1, 1995, a "ZooTV" exhibit opened at the Rock and Roll Hall of Fame in Cleveland, Ohio. Including four Trabants hanging from the ceiling in the lobby, U2's artifacts were the first items visitors saw when they entered the museum.

A subsequent U2 exhibit, called "In the Name of Love: Two Decades of U2," opened in 2002. Speaking of that honor, Edge said to U2.com, "We've been donating stuff to the Hall of Fame over the years, you know. I've been there a couple of times, and I think it's a great facility. It's fascinating to wander around. We give them any help we can."

Bruce Springsteen

On March 15, 1999, Bono inducted Bruce Springsteen into the Rock and Roll Hall of Fame during the annual New York ceremony. In his speech, the U2 singer gave a great overview of a man who became an inspiration to not only him but the other members of U2.

"Here was a dude who carried himself like Brando, and Dylan, and Elvis," Bono explained. "If John Steinbeck could sing, if Van Morrison could ride a Harley-Davidson. . . . It was something new, too. He was the first whiff of Scorsese, the first hint of Patti Smith, Elvis Costello, and the Clash. He was the end of long hair, brown rice, and bell bottoms. He was the end of the twenty-minute drum solo. It was good night, Haight-Ashbury; hello, Asbury Park!"

Later, Bono added, "They call him the Boss. Well that's a bunch of crap. He's not the boss. He works FOR us. More than a boss, he's the owner, because more than anyone else, Bruce Springsteen owns America's heart."

Following up his tribute to Springsteen, Bono joined the all-star jam session at the end of the night, singing part of a celebratory rendition of Curtis Mayfield's "People Get Ready."

Chris Blackwell

On March 19, 2001, Bono inducted Island Records founder Chris Blackwell, the man who co-founded the label U2 has been aligned with since 1980, into the Rock and Roll Hall of Fame. Calling Blackwell a "magician" Bono paid tribute to the man behind the record company that helped make U2 stars.

During the evening's customary jam session at the end of the show, he partnered with Mary J. Blige for a memorable rendition of Bob Marley's "Could You Be Loved," in honor of Blackwell.

The Clash

With Bono sidelined with excruciating back pain, Edge and Rage Against the Machine's Tom Morello inducted the Clash into the Rock and Roll Hall of Fame in 2003.

"There is no doubt in my mind that "Sunday Bloody Sunday" wouldn't— and couldn't—have been written if not for the Clash," Edge said at the New York ceremony.

"They broke through barriers of perception and genre," U2's guitarist added, "and left behind them a thousand bands from garage land who caught a glimpse of what they saw and strove for, including one from Ireland called U2."

U2

After years of supporting the Rock and Roll Hall of Fame, U2 were inducted in their first year of eligibility on March 14, 2005. Bruce Springsteen inducted the group, citing their "beautiful songwriting" and saying of their songbook, "In their music you hear the spirituality as home and as quest. How do you find God unless He's in your heart? In your desire? In your feet? I believe this is a big part of what's kept their band together all of these years."

"See, bands get formed by accident, but they don't survive by accident," Springsteen continued. "It takes will, intent, a sense of shared purpose, and a tolerance for your friends' fallibilities . . . and they of yours. And that only evens the odds. U2 has not only evened the odds but they've beaten them by continuing to do their finest work and remaining at the top of their game and the charts for twenty-five years. I feel a great affinity for these guys as people as well as musicians."

Following the Boss's awe-inspiring introduction, U2 accepted the honor one by one, beginning with Bono, who cracked, "Born in the U.S.A., my arse. That man was born on the North side of Dublin. He's Irish. His mother was Irish, the poetry, the gift of the gab—I mean, isn't it obvious? In fact, I think he's tall for an Irishman."

They played a four-song set that included "Until the End of the World," "Pride" with a snippet of Springsteen's own "The Promised Land," and a segue into a duet with Bruce on "I Still Haven't Found What I'm Looking For." They closed their performance with "Vertigo."

51

Shine Like a Burning Star

ZooTV to 360°: U2's Tours (1992–2010)

ZooTV

On February 29, 1992, U2's ZooTV Tour got underway in Florida. Demand for the first show at the 7,000-seat arena in Lakeland, Florida was high: it sold out in just four minutes. It was an indicator of the success of the tour, as tickets for the March 1 show in Miami sold out in only twelve minutes.

Concern over ticket scalpers forced U2 to only allow telephone ticket sales in most markets and limit sales to two per person. When tickets for the band's Boston shows went on sale, the vendor received nearly a half-million calls in the first hour. Unable to get through, fans would hang up and redial. By the time the show sold out hours later, over two million calls had been made.

Later, in Los Angeles, some four million phone calls for tickets to the Sports Arena gigs caused many customers to temporarily lose service.

As for the show itself, it was unlike any other rock performance ever put on. With its dozens of TV screens displaying satellite transmissions and pre-recorded images—the ZooTV Tour was the perfect companion to the groundbreaking album it was supporting. For most of the first show, Bono performed in the role of the Fly; but by the encore, he changed gears and became the Mirrorball Man, a character dressed in a silver suit.

"He believes in ratings," Bono said of his shiny alter ego, according to *U2 Live: A Concert Documentary.* "That's really all he believes in and . . . he'll say anything that anybody wants to hear. That's kinda like religion is getting these days."

During the course of its extensive run into 1993, U2's frontman also created Mr. MacPhisto, which replaced Mirrorball Man for the encore that

This gig ad comes from the third leg of U2's ZooTV tour. Featuring opening acts Public Enemy and the Sugarcubes, the band's 1992 open-air stadium performances in North America were cleverly subtitled "Outside Broadcast."   *Author's collection*

year. Created as a parody of the devil, replete with devil horns, the character was originally invented as "Mr. Gold" because of the gold outfit he wore before evolving into MacPhisto, named after one of the seven princes of hell, Mephistopheles.

The lengthy trek was full of surprises as Bono phoned the White House after plans to call a phone-sex line fell through—nobody wanted their credit-card number given out to audiences each night. Meanwhile, U2 dueted with a pre-recorded Lou Reed on "Satellite of Love" on most nights and brought a belly dancer they first met in Lakeland during dress rehearsals out on the road with them for "Mysterious Ways."

In March 1992, Bono ordered 10,000 pizzas from a Detro t-area restaurant, but the pizzeria only came through with one hundred. The delivery man brought them into the venue on a trolley as a cameraman followed him and he was put up on the Vidiwall. Before long, the pizza boxes turned into Frisbees that littered the Palace of Auburn Hills.

Celebrities turned out for the ZooTV gigs in New York, Los Angeles, London, and beyond, as the band found itself in the elite company of attendees like Neil Young, Peter Wolf, Dr. Ruth Westheimer, Tatum O'Neal, John McEnroe, Little Steven, Peter Gabriel, Mike Scott, Gary Oldman, Bruce Springsteen, Axl Rose (who joined the band for "Knockin' on Heaven's Door" in Vienna), Jack Nicholson, Dennis Hopper, Robert DeNiro, Julia

Roberts, Elvis Costello, Chrissie Hynde, Salman Rushdie, LL Cool J, and Billy Idol.

Although it was sensational, with psychedelic-painted Trabants—an image of what went wrong with Communism—stuffed with performance lights hanging from the ceiling of venues overhead, the shows were incredibly expensive, costing the band $250,000 per day. U2 would later confess that it nearly caused them to lose their shirts.

"If ten percent less people had come to see us, we'd have gone bankrupt," Bono confessed to the *Dubliner*. "And with those kind of bills you don't go bankrupt a little, you go bankrupt a lot."

Or as Paul McGuinness clearly explained when all was said and done at the end of 1993, the band's swag saved its ass. "We grossed $30 million in T-shirt sales," McGuinness told Bill Flanagan. "Without those we'd be fucked."

PopMart

On February 12, 1997, two weeks before the formal release of *Pop*, U2 descended on the lingerie section of Manhattan's K-Mart store. It was here the band held a press conference to announce the group's forthcoming PopMart Tour of America, which was broadcast on both MTV and VH1.

After it revealed the itinerary, U2 performed a new song, "Holy Joe," beneath the store's infamous Blue Light and amid the panties and brassieres. Ironically, the tune wasn't even on *Pop*; it was the flipside of "Discothèque."

The tour itself was part of a new booking arrangement that eliminated its longtime agents, Ian Flooks for Europe and Frank Barsalona for North America. Although it was a tough decision, considering they'd had working relationships with both since 1980, U2 was a business. After the worries over ZooTV's profit margin, which was in question until its last few shows, the band decided to align with a company that was willing to take the financial risk.

After the lukewarm reception to the *Pop* album, there was plenty of apprehension that maybe the band bit off more than it could chew with its upcoming tour. In 2005 Bono revealed that before PopMart he felt unsure of the band's future and wondered if U2 might in fact fail.

This ticket to the Philadelphia stop on U2's ZooTV Outside Broadcast was the first of two consecutive September 1992 shows at the now-defunct Veterans Stadium. *Author's collection*

Larry was more forthcoming on the eve of the tour, telling *Rolling Stone* in 1997 that the band's struggles to get PopMart ready for audiences had him worried. "I'm scared shitless, to be honest with you. Every night I wake up with this nightmare of getting up onstage and nothing working."

After eight days of rehearsals, the tour got underway on April 25 in front of 38,000 at the sold-out Sam Boyd Stadium in Las Vegas. Taking the stage like boxers entering the ring—with Bono shadow boxing in a satin robe—they walked through the crowd with a security detail as M's 1979 one-hit wonder, "Pop Muzik" played. Despite the fanfare, there were technical problems, including a re-do of "Staring at the Sun" after Bono began it off key. An unforgiving *NME* reporter called it "FlopMart." On the flipside, *USA Today* said the show "outshines Vegas glitz, and with the site of the largest single LED video screen ever built, a one-hundred-foot-high toothpick and olive prop, and the forty-foot mirror-ball lemon that carries the band to the stage for its encores, it's a point that's hard to dismiss." The show cost $250,000 per day to produce.

Celebrities turned out for opening night, including Dennis Hopper, Robert De Niro, Sigourney Weaver, Trent Reznor, Kylie Minogue, Michael Stipe and Mike Mills from R.E.M., some members of the *Friends* television show, and Helena Christensen.

During its four legs and ninety-four shows that kept the band active in stadiums and large arenas until March 1998, the elaborate show was full of humor and self-mockery, and U2's lightheartedness kept the show upbeat, even when problems arose. Just three weeks into the trek, Bono's continued inability to find the right key resulted in the group shifting the then-current single, "Staring at the Sun," from an electric presentation to an acoustic offering it served up on its B-stage in the middle of its stadium show.

Perhaps the most hilarious of all of U2's incidents occurred on August 6, 1997, at the Valle Hovin Stadium in Oslo. The giant lemon that carried the band to the B-stage for an encore shut down while moving with Bono, Edge,

This stub from U2's *Vertigo* Tour is a souvenir from the band's June 2005 gig at Manchester Stadium.

Author's collection

Larry, and Adam inside of it. The door to the giant electronic-fruit replica got stuck as it started to pen; and from the outside, all the fans could see were the group's legs. After a few minutes of pandemonium, they figured out how to get the door to open manually, and the members of U2 climbed down a latter in order to perform their closing numbers.

During the tour, U2 performed in Poland for the first time on August 12. Although the show at the Warsaw Horse Track was poorly arranged—with a mile-long crowd lining up in the afternoon and fans rushing the gates causing injury to two hundred or so fans—it was a triumph. During the gig, Bono paid tribute to Lech Walesa and performed the song that Solidarity leader inspired "New Year's Day." With images of the Polish leader on the screen behind him, Bono told the audience, "This is your song." The crowd's reaction was emotional and uplifting.

Days later, perhaps in response to problems with its mechanical lemon, Bono suggested the idea of bringing such an enormous spectacle on tour in the future might be a mistake in an interview with the *Sunday Times*. "I can't imagine us playing live again. I don't think we would be stupid enough to take this on again. I think this as big as a live show can go. It's a shame but I can't imagine how we could advance a live show beyond PopMart. We will not bring another show the same size on the road again."

His remarks were misunderstood, and reports elsewhere suggested U2 might never tour again. This prompted Island Records to release a statement on August 19 with a clarification from the singer. "Of course this is not U2's last tour," Bono remarked. "The next tour will be different but there certainly will be more U2 tours."

As the stadium trek continued, it was marred by tragedy in Rome when a twenty-eight-year-old fan died, suffering a brain aneurysm in a crush of fans as they entered the venue. It also had its triumphs, including the band's biggest outdoor show ever in front of 175,000 fans on the Reggio Emilia grounds in Northern Italy.

Shows in Kosovo Stadium in Sarajevo, Bosnia and Hayarkon Park in Tel Aviv, Israel were also considered victories as the band played previously untapped and recently troubled cities. U2's presence in these two very different locales was a sign that a semblance of normalcy had returned for the people in these once-terrorized locales.

When all was said and done, U2 walked away with a gross earnings of $170 million from sales of almost four million tickets. But despite the financial reward, the tour left Larry Mullen with a bad taste in his mouth. He knew U2's overconfidence in booking a tour before the album was completed to the band's satisfaction was not only a little arrogant, it was flat-out wrong.

Elevation Tour

On December 5, 2000, U2 played a rare New York club show at Irving Plaza. In order to sustain momentum for their latest album and draw attention to its upcoming *Elevation* Tour, which was three months from its start, the band agreed to play the "free" hour-long concert for radio-contest winners, celebrities like Lenny Kravitz and industry executives.

Broadcast live on U.S. radio, the show marked the first time the band had performed "Won't Get Fooled Again," the song originally done by its heroes the Who that originated on its legendary *Who's Next* album in 1971. When the actual tour got underway on March 24, 2001, at the national Car Rental Center in Fort Lauderdale, the Pete Townshend tributes were gone. But the most significant change was U2's return to indoor arenas over the stadiums it occupied throughout much of the 1990s. When demand existed—as it often did for a band of U2's stature at the arena level—the band played multiple dates in a given venue.

In an unexpected move, the band planned to use general-admission ticketing. Although there were no seats on the floor, fans were excited by the notion of being down on the floor in front of U2 for a mere forty-five dollars—the cheapest tickets for these gigs. With a stage that counted a heart-shaped catwalk that came approximately halfway out onto the floor of any given arena, it allowed for the first three hundred fans on the floor to see the band inside of the structure. But aside from this creation, the band's gigs, like the group itself, were low key. Gone, too, was the gigantic video wall, replaced by four smaller ones that traced the band's respective members in black and white.

The European leg was also an arena presentation, with the exception of a handful of outdoor performances, including a massive Slane Castle show on August 25, 2001, which saw U2 perform for more than 150,000 fans over two nights. Marking the band's first time playing the venue since its 1981 show opening for Thin Lizzy, it was a monumental event for the Dublin band.

Sadly, however, the tour through Europe was a tough one for Bono, who flew home to Dublin to be by his ailing father's side whenever possible. By the time of the Slane gigs, Bob Hewson had lost his battle with cancer. Bono dedicated "Kite" to his dad and introduced his older brother Norman to the audience. It was a bittersweet high point for the U2 frontman.

The third leg of U2's *Elevation* trek got underway in October 2001, just one month after the September 11, 2001 attacks. Starting at the University of Notre Dame in South Bend, Indiana, the shows were a reflection of the somber mood in the world at the time, and included the band performing Marvin Gaye's 1960s social anthem "What's Going On?" and "Walk On."

Three days into these dates, performing in Hamilton, Ontario, U2 began scrolling the names of those who died on the hijacked flights during the terrorist attacks while playing "One." The band quickly expanded the visual presentation to include the names of firefighters and police officers who lost their lives. This presentation was shown for the remainder of the *Elevation* Tour and was reprised in February 2002 during the group's half-time Super Bowl performance.

When the tour closed in Miami on December 2, 2001, U2 had performed a total of 113 shows with the help of opening acts PJ Harvey, Garbage, No Doubt, the Corrs, and others. For its efforts, the band earned $110 million, ranking it as the third most successful tour of all time when *Pollstar* magazine released its tally in 2005.

Vertigo Tour

Following the successful release of *How to Dismantle an Atomic Bomb*, U2 announced plans for its *Vertigo* Tour to launch on March 28, 2005, in San Diego. The band's first run of U.S. dates behind the album ran West to East and counted twenty-eight sold-out arena gigs.

But before the tour—for which the band rehearsed in Vancouver, British Columbia in early 2005—could get off the ground, U2 was embroiled in a ticket presale debacle that upset subscribers of its official website who paid forty dollars for the opportunity to buy tickets in advance of the general public. It turned out that technical problems experienced with U2.com frustrated fans. The band's drummer issued an apology via an open letter on behalf of the band, explaining: "There was a mess up in the way the tickets were distributed."

Eventually expanded to five legs, the *Vertigo* Tour ran through the end of 2006 and was one of the most expensive rock shows ever attempted, with a 120-member crew, 3,000 lights, and five video screens. The band was back to the bombast after its subdued 2001–2002 campaign. When asked about the production—which costs nearly $1 million per show—Bono said to U2.com, "This is our moment. . . . Let's see what a rock band can do when they are right at their prime."

Devised by longtime lighting designer Willie Williams and architect Mark Fisher, the *Vertigo* Tour featured an abundance of LED lights and included a ramp similar to the one used on the *Elevation* Tour, which went out onto the floor and connected to the stage that allowed for several hundred fans inside its "bomb shelter." For the second through fifth legs, held mostly in stadiums, the band supplanted the extended stage loop with two catwalks to B-stages that were built to replicate the "Vertigo Target."

Spiritually, Bono described the shows as part political rally, part gospel tent, and part Las Vegas show. Upon the passing of Pope John Paul, for instance, at the band's Anaheim, California stop, Bono made mention of it, calling the pontiff who once wore his Fly sunglasses "the best front man the Church ever had." He added, "I think I have a little bit of a Pope complex—and he certainly had a bit of a rock-star complex."

Other surprises on the eighteen-month initiative included Bono's onstage collaboration with openers Arcade Fire on Joy Division's "Love Will Tear Us Apart," the return of "Out of Control" to the set after a seventeen-year gap, and the reintroduction of "Au Cat Dubh/Into the Heart," which hadn't been played live since 1984.

In Europe the band sold out three shows at Dublin's Croke Park, shifting 240,000 tickets, and summer stadium concerts there continued to make "Sometimes You Can't Make it on Your Own" a focal point of the gigs in homage to Bono's cherished father. Later in the show, a message of peace built around the COEXIST logo—which embraces a Muslim crescent, the Jewish Star of David, and Christian cross—was used to emphasize the significance of "Where the Streets Have No Name" and "Pride (In the Name of Love)."

A third leg of arenas in North America in the fall of 2005 gave way to U2's early 2006 shows in gigantic Central and South American venues, marking the group's first visit to countries like Chile and Argentina since PopMart. The tour's final leg—which marked gigs in New Zealand, Australia, and Japan—was initially announced in March 2006 but was delayed when The Edge's daughter Sian was struck with a serious but unnamed illness. These stadium performances were eventually

This *Vertigo* Tour ticket is accompanied by pieces of confetti that were dropped on the crowd during gigs.   *Cathleen Penyak*

bumped to late 2006 with a final gig performed on December 9 at Honolulu's Aloha Stadium with special openers Pearl Jam.

This exceptional show marked the appearance of Green Day's Billie Joe Armstrong with U2 on "The Saints Are Coming" during an encore that also counted Pearl Jam's Mike McCready and Eddie Vedder joining in on a rendition of Neil Young's "Rockin' in the Free World."

When all tallied U2's 2005/2006 *Vertigo* Tour was an unbelievable moneymaker. The band sold more than 4.6 million concert tickets and grossed a total $389 million, which was reportedly the second-highest figure ever for a music tour at the time.

The tour also spawned *U2 3D*, a widely praised 2008 concert film featuring U2 performing in Mexico City, Latin America, and Australia during its 2006 *Vertigo* Tour. It was directed by Catherine Owens—the band's lighting director, who had overseen the group's "Original of the Species" clip—and acclaimed filmmaker Mark Pellington, who worked with U2 on "One."

U2 3D was touted as the first live-action digital three-dimensional film. The project was an experiment in a new 3D technology created by 3ality Digital. Shot during seven concerts, U2's second feature film—and first in twenty years—was based almost exclusively on concert footage.

Concerts were filmed in Mexico City, São Paulo, Santiago, Buenos Aires, and Melbourne. The band also recorded a ten-song set, or "phantom shoot," without an audience to allow for close ups. The film's production featured the first-ever 3D multiple-camera setup, and was shot using every digital 3D camera and recording deck that existed at the time.

It previewed at the 2007 Cannes Film Festival, premiered at the Sundance Film Festival in January 2008, and went into international release the following month. Highly praised, the film won several awards; some critics suggested that the 3D effects made the movie more enjoyable than an actual concert or "even better than the real thing." It was the first film released by National Geographic Entertainment, a division of the National Geographic Society.

360° Tour

In support of *No Line on the Horizon*, U2 launched a massive stadium trek to European and North American cities in the summer of 2009. Opening in Barcelona on June 30—where 90,000 tickets sold out in fifty-four minutes in mid-March—the 360° Tour ran for eight weeks of dates in its first leg and included two sellout shows at Dublin's Croke Park.

Humble about that achievement, Bono commented via U2.com on the 180,000 tickets U2 sold, acknowledging, "It's overwhelming, really. It's a very big deal for us to sell-out our hometown at such speed, it's unbelievable." More astounding still was the fact that the group sold 650,000 tickets for gigs on the continent in just seven hours. Anxiety the U2 camp had about the late 2000s' recession and concerns over whether it could still pack massive venues with the modest reception for its latest disc was eased.

Named for its unique 360-degree stage layout, U2's tour offered a strong visual experience for all attendees while offering a larger capacity for attendance than most Stadium shows. Opening with a number of new tunes, including "Breathe" and "Magnificent," the show featured longtime set staples "Beautiful Day," "One," and "Where the Streets Have No Name." For the encore, Bono would take the stage in a laser-laden suit for "Ultraviolet (Light My Way)," "With or Without You," and "Moment of Surrender."

The U.S. leg began September 12 at Chicago's Soldier Field and earned high praise by the likes of *Rolling Stone*—which described it as a hybrid of the ZooTV's visual thrills and the *Elevation* Tour's simple but direct performances. The *New York Times* called the stage's design "part insect, part spacecraft, part cathedral."

The band's political messages were still apparent—including displays of Aung San Suu Kyi, who inspired "Walk On," and apartheid activist Desmond Tutu's promotion of Bono's ONE initiative—but less overt than during previous tours.

Environmental concerns over the gigantic stage were still cause for controversy. It took thirty tractor-trailer trucks to move and required a crew of two hundred men working three and a half days to load in and set up in each venue. Carbonfootprint.com's Helen Roberts told the *Belfast Telegraph* that U2's carbon footprint from its forty-four shows in 2009 was enough to fly its four members the 34.125 million miles to Mars and back.

When all was said and done, Bono—who told a Tokyo audience in 2008, "My prayer is that we become better in looking after our planet"—and his bandmates grossed just over $311 million for those forty-four shows, making the U2 360° Tour the highest grossing tour of the year. It was expected to achieve a total final gross of $750 million by the end of 2010.

The trek marked some record-setting attendances, including a Pasadena show that drew 97,014 to the Rose Bowl. The largest crowd ever gathered for a single headlining act in the United States, it was shown live via YouTube in October 2009 and was being planned for DVD release, according to a March 2010 band announcement. *U2: 360° at the Rose Bowl*, containing material from the penultimate gig of their 2009 tour supporting *No Line on the Horizon*, became available for purchase on June 3, 2010. The Rose Bowl performance was the band's biggest show of 2009.

Before being sidelined by Bono's back injury, the band had announced it would, on June 25, 2010, play the U.K.'s world-famous Glastonbury Festival for the first time. "I used to be skeptical of its roots, the hippie thing" explained The Edge in a press release. He felt that the time was now right to play the fortieth annual event, adding, "It feels like we really have to do it because if we don't do it now, we never will."

This poster promotes the 2008 U2 concert film U2 3D, which was lensed in Buenos Aires, Mexico City, and Australia on the group's 2006 *Vertigo* Tour. Directed by Catherine Owens and Mark Pellington, it premiered in January of that year at the Sundance Film Festival and is considered the first live-action digital three-dimensional film.

Author's collection

52

I Know You're Looking Out for Us

Post-Millennium Honors and Awards

Man of the Year

On January 22, 2000, Bono was given the Man of the Year trophy for his work on behalf of Jubilee 2000 at the NRJ Awards in Cannes, France. Speaking to the crowd, which included Ali and their baby son Eli, he said, "This award is not for me. It's not about the Man of the Year, but it's about an idea, the idea of the year. It's about Jubilee 2000."

Freedom of Dublin

In March 2000, U2 and Paul McGuinness were honored by Ireland's largest city with the Freedom of Dublin distinction by Mayor Mary Freehill. Freehill presented each member of the group with Waterford Crystal renderings of the Joshua Tree in front of a crowd of thousand's at the Smithfield Civic Plaza.

"I'd have thought people would be sick of U2 by now," Bono said, accepting the honor, according to an *Irish Times* report. "It's still moving to come home and see the amount of goodwill toward us." The band topped off the ceremony by performing four songs, including the first-ever live rendering of "The Sweetest Thing."

Harvard

Bono was invited to speak to Harvard University's graduating seniors at its Class Day ceremony in June 2001. "My name is Bono, and I am a rock star," he told the crowd, according to the *Harvard Gazette*. "I say that not as a boast. But more as a confession."

From there he gave a twenty-minute speech based on his thoughts about Third World debt relief. Afterward, the esteemed Ivy League University gave him an honorary degree.

European of the Year

Bono left an array of political leaders and businessmen in the dust to be named European of the Year by Brussels-based *European Voice* magazine. Given an award of $4,458, Bono donated his purse to the Irish charity, Concern.

"A more prosperous world is a more secure world, a more educated world is a more tolerant world and a healthier world is a more stable world," Bono said upon receipt of the honor in December 2001.

Rolling Stone Readers' Top Albums

In October 2002, U2 placed well in a *Rolling Stone* readers' poll of the Top 100 albums of all time. 1987's *The Joshua Tree* rated highest (#4), with 1991's *Achtung Baby* coming in behind it (#10). Its most recent effort, 2000's *All That You Can't Leave Behind*, was clearly the band's artistic comeback in the eyes of fans, as it also did very well (#15).

Stamped

U2 appeared on an official Irish stamp for the first time in October 2002 when Ireland's Post Office issued its Irish Rock Legends series. Aside from the Emerald Isle's biggest-ever band, Van Morrison, Thin Lizzy's Phil Lynott, and Rory Gallagher were represented.

Humanitarian Laureate

Bono became the first rock and roll personality to receive the Humanitarian Laureate Award from the Simon Wiesenthal Center on November 18, 2002. The honor was a result of his international initiative to raise in money for AIDS in Africa and forgive the monetary debt of poverty-stricken Third World countries.

"When the center started its award process this year, only one name came to mind—Bono," the Wiesenthal Center's Eastern director Rhonda Barad said in a press release. "Not only does he address issues, he creates concrete viable plans to make the world a more equitable place."

Person of the Year

Bono was given the MusiCares 2003 Person of the Year distinction that February by the Recording Academy at New York's Marriott Marquis Hotel. A who's who of stars turned out to join Bono, Ali, and their daughters as they sit at the same table with Bill Clinton, Salman Rushdie, and Robert DeNiro. Clinton presents Bono with his ward, praising Bono for his work on debt relief, AIDS, and poverty.

In advance of the event, Bono tells *Billboard*, "MusiCares is about looking after our own kind so that's pretty good. I'm hanging with a lot of un-hip company trying to do the political work that I do, businesspeople, congressmen, and politicians. But this is my own tribe. I feel, in truth, more comfortable here."

Afterward, artists like Mary J. Blige, B. B. King, Wynona Judd, and Elvis Costello perform U2 tunes. Leaving the stage after a rendition of "Kite," Costello calls Bono up to the stage and tells the audience, "Give him the fucking Nobel Peace Prize now!"

The night concludes with a trio of tunes, "That's Life," "Night and Day," and "The Hands That Built America" performed by Bono and Edge.

Salute to Greatness

In January 2004, the King Center honored Bono for his humanitarian endeavors at the annual "Salute to Greatness" Awards dinner held in Atlanta on a day that would have been Martin Luther King, Jr.'s seventy-fifth birthday. Coretta Scott King, the great civil-rights leader's widow, honored U2's frontman.

"This young man we are honoring tonight provides the shining example of a twenty-first century activist/humanitarian," King told the crowd, according to Life.com. "Bono, on behalf of the King Center, I salute you for your outstanding contributions as an eloquent and passionate advocate of the teachings of Martin Luther King, Jr., and for your energetic and dedicated work for numerous human-rights campaigns."

Doctor of Laws

On May 17, 2004, Bono spoke at the University of Pennsylvania's graduation ceremony. His nearly thirty-minute speech was well received by the students and parents in the crowd at Franklin Field, the football stadium where U2 once performed during the PopMart Tour.

Continuing his longstanding fight for AIDS assistance, he urges graduates to take action. "The world is more malleable than you think," the *Philadelphia Inquirer* quoted him as saying. "It's waiting for you to hammer it into shape."

In exchange for his speech and his humanitarian efforts to date, U2's singer was given an honorary Doctor of Laws degree by the Ivy League university.

Person of the Year

Bono and Bill and Melinda Gates were named *Time* magazine's "Persons of the Year" for 2005. According to the publication, the three individuals were selected for "rewiring politics," "being shrewd about doing good," and "re-engineering justice." They all appear on the cover, which had an issue date of December 18. For the piece, Josh Tyrangiel interviews the U2 frontman in his Manhattan apartment.

Knighthood

Two days before Christmas 2006, it was revealed by the British Embassy that Bono would be granted an honorary knighthood by the Queen for "his services to the music industry and for his humanitarian work."

Via U2.com, Bono announced he was "very flattered" by the acknowledgment, which would continue to help with his mission of crushing extreme poverty. Unlike other rock stars such as Sir Paul McCartney and Sir Elton Hercules John, Bono was not given the title "Sir" because he is not a British national.

In March 2007 at the British embassy in Dublin, Bono was given the award. "I would like to thank Her Majesty's Ambassador for pinning this award on me in my home town," Bono explained in a ceremony reported on by the *Irish Times*. Later he joked to the press, "You have permission to call me anything you want—except sir, all right? Lord of lords, your demigodness, that'll do."

NAACP Chairman's Award

In Los Angeles in March 2007, U2's singer was given the NAACP Chairman's Award for his work with the poor in Africa. Bono talked to the crowd about the religious strife he witnessed as a Dublin child. He explained how he found inspiration from Martin Luther King, Jr., "a preacher from Atlanta who refused to hate because he knew love could do better."

A year before he was given his honorary knighthood by the Queen of England, Bono appeared ready for active duty during a gig at the Mellon Arena in Pittsburgh on October 22, 2005.   *Photo by Mike Kurman*

For Those About to Rock

Boston's Berklee College of Music gave The Edge an honorary degree on May 12, 2007, at its graduation ceremony. He encouraged graduates of the music school to find their own voices while performing and creating with others on "the path to greatness."

As he made his exit with his honor, he quoted a 1981 anthem by Australian-bred hard rockers AC/DC. "For those about to rock, we salute you!" he said.

Liberty Medal

On September 27, 2007, Bono and his organization, DATA, were acknowledged when they were given the esteemed 2007 Liberty Medal at Philadelphia's National Constitution Center.

"We can't fix all the world's problems," he explained in a Reuters report. "But the ones we can, we must."

Former President George Herbert Walker Bush gave Bono the honor; and upon receipt of it, Bono happily harked back to the many unanswered phone calls made to the White House back on the ZooTV Tour. In addition to the distinction, he was given a $100,000 prize to benefit DATA.

U2 Way

On Tuesday, March 3, 2009, to coincide with the release of *No Line on the Horizon*, a portion of New York City's West 53rd Street, near Manhattan's Times Square, was briefly renamed "U2 Way." Hardcore fans braved the frigid cold serenading each other with old hits as they waited hours for the band to show up and receive the honor, which was personally bestowed by Mayor Michael Bloomberg. This event occurred directly adjacent to the Ed Sullivan Theater, where the band made an unprecedented weeklong appearance as the musical guest on the talk show *The Late Show with David Letterman*.

On March 3, 2009, New York City Mayor Michael Bloomberg renamed part of West 53rd Street "U2 Way" in honor of the band's new album *No Line on the Horizon*, released in North America the same day. The band was in NYC and in residence just steps away from the rechristened spot near the Ed Sullivan Theatre. U2 performed an unprecedented five consecutive times that week on CBS-TV's Late Show with David Letterman.

© *RD/Dziekan/Retna Digital*

53

We Need New Dreams Tonight

U2's Grammy Awards

1988

In 1988, U2 earned its first two Grammys for the band's artistic achievements on *The Joshua Tree*. It was named Album of the Year, beating out the likes of Whitney Houston, Michael Jackson, Prince, and a collaborative effort by Dolly Parton, Linda Ronstadt, and Emmylou Harris. It also took the award for Best Rock Performance by a Duo or Group with Vocal.

1989

The band's Grammy run continued when it was awarded the Best Rock Duo or Group award for "Desire" and Best Performance Music Video for "Where the Streets Have No Name."

1993

Achtung Baby earned the band its fifth Grammy, again for Best Rock Duo or Group honors.

1994

Zooropa earned the Best Alternative Album gong, as U2 beat out Belly, Nirvana, R.E.M., and the Smashing Pumpkins.

1995

U2 continued its run of Grammy wins when *Zoo TV: Live from Sydney* was named the Best Long Form Video.

2001

In early 2001, "Beautiful Day" won Song of the Year, Best Rock Performance by a Duo or Group with Vocal, and Record of the Year honors. For the band it was just the ego boost it needed after America had lost interest in the band following its *Pop* campaign.

When "Beautiful Day" and its parent album won an abundance of gongs, it was a reassurance for the band both emotionally and from an artistic perspective. If U2 hadn't appreciated its Grammy honors before, its return to the forefront of popular music was not lost on its members.

2002

In February 2002, U2 opened the Grammy Awards—held at the Staples Center in Los Angeles—with a live performance of "Walk On." With eight nominations, the group walked away with four trophies: Record of the Year for "Walk On"; Best Pop Performance by a Duo or Group with Vocal for "Stuck in a Moment You Can't Get Out Of"; Best Rock Performance by a Duo Dr Group With Vocal for "Elevation"; and Best Rock Album for *All That You Can't Leave Behind.*

All That You Can't Leave Behind became the only album ever to have two singles win the Record of the Year distinction in two consecutive years.

2005

U2's single "Vertigo" pulled down three Grammys in February 2005 in the Best Rock Performance By a Duo or Group with Vocal; Best Rock Song and Best Short Form Music Video categories. The ceremony, held at the Staples Center in Los Angeles, brings U2's Grammy count to seventeen in total.

2006

A return trip to the Staples Center in February 2006 resulted in five additional awards as *How to Dismantle an Atomic Bomb* won for Album of the Year and Best Rock Album; "Sometimes You Can't Make It On Your Own" snagged Song of the Year and Best Rock Performance by a Duo or Group With Vocal; and "City of Blinding Lights" was awarded Best Rock Song. Producer Steve Lillywhite also pulled down the Producer of the Year, Non-Classical, honors for his efforts behind the scenes on *How to Dismantle an Atomic Bomb,* resulting in a staggering nine statues for one album, tying a record set by Santana's 1999 album *Supernatural.*

54

The Future Needs a Big Kiss

No Line on the Horizon

Although Brian Eno, Daniel Lanois, and Steve Lillywhite eventually earned the production credits for *No Line on the Horizon*, it was American Records founder and award-winning producer Rick Rubin who first started out with the job. U2 and Rick Rubin had begun working together in July 2006 in both Abbey Road studios and in the South of France on new material, two tracks of which eventually saw release that autumn when the band released new material on its *U218* compilation.

Those songs, "Window in the Skies" and a collaboration with Green Day on the Skids' classic "The Saints Are Coming" surfaced, but the band eventually decided it would abort its efforts with Rick Rubin. The producer and the band had a fundamental difference in approach: Rick wanted the band to bring its finished material into the studio, but U2 was ardent about continuing with its proven practice of piecing material together in the studio.

The band wasn't sure which way it wanted to go stylistically, with Bono quoted by *Billboard* in early 2007, "We're gonna continue to be a band, but maybe the rock will have to go; maybe the rock has to get a lot harder. But whatever it is, it's not gonna stay where it is."

U2 didn't stay where it was, either, leaving Nice for Fez, Morocco by May, where they decided to work with Eno and Lanois in a songwriting capacity. "It's very different, quite experimental and kind of liberating because of that," Larry Mullen told U2.com the following month, after two weeks of sessions held in a Moroccan *riad*. Having been invited to attend the World Sacred Music Festival in the city, Bono suggested his bandmates and collaborators follow him.

The goal was to create "future hymns" and the exposure to Hindu and Jewish music helped the band to craft songs like "Unknown Caller," "Moment of Surrender," "No Line on the Horizon," and "White as Snow." The trip to Fez encouraged U2 to take more musical risks with its new material, but the group also knew that in some point it needed to pull in the reigns, because—according to Brian Eno, "it sounded kind of synthetic . . . like a 'world music' add-on."

Returning to Dublin, but also working in studios in New York and London, U2, Eno, and Lanois continued writing and tracking music for well over a year. With fifty or sixty songs already penned by September but not yet convinced it had a proper album's worth of material, it considered releasing two EPs titled *Daylight* and *Darkness.* Instead it opted to bump the project's release from November 2008 release into early 2009 to allow it time to finish the project.

By November, the group had announced the disc's title, *No Line on the Horizon,* and plans for a companion film by Anton Corbijn called *Linear* was also revealed. But the band was still hard at work perfecting the songs—including some that became known as the "beach clips," after they were uploaded to YouTube but soon taken off the site at the request of Universal Music that same month. The rough-sounding versions of these songs had been recorded by a fan who overheard them emanating from Bono's beach house in Eze, France in August 2008.

By December 2008, the band gathered at Olympic Studios in London where it picked the best songs it had tracked. As a result, songs mentioned in pre-release reviews like "Winter" and "Every Breaking Wave" were left off the album.

The final product marked a new lyrical direction for Bono, who had grown sick of writing in the first-person and instead took on characters that he made up including a junkie, a soldier in Afghanistan and a traffic cop. Able to broaden his outlook this way,

Bono was able to use these subjects—who all took on an intentional ignorance of the rest of the world—as a means to develop the album's central theme of periphery vision.

Stylistically, he explained upon the release of *No Line on the Horizon*—which U2 dedicated to Rob Partridge, who first signed the band in 1979—that there were three sections of the album: the first was "a whole world unto itself, and you get to a very ecstatic place," the third was "a load of singles" and the last consisted of tunes that were "unusual territory."

The Songs of *No Line on the Horizon*

From the relentless groove of the title track to the thoughtful, self-searching aura created by "Cedars of Lebanon" to the sonic fury of "Get on Your Boots," this album may be the most far-reaching in the band's career. "It's very raw and very to the point," said The Edge.

1. "No Line on the Horizon": Unlike most U2 songs, "No Line on the Horizon" was tracked in one take. Originating from a variety of drumbeats that Larry Mullen, Jr. had been working on, Brian Eno sampled them and arranged them to his liking. From there the band began to build from it, with The Edge using a Death by Audio distortion box to craft his guitar lines.

Bono's lyrics were written in response to a photograph of Lake Constance, which is in the Alps between Germany, Switzerland, and Austria that is called the Boden Sea and was taken by Japanese artist Hiroshi Sugimoto. That image was also used as the artwork for the album's cover.

The singer has described it as a place "where the sea meets the sky." The lead track on U2's twelfth studio album is expansive in its sound and passionate in its purpose. The spirited opus did not go unnoticed—*Time* magazine named it the third best song of 2009.

2. "Magnificent": The second single from *No Line on the Horizon* was a surprisingly poor performer when it was released as a single in May 2009. In the U.K. "Magnificent" wasn't, stalling at #42 and becoming the group's worst charting tune since 1982. Initially titled "French Disco," the song emerged from a jam session in Fez, and was upheld by a commanding chord progression. "I think we all knew that it was inherently joyful, which is rare," Edge said later of the song.

According to Bono in the magazine included with some versions of *No Line on the Horizon*, its lyrics were about "two lovers holding on to each other and trying to turn their life into worship." There was also a message of sacrifice that one makes for their art; and while the song has a classic, uplifting U2 approach, it failed to connect commercially. Just the same, Coldplay loved the song, and often played it over the loudspeakers as it took the stage for shows during the final leg of its *Viva la Vida* trek.

3. "Moment of Surrender": Written in Fez in June 2007, "Moment of Surrender" was improvised during the course of a couple of hours and recorded by the band with Eno, and Lanois in a single take. Only the cello part that introduces the song was added later.

Beginning with a percussion loop created by Brian, the group spontaneously crafted the song and fully developed it with each member of the band in a manner so impressive the producer later told U2.com it was "the most amazing studio experience I've ever had." Its end-product sounds as if it could be at home on *The Joshua Tree*.

Topically, Bono slipped into his drug addict character, and transformed himself into a man who was having a crisis of faith. His gospel-like performance was emotional and resonant, prompting *Rolling Stone* magazine to name "Moment of Surrender" the best song of 2009, despite the fact it had never been issued as an actual single. It described it as "the most devastating ballad U2 or anyone has written since "One."

4. "Unknown Caller": Also recorded in a single take during U2's two-week journey to Fez, "Unknown Caller" reprises the drug-addict character of the preceding track, who begins to receive odd, cryptic text messages on his cell phone after attempting to use the device to buy drugs. Bono also draws inspiration from Jeremiah 33:3 in his tale of this spiritually shattered character on the verge of suicide.

The song launches with a birdsong by Moroccan swallows which was captured in the Riad where the song was recorded. A few variations of the track existed in its infancy, but if The Edge is to be believed, the final version was played only one time.

5. "I'll Go Crazy If I Don't Go Crazy Tonight": Initially stemming from the band's visit to Fez, "I'll Go Crazy If I Don't Go Crazy Tonight" was based on a song called "Diorama" that Brian Eno had developed. Reworking it with Steve Lillywhite, the upbeat rock song took on a new shape and meaning with lyrics that were based on Bono's life experience and his observations on Barack Obama's run for the presidency.

With the Black Eyed Peas' brainchild will.i.am assisting in a production capacity, the song earned praise from the likes of *Q*, which called it U2's "most unabashed pop song since "Sweetest Thing" but not everyone was convinced of its greatness. The *Irish Times* called it "U2's most lackluster offering to date."

Featured in a cross promotion with Blackberry for the "U2 Mobile App"—which was developed as part of Research in Motion's sponsorship of the U2 360° Tour—the song was heard most in television commercials. Radio played the song regularly in the summer of 2009 and it was ultimately nominated in the categories Best Rock Performance by a Duo or Group With Vocals and Best Rock Song for the 2010 Grammy Awards. It lost out, however, to "Use Somebody" by its one-time opening act, Kings of Leon, in both instances.

6. "Get on Your Boots": A fuzzy blast of futuristic noise pop first concocted by The Edge at home with GarageBand software, this song—which has been compared in its vocal approach to both Elvis Costello's "Pump It Up" and Bob Dylan's "Subterranean Homesick Blues"—was released on January 23, 2009 as a precursor to *No Line on the Horizon*. Reviews of "Get on Your Boots" were mixed, however, because of its drastic departure from U2's traditional rock approaches heard since the millennium.

Part "Vertigo" and part "Numb," the song's topical inspiration came from Bono observing warplanes overhead while vacationing at his house in France at the start of the Iraq War. Initially titled "Four Letter Word" and then "Sexy Boots," Edge can be seen working on the track in the documentary *It Might Get Loud*, in which he stars with Jack White of the White Stripes/Raconteurs/ Dead Weather and Jimmy Page of Led Zeppelin fame.

At 150 beats per minute, "Get on Your Boots" may be the fastest song U2 has ever recorded but it's also among U2's weakest first-single debuts ever, just cracking the U.S. Top Forty in its first week of release before slipping to #96 on the *Billboard* Hot 100 the next. In the U.K. it stalled at #12.

It does succeed, however, in upholding those aforementioned Costello comparisons. When U2 appeared on the Bravo TV show *Spectacle: Elvis Costello with . . .*, in late 2009, Bono, The Edge, and Costello performed a medley of it with the host's 1978 classic "Pump It Up."

7. "Stand Up Comedy": This song began as "For Your Love" before it was titled "Stand Up" and eventually, "Stand Up Comedy." Originating in the June 2007 Fez sessions, it went through many changes before its completion. At one time, the song counted mandolins and was based upon a Middle Eastern rhythm.

During its first-ever live morning television-show performance, U2 performed on the American program *Good Morning America* on Friday, March 6, 2009, from the campus of New York's Fordham University.   *Photofest*

It eventually became home to one of The Edge's heaviest riffs ever, after the guitarist again felt the influence of Led Zeppelin guitarist Jimmy Page and Jack White—who crafted the 2003 riff-tastic "Seven Nation Army"—during the making of their mutual movie *It Might Get Loud*. At its core, it was held together by a funk foundation poured by Adam and Larry.

Lyrically, Bono said to U2.com, "It's saying, stand up to rock stars. That's about choosing your enemies, too. What are you gonna stand up for and what are you gonna stand up against? I love the notion of standing up rock stars. Because they are a bunch of fucking megalomaniacs."

Bono also cited the "Stand Up and Take Action" event of 2008, which saw 116 million people in 131 countries reminded the leaders of countries of their promise to reduce poverty by 2015, as an inspiration. "It's not a 'let's hold hands and the world is a better place' sort of song. It's more 'kick down the door of your own hypocrisy.'"

8. "Fez—Being Born": A strong contender to open the album at one point, this song—which began on Rick Rubin's watch—was relegated to the back half of the record. And wisely so. Starting with the working title "Chromium Chords" that later became "Tripoli" and finally "Fez," Daniel Lanois and Brian Eno rescued pieces of the slow-tempo number and suggested U2 implement elements of a much faster song called "Being Born."

But the outcome is downright clamorous as the sounds of a Moroccan outdoor market fuse into the "Fez" piece of the song. It's experimental and it's faulty. The song's story is based on Bono's Parisian traffic cop character who travels to the Mediterranean Sea in an effort to see his girlfriend, who is in Tripoli.

9. "White as Snow": The lone political song on *No Line on the Horizon*, the song was written from the mindset of a soldier in Afghanistan who is dying. The tune—which is evidently based on the hymn "Veni, veni Emmanuel"—lasts the length of time it takes for the man to expire after coming into contact with a roadside bomb. Bono has explained that he came up with the idea for the song from the book *Pincher Martin* written by William Golding.

The aforementioned hymn was suggested to Daniel Lanois by fellow Canadian Lori Anna Reid of Newfoundland. Lanois recorded himself playing a piano version of "Veni, veni Emmanuel" and Bono crafted a vocal as part of the group's two-week session in Fez. Adam Clayton pushed for the song to make the record because it offered the listener a calmer moment.

At one point, the band considered starting it with the sound of an explosion but opted against it. As it stands, it's one of the album's finest moments, and among Bono's most underappreciated vocal turns to date.

10. "Breathe": Another song drawing on Edge's exposure to Jimmy Page and Jack White during their collaboration on the film *It Might Get Loud*, it came to the band virtually intact, but after working on it for a while they scrapped it and rewrote it. According to Daniel Lanois, the song was remixed a staggering eighty times during sessions to perfect the record.

Bono also overworked himself for the track, first writing lyrics about Nelson Mandela before opting to write from a "more surreal and personal" perspective. The song is set on June 16, which is a deliberate allusion to James Joyce's novel *Ulysses*.

According to Bono in the bonus promotional magazine for *No Line on the Horizon*, the idea behind the lyrics stemmed from a desire to "become more intimate . . . I want to get away from subject and subject matter [and] into pure exchange. Not even conversation. Often, it's just like grunts or outbursts."

11. "Cedars of Lebanon": The final song on U2's *No Line on the Horizon* consists of a melody based on a sample of "Against the Sky," a song Brian Eno and Daniel Lanois had worked on back in 1984 when collaborating on *The Pearl*, an album by ambient and avant-garde performer Harold Budd.

Lyrically, "Cedars of Lebanon" comes from the viewpoint of a journalist covering the war in Iraq. It's as observational in lines like *"Unholy clouds reflecting in a minaret"* as it critical, in the warning, *"Chose your enemies carefully 'cause they will define you."*

Anton Corbijn's *Linear*

Linear was a companion film to *No Line on the Horizon* that was included in special formats of U2's 2009 album. Directed by the band's photographer, Anton Corbijn, it was contained in the Digipak, magazine, box, and deluxe iTunes versions of the project. The concept came to Corbijn after he worked on a June 2007 video shoot with the group where he asked them to stand motionless while he filmed them.

Using this idea, objects moved around U2 while they remained still, creating what Corbijn called a "photograph on film." By May 2008, the group had commissioned Anton to work on the project, which would allow fans what they described as "a new way to use film to connect to music."

Structured around a story created by Bono and Anton, it revisited characters from the album, including the Parisian motorcycle cop played by actor Saïd Taghmaoui. The music in the film was based on the running order of *No Line* as of May 2008 and, as a result, had a slightly different track listing from the final album. It included "Winter," which was omitted from the final disc.

"As U2 never do anything in half measures," Corbijn explained to U2.com in February 2009, "the record that emerged from the studio in late 2008 was a very different one than the one I'd made images for. Not only had the running order changed, now there were completely new songs on the record while another song had gone, new lyrics without the characters had emerged, and different sounds dominated the songs I had worked on. Disaster!"

Release and Reception of *No Line on the Horizon*

Despite the announcement in June 2008 by Paul McGuinness that U2's new album would be ready for an October release, by the time that month came and went the reality was that the disc with the tentative title *No Line on the Horizon* wouldn't be under any Christmas trees that holiday season.

Bono explained to fans that U2 had "hit a rich songwriting vein" and "there's more priceless stuff to be found" in a post on U2's website. "We know we have to emerge soon but we also know that people don't want another U2 album unless it is our best ever album," he continued.

U2 had aspirations of delivering its most innovative and challenging record yet. When they finally released it on February 27, 2009, in Ireland, March 2 in the U.K., and March 3 in North America, it had been four-plus years between albums, the longest gap since its inception.

Although the band's label, Universal Music Group, did its best to guard against copies leaking by preventing advance copies from getting into the hands of critics, UMG's own Australian arm leaked the tracks two weeks early when it made the album available for digital sale on February 18. Just the same, the group kept a positive outlook about the accidental sale and subsequent leak to file sharing sites. "The one good thing about that is a lot of our fans have already given us their thumbs up," Edge told London's XFM.com. "Even though it was fans getting it for free."

Upon its formal release, *No Line on the Horizon* debuted at #1 in thirty countries including the U.S., the U.K., Canada, Ireland, France, Ireland, and Japan. In the U.S., first-week sales totaled 484,000, and with seven number one albums to their credit, U2 were now behind just the Beatles and the Rolling Stones for the number of chart topping long-players.

Reviews of the disc were strong, with *Rolling Stone* giving the disc a five-star review. Calling it "their best, in its textural exploration and tenacious melodic grip, since 1991's *Achtung Baby*" the assessment seemed over-inflated. *Q* also gave it a perfect rating, and the glowing evaluations came in from *Mojo*, *Entertainment Weekly*, *Uncut*, and *NME*. On the other end of the spectrum, *Time* magazine called it "mostly restless, tentative, and confused."

Pitchfork also panned it, with a 4.2 out of 10 assessment that read, "the album's ballyhooed experimentation is either terribly misguided or hidden underneath a wash of shameless U2-isms."

Despite the production of three singles, "Get on Your Boots," "Magnificent," and "I'll Go Crazy If I Don't Go Crazy Tonight," U2's album sales for the project were a serious disappointment, dipping to its lowest in a decade. With just five million sold worldwide and just over a million in the U.S.—paltry by the comparison to its two predecessors—*No Line on the Horizon* was a commercial flop.

Meanwhile, concert ticket sales for U2's 360° Tour were as brisk as ever. But the band wasn't going for another mainstream-rock album. "We weren't really in that [commercial] mindset," Bono told the Associated Press eight months after the album dropped.

"We felt that the 'album' is almost an extinct species, and we should approach it in totality and create a mood and feeling, and a beginning, middle, and an end," he continued. But in the digital download world of 2009, where pop singles could be had on iTunes at ninety-nine cents apiece, U2 wasn't sure where it—or the traditional rock and roll album format for that matter—fit in any more.

Also speaking to the *AP*, Adam Clayton said in late 2009, "The concept of the music fan—the concept of the person who buys music and listens to music for the pleasure of music itself—is an outdated idea."

Songs for Ascent

With a six-month break between legs of its 360° Tour, U2 continued to make progress on the follow up to 2009's *No Line on the Horizon*. The Edge was promising that the material it had been working on for its as-yet-untitled thirteenth studio set would cover a myriad of styles, from folk to electronic music.

"We are working on a lot of new songs," The Edge told *Entertainment Weekly*. "Some of them are really, really happy. We're convinced that we have something really special. It's like deciding whether we are going to release the album before the tour starts or leave it for a while, we don't really know yet. Literally, within a day of getting off the road [in October 2009] Bono and I were working on new songs. On a roll."

As for the sonic approach, Edge explained they were trying to keep things moving forward. "We are experimenting with a lot of different arrangements, and electronic is one of the things we are playing with. But there are other songs that are very traditional, almost folk. In some ways, that's the thing we haven't figured out yet, is where this album is going to end up. We're having fun with the process."

It wasn't clear at the completion of *U2 FAQ* if this was the same project as the *Songs of Ascent* album previously announced by Bono in a February 2009 interview with the *Guardian*. At that time, Bono had suggested that U2 would release this disc by the close of 2009 and it would be a sister album to *No Line on the Horizon*, much in the way that *Zooropa* had emerged closely on the heels of *Achtung Baby*. At the time, Bono suggested a single, "Every Breaking Wave" might be out by early 2010 although that timeframe came and went.

An interview with the *Irish Independent* in June 2009 found Bono rethinking those plans, admitting that nine tracks had been completed but they would only see release if the group felt the songs surpassed the quality of those on *No Line on the Horizon*.

Is That All You Want from Me?

Quotes About U2

They haven't been very honest about where their influences have come from, have they? A great deal of U2 has to do with early P.I.L. It's The Edge all over, isn't it? That's fine, that's not an insult. He liked it and he took it someplace else. Made it his own. Well, good luck to him. It just gets irritating when people tell me, 'Oh, you're not as good as U2.' Don't you know where they came from?"

—*John Lydon of Public Image Ltd. on the influence of his band on U2*

"Oh, you're a great band. My kids just think you're the greatest, have all your records, listen to them all the time. Yeah, the kids love ya. You know, it would be a great honor if I could tell them that you bought me a drink."

—*Ronnie Drew of the Dubliners to Larry Mullen, Jr., meeting in a bar in 1985*

"Great songs and all that great heart . . . U2's not a pop group. They are in this for real."

—*Lou Reed, 1987*

"Their show is the best around. U2 is what church should be."

—*T Bone Burnett, 1987*

"I think that's one reason U2 were so successful. Their music was big and echo-ey. The minute you heard them you could hear them in a big space. They had big emotions, big ideas. Those things tend to translate well into playing to bigger crowds, which can be a fantastic experience. I've had amazing nights in stadiums, but it does alter what you do. In a club it's much easier to focus. The audience is closer and watching whatever you do. You can tune a guitar or tell a story. A theater retains a concert feeling. In an arena you can still retain a good part of that concert feeling, but the size of the thing broadens what you do. It's the arena and it calls for a big gesture of some sort. You have to be able to switch gears and adjust to the context you're in. Some people are only great in a club. Some, like the Who and U2, are great in a stadium."

—*Bruce Springsteen, 1992*

"I bought *Achtung Baby* and I actually want to do a cover of the third song, 'One.' I think 'One' is one of the greatest songs that has ever been written. I put the song on and just broke down crying. It was such a release. It was really good for me. I was really upset that my ex-wife and I never had a chance because of the damage in our lives. We didn't have a chance and I hadn't fully accepted that. That song helped me see it. I wanted to write Bono a letter just saying, 'Your record's done a lot for me.'"

—*Axl Rose of Guns N' Roses, 1992*

"The only way you can find out about your life and how to live your life is to try a lot of different things and fail at some of them. Probably U2's only failure was *Rattle and Hum*. I'm sure it sold ten million records, but I don't think it did exactly what they wanted it to do. And yet that's good. It opened the door for them to do something else."

—*Peter Buck, R.E.M., 1992*

"They might be all shamrocks and deutsche marks to some. But I feel that they are one of the few rock bands even attempting to hint at a world which will continue past the next great wall—the year 2000."

—*David Bowie, 1992*

"Look at a group like U2. Bono and his band are so egocentric. The more you jump around, the bigger your hat is, the more people listen to your music."

—*George Harrison, 1997*

"I do believe we can eradicate poverty. And, by the way. Bono has come to see me. I admire him. He is a man of depth and a great heart who cares deeply about the impoverished folks on the continent of Africa."

—*George W. Bush, 2005*

"I hate this guy's music, but I like the idea of absolving Third World debt, because otherwise these people are going to die. So if he's using all that rock star power, well, right on. Like he's Mr. Africa Third World Debt Guy, which is a huge issue, but now, he's Mr. AIDS Guy. Well, wait a minute, how did you go from Third World debt to AIDS? It starts to sound like he leaves a lot undone."

—Henry Rollins on Bono, 2005

"I'll leave it to others far more knowledgeable than me to talk about U2's music. All I'll say is that, along with millions of others right across the world, I'm a huge fan."

—Prime Minister Tony Blair, 2007

"Bands all say they want to be as big as U2, but weirdly no one ever says they're influenced by them. That's because there's nothing there, really. They've got good tunes, and you can see that it works on fourteen-year-olds. But I can't see mature people or kids, who are looking for something, something deep—something that you just know it's art and it's going to change your life—caring. For U2, it's always flag-waving and 'Yippee.'"

—Ian McCulloch of Echo & the Bunnymen, 2009

Selected Bibliography

Countless magazines, newspapers, and fanzines have covered U2's lengthy career. A long list of books were consulted in the researching of *U2 FAQ*. For further reading, here are some suggestions:

Books

Alan, Carter. *Outside Is America—U2 in the U.S.* Boston: Faber & Faber, 1992.
———. *The Road to Pop*, New York: Faber & Faber, 1997.
Assayas, Michka. *Bono in Conversation.* New York: Riverhead Trade, 2006.
Bowler, Dave and Dray, Bryan. *U2—A Conspiracy of Hope.* London: Pan Books, 1993.
Chatterton, Mark. *U2—The Ultimate Encyclopedia.* London: Firefly, 2004.
Cogan, Visnja. *U2—An Irish Phenomenon.* Cork: Collins Press, 2007.
Corbijn, Anton. *U2 & I: The Photographs: 1982–2004.* Munich: Schirmer/Mosel, 2005.
De la Parra, Pimm Jal and Van Oosten de Boer, Caroline. *U2 Live—A Concert Documentary.* London: Omnibus Press, 2003.
Dunphy, Eamon. *The Unforgettable Fire.* New York: Grand Central Publishing, 1988.
Fallon, B. P. *U2—Faraway So Close.* New York: Little, Brown, 1994.
Flanagan, Bill. *U2 at the End of the World.* New York: Delta, 1996.
Garrett, Greg. *We Get to Carry Each Other: The Gospel According to U2.* Louisville, Kentucky: Westminster John Knox Press.
Gimarc, George. *Punk Diary: The Ultimate Trainspotter's Guide to Underground Rock, 1970–1982,* London: Backbeat, 2005.
Gittins, Ian. *U2—The Best of Propaganda.* Cambridge, Massachusetts: Da Capo, 2003.
Graham, Bill. *The Complete Guide to the Music of U2.* London: Omnibus Press, 1995.
———. *U2: The Early Days.* New York: Delta, 1988.
McCormick, Neil. *Killing Bono.* New York: Pocket Books, 2004.
McGee, Matt. *U2: A Diary.* London: Omnibus Press, 2008.
Negativland: Fair Use—The Story of the Letter U and the Numeral 2. Concord, CA: Seeland, 1995.

Parkyn, Geoff. *U2: Touch the Flame*. London: Omnibus Press, 1987.

Stokes, Niall. *U2 Into the Heart: The Stories Behind Every Song*. New York: Thunder's Mouth Press, 2005.

———. *The U2 File*. London: Music Sales Corp., 1985.

———. *Three Chords and the Truth*. New York: Three Rivers Press, 1989.

Stokes, Niall, Liam Mackey, and Bill Graham. *U2—In the Name of Love: A History from Ireland's* Hot Press *Magazine*. New York: Random House, 1986.

Taylor, Mark. *U2*. London: Carlton, 1994.

U2 by U2 with McCormick, Neil. New York: It Books, 2006.

U2: The Complete Songs. London: Wise Publications, 1999.

U2: The Rolling Stone *Files*. New York: Hyperion, 1994.

Visconti, Tony. *Tony Visconti: Bowie, Bolan and the Brooklyn Boy*. London: HarperCollins, 2007.

Van Oosten de Boer, Caroline. *Gavin Friday—The Light and Dark*. Utrecht: Von B Press, 1991.

Waters, John. *Race of Angels—The Genesis of U2*. London: Fourth Estate, 1994.

White, Timothy. *Rock Lives, Profiles and Interviews*. New York: Holt, 1991.

Williams, Peter and Steve Turner. *U2 Rattle and Hum—The Official Book of the U2 Movie*. New York: Harmony Books, 1988.

Music Magazines and Fanzines

The Aquarian

BAM

The Big Takeover

Melody Maker

Musician

Modern Drummer

Mojo

NME

Premiere

Propaganda

Q

Record

Record Mirror

Rip It Up

Rock!

Rolling Stone

Sounds

Spin

Star Hits

Strangled

Trouser Press

U2 Magazine

Uncut

Other Newspapers and Magazines

The Boston Globe
British Vogue
The Daily Mail
The Daily Mirror
The Daily Telegraph
The Dublin Evening Press
Entertainment Weekly
The Glasgow Herald
Harvard Gazette

In Dublin
The Irish Independent
The Irish Times
The Los Angeles Times
The Miami Herald
New York Newsday
The New York Times
The Toronto Sun

Music Websites

www.Billboard.com
www.Dropd.com
www.EIL.com
www.Exclaim.ca
www.HotPress.com
www.IrishRock.org
www.ModernGuitars.com
www.MTV.com

www.NME.com
www.Pitchfork.com
www.RIAA.org
www.Rockhall.com
www.RollingStone.com
www.Spin.com
www.Spinner.com
www.XFM.com

U2 Websites

www.u2.com
www.atu2.com
www.interference.com
www.macphisto.net
www.threechordsandthetruth.net
www.u2.se
www.u2achtung.com
www.u2blog.com
www.u2-blog.blogspot.com
www.u2boy.nl
www.u2exit.com
www.u2faqs.com
www.u2france.com
www.u2gigs.com

www.u2info.com
www.u2_interviews.tripod.com
www.u2log.com
www.u2place.com
www.u2star.com
www.u2station.com
www.u2-thespiralstaircase.blogspot.com
www.u2tour.de
www.u2tours.com
www.u2town.com
www.u2wanderer.org
www.u2world.com
www.zootopia.de

Other Websites

www.AP.org
www.BBC.com
www.Carbonfootprint.com
www.FreeRepublic.com
www.Guardian.co.uk
www.Independent.co.uk
www.Life.com

www.Marvel.com
www.Newsweek.com
www.Observer.co.uk
www.Reuters.com
www.TheDubliner.ie
www.TheInsider.com
www.Time.com

Other Media

KZEW interview, June 12, 1983, Bono with George Gimarc

Countdown, Australian TV, September 1984, U2 with Molly Meldrum

Timothy White's Rock Stars, June 1, 1987, Bono with Timothy White

Dave Fanning with U2, "The Nude Interview," RTE, June 25, 1987

San Francisco Press Conference, November 16, 1987

BBC1 Radio Interview, Bono with Roger Scott and Annie Nightingale, October 30, 1988

Sydney Triple M Radio Interview with U2, October 22, 1989

Folkways: A Vision Shared, Promotional Video Interview with Bono, 1990

BBC1 Interview, U2 with Mark Goodier, February 13, 1992

Sydney Triple J Radio Interview with Bono, November 27, 1993

Bono Interview, *The History of Rock and Roll*, Time-Life Video, 1995

BBC1 Radio Interview, Bono with Zane Lowe, 2007

Index